To my dearest [illegible],

my Golden Sister,

my forever, ever friend.

Our friendship is ART
personified....

Sent with volumes
of Love,

Rose

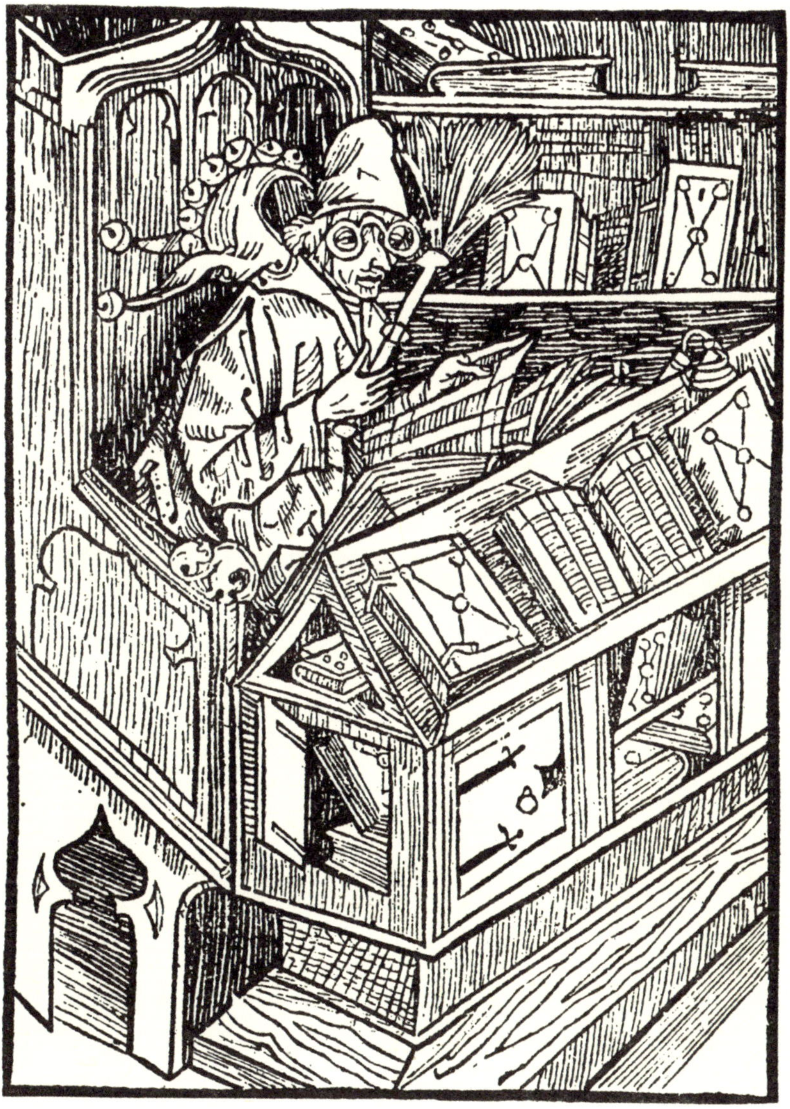

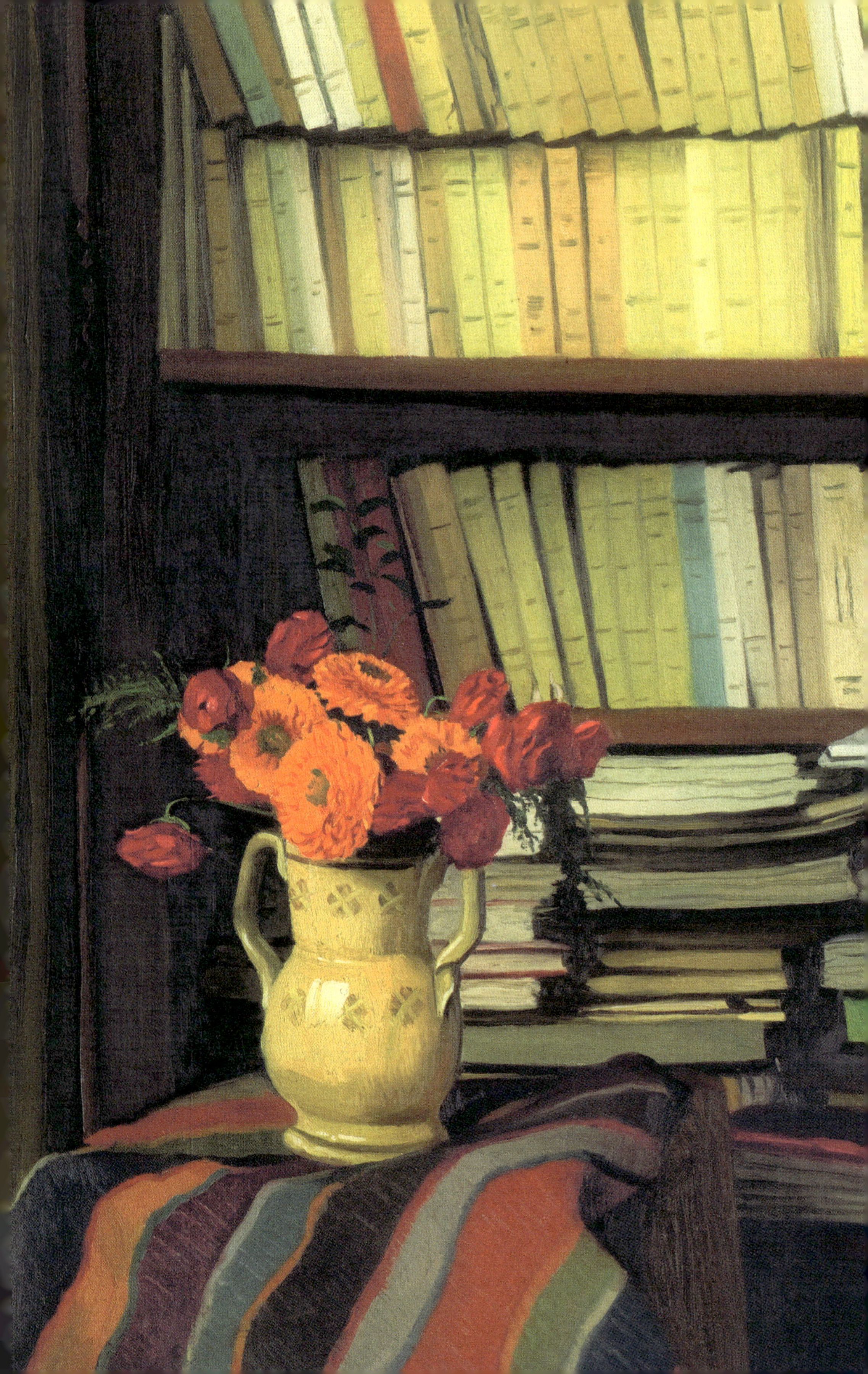

THE ART *of* READING

An Illustrated History of Books in Paint

JAMIE CAMPLIN
MARIA RANAURO

Getty Publications
Los Angeles

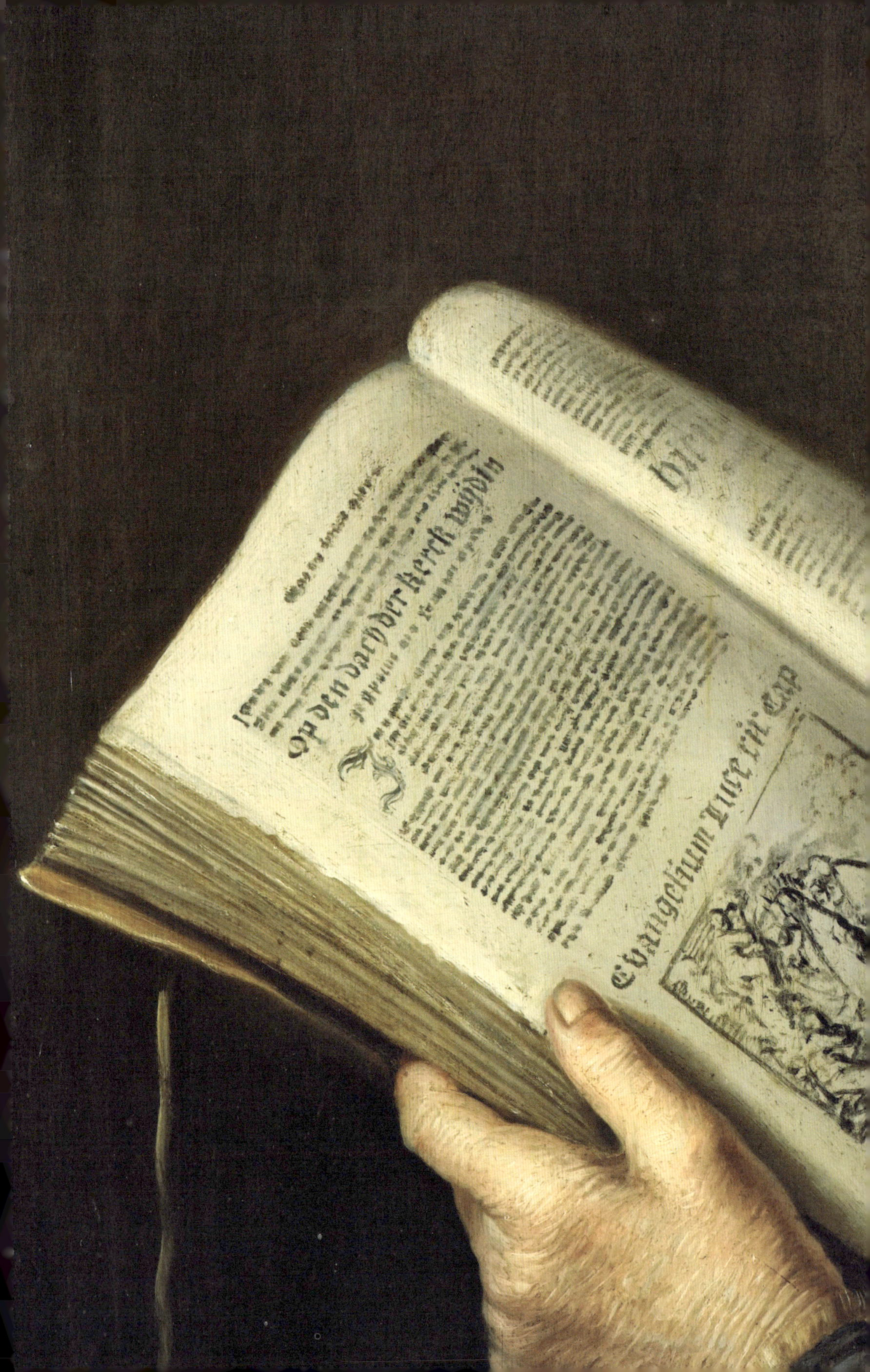

Published by arrangement with Thames & Hudson Ltd., London

Designed by Lisa Ifsits

First published in the United States of America by Getty Publications, Los Angeles

1200 Getty Center Drive, Suite 500
Los Angeles, California 90049-1682
www.getty.edu/publications

Jacket designed by Jim Drobka

Distributed in the United States and Canada by the University of Chicago Press

Printed and bound in China by C & C Offset Printing Co., Ltd.

Library of Congress Cataloging-in-Publication Data
Names: Camplin, Jamie, 1947– author. | Ranauro, Maria, author. | Getty Publications, issuing body.
Title: The art of reading : an illustrated history of books in paint / Jamie Camplin, Maria Ranauro.
Description: Los Angeles, California : Getty Publications, [2018] | Includes bibliographical references and index.
Identifiers: LCCN 2018010808 | ISBN 9781606065860 (hardcover)
Subjects: LCSH: Books and reading in art. | Painting—Themes, motives.
Classification: LCC ND1460.B66 C36 2018 | DDC 751.7—dc23
LC record available at https://lccn.loc.gov/2018010808

Published simultaneously in the United Kingdom as *Books Do Furnish a Painting* by
Thames & Hudson Ltd
181A High Holborn
London WC1V 7QX

Half-title page: Ironically, this woodcut of the 'book fool', attributed to a young Albrecht Dürer, was published in perhaps the biggest-selling book in Europe of the late 15th and early 16th centuries: the humanist Sébastien Brant's satirical *Ship of Fools* (1494).

Frontispiece: Félix Vallotton painted several works in which books were used as decorative devices, exploring contrasts of dull and stronger colours. Here we see *La Bibliothèque* (1921).

CONTENTS

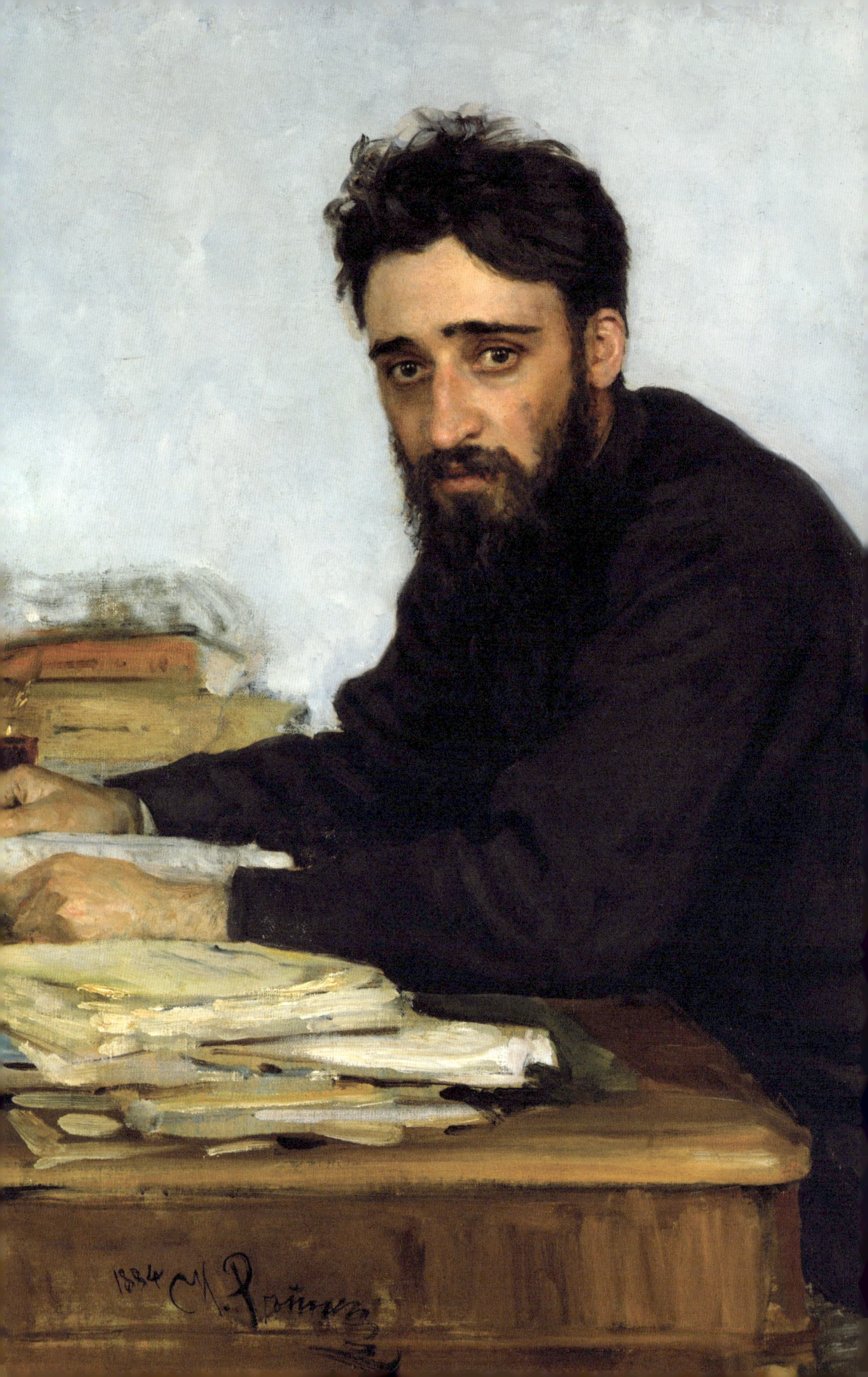

PREFACE

Picture the forlorn and melancholy scene of dead or wounded Russian soldiers on the battlefields of the Crimean War. In the knapsack of each sad figure, the one common object a looter or a voyeur might find is almost invariably a book: a comfort and a solace to those whose lives were in danger.[1]

This book is not all about comfort, but at root about something more surprising in the innovation-obsessed 21st century: it reveals over and over again how continuity in a particular method of communication, despite its staid overtones, fuelled creativity. Bertolt Brecht once stridently argued that 'reality changes; in order to represent it, modes of representation must change'. What was popular in the past is no longer popular; people today are not the people of yesterday.[2] It is of course a truism that tastes and fashions change, but 'the book' managed to defy Brecht's assumption for two thousand years without any hint that it was an outdated communication tool. It accommodated Baroque, or Barbizon, or Bauhaus, or – for that matter – Brechtian at its ease. Art, science, technology, religion, politics, social life, philosophy, entertainment – all were encompassed.

Writing, without whose invention there would have been no books, was reverenced from the beginning. The ancient Egyptians, whose word for the script we call hieroglyphics translates as 'words of God', believed it had been given to them by a goddess, the Chinese that a dragon had come from heaven with characters on its back. The first books also acquired a distinctive esteem. An inscription on the great library at Alexandria, founded in 3000 BCE, read: 'The nourishment of the soul; or, according to Diodorus, the medicine of the mind'.[3] And there is an all-pervading sadness so many years later when, at the end of one of the poems in Victor Hugo's *L'Année terrible* (1872), the communard who has brought destruction to a Parisian library responds to multiple lines of almost delirious homage to the book with, 'Je ne sais pas lire'.[4]

Books have been 'the best of friends, the same today and for ever' (as Martin Tupper's *Proverbial Philosophy* found them in 1838); like Hope Summerell, sitting on the porch of her home in North Carolina in the 1880s in thrall to *Alice in Wonderland*'s White Rabbit (an experience vividly remembered nearly sixty years later in her memoirs, *This Was Home*), they have been a rock for the turbulent business of growing up for uncountable generations of children. For one artist, they even triumphed over man's faithful companion – his dog. Samuel Palmer, when walking in the country, found them preferable to his 'not unbeloved bull terrier', for 'Milton never fidgeted, frightened horses, ran after sheep, or got run over by a goods-van.'[5]

The fact of the matter is that, through innumerable changes of regime, belief, taste and technology, books have been 'the necessaries of life', as the American writer and preacher Henry Ward Beecher said in the centennial year of 1876. Even when Samuel Richardson, still making the news in the *New Yorker* in 2016 as 'The Man Who Made the Novel', created his tragi-heroine Clarissa (1748), it seemed natural that she was depicted in Charles Landseer's painting of 1833 completely wretched, jailed for debt, but still accompanied by her book – a small object, but somehow substantial at the same time.[6]

Leigh Hunt, in an article in the *Literary Examiner* in 1823, agreed that books were 'so small', yet they were also 'so comprehensive' – 'so slight, yet so lasting, so insignificant, yet so venerable'.[7] And if artists sometimes used them simply as props, they were excellent for that purpose, too.

In this volume we have set out to explore the many-sided and astonishingly long-lived story of books, the ways in which artists have depicted them – and the reasons why they felt compelled to depict them. In some ways this is a bit like telling the whole history of Western art, or even of the Western world, from a particular perspective. For that reason, although happiness and contentment are found aplenty, so too are all other areas of life. In Augustus Leopold Egg's *Past and Present, No. 1* (1858), a wife lies on the floor, in a state of collapse at news of her adultery reaching her husband;

THE CLOSE CORRESPONDENCE between art, literature and life was exemplified by Ilya Repin – the Tolstoy of Russian art – in his painting of his friend Vsevolod Mikhailovich Garshin (1884). Garshin, whose father and brother had committed suicide, killed himself four years later.

her daughter's house of cards is coming down; and there on the chair is the guilty corrupting influence, at least according to the moralizers of the day: a yellow-coloured book bearing the name 'Balzac'.[8]

There is much to be said about what books in paintings reveal with regard to male attitudes to women. Ruskin sets the scene for us when he writes in a letter that Egg's representation of the adulterous wife suggested someone who would be prey for any 'sham count, with a moustache', and whose normal reading – the historical romances of the prolific William Harrison Ainsworth – would preclude any understanding of Balzac's subtlety.[9]

Most of the time, both books and art have been great civilizing forces, but that doesn't mean there has always been harmony and balance between art and literature. Many extreme opinions have been expressed through the centuries: Ruskin – never short of colourful opinion – insisted that the great writers had the power of 'self-annihilation', so that when we listen to the wailing of Lear, we are not conscious of Shakespeare. But as to artists, he accused them of using their subjects as 'mere themes on which the artist's power is to be displayed'.[10]

There has also been much national or regional difference in both painting and the novel. French and English artists had had little to do with one another for four centuries when the painter Théodore Géricault spent several years in London in the 1820s, or when the Paris salon showed Constable's *Hay Wain* in 1824.[11]

Nevertheless, books show up in almost all painting genres in all nations. Perhaps not on the battlefield, where they might be hidden in Crimean knapsacks, or saving the lives of at least some soldiers in the English civil wars with Bibles in their pockets impenetrable to bullets,[12] but their intimate connection with what makes us civilized (the literature of hatred excepted), and civilization's intimate connection with what it is to be human, usually signifies that a human being will be present in the painting. Portraits are not always honest, but where they include books, that part of the image does not lie. This does not mean that only portraits show books; landscapes, history paintings, religious scenes, those of everyday life all contribute to the genre. Still lifes, too, but these are usually accompanied by other important objects in our lives.

The footprint of books is everywhere in history, and their visual depiction is – quietly but insistently – everywhere in art.

To how and why this happened, we now turn.

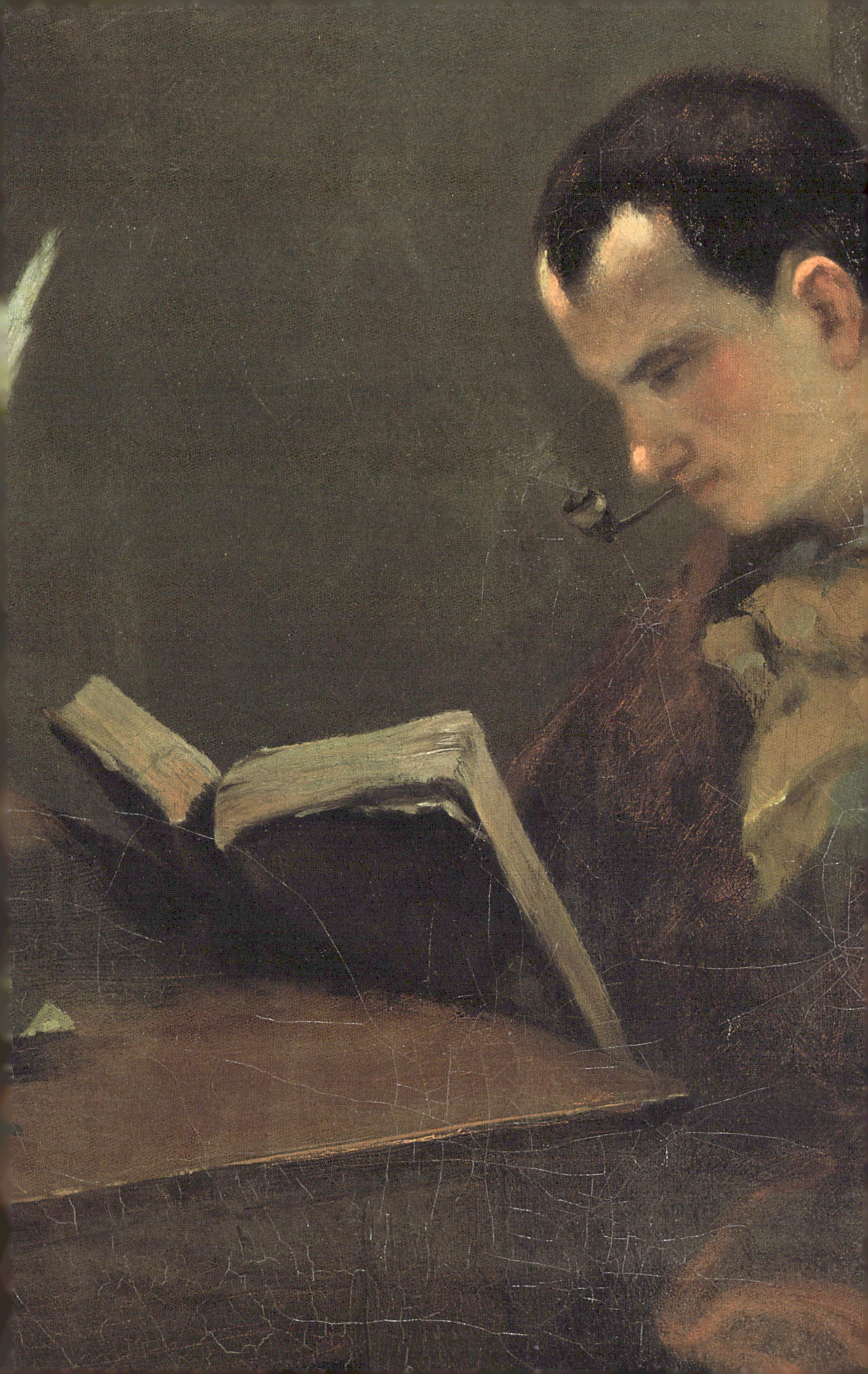

Part One

WHY *do* ARTISTS LOVE BOOKS?

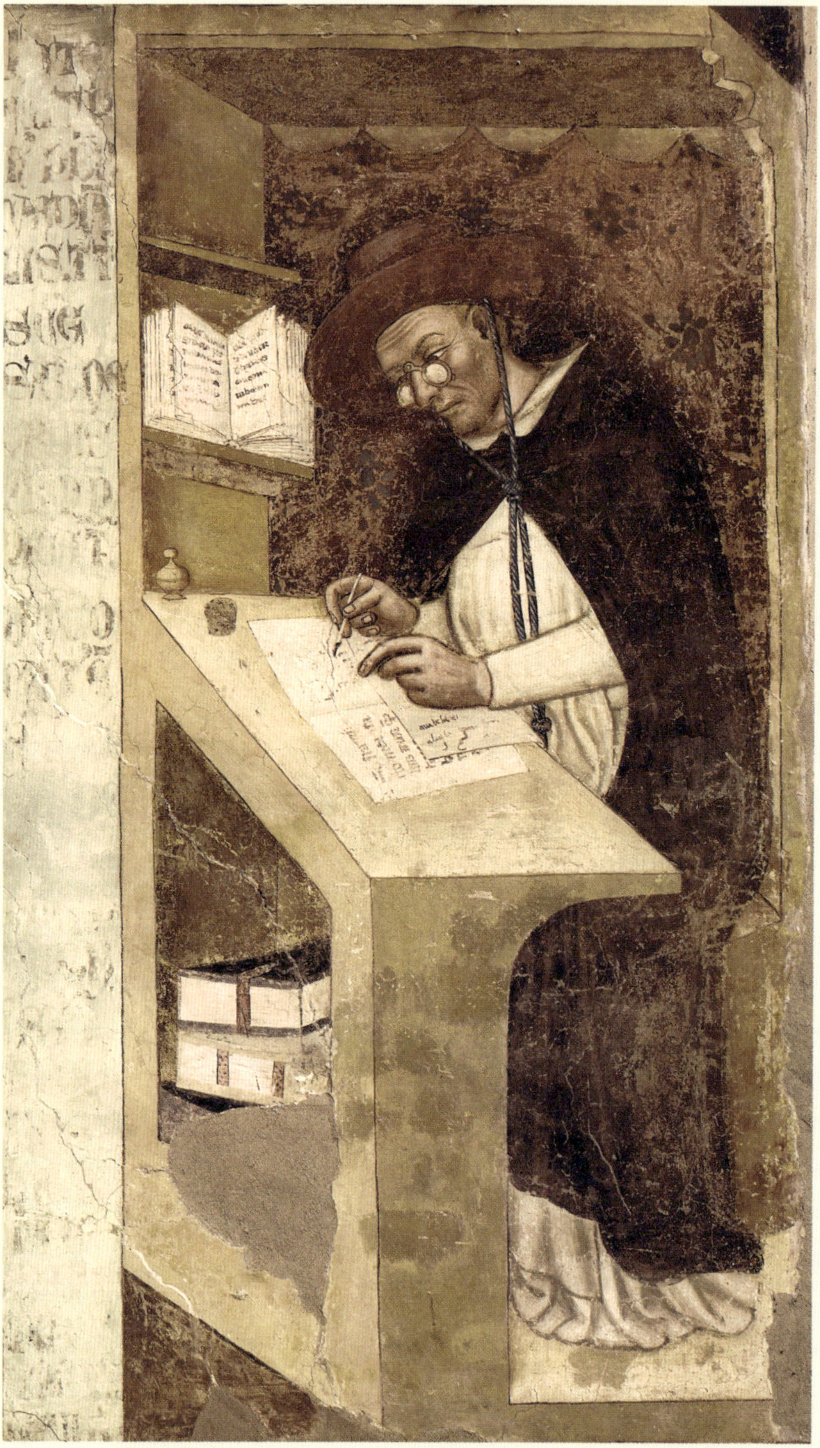

CHAPTER 1

HOW *it* ALL BEGAN

THAT SUMMER – of 1438 – Johannes Gutenberg was a worried man. It had all seemed such a good idea. Every seven years, thousands of pilgrims flocked to Charlemagne's great capital, Aachen, to seek the miraculous power of many of the Church's most sacred relics: the loincloth of the crucified Christ, for example, or the cloth in which the severed head of John the Baptist had been wrapped, shown to the faithful from the golden Marienschrein in Aachen's cathedral.

In woodcuts and illuminations, we see the eager pilgrims holding their holy mirrors upwards. These mirrors were of polished metal, not of glass, and their owners hoped to catch the rays from the relics and take their virtues home. The Aachen goldsmiths had made a good income from making and selling the mirrors, but could not cope with the sheer number of pilgrims. It is thought that Gutenberg, primarily remembered today as the inventor of printing in the West, trained as a goldsmith and – in partnership with other investors – made not a few hundred but tens of thousands of mirrors, suggesting that he must have been employing at least a semi-mechanical method.

The venture was a disaster. Plague spread from Italy to Aachen, and the pilgrimage was delayed. The city's warehouses were full not of a large inventory of unsold books, like those of so many of Gutenberg's publishing heirs, but of unsold holy souvenirs.[1]

THE DOMINICANS, whose mendicant order was founded circa 1216, were noted for pioneering scientific development in the Middle Ages. Spectacles, probably a Florentine invention of the 1280s, quickly became associated with learning. In this first depiction of them, by Tommaso da Modena in 1352 – one of forty parts of a fresco cycle of Dominican scholars – Hugh of St Cher (Cardinal Hugo of Provence) is anachronistically bespectacled (he died in 1263) and reads in a scriptorium.

The relationship between art, artists and books is a captivatingly close and multifarious one. Gutenberg's artisanal activities and subsequent invention of printing provide a pivotal point from which we can look back to glimpse the symbiosis of artist and pre-printed book, and forward to see the ironic consequences of the invention of printing unfold over five centuries.

For printing first shattered the direct relationship in which the artist made the book (a relationship that was later, especially in the modern era, recovered). Yet at the same time books played a key role for artists in establishing individual identity, and then, eventually, became associated with such a cornucopia of knowledge, authority, education and entertainment that they became a favourite subject for so many artists.

But first there are two questions to be answered. How and why did the deep-seated cultural significance ascribed to books develop? And even more fundamentally, what do we mean when we speak of 'a book'? The Greek tyrant Histiaeus gave a good lead to today's artists, some of whom have turned books into installations: don't neglect humans. He used tattoos on the scalps of his messengers to send secret orders, secret because the missive-bearers were not dispatched until their hair had grown over the tattoos.[2]

Still, if this was communication, albeit slow for contemporary tastes, it was not a book. Were ancient Asian dried palm leaves, held together by string and with texts written in ink,'books'? In Mesopotamia, were the clay tablets in some sense 'books'?

Some would say so. But in the Western tradition at least, the choice of material for writing on, and the form of the resulting document, were to prove a decisive influence until the digital era. Papyrus sheets were first used in the Nile valley, and the scroll became a widely used form for presenting the data preserved on them. The latter provided an early link to art in a painting of the baker Terentius Neo at Pompeii; he holds a scroll, while his wife is about to write with a stylus on a wax writing tablet.[3] There are several other such paintings of scrolls that survive from Pompeii. Rome had given a boost to the scroll as it sought to assimilate plundered Greek libraries and developed a literature of its own. Nevertheless, it was the codex in the early centuries of the Christian era that properly began our millennia-long love affair with the cultural artefact we call 'a book'. Made of folded pages held together, with text on both sides of the sheet, it was practical, portable, convenient to use, versatile in not being dependent on a particular raw material.[4]

In a sense, the only major changes for the next two thousand years were inventions that helped widen distribution – notably printing – and, again, raw materials. Parchment, whose introduction is ascribed to Eumenes II of Pergamon (r. 197–159 BCE), was smoother and had greater longevity than papyrus; eventually, vellum (from the Old French for 'calf') enabled the use of an even finer surface. Paper, the decisive material, came later, although in Asia notable progress predates these Western developments, first with the beginning of a written language, using bone and tortoiseshell (later silk) as the writing surface. China's first dated book, the 'Diamond Sutra', is from 868 BCE. Paper was also invented earlier in China, around 100 CE. Today we take it for granted, but the secrecy in which the Chinese shrouded its making and the value given to it by all-conquering Islam should have given Peter the Venerable a clue that not everything foreign should be distrusted; the 12th-century French abbot raged against a substance made from 'the rags of old cast-off undergarments, or rushes out of Eastern swamps, and some other vile material'.[5] China also invented a form of early printing, using wood blocks on cloth, in the 3rd century CE. In Korea, there is even evidence of the first printing with movable type at the beginning of the second millennium.

The fact of the matter is that a book in all civilizations may be many things: a physical object; a series of texts, sometimes with images; a work of art in itself; and, as we might conclude, an encounter with something more meaningful than pure action. As a material object, it is principally relevant to our subject because – as we shall see – it will help us answer the question of why Gutenberg's invention of printing with movable type was to become significant for artists. At the same time, it will help us understand the relationship between artist and artisan.

In our own time, despite abundant evidence of the continuing creativity of artists, we answer the question 'What makes an artist?' by stridently stating a tautology: art is everything we say it is.

It was not always so. Before Gutenberg, the medieval centuries, especially the later ones, were the first great age of the artist and the book, whether made of parchment, vellum or paper. Anonymous artists depicted the book, sometimes marvellously so – as in the case of folio 291v of the Book of Kells, in which Christ holds a red binding with decorations provided by twilling, a weaving that produces parallel ridges.[6] It had been the Roman statesman Cassiodorus who, after serving the Ostrogoth king Theodoric the Great, had eventually founded the monastery school that paved the way for these developments. Via his 6th-century *Institutiones*, Cassiodorus encouraged the preservation and transmission of knowledge through the copying and study of both religious and lay texts.[7] The message was an influential one:

a book of sermons by the German Benedictine monk Haimo of Halberstadt was apparently worth 200 sheep, 3 bushels of grain and some marten furs to one of the countesses of Anjou. Books were endowed, at the hands of artist scribes and illuminators, with visual power; and at the hands of no lesser 'artists', the artisans, books were made tactile by using precious materials – jewels, carved ivory, enamel – to adorn the materials that encased the pages, first wood, then leather.

It would be a mistake to see the centuries after the first millennium as a period of little significance until the invention of printing. Books became, in the widest sense, a symbol for the world, a *speculum mundi* through which it could be discovered.[8] We might say that the book, made by artists of various kinds, marched towards the destiny that printing was eventually to give it. Practical inventions helped: chapter titles, paragraphs and indexes made reading easier or, in the case of spectacles, possible – as demonstrated by Hugh of St Cher in Tommaso da Modena's portrait of the friar from 1352 (p. 14).[9] No matter that books were sometimes 'fashion accessories',[10] as in the Flemish miniaturist Simon Bening's illuminated genealogy of the kings of Spain and Portugal (1530–34).

Aristocracies could parade their courtliness, their sophistication, their faith and their riches with books that made use of special leather and jewels in their bindings and gold illuminations in their illustrations.

Faith and the book went very well together. They have lasted for centuries at the tomb of the great Eleanor of Aquitaine in the abbey of Fontevraud, where her effigy holds an open book.[11] And for faiths that proscribed the representation of humans, there were ingenious solutions: a 14th-century German Haggadah replaced the cantor's face with a bird at the reading desk in a synagogue.[12] In the Christian church, innumerable works of art sent symbolic messages. Prophets and patriarchs, because they lived before Christ, were shown with scrolls – distinctly inferior as a medium because their content reflected their pre-Christian status. A Gospel would be placed on an altar, it being a symbol of the New Testament. William Durand (*c.* 1230–1296), a canonist whose career took him from Paris to Italy and the Roman Curia, set out the symbolism and its origins in his *Rationale divinorum officiorum*. No wonder that some sixteen images of books can be found in Duccio's great altarpiece, the *Maestà*, commissioned by the city of Siena in 1308.[13]

The monasteries had kept learning alive through many dark periods. In scriptoria, peaceful rooms developed for the task, the scribes carried out their patient work of copying on folded vellum sheets. Their texts were literally sacred – God's Word – and it was natural for them to be decorated with gold and silver and vibrant colours, with painted miniatures as illustrations. In time, specialist skills developed, with copyists, rubricators (those who prepared initial letters and headings) and illuminators plying separate arts. There was even a form of tracing paper, *carta lustra*, to allow for copies of a particular design.[14]

The book thus provided the means by which the Word of God could be spread and, within the power structures that humans appear to need, supported the Church's hierarchy. But long before print, merchants, lawyers and other members of an incipient bourgeoisie fuelled the development of the book, whose status worked for them as it did for aristocracy and church. Herbals, histories and many other subjects widened the range of books, and private collecting began in earnest in the 13th century. In this and succeeding centuries, education further proselytized for the book, even if the student was unwilling: an illuminated miniature from the late 15th century in the Bibliothèque Nationale shows a teacher poised to punish his pupil, who is holding a French translation of Aristotle's *Politics* (p. 23). Use of vernacular languages speeded up the widening of education, whether or not the students were keen.[15]

In Paris, whose size and dominance provided wealth and literacy sufficient to encourage the new profession of producing manuscripts to order, a painstaking study of tax records in the 1290s shows a concentration of booksellers in the Rue Neuve Notre Dame, a street now absorbed into the parvis of the cathedral.[16]

Did artists read? There is little evidence that they did, although Ghiberti (1378–1455), creator of the bronze doors of the Florence Baptistery, was an exception.[17] Their role became professionalized through the guilds, but they were largely anonymous craftsmen. Intellectually, they were excluded from the seven 'liberal arts', which, as codified in the 5th century by the grammarian Martianus Capella, included logic, rhetoric and geometry. When, in the 12th century, Hugh of St Victor and others developed an analysis of the equivalent 'mechanical arts', painting was a mere subdivision of the one devoted to supplying shelter and tools, *armatura*. Art, as we understand it, stood very much below poetry, whose discourse was encompassed in rhetoric. For Dante (*c.* 1265–1321), *artista* could easily have referred to a cook as much as an artist, although he did praise Giotto in his *Purgatorio*.[18]

Nevertheless, artists being artists regardless of cultural status, hints of personal style are sometimes visible. We are far from the 'divine' Michelangelo in the 16th century. Yet the illustrations created by Jean Pucelle between 1325 and 1328 for a book of hours for Jeanne d'Evreux, third wife of Charles IV of France, were ascribed to him in her will.[19] And the 'artist' Master Guglielmo was the happy recipient of eight gold florins for the illuminations commissioned by Ludovico III Gonzaga of Mantua for his niece in 1469.[20]

Devotional books flourished for three hundred years after the mid-13th century, and it was artists, albeit mostly anonymous, who were central to creating what became in effect the biggest bestsellers of the later Middle Ages. Thus, whether it was the Virgin reading her book of hours in innumerable Annunciations, or royal ladies doing the same, artists and books became closely associated. While illuminations are found as early as the 7th century, that was some distance from what has been colourfully called 'an all-singing, all-dancing illuminated manuscript'.[21] But by the 15th century certainly, hand-created books had become a magnet for the best miniature painters.

There were other reasons for the evolution of the book, some of them practical. The new universities, from the middle of the 14th century, could not survive without them. Even in 1424, the entire library of the University of Cambridge consisted of 122 books. They were expensive – so expensive! Nevertheless, the astonishing quantity of more than two thousand copies of the works of Aristotle survives today from the 13th and 14th centuries.[22] The rediscovery of pagan classics, helped by Greek refugees from Ottoman expansion in the period leading up to the fall of Constantinople in 1453, gathered pace, while the questioning of the Church that accelerated as the Reformation approached further fuelled demand for books.

A 'History of the World in 100 Materials' would certainly have to include paper. Peter the Venerable's strictures apart, paper came late to Europe. Through the Islamic conquests, some local production began in the middle of the 12th century before spreading to France and Italy, where the Fabriano mills were renowned by the end of the following century.[23] Paper was much cheaper than parchment, and certainly than vellum, and in many ways more versatile. On the eve of the invention of printing, it was widely available as a suitable medium for anyone who could envisage mass production – or any machine that could enable it.

The technical details of how printing developed need not concern us. That is as well, since the historical record is very murky. It may be dubious to say that it was an invention waiting to happen, but woodcuts were being used for text-based book blocks, as well as by artists, in the decades leading up to Gutenberg's breakthrough. Gutenberg, evidently an interesting mix of brilliant artisan and ambitious, not to say greedy, entrepreneur, operated in great secrecy; he also managed to fall out with his partners and financiers on more than one occasion. At the time of the pilgrim-mirrors fiasco he was living in Stuttgart, and no one knows how far his experiments had taken him before he moved back to his birthplace of Mainz. It is thought that what became known as the Gutenberg Bible, produced around 1455, was the first substantial book printed from movable type, with 3 million characters and 1,282 pages: a brave venture by any criteria.

In a tangled story, no one was entirely reasonable. Gutenberg was nevertheless pushed out of the tale until modern times. What he had realized, that money could be made from printing, quickly became a reality. There may have been others, but he certainly played a key role in how to manufacture – relatively quickly, relatively consistently and with the greater longevity of metal – the printed text or image. He also used inks more appropriate to metal type than the water-based materials used by the Chinese, just as the Netherlandish masters made good use of the viscosity of oil paint, which came eventually to dominate European art.[24]

Gutenberg died in 1468, and even by the end of the century Western Europe had acquired nearly 240 printing presses. All the most vibrant ideas of a great age of discovery were drawn to it as the perfect medium for disseminating information, practical guidance and inspirational ideas. Guillaume Fichet, theologian and humanist, summed it up perfectly in an epistle to fellow humanist Robert Gaguin in the early 1470s. Gutenberg's invention, Fichet observed, 'furnishes characters by the aid of which all that is said or thought can be written, translated and preserved to the memory of posterity'.[25]

And artists were among the groups that benefited hugely. Sales of block prints on paper had long since become a flourishing trade. Printing, however, greatly enhanced the recognition and value of the works of the individual artist. While Dürer, Titian and others used woodcuts creatively, this was a medium subject to wear, and did not have the subtlety a great artist could exploit to the full. By contrast, making prints from engraved copper plates – an invention ascribed by Vasari, some say erroneously, to a Florentine goldsmith, Maso Finiguerra (b. 1426) – provided much more scope.[26] Marcantonio Raimondi (*c.* 1480–*c.* 1534), an Italian, specialized in prints that copied paintings, and was eventually to have a close working relationship with Raphael.

Artists, as through all history, were given new options via technology geared to human needs. But what happened next changed their status forever.

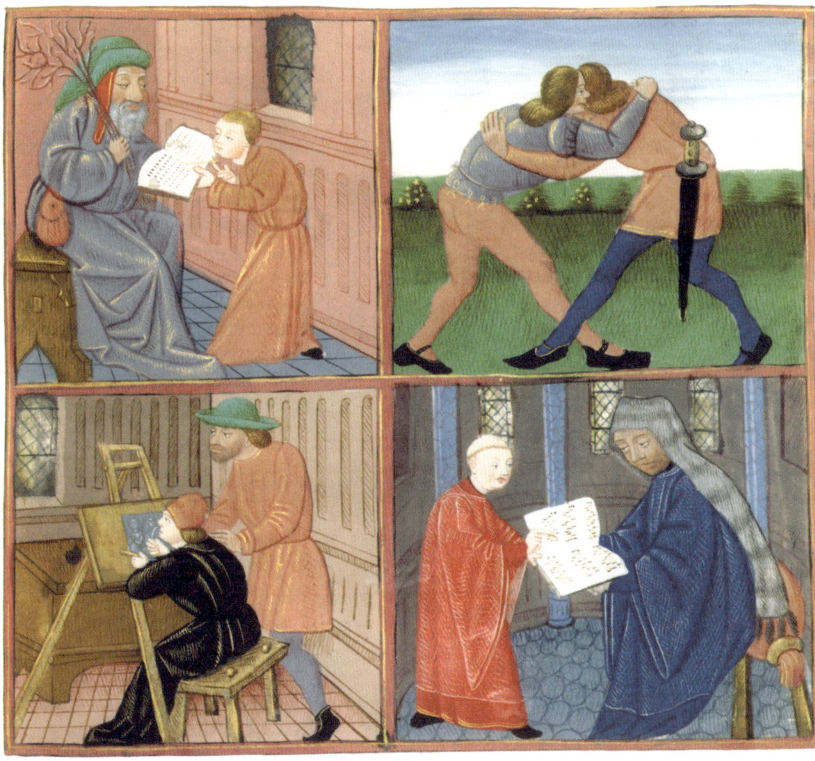

BATTLE, SONG, DRAWING – AND READING: a late 15th-century education. Aristotle's *Politics* (top left), unknown in the Arabic world, was prescribed, with his other works, by the University of Paris as early as the 13th century, but its translation from Latin to French the following century paved the way for its wider use during the flowering of humanist teaching in the Renaissance.

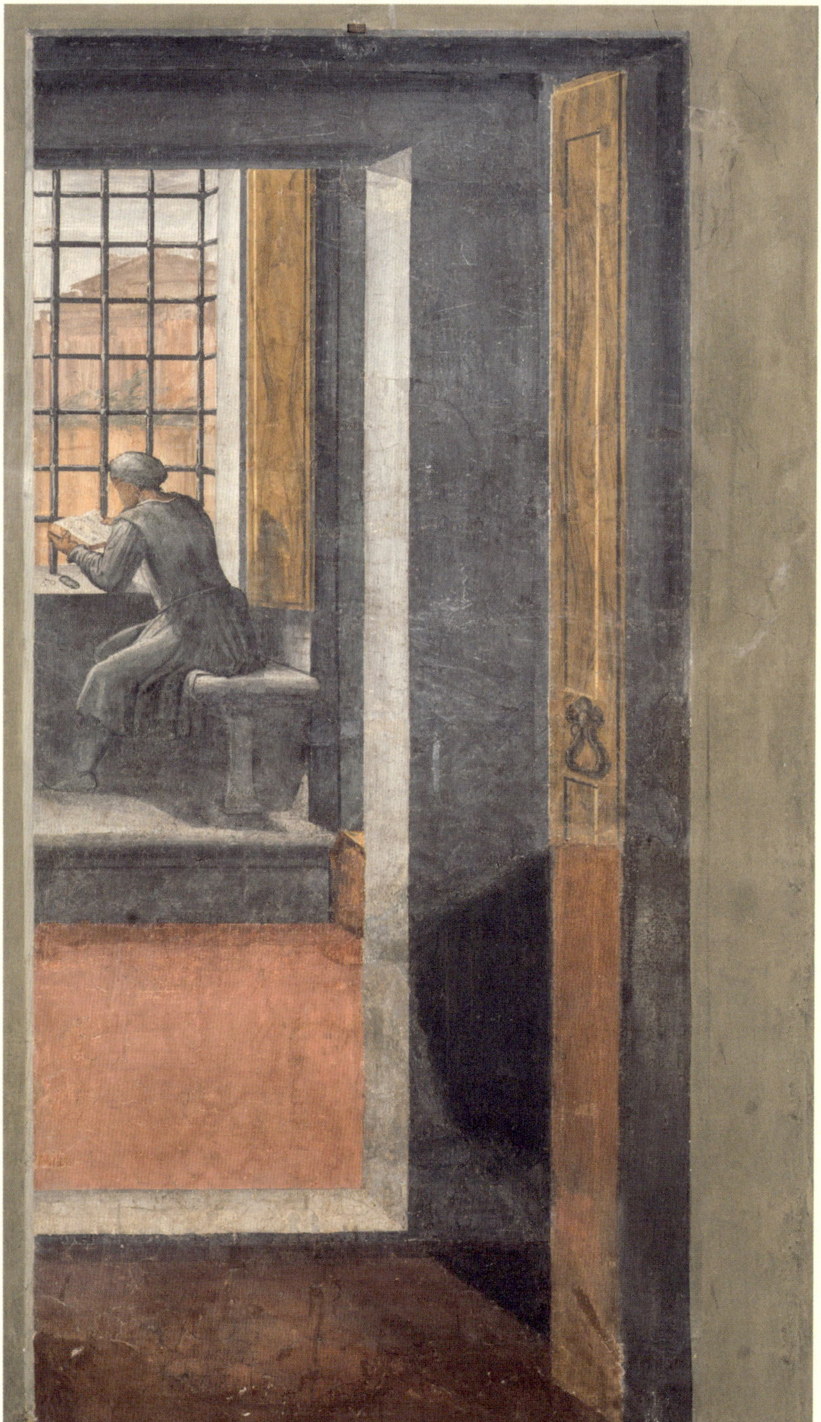

CHAPTER 2

WHO INVENTED '*the* ARTIST'?

THE RENAISSANCE, in the most basic sense, would serve both artist and book, and would provide a link between them and our evolving history that, in many ways, has continued for six centuries. The Florentine humanist and bookseller Vespasiano da Bisticci (1421–1498) recorded the way that libraries came to be associated with wealth and status. A famous portrait of Federico da Montefeltro (1422–1482) with a codex in his hands and his son at his knee, thought to be by Justus of Ghent, was just one of a number of this ruler of Urbino that included books.[1] There was a shrewd recognition that it was through books especially that the names of the rulers and great men of antiquity had survived.

The Venetian artist Vittore Carpaccio (1460s? – *c.* 1526) painted in loving and exquisite detail the book bindings and prayer-book miniatures in his *Vision of St Augustine* (*c.* 1502). While secular themes did not come quickly, domesticity was more than implicit in, for example, the Virgin's room in Carlo Crivelli's *The Annunciation, with St Emidius* (1486), with its books, bowls, carpets, cushions and cucumbers. An analysis of inventories in Valencia between 1474 and 1550 shows that books are mentioned in one in three; and if nine out of ten clerics died with books, then aristocrats, merchants and even some labourers had some.[2] Wives, as for so long, were kept in their own world; patriarchial disdain was apparent in the case of Camilla Bartalo, wife of a Sienese philosopher and doctor, whose 1483 inventory included 'a small book for women'.[3]

GIORGIO VASARI, WHO DID more than anyone to create a history of art that put the artist centre stage, and used a book – his *Lives* – to do it, symbolized his own endeavour in this self-portrait, entitled *The Reader* (*c.* 1542–48). When writing about the 15th-century Bellini family of artists in the second edition of *Lives*, he asked whether anyone could not feel 'infinite pleasure and contentment' when seeing 'images of his ancestors'.

Not all artists, even the great ones, cared for books. That was certainly true of Masaccio in the early 15th century; but then, like so many artists, anything other than his art was irrelevant to him.[4] Late in the century, in 1498, the Florentine brothers and sculptors Benedetto and Giuliano da Maiano owned twenty-nine books, including some from antiquity, as well as works by Dante and Giovanni Boccaccio. Leonardo da Vinci had many more, with vernacular literature alongside maths and astronomy, although he was hardly representative.[5]

In fact, Leonardo – when writing about art in his notebooks, first published in 1651 as *Trattato della pittura* – was clear that music or poetry or history could not match painting, and related this to the idea that the visual impact of art was instant, and yet its contemplation need have no limit.[6] In a sense, there was a certain acknowledgment or evolution of this idea centuries later when André Malraux's *Psychologie de l'art* (1949) reproduced a Giotto fresco, *The Raising of Lazarus* (1304–06), upside down. Malraux took the view that the focus of his discussion would be lost if the reader's eye went straight to the image.[7] Nevertheless, back in the Renaissance, an obstacle to reading for those who found the visual more natural than the written was removed through the humanist encouragement of a more visually pleasant script, albeit in reaction to what was seen by Petrarch and others as Gothic inaccessibility and ugliness.

Change in status for artists must sometimes have felt, for them, far away. Most came from humble backgrounds – Titian being an exception. They had to be members of a trade guild, with strict apprenticeship. But there were at least some portents for the future. Giovanni Villani, chronicler of medieval Florence, made a separate list of painters as early as the 1340s. At an uncertain date early in the next century, Cennino Cennini produced *Il libro dell'arte*; although predominantly a manual, to an extent it identified a new model for the artist, with painting and sculpture seen as liberal arts. Leon Battista Alberti's *Della pittura* (1436) went further, in both vernacular and more scholarly Latin editions, raising the artist and the art of painting to the sphere of godlike powers, as well as linking them to rules derived from rhetoric and making them intellectually respectable.

With the humanist rediscovery of Pliny the Elder's account of the status of artists in antiquity, and other pro-painting statements from such classical thinkers as Galen and Philostratus, a new recognition for the artist at least came into sight. No matter that, except perhaps in 4th-century BCE ancient Greece, artists in the classical world were seen at best as artisans, or that the great painting- and sculpture-commissioning emperors did not encourage their admission to the liberal arts. The sisterhood of painting and poetry, proclaimed by the Roman poet Horace in his *Ars poetica*, was a useful device to the extent that Bartolomeo Facio, a Ligurian humanist who eventually became secretary to Alfonso of Aragon and died in 1457, could declare: 'A picture is nothing but a silent poem.'[8] The same suggestion is in fact found variously in antiquity, as when the poet Simonides, reported by Plutarch, declares that 'painting is mute poetry and poetry speaking painting'.[9] It remained true that the great achievement of the artists of the ancient world – and it was true of the medieval centuries also – was their work, not how they were regarded.

The tangled story of print, the book and the artist was not so tangled as to obscure a fundamental change from all that had transpired in the past: a new status for the artist. It was related to the invention of the printed book, but more specifically to one in particular: Giorgio Vasari's *The Lives of the Most Excellent Painters, Sculptors, and Architects*, first published in 1550.

History is never neat. The fact that 'China's Gutenberg', Feng Dao, announced in 932 the printing of 150 volumes of Confucius does not minimize the impact of Gutenberg.[10] Moreover, 'revolutions' are awash with continuities that do not weaken their role in making decisive change. Before printing in the West, scribes had not been unconscious of markets and what was popular; for that matter, printing did not necessarily bring riches. In Ulm, Lienhart Holle was only one of many printers who quickly became bankrupt, as he did in the 1480s, despite targeting rich, secular clients.[11]

Who were the printers? Some were themselves originally scribes, from Peter Schoeffer in Germany to Antoine Vérard in France, hypnotized by this new version of Cicero's 'teacher of all the arts'. Johann Bämler of Augsburg variously appears in records, including his own, as *artifex* (artist), illuminator, *schreiber* (scribe) and, in 1477, *trucker* (printer).[12] It may have been that some of the great Florentine princes initially had a disdain for the printed book, but Urbino – despite its reputation in this respect – sponsored an early printing press in 1482.[13] The story of artists, books and technology is a human one, and thus either messy or beautifully variegated, according to your taste.

The overall impact of printing cannot be disputed. Among the scholarly printers of the 15th and 16th centuries, the career of Johann Weissenburger in Nuremberg is not untypical: university-educated in Ingolstadt, later a priest, printer of theology – but also, through printing, encouraging Nuremberg merchants to make outposts in Lisbon following the Portuguese discovery of a new route to India, taking trade away from Venice.[14] The text in which he did so was in Latin, but printing also greatly furthered the dissemination of vernacular texts. The power of the new medium unfolded over centuries. Isaiah Thomas, in his *History of Printing in America* (1810), compared it to that of the philosopher's stone.[15]

For a long time also, artists, writers and printers continued to probe ultimate questions, expressed through theological discourse; the Reformation, as much as secularism, provided a strong boost. Martin Luther, writing to the leaders of the German states in 1524, proselytized for 'good libraries and bookshops'.[16] The two 'p's, Protestantism and printing, assisted Holbein, Cranach, Dürer and others in enhancing their success.[17] It helped that, in Germany, printing became dispersed to a number of cities, with the book benefiting most from the Reformation; in England, where London was the dominant printing location, the effect was less obvious, and in France the Catholics offered a vigorous response to Protestantism.[18] But if Europe, as ever, was not a unity, it remained true to an extent that a third 'p' went naturally with Protestantism and printing to make a triumvirate: progress.

By 1500, if images, words and numbers could all be reproducible and also interact together, a discerning observer of the cultural universe might have deduced that something irreversible could at last be in sight for artists and their status. The human mechanism for that irreversible change was precisely Giorgio Vasari. The great thing about *Lives*, as his friend Paolo Giovio – who had himself written about Leonardo in the 1420s – suggested, was that it would give its author immortality. Time would certainly ravage his new wife's beauty; even his newly completed paintings in Naples would not be immune.[19] Here, then, was a case of the proposition being as beguiling as it was true – for Vasari, and, as it transpired, for the artists about whom he wrote.

Vasari was himself a painter and an architect, working in particular for Cosimo I de' Medici, Grand Duke of Tuscany. The first edition of *Lives*, published in March 1550, provided the biographies of 142 artists, from Cimabue to Michelangelo, in two volumes totalling more than a thousand pages. Vasari emphasized, in his epilogue and in his presentation to the duke, his decade-long research and travelling. Modern art historians have uncovered a variety of unacknowledged sources or identified the work of multiple authors, as if expecting a Renaissance author to follow modern copyright and etiquette. The point instead is the influence of *Lives*. It was fun, captivating, informative, brilliant propaganda for artists everywhere. And it was a book.

Although it contained some practical information, Vasari gave short shrift to a Flemish correspondent, Dominicus Lampsonius, who wanted him to add detailed instruction, by stressing that this was a book about the people, the artists, their lives, their achievements.[20] He may not have said it, but Vasari was effectively creating a form of celebrity culture of great significance for the whole subsequent history of Western art.

The second, enlarged edition of *Lives* (1568) also contained portraits of each artist, with only eight omitted because no likeness survived. Churchmen believing they could recognize the face of a sinner, and humanists thinking that personality shines through the image, were hardly unusual; but in giving apparent authenticity to his artist subjects, whether or not it was a true likeness in any particular case, Vasari was doing only what became a very effective commonplace for portrait painters – who, as we shall see, often included a book in their works – through to the present day.

Also significant for the future was Vasari's link with writing and the literary world. Vasari himself left a legacy of more than a thousand surviving letters – to writers, aristocrats, businessmen, churchmen, including six popes.[21] In scope, at least, here was a corpus of written material to rival that of the acknowledged literary gods of the time, Petrarch and Pietro Aretino, both – like Vasari – born in Arezzo in Tuscany.[22] In Casa Vasari, Arezzo, there is a painting by Vasari entitled *The Reader* (*c.* 1542–48; p. 24). And in *Six Tuscan Poets* (1544), commissioned by his friend Luca Martini and encouraged by Bronzino – another friend – he depicts Dante, book in hand and pointing at another, with Petrarch, Boccaccio and other towering Tuscan figures. Two more books lie on the table in front of them.[23] No wonder that Annibale Caro, quintessential literary figure of 16th-century Italy, who read parts of the final draft of the first edition of *Lives*, could praise Vasari for his excursion into 'another's profession':[24] painter turned writer.

The Renaissance was meant to represent a triumphant culmination for art. In fact, what had started out casually, said Vasari, at a dinner party in the Palazzo Farnese,[25] was a splendid beginning to a whole new trajectory for artists – and for books. Real revolutions, despite their reputation, tend not to be instant affairs; most artists continued to come from craft or other segments of the lower orders, just as most writers of all kinds came from the elite. According to Le Comte de Laborde, writing in *La Renaissance des arts à la cour de France* in 1850, artists at the French court of the 16th century were ranked merely as *varlets de chambre*.[26]

Moreover, while Vasari's significance for artists would be profound, immediately after the introduction of printing it might have seemed that they had lost a role: as creators of the physical book. As a medium in its own right for artists' work, it seemed to have severe limitations. Early books have been endowed with great monetary value by collectors, and with great praise as objects of beauty by typographers. But it took a great artist of the 20th century, Georges Rouault, to echo the stark blackness of those first books in the illustrations he laboured over for 15 years for Ambroise Vollard's *Réincarnations du Père Ubu* (1932). And in doing so, he was reflecting further technical progress: these were gouaches photographed on printing plates, then further worked on with aquatint, etching and drypoint.[27]

In the second half of the 15th century, therefore, the visual (in the history of the book) gave way to the primacy of the text. If each colour had to be printed separately, the rich use of colour in the handmade book became impossibly expensive. Some printers left space for decorated initials later to be replicated in colour, but most often engravers started cutting relief blocks of initials for black printing.[28] It would be a mistake to assume that, in these early years, the artist's motive for including representations of books in their paintings was because the medium itself seemed ideally suited to their skills.

Nevertheless, it was Albrecht Dürer (1471–1528) in particular who showed what could be achieved by practical and creative verve in a limited landscape. In his early twenties, he almost certainly produced woodcuts for the printer-publisher Johannes Bergmann of Basle. Dürer's woodcut vehicle was the humanist Sébastien Brant's *Das Narrenschiff* (The Ship of Fools). At least one of the woodcuts depicts books, although not in a complimentary way. The frontispiece showed the Büchernarr, or 'book fool', expressing the folly of a scholar's life spent with books (p. 1).[29]

Dürer was not only the son of a Nuremberg goldsmith, but also the godson of Anton Koberger, a man described by Elizabeth Eisenstein, historian of the cultural changes brought about by printing, as 'the greatest entrepreneur of the printed book-trade in the 15th century'.[30] Dürer was thus linked to Gutenberg by his father's craft, and to the evolving world of books through Koberger, who, by about 1470, had twenty-four presses in Nuremberg. Dürer certainly owned books, including Luther's tracts and Euclid's *Elements*; there is also a record of him buying ten from one Bernhart Walter in 1523. Eventually, Dürer provided a useful corrective to the idea that, henceforward, the text would have absolute primacy in the book. In fact, his wonderful series of woodcuts – *Apocalypse*, *The Great Passion* and *The Life of the Virgin* – were first published as prints, beginning in 1498 and continuing over the next dozen years. After that, he worked closely with the official printer to Maximilian I.[31]

As Elizabeth Eisenstein has drily observed, caveats notwithstanding, 'The conditions of scribal culture [had] held narcissism in check.'[32] Now, even the accurate likeness of the artist – at least, the living artist – which was clearly an important component of individual identity, could be recorded in woodcut portraits. Printing and the printed book had released the artist from the shackles of being merely 'a purveyor of goods', to use Anthony Blunt's phrase; the artist was now 'an individual facing a public'.[33] The seeds had been planted for a positive relationship between artist and printed book, in due course to be expressed via literally thousands of paintings in the centuries that followed.

Vasari could not please all the people all of the time. The copy of *Lives* owned by the Carracci (Bolognese artist-brothers Agostino, Annibale and Ludovico) contained hand-annotations calling him 'a shitface'.[34] Professional art history has not always been kind, either, far removed as it is now from what Vasari achieved: the creation of the artist as hero. The accompanying love for self, others' applause fuelling the individual's own self-esteem, was a widespread Renaissance development, and it was not surprising that Vasari was much imitated in Italy – by Carlo Ridolfi and his *Meraviglie dell' arte* (Marvels of Art) in Venice the following century, for example. Autobiography was also in evidence independently, from Michelangelo, Benvenuto Cellini and the Florentine sculptor Baccio Bandinelli.[35]

Nationalism and regionalism influenced the focus. Vasari praised the Tuscans, Arnold Houbraken the Netherlandish masters. Karel van Mander's *Het Schilderboek* (The Book of the Painter) was widely influential after its publication in 1604; indeed, it was one of the few books owned by Rubens. Van Mander suggested that it was through Dürer that Germany 'shed its darkness'. We know that Dürer himself was planning a substantial volume on painting in about 1512, and the pieces that were written include considerable reverence for earlier artists.[36]

What Vasari and the others produced had ramifications for centuries. Students settling down with the American college professor John C. Van Dyke and his *Text-Book of the History of Painting*, first published in 1894, were simply told that if they wanted 'the lives of the painters', they should use Vasari.[37] Technology reinforced the approach: Herman Grimm's *Life of Michel Angelo*, published by Smith, Elder & Co. in London in 1865, contained a photographic frontispiece reproducing a portrait in the Vatican. But in a nice little irony, only the art historians and publishers seemed reluctant to explore artists' work by using visual evidence. Luigi Lanzi's six-volume history of painting in Italy, translated into English in the 1820s, was typical in having none.[38] Of course, their decision was heavily influenced by cost and the state of printing technology, and it was only way into the 20th century, just as art critics fell into the abyss of deep theory, that the art book fought back with the enabling technology and images became its defining feature.

Naturally, Vasari was not entirely responsible for the two great changes to the status of artists in the Renaissance: in the esteem given to them, and in their education. Baldassare Castiglione's influential *Book of the Courtier*, published first in 1528, firmly established the notion that art was a natural subject for an aristocratic community; after all, as Ingres recorded in a renowned 19th-century painting, Leonardo had died in the arms of Francis I in 1519. Even if records of their ownership are scanty, books must have had a key role in spreading ideas. Castiglione's *Courtier* is known to have been in the library of the Mannerist artist Rosso Fiorentino, whose attributed portrait of Machiavelli (p. 203) has his subject pointing at a copy of his treatise *The Prince*, immediately after publication (just as 'Il Rosso' was later included by Vasari in *Lives*).[39] While the greatest artists were, by definition, not typical, it was something for Titian to be given the hereditary title of Knight of the Golden Spur and Count Palatine by the Holy Roman Emperor in 1533; and Raphael, friend of Castiglione, lived in a palace when he was in Rome.

Both Vasari and Cellini, each an artist and an author, were involved in the foundation of the Accademia delle Arti del Disegno in Florence in 1563. Bandinelli had opened a precursor to this first 'modern' art school in Rome in the 1530s. It was also natural that when France began to dominate European culture in the 17th century, it saw the opening of two major art institutions: first, in 1635, under Cardinal Richelieu, the Académie Française; and then, in 1648, under Cardinal Mazarin, the Académie Royale de Peinture et de Sculpture, the latter hastening the demise of artisanal guild control of artist development.[40]

As a subject for artists, books had originally found favour partly because of their association with art, or at least artistry, in the era of the hand-created book; partly because of their role, in the era of printing, in instruction; but even more in identifying, appraising and applauding individual artists and disseminating their work to much larger audiences.

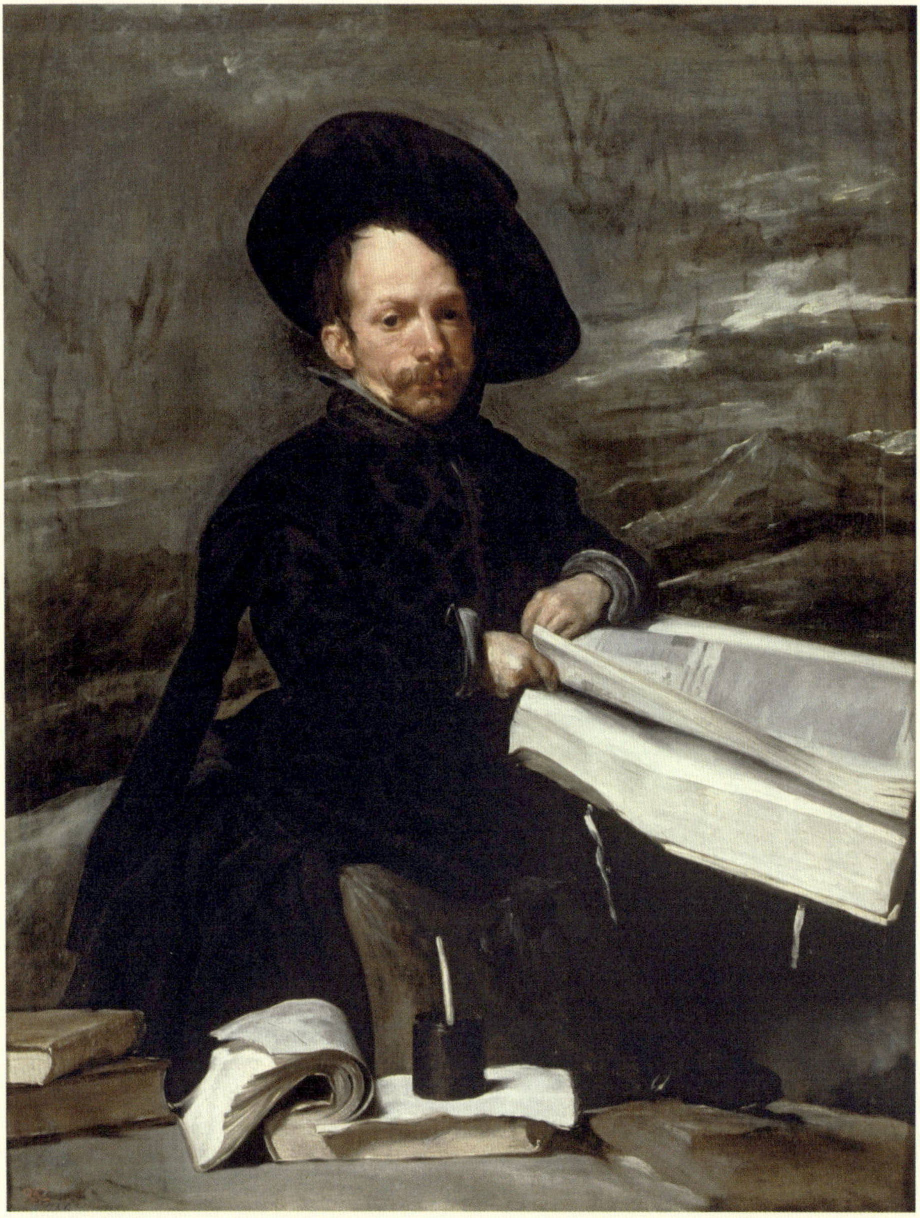

CHAPTER 3

COURTLY CULTURES *and* *their* UNDER-CURRENTS

THE RENAISSANCE had left artists and books poised for far-reaching influence on society, as well as linking the two in a very positive relationship. The later 16th and 17th centuries, turbulent in so many ways, were more quietly significant for the artist–book interaction. The pattern of growth for books across Europe was not even, but the Valencia book inventories mentioned in the previous chapter, which showed books in one in three households, had by 1620, in Canterbury, become one in two.[1]

We know only a limited amount about artists' libraries, beyond the variation in their size. Rembrandt, who included books in many of his works, apparently had few: a Bible, Dürer on proportion, some 'art books' that were in fact prints bound together for reference. El Greco, whose first surviving portrait included a book (the Farnese Hours, *c.* 1571, illuminated by the portrait's subject, Giulio Clorio), and who made a huge book the dominant motif in his hauntingly real but otherwise sparse *Self-Portrait as St Luke* (*c.* 1602–06), had his probably typical inventory recorded by his son in 1614 – mostly volumes that would help in complex religious, mythological or historical works.[2] Velázquez had a much more diverse collection, ranging from philosophy to hydraulics, often useful, but also including Castiglione (still influential) and Roman classics translated into the vernacular. The Genoese artist Domenico Parodi (1672–1742) certainly stands out as 'a lover of letters and sciences'; he spent all his fees on some seven-hundred rare books.[3]

ALL IS NOT WHAT IT SEEMS in Velázquez's *The Dwarf Diego de Acedo* (*c.* 1645). At first sight, it might be thought of as ridiculing the jester at the court of Philip IV of Spain: the size of the book, traditional attribute of a gentleman, stresses the slightness of the figure. Yet Velázquez conveys an air of quiet dignity in the face of his subject, for Don Diego was both a scholar and keeper of the royal seal.

This being the era of the great courtly cultures, the court became the centre of the universe for many Baroque artists. The guild was replaced by the prince. These monarchs loved images that oozed power and authority from every inch of the canvas; books were not absent, but it was a discreet presence, unlike the cacophony created by the celebration of a great victory. The books themselves, also discreet in their content, were often opulently presented, with plentiful use of expensive leathers and precious metals in their bindings. Some of them, from the 1650s, even featured a new form of fore-edge painting – one that could be seen not when the book was closed, but only by fanning the outer edge. But in some sense both writers and artists were servants, pandering to the tastes of majesty, with a leavening of beautiful princesses. Did the image have equality with the word? There were mixed opinions. In England, in 'The Parallel of Poetry and Painting' (1695) – the preface to his own translation of a Latin poem – Dryden restated the position that poems are like silent paintings and paintings like poetry read aloud.[4]

What changed? The new impact given to books by printing was slowly reinforced in many ways. While books and artists continued to be linked firmly to religion as their subject matter, religion could encourage literacy. For example, what is sometimes called the 'Second Reformation' in Germany, in which the Pietists insisted from the end of the 17th century that the content of the Bible must be studied, had in the next hundred years a remarkable effect on the literacy of peasants in eastern Prussia.[5] And the 17th-century English curriculum, with its hornbook (a page of text mounted on a wooden board with a handle) to introduce reading, plus the Bible and other religious literature, went to America; between its first publication in 1690 and 1830, *The New-England Primer* is believed to have sold between 6 and 8 million copies.[6] Religion helped to endorse the value of books. When John Osgood of Andover, Massachusetts, left money in April 1650 'to buy a cushion for the minister to lay his book upon', there were sufficient funds to purchase a cushion costing perhaps three and a half times as much as the Bible itself.[7]

Education also moved on, but slowly. And that was reflected in painting. Jan Steen's *The Schoolmaster* (*c.* 1663–65) showed teacher, book – and unhappy boy about to receive a smack with a spoon.[8] The subject matter of books did expand during the Baroque, but because neither noble nor scholar had an interest in communicating widely, and because the confidence that merchants and lawyers exhibited professionally did not yet extend to a similar security about the intrinsic interest of their lives, the era in which books would become a central part of the culture of all classes and a completely natural accompaniment to the painter's composition remained far off.

The German writer Grimmelshausen emerged from the Thirty Years' War (1618–48) to beguile, later in life, a wide public with his *Simplicissimus* adventures, but François Fénelon (1651–1715), archbishop of Cambrai from 1695, was hardly speaking as a populist when he said: 'If the crowns of all the kingdoms of the Empire were laid down at my feet in exchange for my books and my love of reading, I would spurn them all.'[9] Fénelon was a tutor to the Grand Dauphin's eldest son, Louis, Duke of Burgundy – a very sorry figure when depicted by Alphonse de Neuville in the 19th century, uncomfortable, book and quill on the floor, being lectured by his mentor.

Bookshop development was also slow. The cloth dealer, according to the German commentator Adrian Beier in 1690, managed to distinguish between producer and consumer; the book dealer was both producer and – as a scholar – consumer.[10] It was perhaps remarkable that there were three bookshops in Piacenza in 1631, and that their stock was not entirely religious or locally produced, but hardly a revolution.[11] And as for women, Juan Luis Vives, attached to Catherine of Aragon's court in the 1520s, had set the tone for centuries to come when he said that women should beware of romances in book form 'like as of serpents and snakes'.[12]

In one prominent area of painting, the book was almost an essential. It is true that many things are much older than they seem, and what eventually became, at various times, *Still-leven* in Dutch, *Stillleben* in German and *nature morte* in French is found as early as 1337–38 at Santa Croce, Florence, in niches painted in fresco by Taddeo Gaddi;[13] or, for that matter, is known in the classical world, although no examples survive. But in the 17th century, the sense of mortality that printing (the great preserver) threatened needed a corrective. Thus, in the still lifes known as vanitas, the skull symbolized the transience of life, the hourglass the injunction to spend time well, and books the temporary character of human knowledge.

In Jan Lievens's *Still Life with Books* (*c.* 1627–28), the books have become mere empty bindings, without lasting substance. In *Allegory of Vanity* (1660; opposite) by Juan de Valdés Leal, a putto blows a fading bubble at Vicente Carducho's treatise *Diálogos de la pintura*. So much for human achievement.

Nevertheless, books would not have been shown if they were not important; and where the skull was crowned with laurel (symbol of resurrection) and book, there was perhaps a suggestion that, after all, if life was limited, the findings of the intellect were not.

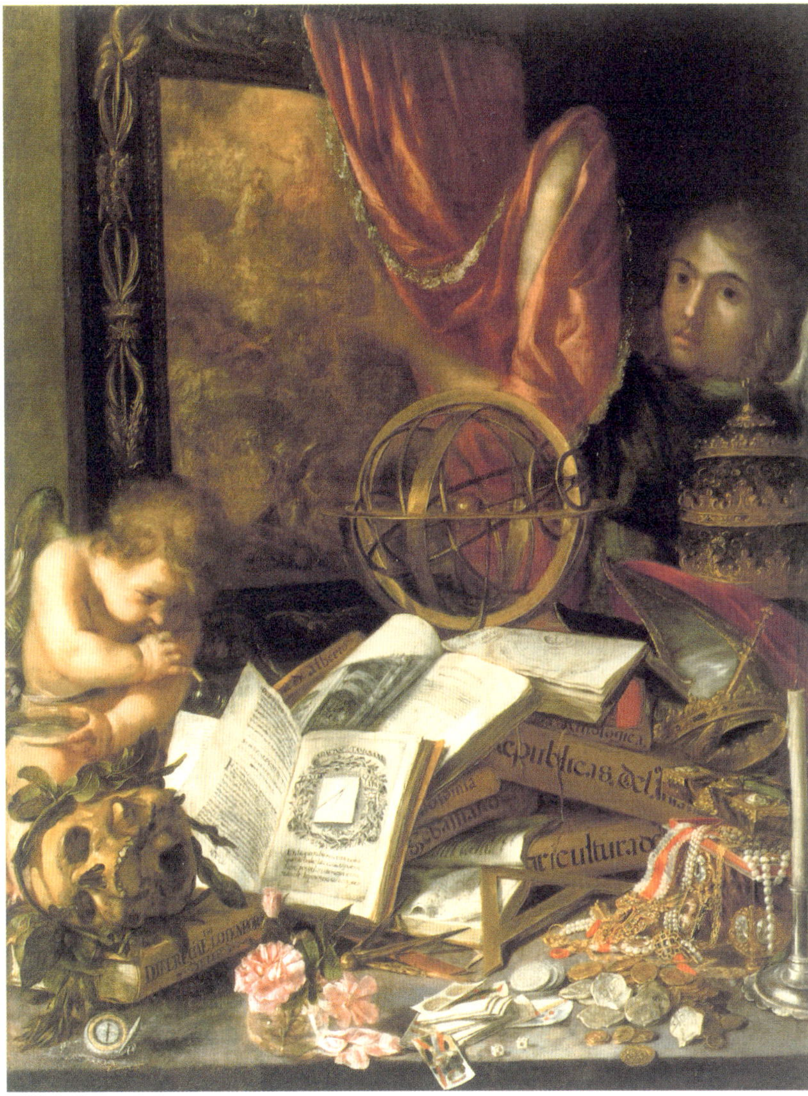

IN JUAN DE VALDÉS LEAL'S *Allegory of Vanity* (1660), a skull rests on a copy of a book by Father Juan Eusebio Nieremberg, distinguishing the temporal from the eternal. The jewels, the money, the gambling tools; the crown and papal tiara of man-made power; even the books, ranging from Jéronimo Román's history *Las Repúblicas del mundo* to Vicente Carducho's *Diálogos de la pintura* – all become meaningless at the Last Judgment, depicted in the painting in the background.

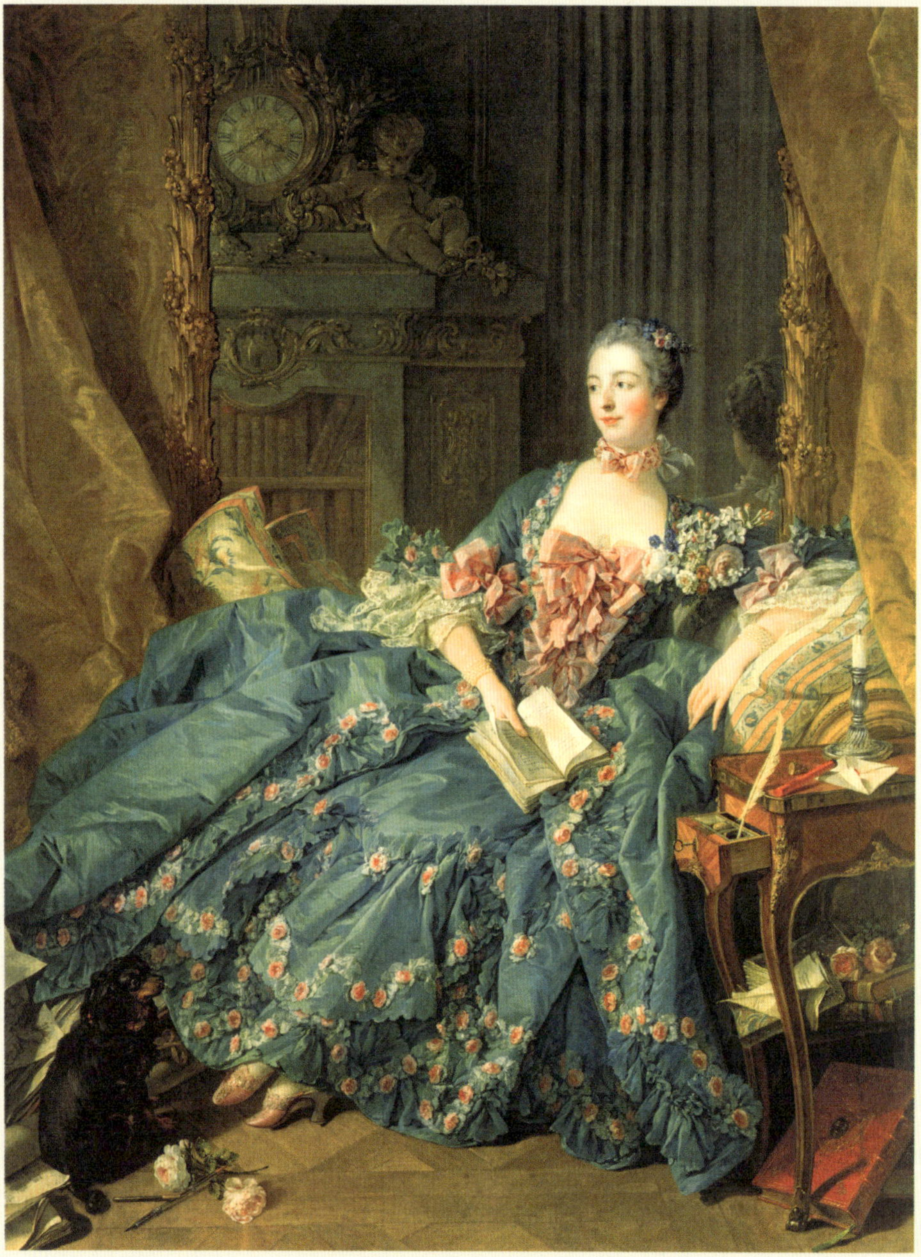

CHAPTER 4

'PEOPLE *are* STUFFED *with* READING MATTER'

THE 18TH CENTURY was not just an era of enlightenment and revolution. 'Here people are stuffed with reading matter in the same way that geese are stuffed by noodles', Luise Mejer, a lady's companion staying with the Countess of Stolberg in Holstein, wrote to a friend in 1784.[1] Hubert Robert (1733–1808) painted the female Enlightenment intellectual Madame Geoffrin at breakfast. Her valet, with broom behind him, reads to her, fulfilling a new servant duty.[2] With the rise of the professional writer, Johann Gottlieb Fichte (1762–1814), son of a ribbon-weaver and descended from generations of peasants, yet one of the founding fathers of German idealism, was able to record in 1805 that reading had taken the place of the other fashionable pursuits of the previous fifty years.[3] 'Fashion' was an appropriate word: Rousseau, in *La Nouvelle Héloïse* (1761), compared the rational and thoughtful readers of his home town, Geneva, with Parisians who 'read' a lot by leafing through books in order to inform themselves for social discourse.[4]

It was a century in which there was increasing questioning by the bourgeoisie of state and church control of people's minds, although change was uneven. The Zurich censors banned as dangerous a translation of Milton's *Paradise Lost* in 1732, but Daniel Defoe's *Robinson Crusoe* (1719), with readers – according to Defoe himself – 'of the middle sort', was a best-seller across Europe, with three translations in Germany within a year of

---

BOOKS ON SHELVES, books scattered, a book with a simple, drawn-on cover emphatically to be read and not for show in the subject's hand – François Boucher's life-size portrait of Madame de Pompadour (1756) shows not a mere mistress of Louis XV of France, but a true intellectual. The *philosophe* Hélevetius was received with hostility for proposing male–female intellectual equality, but education provided by books would, eventually, prove him right.

publication.[5] The bourgeois sense of time, through which anything, including reading, could be allocated a space, helped; so did the writers of fiction themselves, in an almost tangible relationship to their readers – the middle classes, reassuringly, could recognize themselves while being entertained. The *Leserevolution*, the reading revolution, was even encouraged by some Protestant clergy, thus effectively publicizing Defoe or Samuel Richardson.

Richardson, although quintessentially English, received extravagant praise from Diderot and other French *philosophes*. Female virtue, when threatened, as in *Pamela* (1740) and *Clarissa* (1748), was a beguiling topic; the Italian dramatist Carlo Goldoni took the plot of *Pamela* and turned it into a play.[6] No wonder that Joshua Reynolds painted his niece in a work entitled *Theophila Palmer Reading 'Clarissa Harlowe'* (1771).[7] Conceivably, since artists have many things to consider, the choice of 'Offy', as Reynolds's favourite niece was known, was also influenced by the fact that she had 'the most pleasing face', according to Fanny Burney, even if she did not have the same 'understanding' as her elder sister. But we can see she is enjoying her book by the careless way the pages are opened and the spine not supported.

This was also the period in which, in one of history's familiar ironies, the professionalization of the writer and the artist fuelled a wider, non-specialist interest in exhibitions, collecting, art and literary criticism. At first it may have been the mansions of the elite that displayed paintings and books on drawing-room walls, but as Swiss-born Henry Fuseli, who had a special interest in literary painting, wrote in 1788, readers had also become spectators.[8] Fuseli himself had arrived in London in March 1764 in his early twenties with literature as his chosen profession, and it was Reynolds who later encouraged him to study art in Italy.

Fuseli, in thrall to fellow Swiss Johann Jakob Bodmer and his attempts to revive German literature using English precedents, translated some of Shakespeare into German. But his main obsession became Milton; his Gallery of the Miltonic Sublime opened in Pall Mall in 1799 with forty-seven paintings (it was not a success: artists, like publishers and writers, are prone to overdoing a genre).[9]

In France, the abbé Charles Batteux had paved the way in 1746 for the acceptance of the fine arts as a separate category in his treatise *Les Beaux-Arts réduits à un même principe*. The attempt in the *Encyclopédie* (1751–72) to provide all the world's knowledge aided the spread and acceptance of the activity undertaken by artists and sculptors. Montesquieu did not question the existence of 'fine arts' in his essay on taste (he also noted that the love of reading allowed the *heures d'ennui* to become *heures délicieuses*). And in 1816, the academies, which also included music and architecture, became the Académie des Beaux Arts.[10]

The way women were depicted in paintings in all countries, at this time and all others, was very revealing. At best, as in Reynolds's portrait of Emily, Duchess of Leinster (1753) – a woman of many interests – the female subject has her finger in a book, holding the place, but there is no real hint of erudition, unless it comes from the heavier volume on a table, such as the one on which Reynolds has the duchess resting her arm. The Scottish portraitist Allan Ramsay did show her reading, intently, from a large volume, but both artists created a far more formidable figure when they painted her husband. Reynolds painted him grandly in front of his Irish estate, Carton House, Ramsay as a martial figure in red uniform. It would not have been visually apparent that Emilia, as she was born, was heavily involved both in the duke's public life and in the running of the estate.[11]

In the 19th century, neither sex would come out well when artists reflected the evolving moral views of their society. The nonconformist Samuel Colman's crowded scene *St James's Fair* (1824) does include a boy reading to his mother at an open window, but there is a brothel on the other side of the picture. At the bookstall, neither the Bible nor Hannah More's *Poem, On Slavery* (1788) attract attention from the male customer, intent on the *Racing Calendar*.[12]

In the century before Colman's painting, depictions of women evolved from the good manners of the demure girl in *Liseuse* by the French artist Alexis Grimou (1678–1733) – not that he showed good manners to his fellow artists – to something more sinister, the root of which was expressed by the essayist Vicesimus Knox (1752–1821) when he suggested that 'sentimental affection', of the kind you might find in Richardson's novels, was 'but lust in disguise'.[13]

Artists often showed women lost in the emotions of the novels they were reading, implying that they were either easily influenced or empty-headed, or both. But the erotic gaze of the male artist and the viewers of his work was more or less explicit – very much so in works by Pierre-Antoine Baudouin (1723–1769), François Boucher's pupil and son-in-law, who exhibited in the Salon in the 1760s, but carried with him the air of the libertine, as Diderot said. In Baudouin's *La Lecture* (*c.* 1760; p. 106), any 'serious' books are discarded to the left; the guitar and small dog to the right perhaps represent the undemanding pleasures 'appropriate' for a woman. And in the centre, in front of a screen blocking off the door, is a woman sprawled back in her chair, a novel about to slip from one hand, while her other hand is inserted into her gown intent on masturbation.[14] In another version of the work, *Le Midi*, engraved as part of a series by Emmanuel de Ghendt – a similar scene but in a garden, with the novel dropped to the ground and the girl's umbrella abandoned at the side – the focus is even stronger.[15]

Whatever else, the rise of the novel in the 18th century changed the world of books and provided plentiful subject matter for social commentary by artists. In a commission from the Prussian Crown Princess of Sweden, Louise Ulrique, in 1745, Chardin contrasts a woman at work on household costs (in one painting) with the same woman caught unawares with a different kind of book resting on her knees (in a second).[16] And everywhere the progress of books went further into society – a worry to some as (with a little exaggeration) reading became an addiction (*Lesesucht*) or a mania (*Lesewut*).[17]

Catalogues from the Leipzig Book Fair indicate that, in 1650, 41 per cent of books had theology as their subject and 71 per cent were in Latin. By 1740 Latin had dropped to 27 per cent, theology less so (to 31 per cent).[18] But there was also a division between Roman Catholic and Protestant regions. Lutheran cities, such as Tübingen, show a very high proportion of inventories with book ownership in the middle of the 18th century, unlike Catholic Paris. In puritan America, books were central to family life from the beginning; and if the *Bay Psalm Book*, after its first publication in 1640, went through twenty-four editions in the next ninety years, *Robinson Crusoe* could be found in forty-four editions between its first New World appearance in 1757 and the end of the century.[19] At the time of Independence, there were more English books in America than in the whole of Europe; Noah Webster's *American Spelling Book* (1783) was one of many signs that books would play an important role in the New World – and thus would be an essential subject for artists.[20]

The progress of books was visible from many perspectives in the 18th century. Berlin had a lending library as early as 1704 and many more followed, at least in the Protestant centre and north. A similar process took place in Great Britain, beginning in Edinburgh in 1725.[21] The quality of book production was often high, a sign of the book's status, although some – notably the Swiss bookseller and critic Johann Georg Heinzmann at the end of the century – complained about all the 'chintz and glitter'.[22] Nationalism sparked creativity in typography: Italy had its Giambattista Bodoni, France its François Didot.[23]

Germany took a lead in the development of publishing as a business, with the beginnings of modern marketing and distribution. The gulf between Christoph Gottlieb Nicolai, a publisher of the Baroque era, and his Enlightenment son Friedrich was a chasm. Friedrich, a mix of publisher, bookseller, critic and author – an *Aufklärer*, a German *philosophe* – helped to shape a market, as well as responding to consumer needs. Between 1759 and 1811, he published some 1,100 volumes – theology certainly, but also textbooks, science and technology, travel and novels.

Not that he was always popular: as Goethe and Schiller's epigram had it: 'Little as you have done for the education of the Germans / Fritz Nicolai, you have earned a great deal in the process.' Nicolai was certainly drawn to feuds, although sometimes with good cause, as in the case of Heinzmann, who also attacked Goethe and Schiller and the entire writing establishment in Berlin and the rationalist north of Germany. Heinzmann's *A Plea to My Nation: On the Plague of German Literature* (1795) complained that too many books were published, that they prevented people from thinking for themselves, and that they showed no respect or interest in the past. The obsession with reading resulted in 'oversensitivity, susceptibility to colds, headaches, poor eyesight, heat rash, gout, arthritis, haemorrhoids, asthma, apoplexy, lung disease, poor digestion, constipation, nervous disorders, migraines, epilepsy, hypochondria, and melancholy'. A more balanced view might be that, on the whole, in France, England and the new United States, the spread of books throughout society was welcomed; in the German lands, Nicolai seemed to threaten the elite with what they saw as a wave of superficiality.[24]

Either way, nothing was going to stop the march of books. In 1796, the Erfurt clergyman Johann Rudolf Gottlieb Beyer declared that 'no lover of tobacco or coffee, no wine drinker or lover of games, can be as addicted to their pipe, bottle, games or coffee-table as those many hungry readers are to their reading habit.'[25] In France, the utopian plan of visionary architect Etienne-Louis Boullée to create a gigantic reading room for the king (1785), in which all knowledge would be stored and studied, took the form of a basilica. In a sense, the sacredness of church buildings was being transferred to the book.[26] Artists might take note of Kant's 1798 truism – that 'incessant reading' was now one of life's essentials.[27] In *Le Bon Genre* (1817), a collection of prints depicting, often satrically, the lives of the Parisian bourgeoisie, there is a telling illustration of this: in a drawing entitled 'Luxury and Poverty', a woman lies in bed in a sad, poor room, her luxurious clothes – and her book – beside her.[28] Chardin's commission from the Crown Princess of Sweden had depicted a woman in a *bergère*, wearing a *liseuse*: chair and clothing both designed for a world of books.

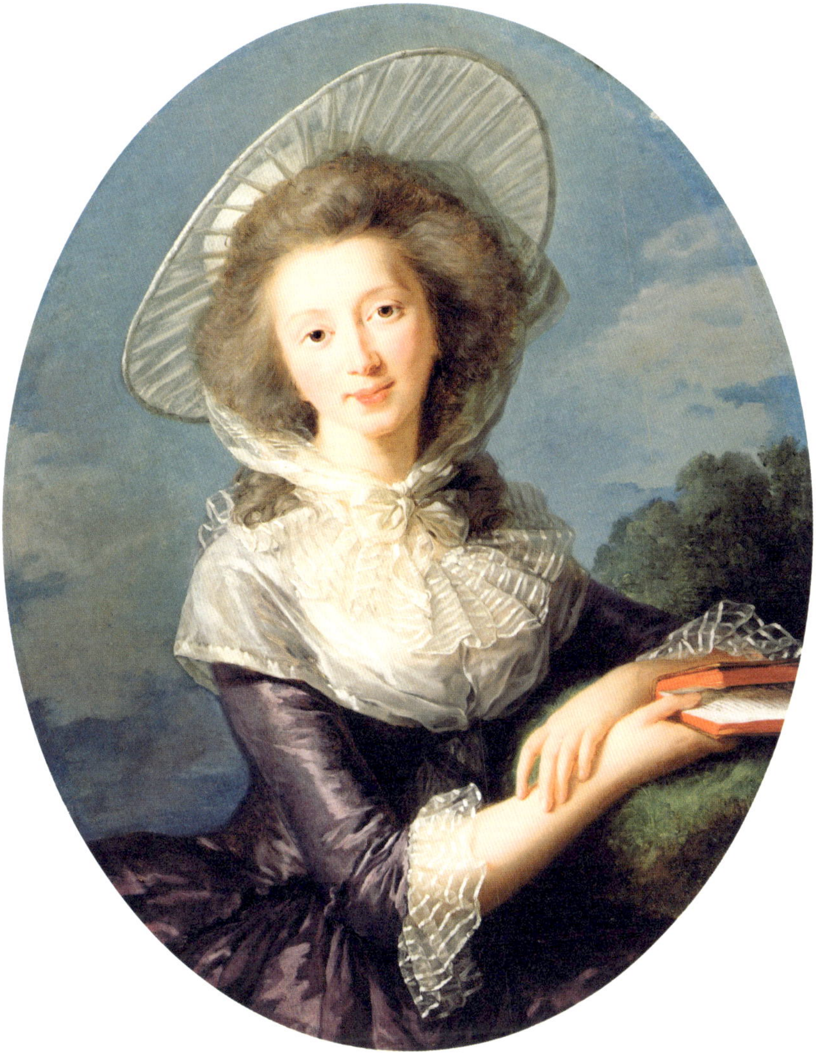

ELISABETH VIGÉE LE BRUN had to make her way as a female artist not only in a man's world, but also without the help of her portrait-painter father, Louis Vigée, who died when she was twelve. Her early critics were divided: her work showed taste and liveliness, but was there a tendency towards bright attractiveness more than reality? Her 1778 portrait of the French queen, Marie Antoinette, settled any career doubts. By the time of this portrait of the Vicomtesse de Vaudreuil in 1785, the artist's accomplished ability to portray refinement – and its natural accompaniment, a book marked by a finger indicating the point reached – was fully demonstrated.

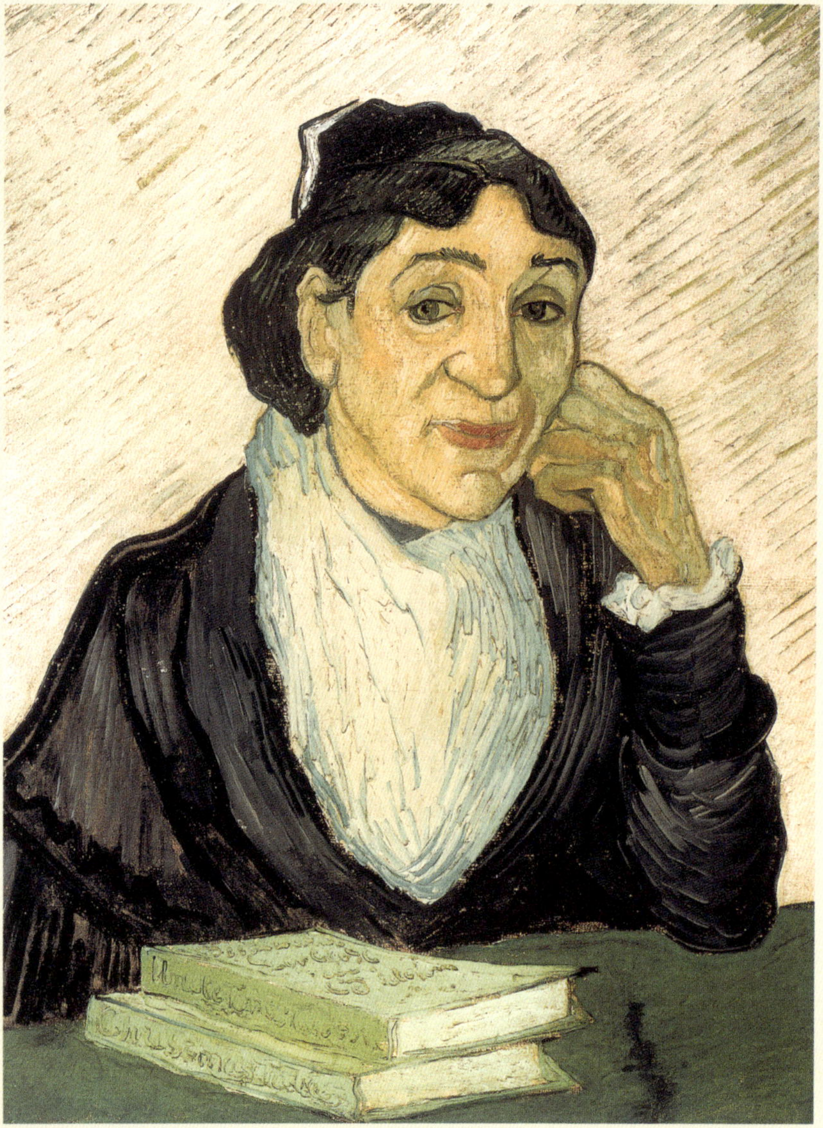

CHAPTER 5

BOOKS *and the* PAINTING *of* 'MODERN LIFE'

THE 18TH CENTURY may have ended in revolution and a rampant Napoleon, but books and artists, in their quiet way, were not to be deterred. Soon it would be the most natural thing for Dickens's manipulative businessman in *Dombey and Son* (1848), Carker, to adorn his home both with lavishly bound books and with their 'companions', prints and pictures, just as his death on a railway track reflected a new environment for suicide, murder or accident.[1] The middle classes were at home in providing not only writers and artists but also customers for the books and paintings that resulted. Once the bourgeoisie had a literature of its own, it was a small step for it to have an art of its own.

Books fulfilled multiple roles – in the early 19th century, often to entertain and to educate, then more and more to parade bourgeois values and virtues. When the century moved to its close in some uncertainty and doubt, they were comforting and reassuring. Often they were all these things, and each was expressed in paintings of the period, literally and symbolically.

Increasingly, the art patrons came, as the *Art Journal* reported in 1869, from 'among the wealthier sections of the middle class of society'.[2] One of those enjoying a natural relationship between books and art was the art collector Benjamin Godfrey Windus, whose library in his house on Tottenham

---

VAN GOGH FIRST MET MADAME GINOUX in May 1888, when he began lodging in Arles at the café she ran with her husband. Of the six portraits titled *L'Arlésienne*, this one – painted in the asylum at Saint-Rémy in 1890 – was once owned by Albert Aurier, whose article in *Mercure de France* in January of that year was the first to take Van Gogh seriously. On the table are books by two of the artist's favourite authors: Harriet Beecher Stowe's *Uncle Tom's Cabin* on top, and Dickens's *Christmas Books* (here called *Christmas Tales*, a retranslation by Van Gogh of *Contes de Noël*) beneath.

Green, north London, was painted in watercolour by John Scarlett Davis in 1835. It was in this room, which had Turners on the wall, as well as containing books, that Ruskin studied while researching for the first volume of his *Modern Painters*. In the watercolour, two of Windus's grandchildren look at other artworks in an album, in front of a wall of paintings and books.

Not for the last time, an entrepreneur, with friends from multiple businesses, distorted the art market: Windus, who had bought 650 drawings by David Wilkie, released a large number of them on to the market soon after the artist's death in 1841.[3] Wilkie himself painted many subjects, but naturally they included books of many kinds. *The Cotter's Saturday Night* (1837) shows the family's patriarch reading to his attentive family; *The Rent Day* (1807) focuses on an elderly farmer and his son, but this time the 'book' is a record of rent and the steward is in conflict with the tenants.

During the 19th century, novels embraced all the subject matter of what, in art, would become the painting of 'modern life', to use Baudelaire's phrase. In France, the new urban landscapes were an appropriate setting for Balzac or Zola to tell their tangled tales of love, power and money. In Germany, the 4,505 new titles on all subjects of 1821 had become 31,281 in 1910; in the latter year, the United States had 13,470, France 12,615 and the UK 10,804.[4] The scale of the change in the vastness of America had been particularly striking. News of George Washington's death in 1799 took almost four weeks to reach Frankfort, Kentucky.[5] But even by 1825, the memoir of Catharine Brown, a Cherokee Christian convert, could get sufficient distribution to allow for nine printings in seven years (and in the frontispiece, its subject lies on her sickbed, accompanied by her essential companion: a book).[6]

The United States quickly became unique, as the United States is, in finding an efficient way for all segments of a market to obtain what they wanted. In American publisher G. P. Putnam's 'Railway Classics' series of the 1850s, one could buy Washington Irving's satire on New York culture from early in the century, *A History of New-York* (1809), for just 50 cents. The railway magnate Henry E. Huntington probably surpassed everyone in his collecting of incunabula, pre-1500 printed books – a sure sign that new societies were giving as much primacy to the book as the old.

Booksellers became a suitable subject for artists; for one thing, there was no trace of cynicism in their enthusiasm for their product, as we might judge from the title of Honoré Daumier's *Bookseller in Ecstasy* (1844).[7] And new media? William Henry Fox Talbot's *The Pencil of Nature*, published in parts between 1844 and 1846, was the first printed book to contain photographs;

and it included a photograph of ... books.[8] Still life had thus gone from canvas to a new art form, the photograph – albeit without commercial success, since modest sales of each successive part of Talbot's work tailed off. In 1889 the French wallpaper manufacturer Isidore Leroy even produced wallpaper depicting books by Jules Verne, Cervantes and Walter Scott.[9]

Was this a tale essentially of the middle classes? Not by the end of the century, and often earlier. In 1865, Catherine Laura Johnstone described the cottage interior of an old and infirm Russian peasant in which six to eight grandchildren were 'absorbed in their books'. Expectations of 'barbarism, sloth and ignorance' were belied by the presence of Nikolay Karamzin's *History of the Russian State* and the *Memoirs* of the French diplomat and politician Bourrienne.[10] The UK enjoyed about 70 per cent male literacy in 1850 (55 per cent female), Germany 88 per cent overall in 1871.[11]

The realist painter François Bonvin showed the spread of reading through the classes in *On the Pauper's Bench* (1864), with its two white-capped and presumably homeless women, and also in *La Servante indiscrète* (1871). They are both works of moderate achievement, influenced by the Dutch masters, but significant for their subjects' patent involvement in what they are reading and the low social status of those subjects. Bonvin's *Grandmamma's Breakfast* (1865) puts its emphasis on a large book on the elderly lady's lap, with breakfast relegated to the background, arriving through a door. The working men painted by Edgar Bundy in *The Night School* (1892) are almost all completely engaged in their books; if one is distracted, he may well be dreaming of the escape education might provide.[12] Workhouse life, as depicted by Hubert von Herkomer in *Eventide: A Scene in the Westminster Union* (1878), certainly revealed the aged residents animated by drinking tea and perhaps sewing. It would, however, have been incomplete without a figure on the floor, book on lap, and another in the background.[13] Laps were made for books, or vice-versa.

In January 1866, the Cuban newspaper *La Aurora* reported on readings in a cigar factory, which had been proposed by the proprietor: an encouragement to work and an introduction to books that would be a 'source of everlasting friendship and great entertainment' for the workers. Alas, the experiment did not last, since the political governor of Cuba believed that books were politically inflammatory.[14] More far-reaching, if all too incomplete, is what happened in post-bellum America: Dickens, Shakespeare and Louisa May Alcott may not have been appropriate fare for the eighteen-year-old Ida B.Wells – daughter of Mississipi slaves and future civil rights activist – when she went to school in 1880, but they were perhaps a start.

Up from Slavery, the 1901 autobiography of African American educator and leader Booker T. Washington, detailed the story of a generation and their passion for learning, writing and reading.[15] And while Winslow Homer's *The New Novel* (1877; pp. 182–83) showed the carefree mood (of the subject, not in this case of the artist, as we shall see later) a book could provide for the white middle classes, his *Sunday Morning in Virginia* (also 1877) showed the rapt – we might say spellbound – attention of three black children in response to the book being read to them.[16]

Similarly, in France, while publisher Michel Lévy pioneered less expensive books for the middle classes or high-selling writings by Victor Hugo, George Sand or Charles Augustin Sainte-Beuve, instalment publishing of sensational fiction widened the social basis. Calmann Lévy, brother of Michel, encouraged the process, and their firm published more than a thousand new and reissued titles in 1872. Although education developed painfully slowly across the Western world for the less advantaged sections of society, Louis Hachette's textbooks and dictionaries provided suitable tools.[17] Hachette also became especially interested in helping the poorer classes to escape: after food and housing, the book was the special ingredient.

Education at home could supply a strong foundation. In Fort Wayne, Indiana, the Hamilton sisters – Edith, Alice, Margaret and Norah, all of whom would excel in their chosen field – were taught by their mother in the 1870s and 1880s; there was much reading aloud and the use of people in fiction to underpin the writing of plays, or even as part of role play in family life.[18] Of course, older children could use books to assert their independence. In *Interior at Arcachon* (1871), Manet depicts his wife and son cut off from each other not just by a window but by Leon's evidently far-away thoughts, stemming from the book resting on his knees.[19] Reading groups, however, encouraged friendship and social bonding, although sometimes with more serious professional intent, as is visible in Théo van Rysselberghe's pointillist *The Reading* (1903; p. 232). The Belgian artist also painted his wife, book in lap, in a garden (p. 188), and again, in a similar pose, inside, although this time with his daughter, who, alas, looks bored, rather than engaged in her mother's pleasure.

Once François Guizot had encouraged the creation of public schools in France in the 1830s, artists had a new subject – not that the growth in the number of schools was immediately visible in any country, or that, judging by the British artist Henry James Richter's 1823 watercolour *A Picture of Youth, or The Village School in an Uproar*, everything went smoothly. Richter's absent teacher, cane in hand, is about to return to find books flying in all directions. In fact, this image would be widely used in educational propaganda directed at all sections of society in Germany, France, Spain, Italy and the United States, making use of low-cost lithography. In general, the influence of the book, and its suitability as a subject for artists, were bound to reach new heights if the numbers in public schools could increase from 1.8 million to 17 million, as they did in America in just forty years from 1840.[20]

Gender remained very much a preoccupation. Leigh Hunt, a key figure in the English Romantic movement and the son of American Loyalists who settled in Great Britain, may have been unconsciously hinting at the dark side of 19th-century society when he called his books his 'mistresses'. Ruskin was not alone in seeing books as women: first clothed, then opened up, viewed, touched, smelt, owned.[21] His own sexual relations reveal a disturbing – and ever since much-debated – attitude to innocence. He met his only wife, Effie, when she was twelve and later failed to consummate the marriage. He met Rose la Touche in 1858 when she was nine and proposed when she was in her teens, only to be rejected. A kind view might be that he wanted an ideal and – being a man given to extremes – could not deal with its absence. The 20th century would go further, as the 20th century did, in a Duchamp catalogue in 1947, its cover featuring a foam breast in 3D with the invocation, *Prière de toucher* (Please Touch).[22]

It appears to have been John Ferriar, a Scottish physician at Manchester Royal Infirmary, who invented in 1809 the term 'bibliomania': the 'wild desires' of 'the hapless man, who feels the book-disease'. At the end of the century, the grandson of the great essayist William Hazlitt (1778–1830), William Carew Hazlitt, a lawyer and an editor, traced the spread of addictions in his *Confessions of a Collector* (1897).[23] But perhaps the mania's root was collecting – not books as such – and Hazlitt himself declared that 'paintings and prints were the greatest snare of all'.[24]

The French writer and publisher Octave Uzanne would probably have disagreed. In 1892, some ninety-five of the bookstall-keepers on the left bank of the Seine were given a banquet from money provided by M. Xavier Marnier of the Académie Française. Uzanne's *The Book-Hunter in Paris: Studies among the Bookstalls and the Quays* was published the following year. If 'Lovers are but hunters after women', no chase was 'more insatiable in triumph', 'more abundant in joys', 'more obstinate in ill-success' than the search for books. For one thing, physical pleasure was 'not entirely absent', derivable from fondling a binding.[25] It was Uzanne, however, in an article for *Scribner's Magazine* in 1894, who, in writing about phonography, came close to predicting the new broadcast media of the 20th century, the article's title a mistaken assumption: 'The End of Books'.

How did women react to all of this? So much of it was very extreme. Writing in his early 20th-century treatise *The Sexual Life of Our Time in Its Relations to Modern Civilization*, the German psychiatrist who rediscovered the manuscript of the Marquis de Sade's *120 Days of Sodom*, Iwan Bloch, referred to bibliomaniacs and erotomaniacs who bound books with female breast skin.[26] Women also had to face the fact that many males in all countries stressed the 'False Morality of Lady Novelists', to borrow the title of W. R. Greg's *National Review* article of 1859, with a heavy emphasis on female inability to apply critical, rather than emotional, judgment.[27]

There was the occasional diversion, although it was still the men who got what they wanted. The Reverend Thomas Frognall Dibdin's *Bibliomania, or Book Madness* (1809) confounded the apparently obvious suggestion that male collectors viewed women as objects by finishing with a tale of two bibliophiles who are encouraged in their mania by two sisters intent on seducing them. The men become enamoured by the books – and only the books.[28]

Yet, as so many paintings suggested (there was no one more involved and content than a woman with book in a Henri Fantin-Latour portrait), women would not be deterred by the historian and journalist Charles de Mazade's complaint in 1867 that the modern novel seemed to be 'the privileged domain of women' (or men either, since they elected him to the Académie Française later in his career).[29] The palpable excitement of reaching the end of a book animates *The Last Chapter* (1863; p. 119) by the Pre-Raphaelite Robert Braithwaite Martineau.[30] The Renaissance tradition of showing the Virgin reading devotional literature was nevertheless perpetuated in such works as the Raphael-influenced *Madonna and Child* by William Dyce (1845), 'so chaste & exquisitely painted', as Queen Victoria reported in her journal.[31]

Overall, we would have to say that the artist's male gaze had decided that women, in their relationship with books, were either impressionably lost in a fictional world or upholders of undemonstrative, deeply moral conduct. As the century progressed, greater subtlety developed, at least in the work of some artists. In his paintings of women and girls reading, of which there were many, Renoir began to leave an impression that 'female' did not spell 'stereotype'; nor did Toulouse-Lautrec's 1887 portrait of his mother reading exhibit either frivolity or a heavy moral aura.

Of course, although the 19th century was so confident that 'truth' was a reachable reality, its writers and artists, whether consciously or not, provide us with abundant evidence of opinion, belief and prejudice but not of truth; their successors, in the 20th century, would in any case strongly dissent from the idea that representing reality was their function. When Auguste Toulmouche painted *Forbidden Fruit* for the Paris Salon in 1867, were its four young girls – two reading, evidently delighted by illicit literature, a third listening at the door and a fourth reaching for the higher shelf where such delights were to be found – the subject of an implicit male reprimand? Or were they just using their guile, independence and enthusiasm to get what they wanted?[32] Our own era can safely give them applause for their spirit, given that, at about the same time, a monster like Heinrich von Treitschke in Germany, with his own fantasized version of history and of women's intellects, could praise Gustav Freytag's *Bilder aus der deutschen Vergangenheit*, on the Teutonic past, as 'one of the rare historical works that women can read and understand'.[33] A milder form of Von Treitschke's rabid prejudice against women could be seen everywhere: Richard Westall's *Milton Composing 'Paradise Lost'*, exhibited at the Royal Academy in 1802, showed the poet's two daughters recording the epic verse on paper; in fact, neither had been taught to write, a common fate for the girls in a family.[34]

Despite all, there is more to be said about the love of books than what it tells us about gender differences and male behaviour. Leigh Hunt, in his 1823 article 'My Books' for the *Literary Examiner*, spoke for many when he reflected, as he sat warm by the fire one winter, on how he loved authors not only for giving him imaginative pleasures but also for making him 'love the very books themselves': 'Take me, my bookshelves, to your arms / And shield me from the ills of life.' Just as he spoke of contact with his books in a literal sense – he liked to lean his head against them – it is moot as to whether that was an innocent human pleasure or some conscious or unconscious confusion of book and woman.

Perhaps the truth of the matter is that there was both innocent pleasure and something far from innocent in the feelings of many bibliophiles. Isaac D'Israeli, whose *Curiosities of Literature* went through fourteen editions between 1791 and 1849, referred to raging 'BIBLIOMANIA' and compared books to 'eastern beauties peering through their jalousies'. Nevertheless, he described his collecting motives as simple utility and pleasure, and in an essay in the same book defended women against those aspects of Christianity, Islam and Judaism that reduce their role to that of 'multiplication and pleasure'. And Ruskin, in *Sesame and Lilies* (1865), complains that lovers of books are pronounced mad, whereas we don't speak of gamblers being 'horse-maniacs' even though the habit ruins them.

The prolific Scottish author Andrew Lang wrote of the erotic effect of touching books, but he ascribed that phenomenon to the fact that they had sometimes been touched by kings, or cardinals, or scholars, all of whom were men. It was left to the Liberal politician Augustine Birrell to pour scorn on the otherworldly maniacs: 'To listen to some people you might almost fancy it was within their power to build a barricade of books, and sit behind it mocking the slings and arrows of outrageous fortune.'[35]

The long debate about whether art or literature was superior continued. The English essayist and poet Charles Lamb, at his most strident, argued that the immediacy of art stifled interpretation: once you saw, in a painting, Falstaff as 'Plump Jack' or Othello as 'a Blackamoor', you acquired immovable and unsubtle preconceptions.[36] But Ruskin, possibly the coiner of the term 'word painting', was perfectly represented by Dickens, who was adamant that 'I don't invent it – really do not – but see it, and write it down.'[37] The novelist's own opinion had an interesting endorsement from Van Gogh in March 1883: 'There is no writer, in my opinion, who is so much a painter and a black-and-white artist as Dickens.'[38] It was the Romantics earlier in the century who had abandoned Gotthold Ephraim Lessing's 18th-century desire to make a demarcation between painting with a primary concern with space and writing with a primary concern with change over time, expressed in his *Laocoön* (1766).

On the ground, painting and reading often went happily together. In Russia, Grigory and Nikanor Chernetsov were commissioned by the Ministry of the Imperial Court in 1838 to paint interesting places on the Volga. In their painting of the barge on which they spent half a year, and on which they had many mishaps, one brother reads and the other writes or draws.[39]

Sometimes, artists and writers were able to inspire one another. Robert Browning's painterly poems, 'Andrea del Sarto' or 'Fra Lippo Lippi', feel as though they come from the artist's work itself.[40] Dostoevsky's second wife, Anna, recorded how he had remained completely still, as if in the first stages of one of his epilectic fits, in front of Holbein's *Body of the Dead Christ in the Tomb* (1520–22). Later, the writer's notes for *The Idiot* are full of preoccupation with the dead Christ; the Holbein, in a copy, hangs in the house of the icy killer, Rogozhin, while the Christ-like hero, Prince Myshkin, has seen the original in Basle.[41]

Just as it has often been remarked that novels are great inspirers of the visual because of the way the words – the story – evoke an image, so painting often provides the backbone, or even the plot, of a novel. Published in 1890, Oscar Wilde's *The Picture of Dorian Gray* (what could be more visual?) was an early example of a genre that gathered pace the following century, two more recent examples being Tracy Chevalier's *Girl with a Pearl Earring* (1999, about Vermeer) and Donna Tartt's *The Goldfinch* (2013, at the heart of which is Carel Fabritius's painting of the same name from 1654). Another good example is Anthony Powell's *Books Do Furnish a Room* (1971). Powell's novel was one of a sequence that he called *A Dance to the Music of Time*, a title itself derived from a complex story that began with Giovanni Pietro Bellori in the 17th century. Bellori, Poussin's first biographer, wrote his own version of Vasari's *Lives*, and entitled the work by Poussin now in the Wallace Collection, London, *The Dance of Human Life*. Today, after cataloguing by the curators at the collection in the early 20th century, we know it by the name used by Powell: art reflected in literature, just as literature was reflected in art.

For artists, books were a rich source of imagery. William Powell Frith's autobiography records his extensive reading of the works of Cervantes, Molière and Oliver Goldsmith, looking for subjects.[42] In the UK alone, it has been established that at least 2,300 paintings from 1760 to 1900 are of scenes from Shakespeare. The technical progress in engraving and printing enabled artists to use books and prints to reach larger audiences. In the United States, Eastman Johnson's *Barefoot Boy* (1860), a portrait of the eponymous subject of a hugely popular poem by John Greenleaf Whittier, became an iconic image in 1868 thanks to chromolithography.[43]

We were not yet in the era of the creative use of the book form by artists, but Delacroix's illustrations for an edition of Goethe's *Faust* (1828; 'he has surpassed my own vision', said Goethe), or Manet's for a French translation of Edgar Allan Poe's *The Raven* (1875), were two examples from many – not that the latter was successful, despite its Mallarmé translation. Delacroix had himself failed as a young man to get two novels published, and records in his journal in 1824 his wish to explain the difference between art forms.[44] He never did; and while he, like others, was concerned that painting and illustration left the artist under the yoke of literature, he too used Shakespeare and other writers. And who could resist John Watkins Chapman's *The Old Curiosity Shop (or Little Nell and Her Grandfather)*, exhibited at the Royal Academy in 1888, with (of course) a book on Nell's lap, as well as plentiful books among the disorder.[45]

Many artists continued to be of humble origin; to be one of the *bohèmes* at the Café Guerbois in Paris, where Manet presided and was able to display both his erudition and his speed of thought, was not always a comfortable experience for the son of a mere grocer, as Monet was, or the sixth son of a struggling provincial tailor, as Renoir was. But other artists could, at their ease, display a considerable knowledge of classical or Renaissance literature, as Degas did, although that was sometimes at the Café Guerbois also. Many writers could draw, which might be a useful distraction (as well as bearing out Napoleon's dictum that 'a good drawing is worth more than a long speech'): Turgenev, who in 1863 met Flaubert in Paris – as one did in the close-knit, comradely but sometimes competitive and explosive international world of artists and writers – is relatively cursory in writing his condolences at George Sand's death, but the most interesting part of his letter is a lively sketch of his Russian estate, Spasskoye.[46]

For Victor Hugo, drawing was more than a distraction, although he took good care to keep it in private, so that it was his writing on which others focused (an unnecessary precaution, given that his corpus of written work amounted to what most people could not begin to match in quality and quantity in many lifetimes). He left some 4,000 drawings, and shared them selectively, as we might gather from the letter he wrote to Baudelaire in April 1860 expressing happiness that the latter thought kindly of them, and explaining that his materials included 'all sorts of bizarre concoctions': not just pencil and charcoal, but coal dust and soot. He also used coffee grounds, and rumours had it that his own blood was employed for the purpose too. His son Charles, whose death of a stroke in that turbulent time of Franco-Prussian war and the Paris Commune helped to occasion *L'Année terrible*, may have been *parti pris* when he compared his father's drawings to etchings by Rembrandt and Piranesi, but the writer certainly won Delacroix's praise as a potentially great artist.[47]

It would be going to far to suggest, as Sainte-Beuve did in the heady days of Romanticism, that the avant-garde painters had become 'our brothers'.[48] Nevertheless, artists often painted authors: Gustave Courbet's *Portrait of Charles Baudelaire* (1848; p. 223) shows the writer reading intently, although Baudelaire's distaste for realism put limits on their friendship.[49] Manet and Zola had no such difficulty, especially after Zola criticized Manet's omission from the Salon in 1866. Their friendship, or at least their mutual desire for success, was enhanced in conversations at the Café de Bade, and Manet's portrait of Zola from 1868 (p. 228) includes a variety of books – among them, and open in front of the writer, one of the artist's favourites, Charles Blanc's *L'Histoire des peintres*. The portrait also includes a reproduction of Manet's *Olympia* (1863), which Zola had praised, and Zola's published defence of Manet, with its blue cover: a painting of multiple *homages*, cemented by a mutual desire for applause.[50]

In this universe, artists also painted other artists reading, whether or not they were well read – Renoir's portrait of Monet smoking his pipe and intent on his book (1872; p. 229), for example. Sometimes, as in Marcellin Desboutin's *Edgar Degas Reading* (1884), the cap fitted, for Degas was exceptionally learned, even if on this occasion it was a newspaper or magazine in his hands.

And Van Gogh's expressions of book connections were as poignant as anything in the *oeuvre* of this troubled genius. His *Still Life with Bible* of 1885 (p. 231), with its prominent, dominant open Bible – literal symbol of the fierce Calvinism of his father, Theodorus – contrasting with the small, battered, subdued-yellow (subdued but still a contrast) copy of Zola's *La Joie de vivre*, represented a conflict to be resolved by a victory, of sorts, for the latter.[51] The Bible was open at Isaiah, with its powerful sense of sin and the need for repentance: no *joie de vivre* allowed. Van Gogh, disillusioned with the Church after his time in the Borinage in Belgium, and newly intent on becoming a painter, nevertheless did not find it easy to break with his father and his stern world view; his *Still Life* was painted just after Theodorus's sudden death.[52]

Vincent's love of books, he said in one letter, was as sacred as his love of Rembrandt.[53] Their usually clear depiction in his works revealed how widely he had read (Dickens, for example), although sometimes their presence was in fact a reflection of a current preoccupation, one of which was his health, as in *Drawing Board and Onions* (1889), with its *Annuaire de la santé du Docteur Raspail* prominent on the table. The six similar paintings entitled *L'Arlésienne*, of Van Gogh's landlady in Arles, were sparked by the arrival of Gauguin, who drew her while Van Gogh dashed off a painting with gloves and umbrella, to be replaced by books in the other versions.

Two of Van Gogh's paintings, one of his own chair and one of Gauguin's containing a candle and two books, dating to late 1888 and Gauguin's departure for Paris, have spawned a vast interpretative literature. Theirs was too intense a relationship for longevity, but what Van Gogh called Gauguin's 'empty place' – his chair – in a letter to the art critic Albert Aurier[54] was not inappropriately represented by modern novels and a candle, knowledge and light, yet otherwise in a sombre setting. The dynamics of artist, book and human relationships were more alive, more subtle and more in evidence than ever. The presence of the book in painting, natural for so many centuries already, was an essential for the representation of 'modern life'.

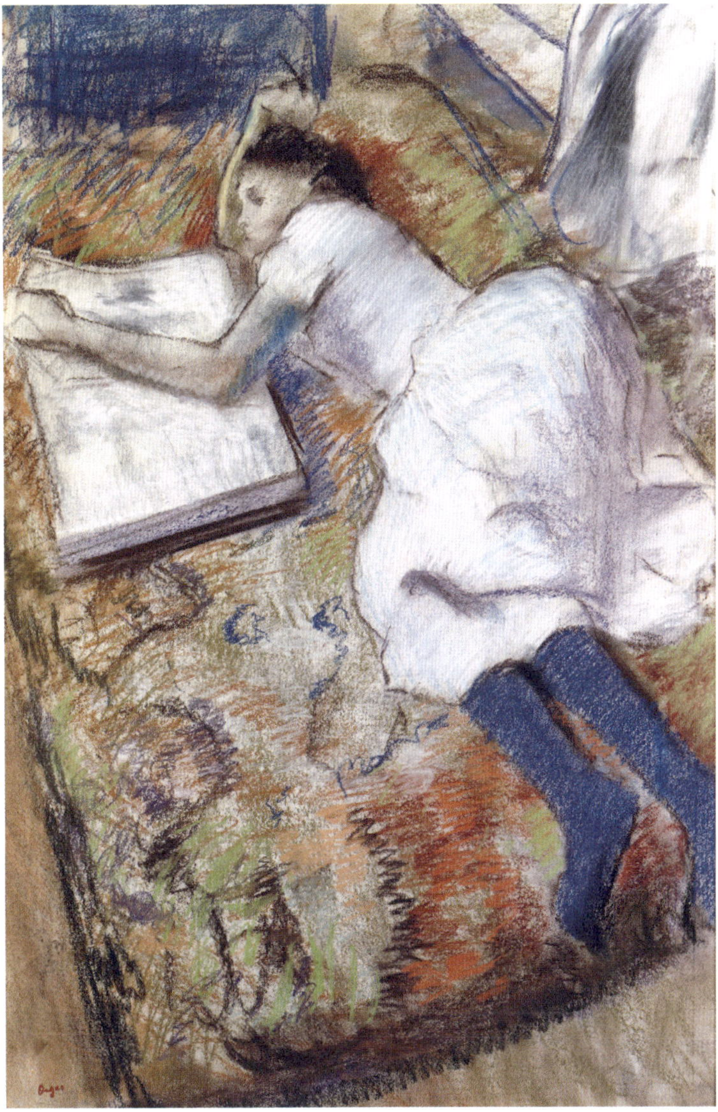

DEGAS'S PASTEL of a languid young girl (*c.* 1889) – probably a daughter of his sister Marguerite de Gas Fevre – shows how versatile bound volumes of any kind could be in their human effect, no matter whether education or pleasure was the purpose.

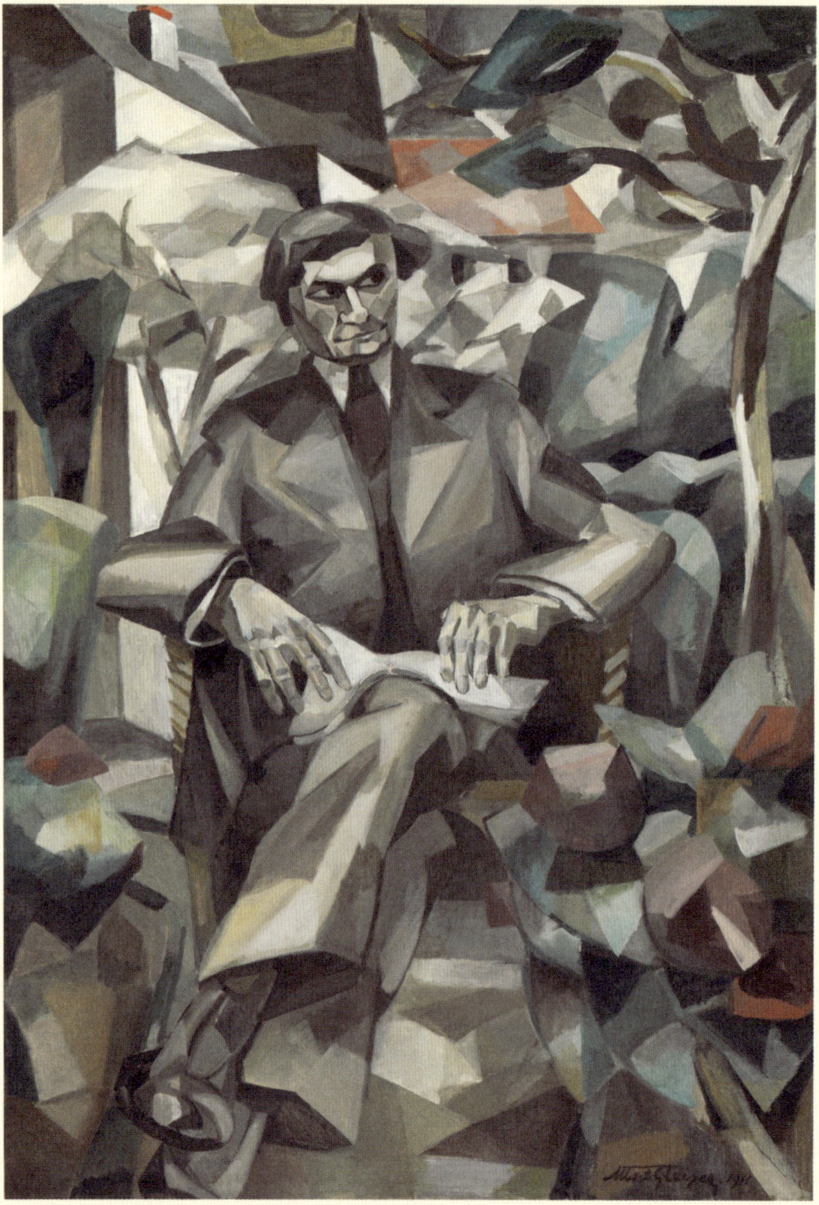

CHAPTER 6

THINGS *hold* TOGETHER

I F THERE HAD BEEN any doubt about it before, there could be none as the 20th century began: the book was versatile enough to be an individual, a family, a community, a national and a global tool. It served the needs of education and entertainment in all subject areas; it could provide information, an aesthetic experience, a moral structure and access to the forbidden.

For those battered by the newly unleashed forces of modernity, it was also a comfort. In Germany, *Der stille Garten* (1908) gave reassurance in its account of German painting in the 19th century. The art historian Max Sauerland presented not a bustling but a tranquil bourgeois world, unindustrialized and also with humans at peace with nature. The following year, at Christmas, it was sold as part of a boxed set with *Das Haus in der Sonne*, which brought international fame to the Swedish artist Carl Larsson. That served as a distraction from an uncertain reality – another function of books, potentially sinister perhaps, but more effective for many than Mr Freud's new analysis (although the depression that Larsson suffered from in later life might have benefited from the latter's books).[1] Books also symbolized social status. In the United States, by the time of William Channing Gannett's *The House Beautiful* (1897), there was no doubt that guests needed to be – and were – impressed by books.[2]

ALBERT GLEIZES USED HIS GARDEN at 24 Avenue Gambetta, Courbevoie, for the background of his 1911 *Portrait of Jacques Nayral*. It was reproduced in Cubism's only manifesto, *Du 'cubisme'*, written by Gleizes and Jean Metzinger and published in 1912. Nayral, a pseudonym of the Modernist writer and publisher Joseph Houot, would die in action in December 1914; a poignant postcard from his friend Gleizes, never received, reads: 'it is impossible that this war can endure much longer.'

Nevertheless, throughout the 20th century, and long before the digital age, siren voices – some of them surprising – suggested that the book was in danger. Because of film, radio, sport and other leisure activities, the publisher Samuel Fischer declared that the book was 'currently one of the most unnecessary things of everyday life'. But 'currently' was an important word, for this was 1926, era of depression and inflation in Germany. In fact, mass-market books, first seen in the 19th century in the form of Reclam's Universal-Bibliothek series, could now combine mass appeal with quality of presentation, as in Insel Verlag's series launched in 1912, which even included the art of a master, Hans Holbein. The book could reflect unreality and fantasy, but also – when needed – not shirk reality; *Bilder des Todes*, a collection of Holbein's images of death, was published by Insel in 1917, a grim point in the First World War.[3]

It is one of the ironies of the 'modern era' that books had their ultimate triumph as it unfolded; in the broadest sense, their continuing depiction by the likes of Picasso, Léger or Juan Gris reflected that. For a while, the world had moved on from Alexander Pope's 18th-century 'The proper study of mankind is man' to Aldous Huxley's 20th-century 'The proper study of mankind is books.' The sense of excitement they generated was brilliantly conveyed by Chinua Achebe's *No Longer at Ease* (1960), when this gifted symbol of African literary creativity described an Igbo village in which only one man knows how to read – not that, in a period of colonial transition, this is in any sense a happy story.

In the Western world, the trailblazing American publicist Edward Bernays was early to discern – in the 1920s – that other media, far from threatening the book, would almost become locked in a dependency culture because books, acknowledged or not, would provide so much of the content their readers craved.[4]

Above all, the idea that books were a conservative medium would have made the great 20th-century dictators laugh. Self-conscious modern suspicion of old technology and old activities could not deflect books' power to shape history. The 19th-century Russian realist tradition of Ilya Repin's famous painting of exploited working men, *Barge Haulers on the Volga* (1870–73), was renewed when the work appeared on the wall of a cruise ship in a Stalinist-era painting. A young Pioneer – a member of the Communist youth movement – reads Nikolay Nekrasov's *Who Can Be Happy and Free in Russia?* while his mentor points to the total regeneration of the great river by the might of Soviet industry.[5] Stalin himself, in a portrait by Boris

Karpov, is the model of a comforting leader, pictured in front of an open door to a garden, with a chair behind him to the right, on which – too visibly to be insignificant – is a book.[6] This was one of many portraits of Stalin by Karpov; another has him at his desk, open book in front of him. After meeting Tolstoy in 1880, Repin had given much thought to the ways in which art and literature might find different paths to truth; for tyrants, at least, their collaboration worked very well.

Would it have been different if the great dictators of the 20th century had lived in the era of social media? Of course, social media have the virtue of spreading a message quickly, and in principle with no geographical limits. But it is no accident that instant methods of communication, giving no value to accuracy or truth, have no longevity, especially if they have no physical existence. Would the Ten Commandments have acquired the same authority if they had been recorded on iPhones rather than stone tablets, even symbolic ones? And once the Codex Alexandrinus or the Codex Sinaiticus, both surviving today and dating from the early centuries of the Christian era, had made available the New Testament in book form, the Bible could embark on its long, long journey influencing so many human minds, reinforced by the sense that it was expressing God's word tangibly.

The lesson was not lost on modern tyrants, who stole the authority of the book, as it were, for less commendable purposes. In Mao Zedong's *Little Red Book*, first published in 1964 by the People's Liberation Army, Mao included in his aphorisms the statement that a revolution is not a matter of writing an essay, or painting a picture, but 'an act of violence by which one class overthrows another'. But the many photographs and paintings of his disciples (which, in effect, included everyone, since adherence to its maxims was compulsory) waving the book are a reminder of the power of the latter. Substitute an iPhone for the book and you substitute a soon-to-be obsolete piece of technology for a medium that 'authorizes' any message it might provide. To date, it is believed that more than a billion copies of *The Little Red Book* have been distributed.

Dictators apart, both writers and artists continued to provide images of reading of varying intensity – Elizabeth Jane Howard, for example, describing in her 2002 memoirs her friend Carol's mother in characteristic pose, lying on a sofa with a lamp illuminating her novel; or, rather differently, the Czech Expressionist Emil Filla and the tormented subject of his *Reader of Dostoevsky* (1907), which reminded Gustav Janouch so much of Kafka at his own desk.[7] Janouch, who struck up a friendship with Kafka in his teenage years, also pointed to him as yet another great writer with considerable drawing skills. Kafka was adamant that his spare artworks were the remains of an old passion. 'It's not on the paper. The passion is in me. I always wanted to be able to draw. I wanted to see, and to hold fast to what was seen. That was my passion.'[8]

In the modern period, there were also many ways in which artists became more adventurous in their interaction with books. While it might be said that there were many precursors of the *livre d'artiste*, such as Goya's *Los caprichos* (1799), the artist now was not 'just' an illustrator but actively engaged in applying graphic ideas and techniques. The catalyst, at the end of the 19th century, was the Parisian dealer Ambroise Vollard, who, he said, began to dream of publishing, but felt that 'they [the books] must be done by "painter-engravers"': artists who were not by profession engravers but would apply their creative skills.[9] Together with the German-born collector and dealer Daniel-Henry Kahnweiler a little later, Vollard had begun something that would prove that, of all methods of communication, none is more versatile or many-sided than the book, the ever-flexible book, whose physical form – forms – can operate not as a constant but as a portal into a richer world.

Artists, so 'knowing' as humans, understand this; at least, it was convincing to Bonnard and Braque, Matisse and Picasso, and to almost all the art movements of the 20th century. Oskar Kokoschka almost got there independently with his 1908 *Die träumenden Knaben*, on one level a children's book, on another a highly erotic homage to a woman who appears as Li in the story and about whom he fantasized as a student.[10] Max Ernst was one of many who took the genre further in a number of works, including *Une semaine de bonté* (1934), a collection of 182 horror images made by cutting up illustrations from 19th-century novels and reference books.[11]

Throughout the modern era, words intruded into images, to the extent that, in 1960s and 1970s Conceptualism, the words became the art: idea replaced form. Between 1961 and 1970, Dieter Roth, who once insisted that he was an artist only to support his writing habit, used a traditional recipe to create 'literary sausages' out of boiled, shredded paper; the books from which the paper came ranged from Marx to mass market. Today, there are book artists all over the world, working to many scales: Mike Stilkey, in Los Angeles, created a 7.3-metre (24-ft) artwork, *Discarded Romance* (2012), with 3,000 abandoned library books – 'I'm putting my story on someone else's story.'[12] M. C. Escher even managed a self-portrait, *Hand with Reflecting Sphere* (1935), in which 'the self' is just part of a crowded world of curved room, pictures and, of course, books.

All this happened during a period of rapid expansion for the book. Between 1940 and 2000, Harvard's library increased from 4.3 million books to 14.4 million, Berkeley's from 1.1 million to 9.1 million.[13] By 1957, the first ten titles in Pocket Books' new mass-market paperback format, introduced by the company in 1939, had sold more than 8 million copies.[14] Only 317 art books were published in the United States in 1950; at the start of the new century, the figure had become 5,000 plus.[15] In 2003, 2.75 billion books were sold globally, and almost one million new ones published.[16] But while the digital world, despite predictions, did not threaten books, it did (and does) change perceptions, most perniciously, as we have now found – for books but also for humans – in ushering in a 'post-truth' age. Already, before digitalization took hold, a profound loss of faith of all kinds, perhaps largely engendered by the human inability to control destructive technology, was reflected in the sculptures of Anselm Kieffer. If they are part expression of the brilliant intensity of a great artist, they are also – for anyone seeing the book as our sure repository of the world's wisdom – a sign that a new world might not take reassurance from them anymore. Perhaps, in the end, the loss of comfort provided to those Russian soldiers in the Crimea is the worst loss of all.

Today, the artist has – in the main – lost church, patron, academy. The resulting freedom often seems an unhappy one. The books found for so many centuries in paintings were often solid, supportive, informative, creative torchbearers; lose them, and some foundations are also lost. Whatever else, books will never be all about bleakness, even if they – and artists showing them – must not exclude that. We don't need to be living in ancient Greece to appreciate the beauty of a Greek sculpture or the profundity of Plato; books continue to help us to understand them and, as the ever-pithy Walter Savage Landor (1775–1864) said, 'The writings of the wise are the only riches our posterity cannot squander.'[17]

The terror of the blank canvas cannot easily be assuaged by the genres of the past, but perhaps there is a better understanding that both art and literature have it within their gift to depict actual things, but also thereby to convey any manner of feelings or ideas. The genre of novels about paintings continues, and in Katie Ward's *Girl Reading* (2012) the narrative is entirely constructed around stories from actual paintings throughout history depicting women reading, inspiring an online fan's imagination to ask the question, 'What if we could interact with works of art?' Artists and writers are not about to be made redundant with the popularization of virtual reality; their creativity speaks to something deeper than technology can supply.

As Gilbert, of the inseparable artist duo Gilbert & George, recently mused, death was no threat because they would leave their art, their foundation, their collection – and their books.[18] Taking the title of their work from an essay by Walter Benjamin, 'Unpacking My Library' (1931), in which the philosopher and critical theorist writes of the time before the books are put on their shelves, so 'not yet touched by the mild boredom of order', Jo Steffens and Matthias Neumann have examined how important both books and reading are in the lives of such contemporary artists as Ed Ruscha and Tracey Emin. They also reprint Marcel Proust's 1905 essay 'On Reading', which begins with remembering how the fullest days of childhood were those in which there was no living, but time spent with a favourite book.[19] Thus we are taken back to where we started in the preface, with Hope Summerell and *Alice in Wonderland*'s White Rabbit.

At one point in Robert Harris's bestselling trilogy on the life of Cicero, the wife of the Roman statesman and scholar exclaims with great contempt: 'Books! ... Where is the money in *books*?' The reasons that artists included so many books in their paintings (they do not, on the whole, seem moved to depict computer screens, despite their role as the furniture of our time) are largely unconnected with money and largely unconnected with technology, which are therefore not the only things that make the world go round. Their patrons and customers put great value on both paintings and books, but the two media had their millennia-long relationship for other, more important reasons. Those reasons begin, and end, with comfort and solace, but – as we have seen – also embrace almost everything else human beings have found to be of value. Happy or sad, no reader of a book, or painter of a book, ever forgot that they were human. Despite Yeats, things did not always 'fall apart'.

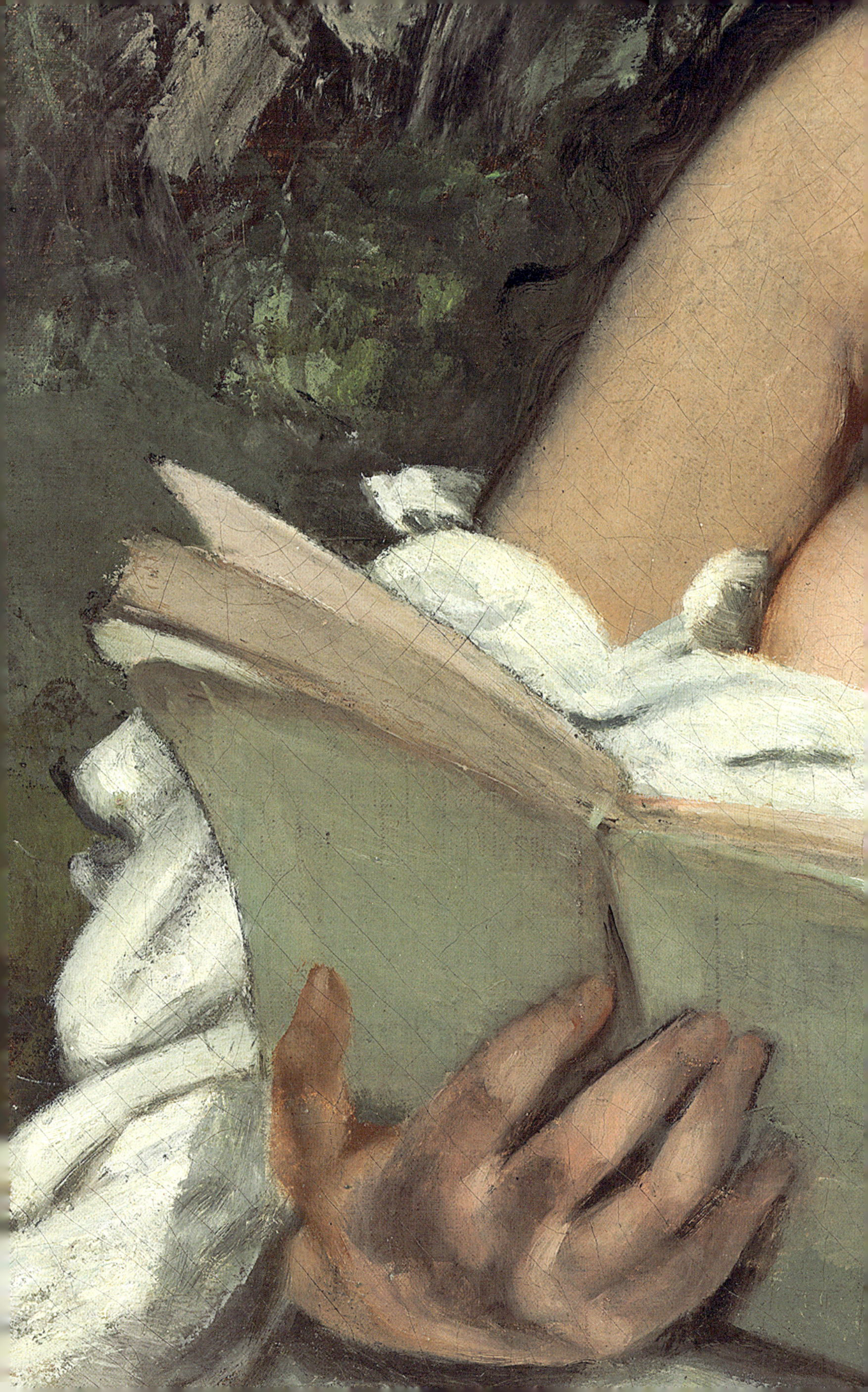

Part Two

PAINTING *is* 'LIKE *a* BOOK... *which* NEEDS *to* GIVE UP *its* RICHES'

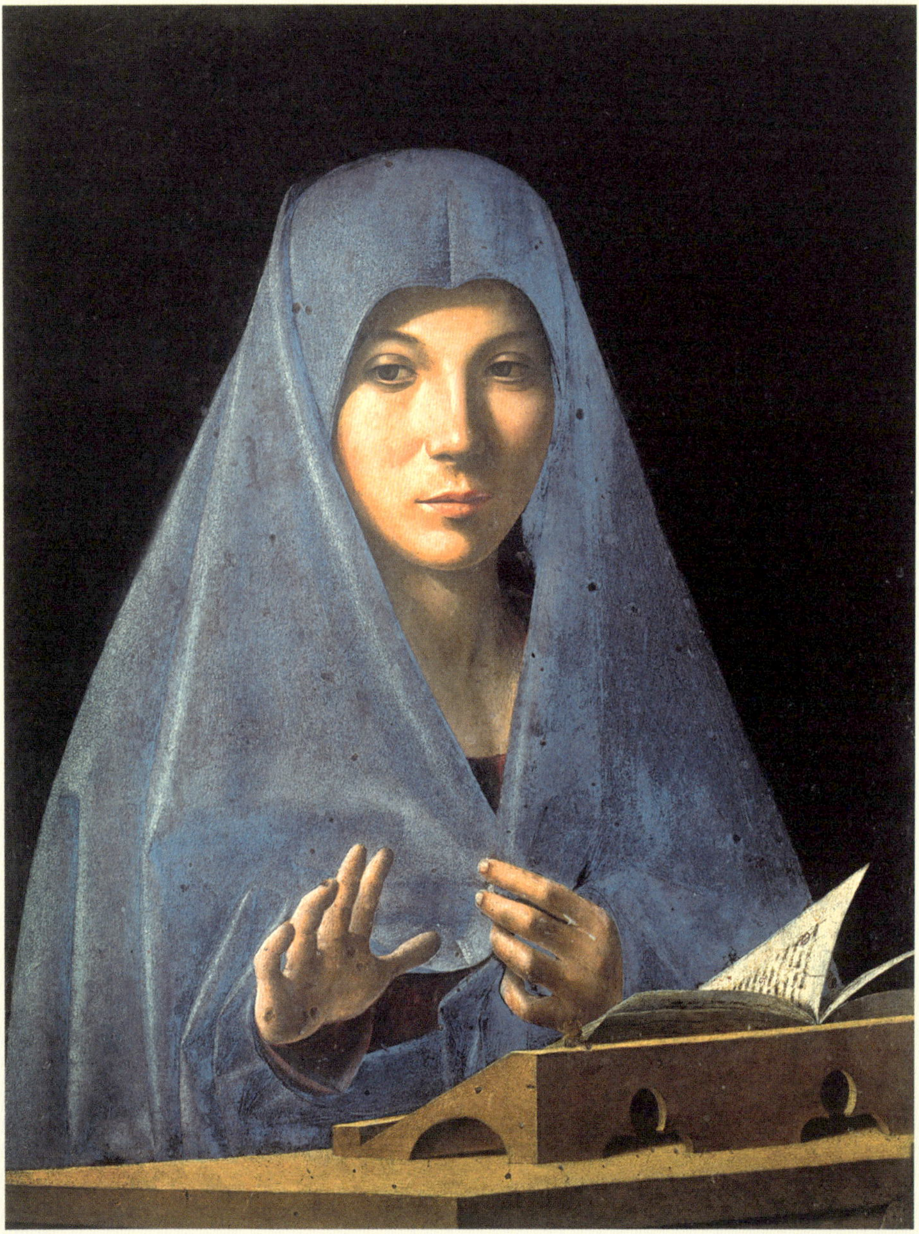

GALLERY 1

THE WORD *of* GOD

WHY SHOULD the Devil be frightened of a book? St Geneviève, patron saint of Paris and twice an inspiration to its inhabitants in the 5th century when the city was threatened first by Attila the Hun and then by invading Franks, was walking to church after dusk – so legend has it – only to have her way threatened by a devil seeking to extinguish her candle. St Geneviève became revered in other parts of Europe, in south-west Germany and England, for instance; she was also patron saint of several Flemish guilds. In the 15th century the Flemish master Hugo van der Goes created a great diptych, with *The Fall of Man* on one side and *The Lamentation* on the other. Its commissioners would also have seen St Geneviève on the back of *The Fall* (p. 82), with a devil seeking to prevent her reading a book by putting out the candle. And why? Because the book was the Word of God. Perhaps it is no surprise that, like other diptychs with an image on the reverse, this work could be opened like ... a book.[1]

Those in the secular West who write off the role of religion in shaping history, or the extent to which belief, far from being otherworldly, had highly practical social, economic and political implications, can be easily disabused by the history of the book. Even before Christianity, ancient Egyptians wanted to be buried with the Book of the Dead to ensure their journey to the afterlife was secure and protected. But once the Roman emperor Constantine had been converted to Christianity, the book became an essential part of the

---

WAS THERE EVER such an alluringly enigmatic expression of face, eyes and hands? In Antonello da Messina's painting (*c.* 1476), the Archangel Gabriel has just brought news to the Virgin that she is to be the mother of Christ, a startling interruption of her reading of her Book of Hours or Bible.

iconography of a religion – and its associated art – that would know no geographical boundaries. It should perhaps be noted that, while the Christian world elevated the book to a new pinnacle of authority, the process was not accompanied by the tolerance of free thought of the preceding pagan era, whose literature and practices were at odds with a sexually repressive Christian culture.[2]

The role of the book was not limited to iconography; it acquired its own power when associated with saints. In 827, legates of the Byzantine emperor arrived at Saint-Denis near Paris with a copy of St Dionysius's works; by morning, nearly twenty miraculous cures had been effected. A 20th-century painting by the German artist Hermann Nigg shows St Benedict in the 6th century writing the rules to be used by Benedictine monastic communities; since they included four hours of daily reading, the practical consequences were to encourage – long before printing – the copying of books. We could almost say that books were as valuable to the Church as the institution itself – or, at least, that they became the vehicle that facilitated contact with God, knowledge of Christian tenets and conversion; guided Christians on how to live their lives; and increasingly became a symbol of authority for the Church's officers and hierarchy. In a sense, the Bible is the story of our world as a book, one that opens with Creation and closes, in Revelation 6:14, when 'the heaven departed as a scroll when it is rolled together'.[3]

There was, from the beginning, a strong link with painting. In the 6th century the bishop of Marseilles expressed his concern to Gregory the Great that images of pagan idols influenced the faithful; the Pope made clear in his reply that, while 'the written word is for readers', everyone else – literacy rates being low – needed images.[4]

Not everyone was persuaded – a variant of the millennia-long battle between the word and the image. Isidore of Seville (d. 636) influenced many in his *Etymologiae*: 'painting ... is often a feigned representation, not the truth.'[5] But in practice there were many images that included books for their symbolic value. Certainly, by the Renaissance the representation of God Himself – previously associated with sacrilege – would often include a book. Books seemed as natural an accompaniment to paintings of Christ as cross and stigmata; they might be closed to show that Christ alone was ultimately adequate to present the Word of God, or open, for there you would see that He was the redeemer.[6] They also reinforced the idea of Christ as a teacher and the source of authority; if St Paul had never known him, he could be shown receiving that authority by being given a book.

Archangels, being leaders, appeared with scrolls or books because they could interpret judgments and prophecies; the prophets themselves used scrolls to record their prophecies. Many saints, from St Bernard to St Sylvester, revealed their holiness through their books; in the case of some, such as St Catherine of Alexandria or (as depicted by Tommaso da Modena in the church of San Niccolò, Treviso) the Dominican saints, their learning and wisdom were also indicated.

The scholarship of the evangelists and of the Church Fathers was represented by reading or writing. It has to be observed that, mostly, a very male view of the wisdom of God is being expressed. In Rogier van der Weyden's *Virgin and Child* of 1435–38 (the Durán Virgin; p. 83), the child crumples the pages of the Old Testament, for the male Jesus is the one to replace the Old with the New Testament. Nevertheless, the mother of the Son of God is frequently represented with her prayer book, her Book of Hours, as in one of the frescoes by Giotto in Padua's Arena Chapel from the beginning of the 14th century.

The dissemination and visibility of such works was enhanced hugely in the Renaissance. Before Pope Nicholas V, the Vatican owned only some 340 manuscripts; within twenty-five years of the Pope's death in 1455, that figure had grown tenfold.[7] Also in the 1400s, woodblock prints, often put in book blocks, showed scenes from the Bible or the lives of the saints. It was likewise common, as in Hans Memling's Moreel Triptych (1484), for the donors and their families to be shown in the left- and right-hand panels holding prayer books.[8]

Many artists depicted St John the Evangelist on the island of Patmos, among them Bosch, Correggio, Poussin and Velázquez, but a 17th-century Russian broadside in the British Library actually shows John being told to take a book from an angel and eat it.[9] If this was still a long way from a secular world, the concept of divine instruction was widened as a result of humanism to something that might be called 'divine inspiration' and applied to scholars and writers whose lives were so closely entangled with their books. Moreover, as the great French historian Elie Halévy said, Protestantism was a 'book religion'.[10] Luther's *Flugschriften* were doctrinal or proselytizing booklets that were inexpensive, in the vernacular and instantly successful.[11] Pierre-Robert Olivétan, a cousin of John Calvin, modestly suggested at the beginning of his Bible translation (1535) that trying to make Hebrew and Greek 'eloquence' speak French was akin to teaching 'the gentle lark to sing the song of the croaking raven', but opinions on that matter were soon reversed.[12] From that time on, the Catholic Church, if not universally, was less enthusiastic about, for example, depicting the Virgin Mary reading. For giving books to the laity just resulted in heresy.[13]

The book had acquired status and authority from its prime use by the Church. The Protestant encouragement of reading crossed the Atlantic; *The History of Holy Jesus*, first published in Boston in 1745, contained an engraving entitled 'The Careful Mother Instructing her Children'. Ironically, one result was to fuel the secular appetite, and respect, for books of many kinds.[14]

John Stuart Mill once observed that 'one person with a belief is a social power equal to ninety-nine who have only interests.'[15] That is part of the reason why Christianity flourished into the modern era. The book was used as its advocate, but equally Christianity became an advocate for the book. Artists, as ever, reflected and interpreted this strong current in human societies; and they did so again sometime later in the era of the new religions – the totalitarian regimes of Communism and Fascism – which (in the selective way that results from combining belief and interests) found that the book could help them, too.

Henri Matisse put it best: a painting, he wrote, is 'like a book on the shelf of a bookcase, showing only the few words of its title, which needs to give up its riches, the action of the reader who must take it up, open it, and shut himself away with it'.[16]

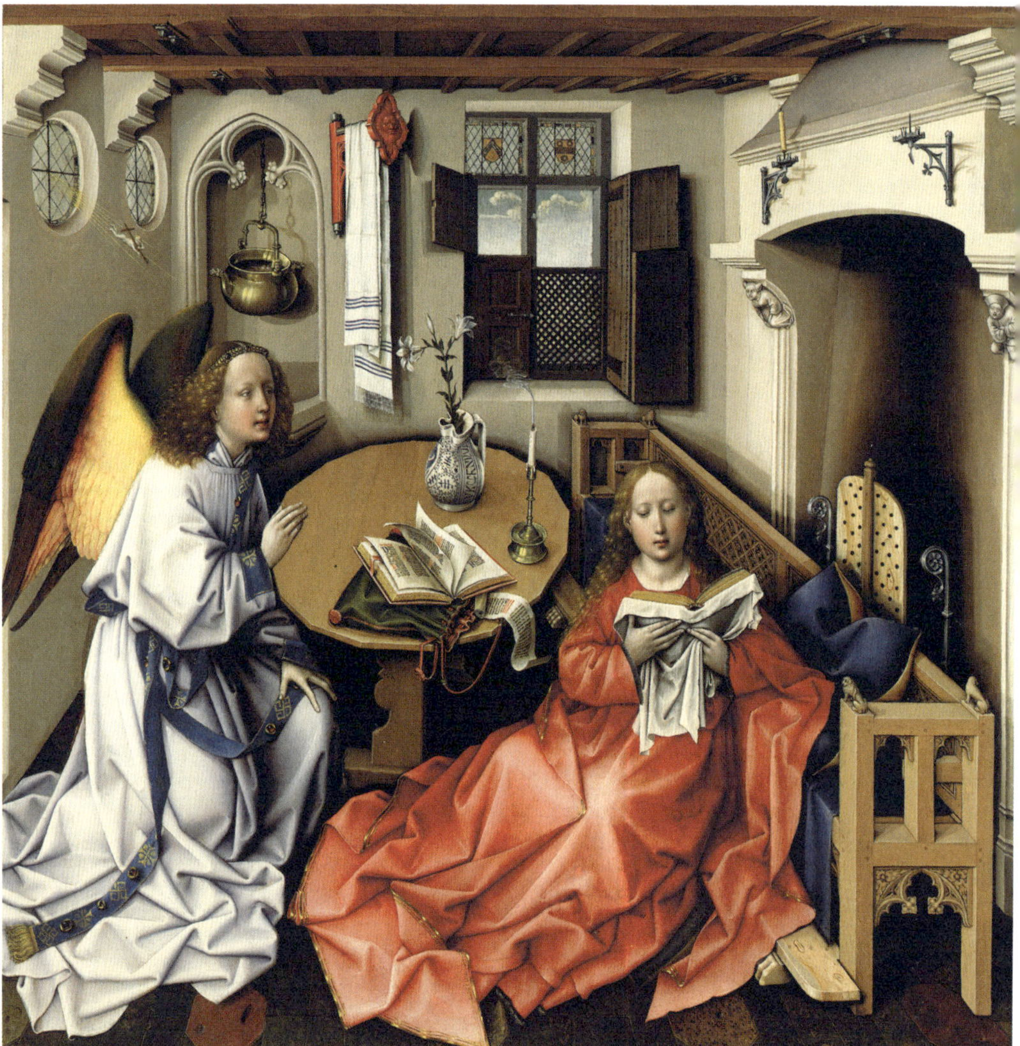

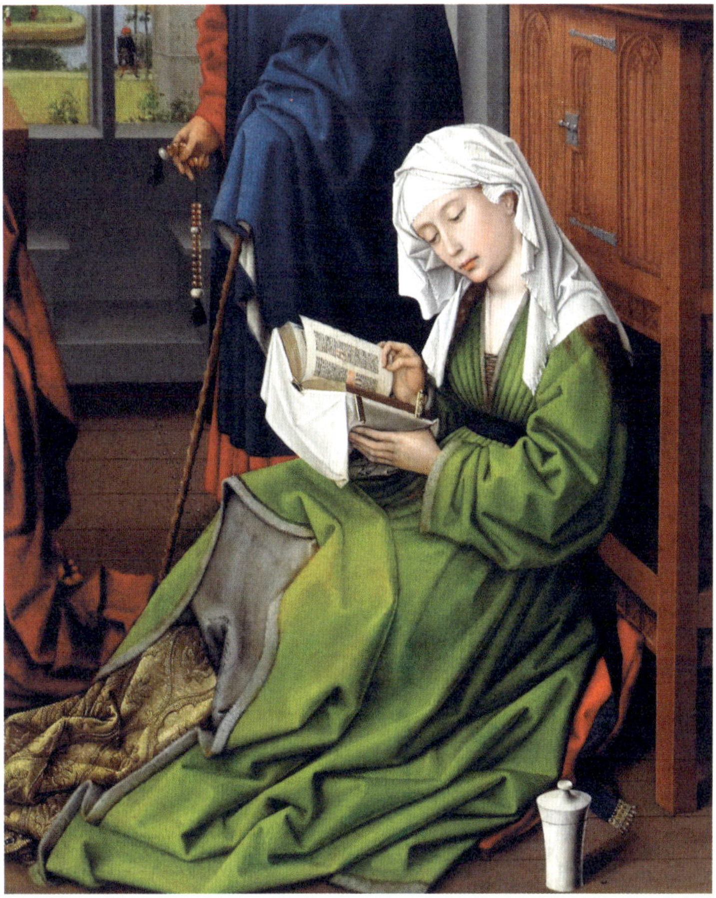

THE VIRGIN MARY, OFTEN WITH BOOK, was depicted in Renaissance painting more frequently than any other religious figure, except Christ. But was this Annunciation (*c.* 1425–30; OPPOSITE) by the Master of Flámalle, or by Robert Campin? Or were they the same person? Before Vasari and printed books, the subject matter of artists had greater clarity than their identity. And was *The Magdalene Reading* (1438; ABOVE) by Rogelet de la Pasture, the Flámalle Master's pupil, and was he the artist we know as Rogier van der Weyden? The only certain thing, revealed by microscope, is the remarkable skill used in the detail and colour of the open book pages and minute bookmarks.

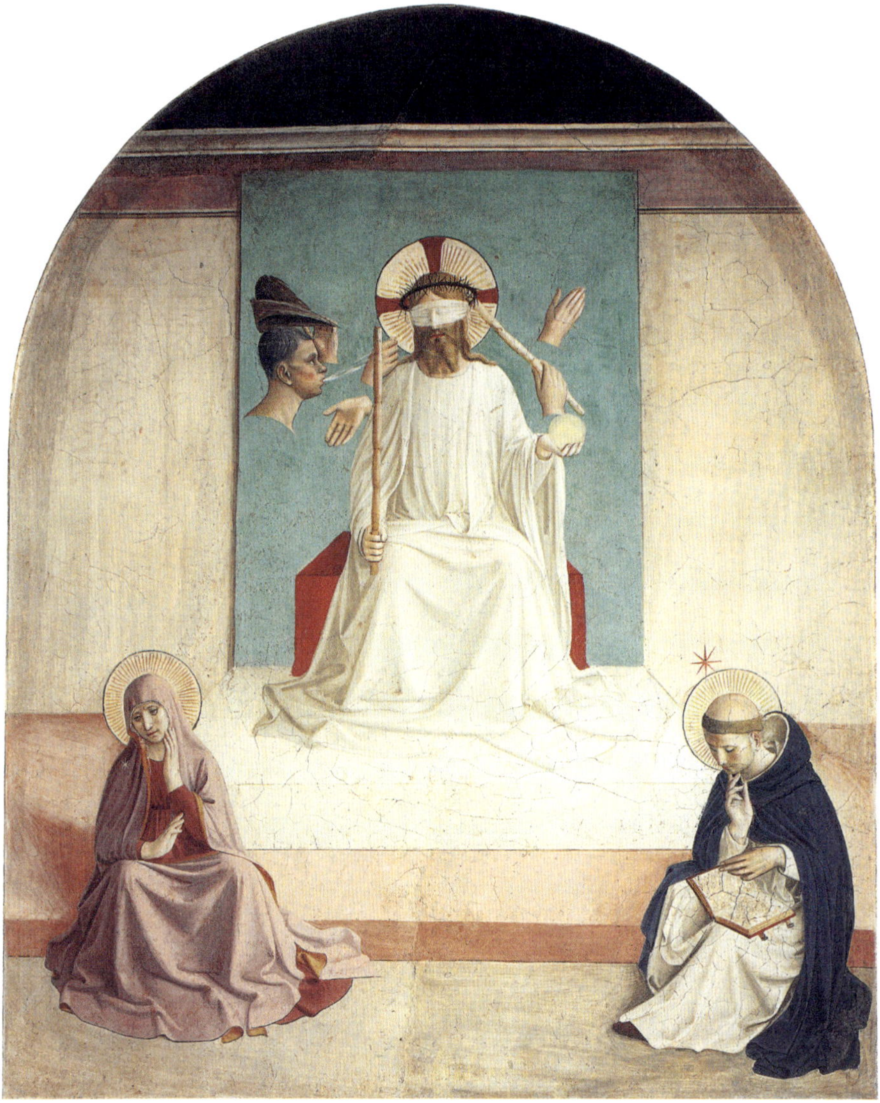

LIKE SO MANY GREAT PAINTINGS, *The Mocking of Christ* (1440), a fresco in the Convent of San Marco, Florence, by the artist we have known since the 19th century as Fra Angelico – the Dominican friar Guido di Pietro – can be read in many different ways. But the literal reading of the book by St Dominic (bottom right) is one key. The fresco was painted for a monk's cell to aid meditation, and the saint concentrates – for practical, not intellectual reasons: the Bible contains the Living Word – on understanding the meaning of Christ's suffering. The deep authority associated with 'the book', unlike the other religious symbols, could later be appropriated for secular knowledge. And part of the underpinning of this authority stemmed directly from the artist, Fra Angelico, a man – said Vasari – who wept every time he painted a crucifix.

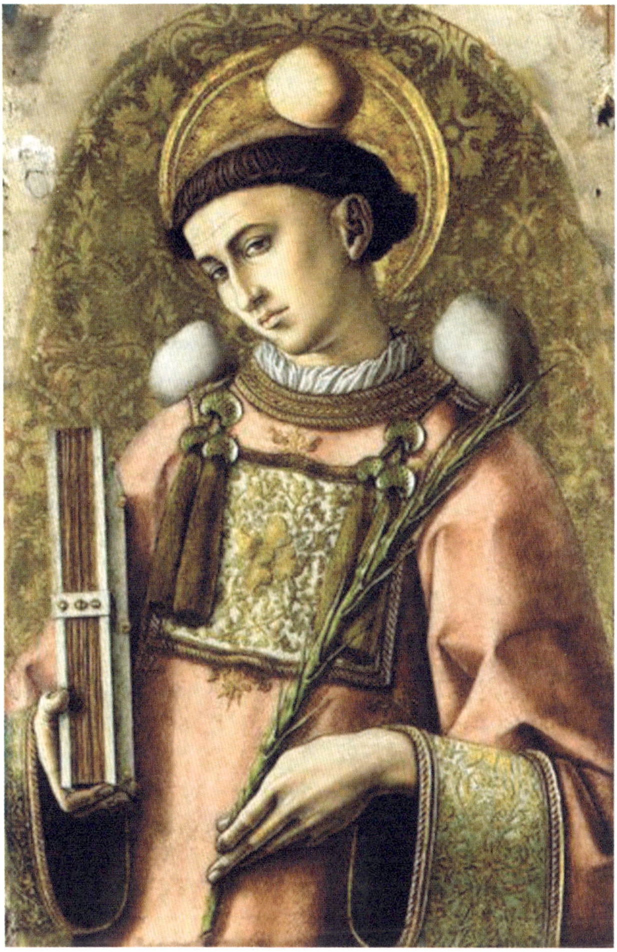

THE STONING TO DEATH of the first Christian martyr, St Stephen, in *c.* 34 CE, witnessed by St Paul, became a much-painted event. In the early Renaissance, it is found in Uccello's 1435 work for the Duomo in Florence; St Stephen formed the subject of Rembrandt's first signed painting at the age of nineteen; and later it appealed to the Pre-Raphaelites, including Burne-Jones and Millais. Here, in one of many panels prepared for the high altar of San Domenico, Ascoli Piceno, in the Italian Marche (1476), the Venetian-born Carlo Crivelli shows St Stephen with the attributes of palm, for his spiritual triumph over martyrdom, and book, for his learning.

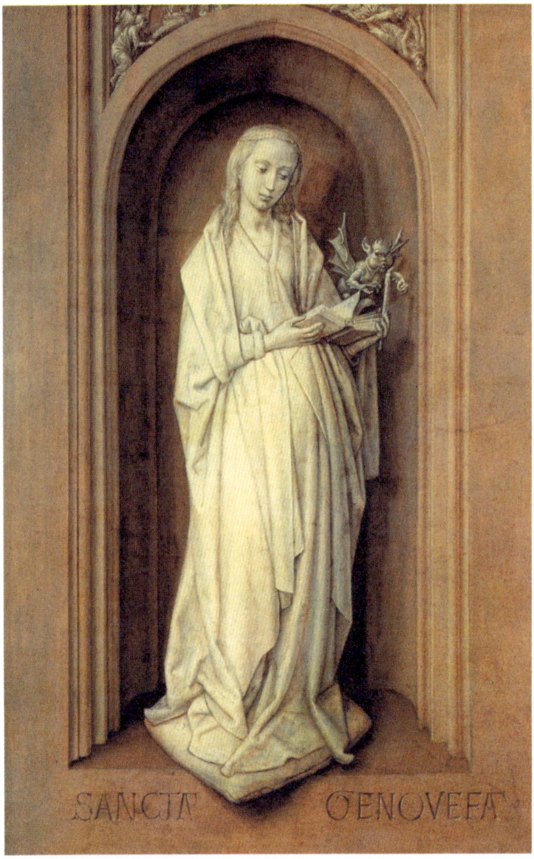

ST GENEVIÈVE, who managed to save Paris first from Attila the Hun with a prayer in 451, then from the Franks thirteen years later by breaking the Frankish food blockade, will not allow a disconcerted devil – disconcerted by a book – to interrupt her study of scripture. Her reputation reached beyond France; in Flanders, she was the patron saint of a number of guilds, although this panel from Hugo van der Goes's *The Fall of Man* (after 1479) is the only Flemish depiction of her. The miniaturist Alexander Bening (d. 1519), who was married to a niece or sister of Van der Goes, used the painter's preliminary drawings from *The Fall of Man* for the illuminated manuscripts of the Ghent-Bruges school. Centuries later, Van Gogh, 'haggard of late', wrote several times to his brother, comparing himself to Van der Goes, who – convinced of his worthlessness – retreated to a monastery and spent all his time reading books, inspiring the late Romantic Belgian artist Emile Wauters to paint *The Madness of Hugo van der Goes* (1872), to which Van Gogh referred.

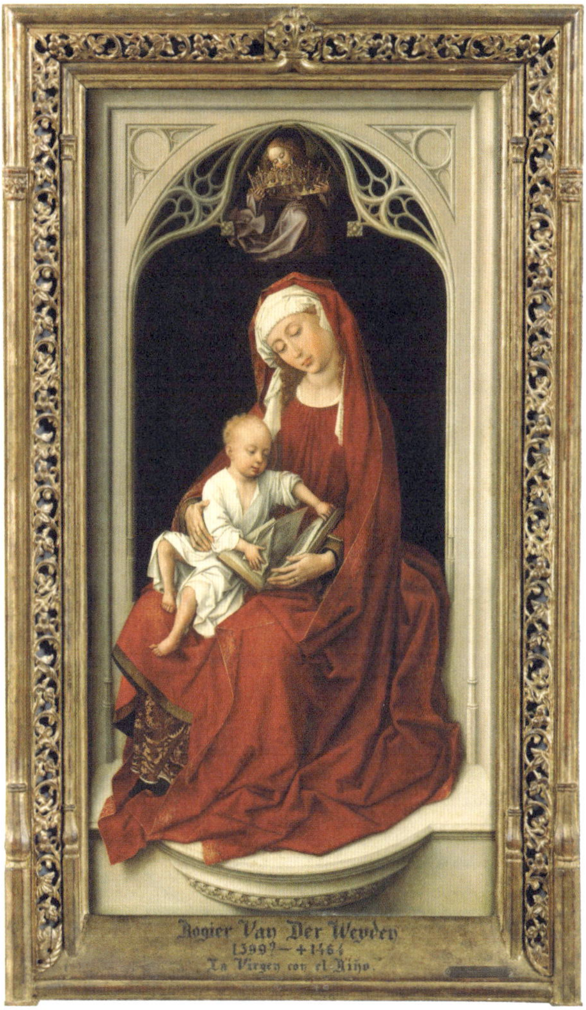

E AGAIN A BOOK is centre stage, here in the Durán Virgin by gier van der Weyden, painted between 1435 and 1438 on two boards of Baltic oak from the previous century. The Virgin Mary's wisdom is often represented by a book, and the fragment of an altarpiece showing *The Virgin and Child with Six Saints*, entitled *The Magdalene Reading*, is reproduced on page 79. But here attention switches to the young Jesus Christ, and some scholars have suggested that he is leafing the Old Testament backwards to the Fall of Man in Genesis to symbolize his redemptive mission. Only a blue initial 'B' is viewable in the work itself.

IN HIS TWENTIES, Raffaello Sanzio, Raphael, was encouraged to leave Florence and help in the biggest project of his life: decorating the Vatican. The humanist and historian Paolo Giovio, whose footsteps are all over the first half of the 16th century, provided a private commission for Raphael to paint this image of the Virgin Mary (*c.* 1510), a work that became known as *The Alba Madonna* in the 18th century because of its ownership by the Spanish House of Alba. A triumph of form and meaning in perfect harmony, it exudes the quintessential High Renaissance: the figures of the Virgin Mary (in classical clothes), Jesus and John the Baptist are against a background of the Italian countryside; what was to follow is foretold in the cross held by the young Christ, while his mother keeps her place in the holy book she holds.

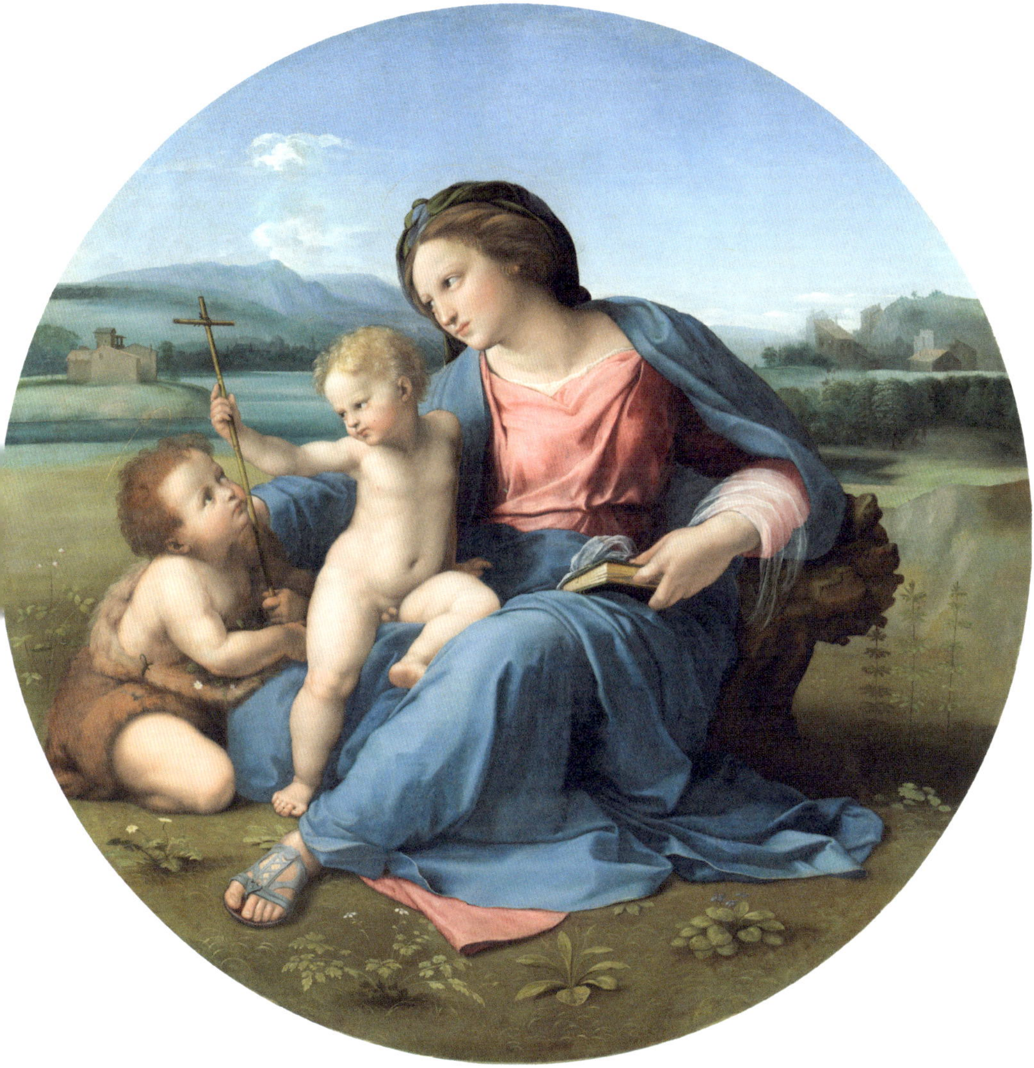

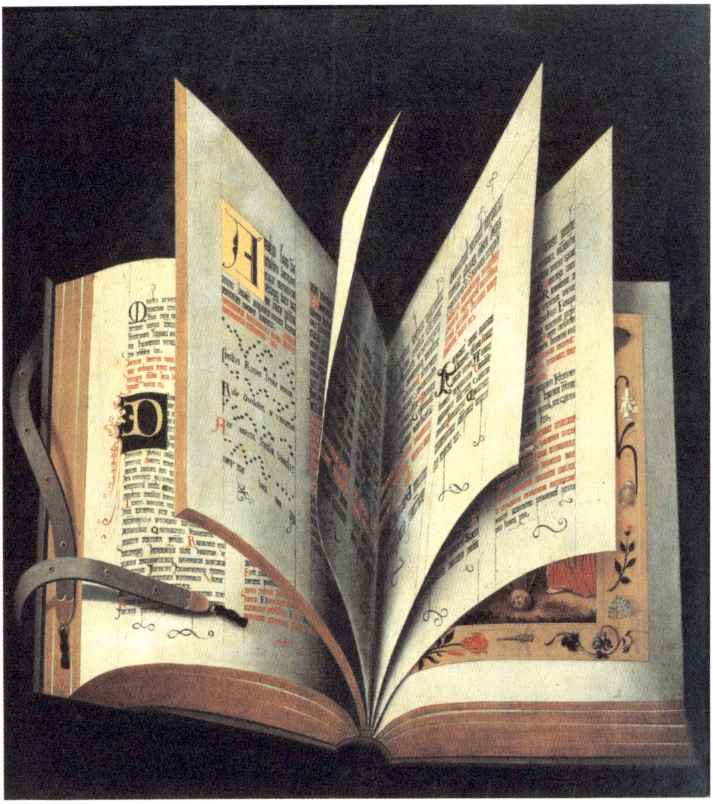

THE TRADITION OF ILLUMINATION that first fully flowered in the time of Charlemagne did not come to an end with the invention of printing. The beauty and significance, religious and social, of illuminated books was justification enough for an unknown but brilliantly skilled artist to create this *trompe l'œil* still life of an early 16th-century German vellum-bound volume, in which we can just see a small part of a Crucifixion scene – with a skull at the foot of the cross and a figure representing St John – on a right-hand page. It appears in the inventory of the Villa Medicea di Lappeggi near Florence in 1669, shortly after the death of the villa's then owner, Prince Mattias de' Medici, governor of Sienna, whose mother was an Austrian Habsburg and whose maternal grandmother was Bavarian. The panel may have been intended as a door to a bookcase in the Northern tradition, but influenced by Italian marquetry. Some identified artists produced very similar works, including Ludger tom Ring the Elder (see p. 196) later in the 16th century.

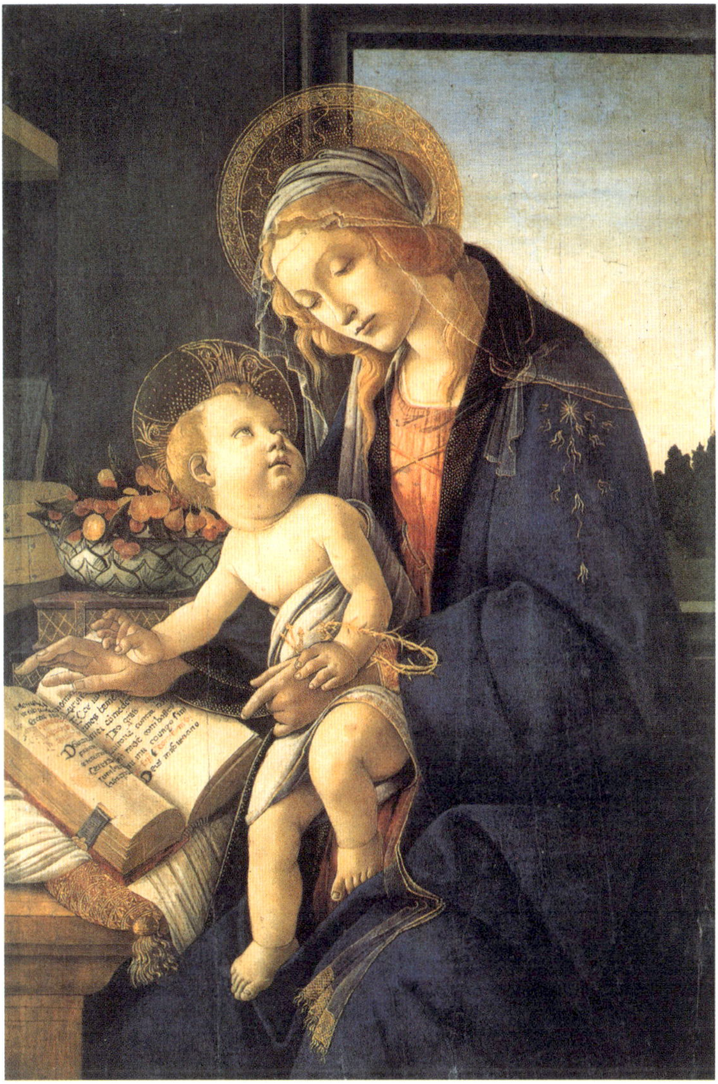

BOTTICELLI PAINTED *The Madonna of the Book* in tempera on a panel in 1483; by then, the *Horae Beatae Mariae Virginis* was just one of many Books of Hours used as prayer books. The detail in the book, as also in the rest of the painting, is extraordinary in the true sense of that word. The book appears to be open at two passages from Isaiah prophesying Christ's conception and birth, and Mary's hand is over the words 'Be it unto me according to Thy word'. In another respect, Botticelli looked to the future; his interest in developing a printed book from his illustrations to Dante's *Divine Comedy* was highly unusual for his time. Later artists became captivated by the idea of combining art and book.

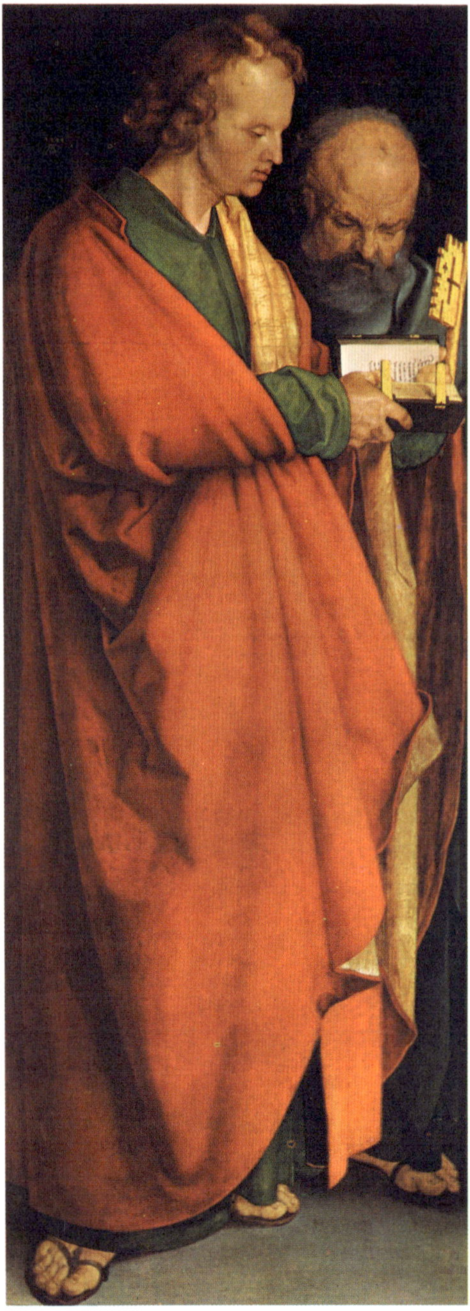

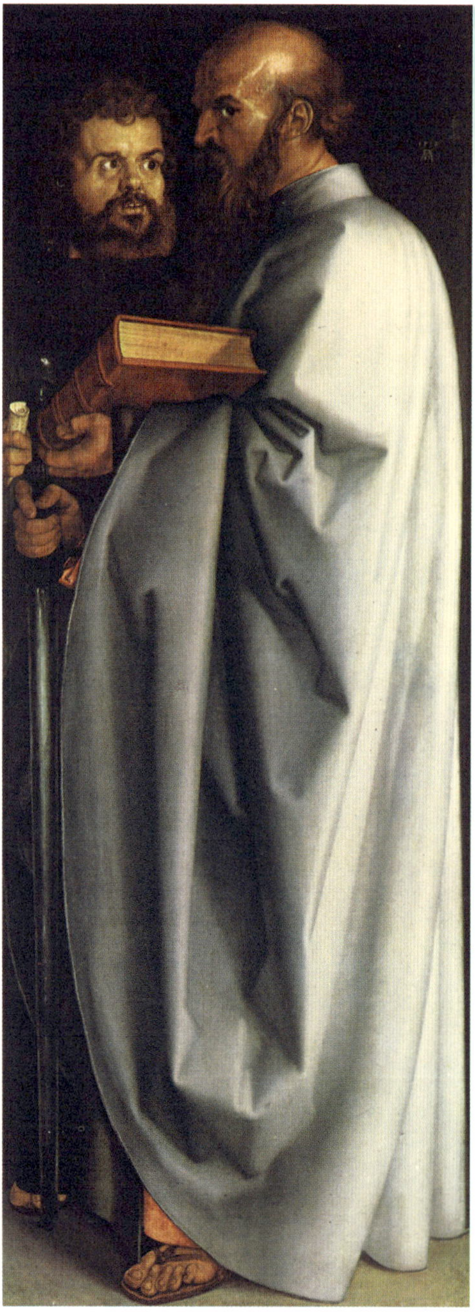

WHEN GOETHE STOPPED OFF in Munich on his way to Italy in October 1786, he recorded the '*unglaublichen Grossheit*', the 'incredible grandeur', of Dürer's larger than life-size panels of *The Four Apostles* (1526). The work was begun in 1517, the year in which Luther nailed his 'Ninety-five Theses' to the church door at Wittenberg Castle. St John (at the far left of the four figures) and St Paul (at the far right) were Luther's favourite disciples. The open book was a symbol of St John, and here the Protestant emphasis on the Word, not the Church, is transparent in his Gospel: '*Am Anfang war das Wort*', 'In the beginning was the Word'. St Peter, next to St John, has to take guidance. St Mark's Gospel begins with the declaration that Jesus is the Son of God, but – St Mark is next to St Paul here – it is St Paul who will provide the interpretation.

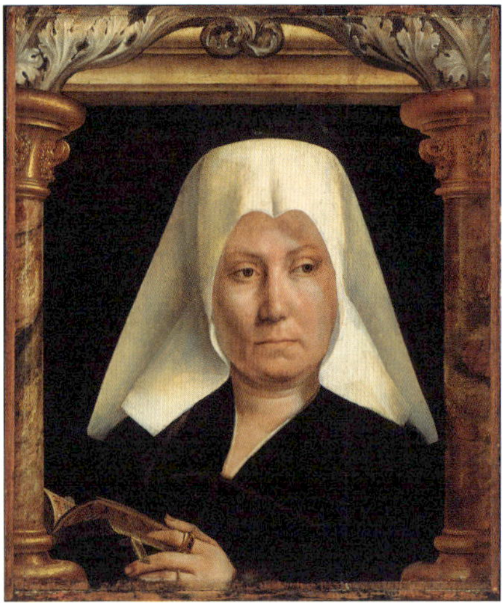

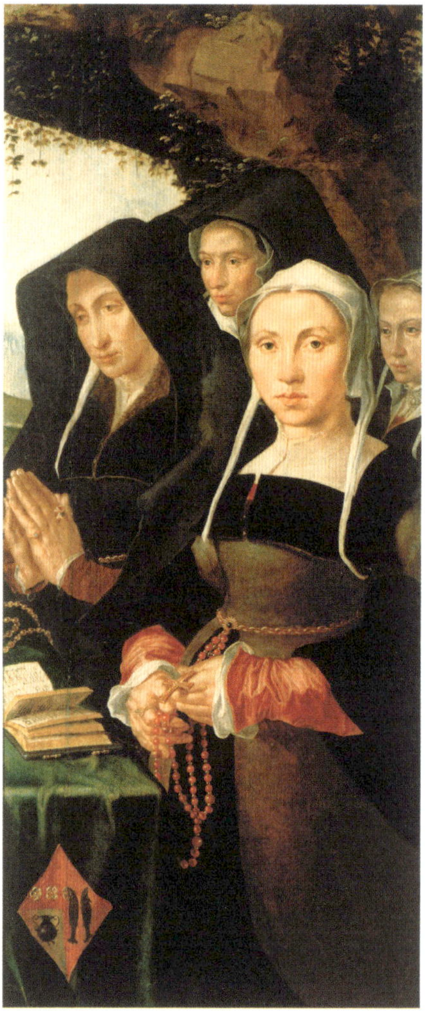

WHETHER IN PAINTINGS imbued with a humanist spirit (ABOVE LEFT, a work by Antwerp's Quentin Metsys, who also portrayed Erasmus with a book), or bringing an Italian Mannerist feel to Northern Europe (ABOVE RIGHT, part of an altarpiece by Maarten van Heemskerck), or from an artist fully faithful to the Counter-Reformation (OPPOSITE, the founder of a Carmelite convent near Bergamo by Giovanni Battista Moroni), books continued to express female piety.

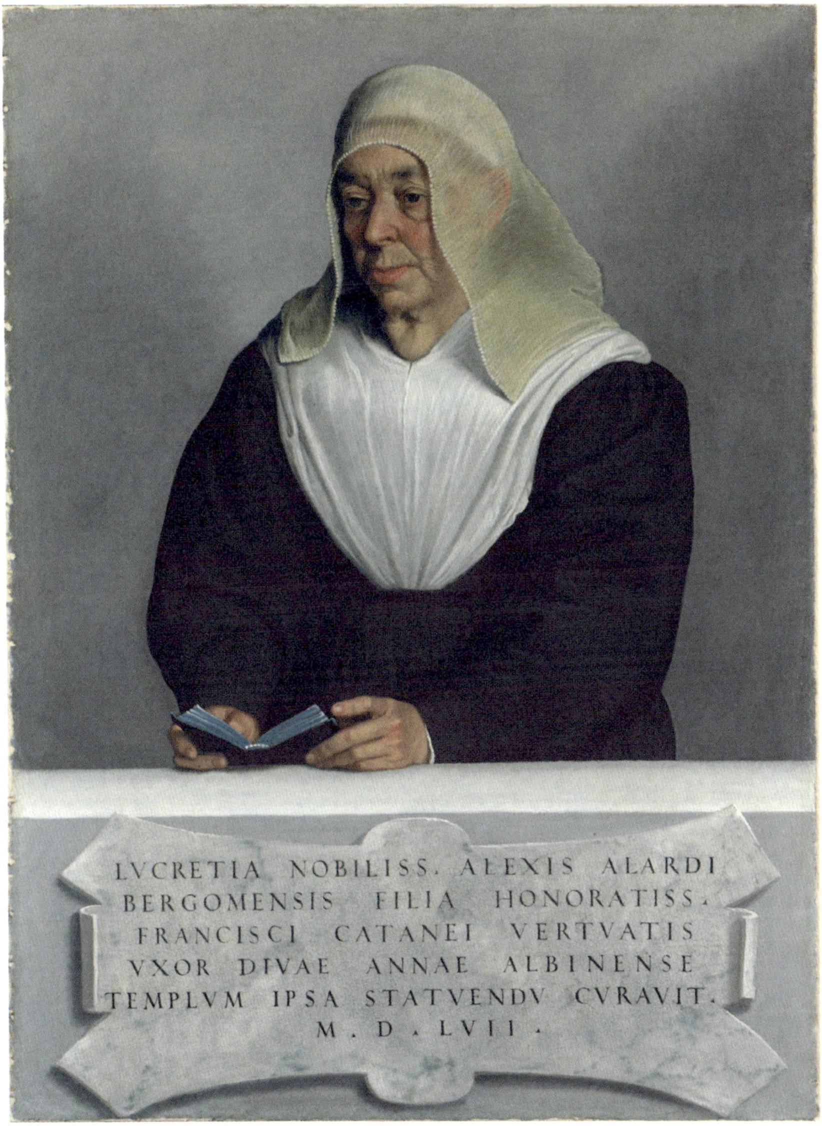
LVCRETIA NOBILISS. ALEXIS ALARDI
BERGOMENSIS FILIA HONORATISS.
FRANCISCI CATANEI VERTVATIS
VXOR DIVAE ANNAE ALBINENSE
TEMPLVM IPSA STATVENDV CVRAVIT.
M . D . LVII .

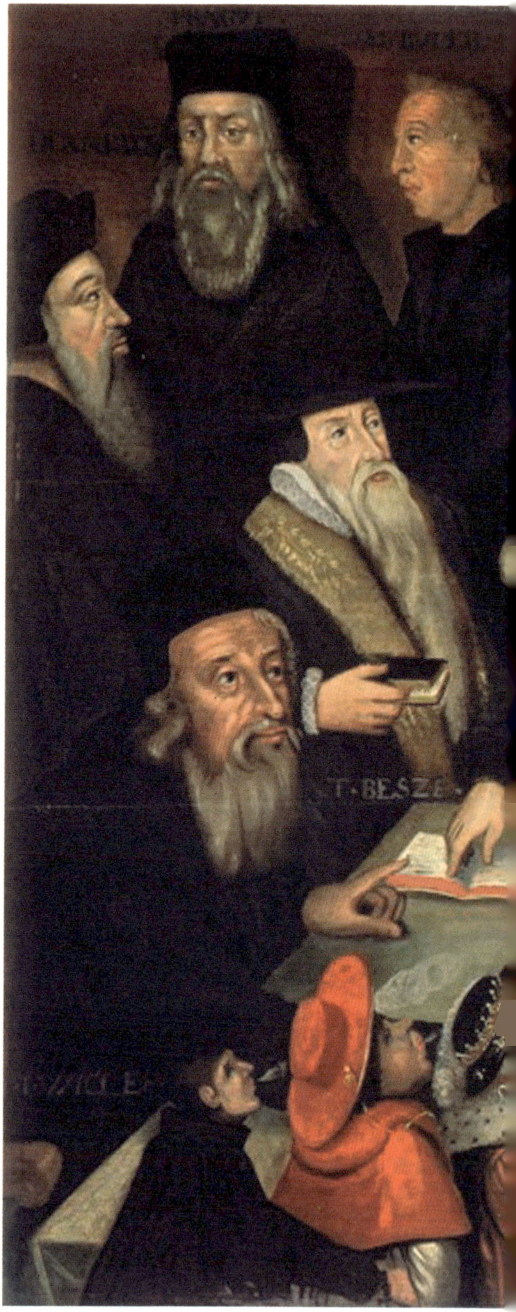

THE RAMIFICATIONS OF the Reformation are depicted in an anonymous German painting entitled *Martin Luther in the Circle of Reformers* (1625–50). Luther has John Calvin, Protestant spearhead in France and Switzerland, to his right, Philip Melancthon, intellectual leader of the Lutherans, to his left. The consequences of their actions have unfolded up to the present day: as far afield as what became the United States in the 17th and 18th centuries, and what we know today as South Korea and Tanzania from the 19th century, while China has a fast-growing Protestant population today. In the foreground of the painting, the Pope looks on, the Devil to his right. But the support for the triumph of books that came as a by-product of the Reformation and printing did not mean that Luther himself approved of all books, only of those connected to scripture. And it was not only Catholics who used books to combat Lutheranism. The humanist and polemicist Johann Cochlaeus, whose *Brevis Germaniae descriptio* (1512) praised printing for reviving classical literature, not the Faith, had a long and hostile debate with the founder of Protestantism.

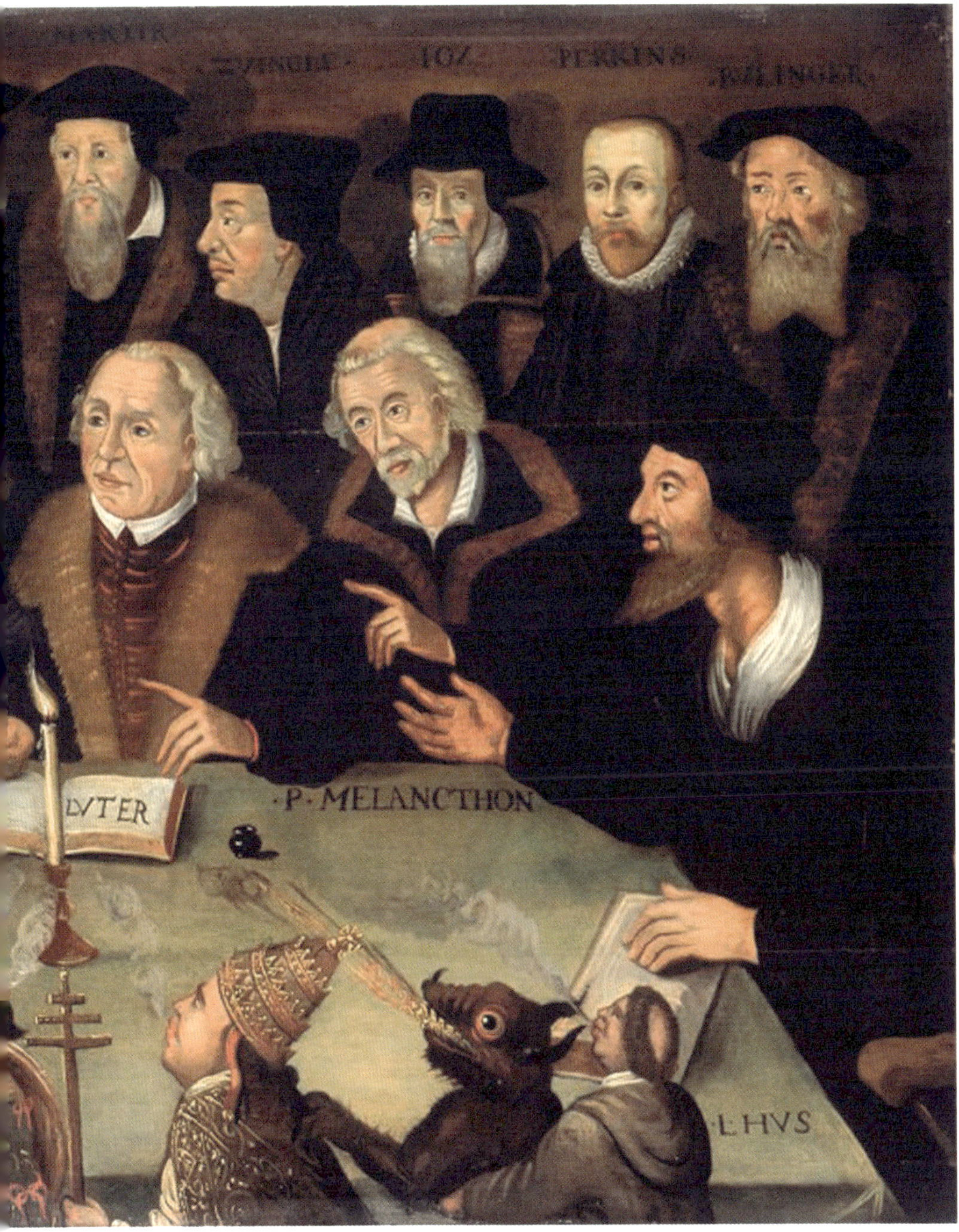
LVTER
·P·MELANCTHON
·L·HVS

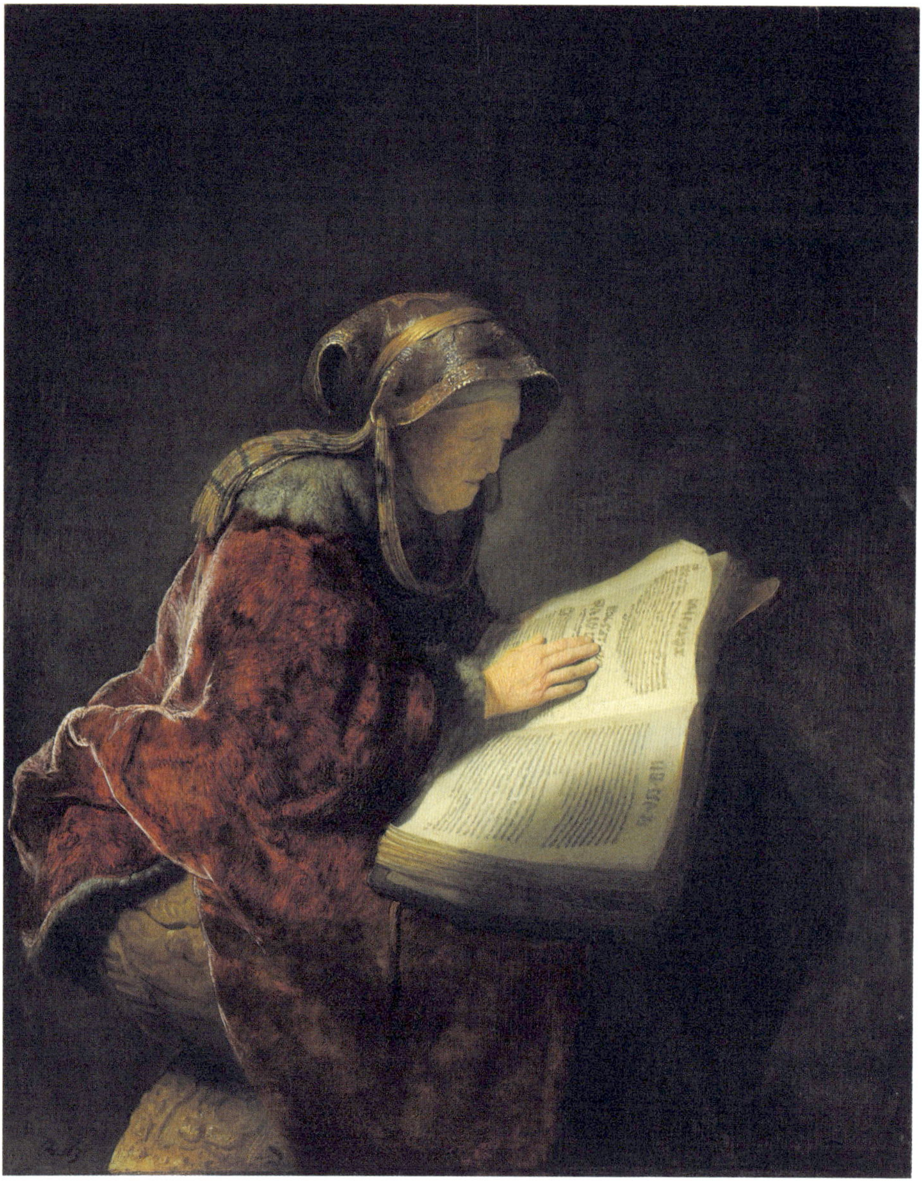

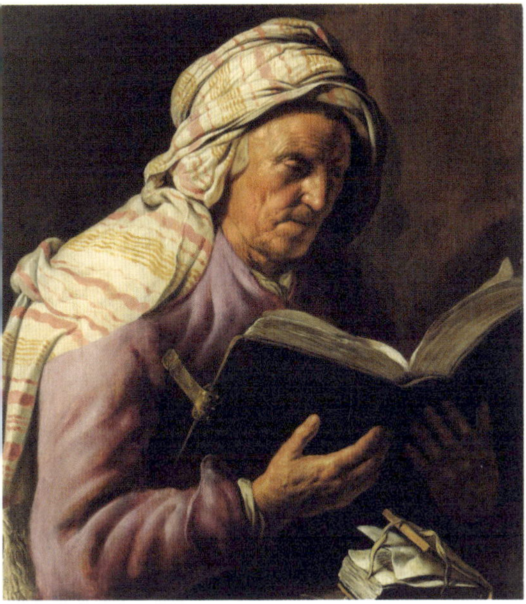

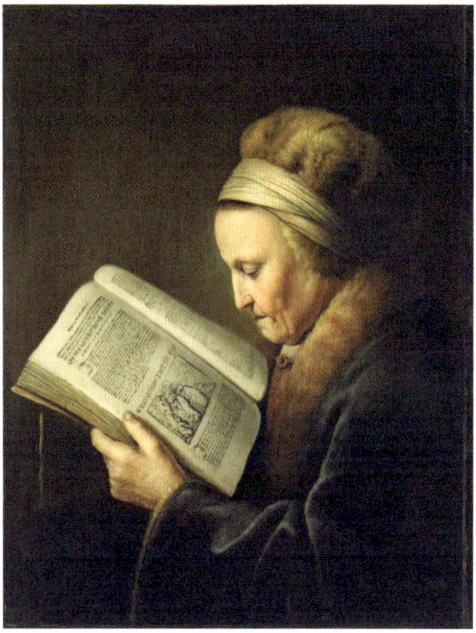

THREE CLOSELY ASSOCIATED 17th-century artists often depicted old women reading (not that men didn't receive, in other works, the same treatment). Rembrandt (OPPOSITE) is generally acknowledged to have used his mother as the model for his painting of the prophetess Anna, and the same person is evident in the painting by Gerard Dou (ABOVE RIGHT), who joined Rembrandt's studio on his fifteenth birthday, but who renders pages from St Luke in much greater – indeed exquisite – detail. Jan Lievens (ABOVE LEFT), friend and rival to Rembrandt in Leiden, further emphasized the theme.

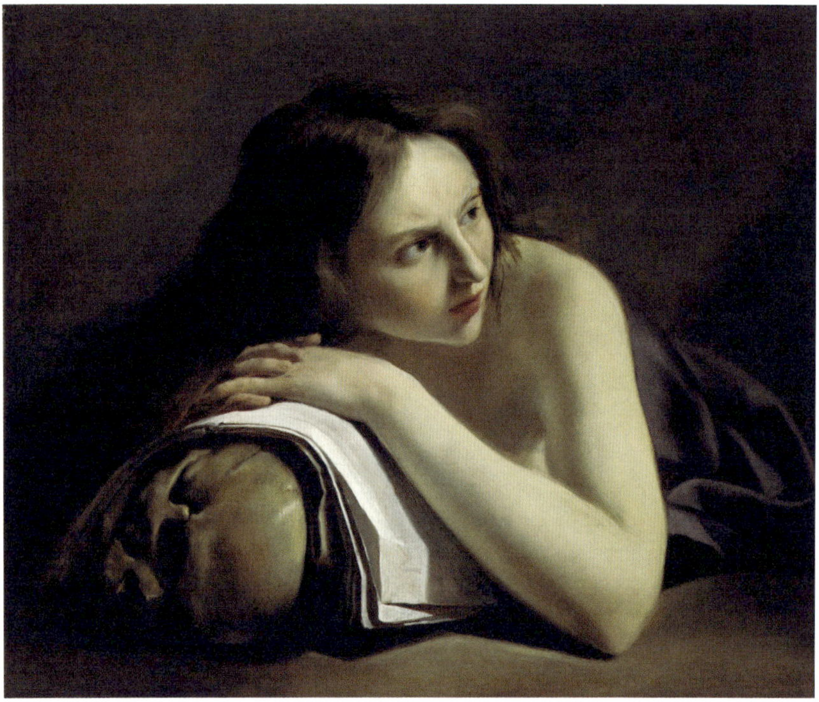

THE MAGDALENE has been disrespectfully called a supermodel and, with even less respect in *The Da Vinci Code*, the wife of Christ. These two works by Baroque artists, one (ABOVE) by Paulus Moreelse (the first head of the Guild of St Luke, a painters' guild in Utrecht that moved artists on from their status as mere members of the Saddlers' Guild), the other (OPPOSITE) by the Frenchman Georges de la Tour, give clues as to why her allure for artists has never waned. The books and contemplative demeanour suggest that Mary – 'out of whom seven devils were gone forth' – had found repentance; the lack of clothing and the smoky candle flame suggest that penitence does not come easily.

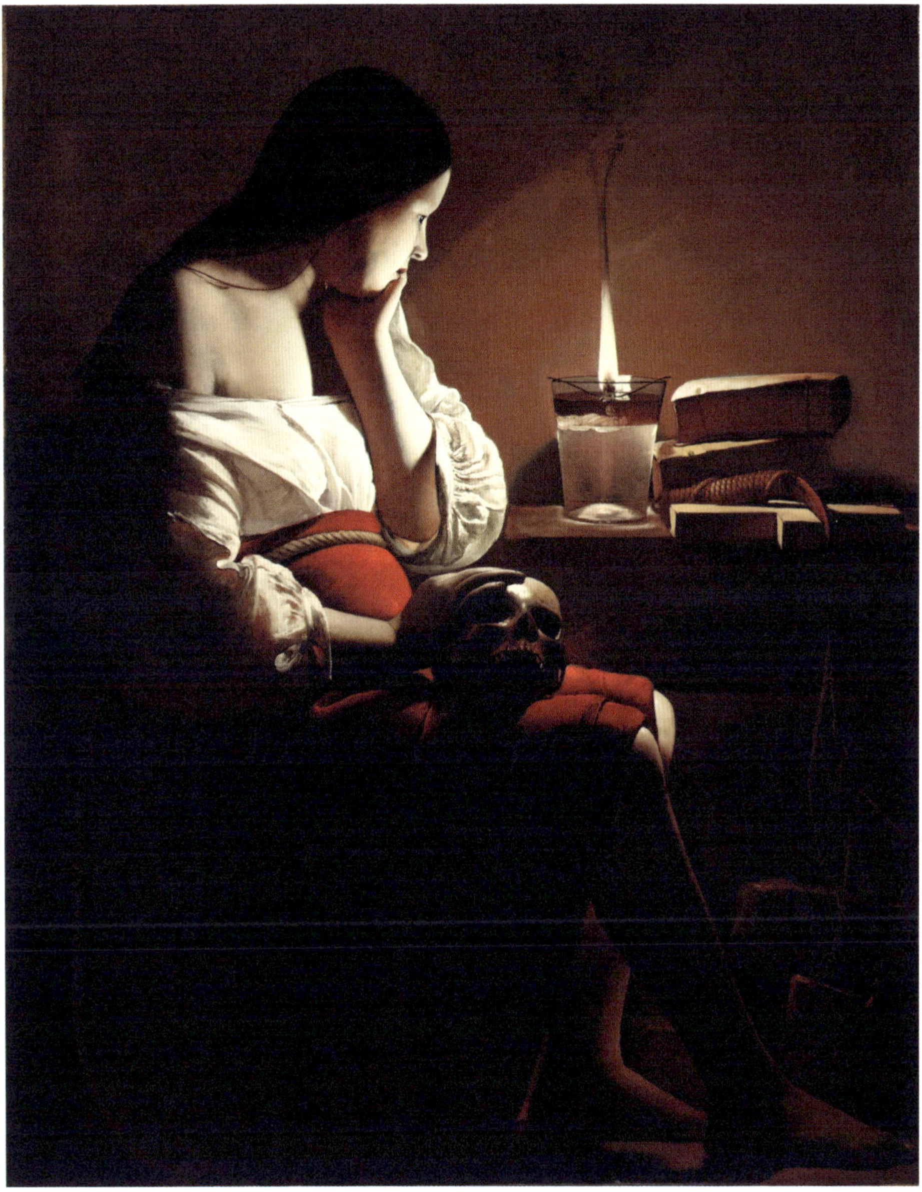

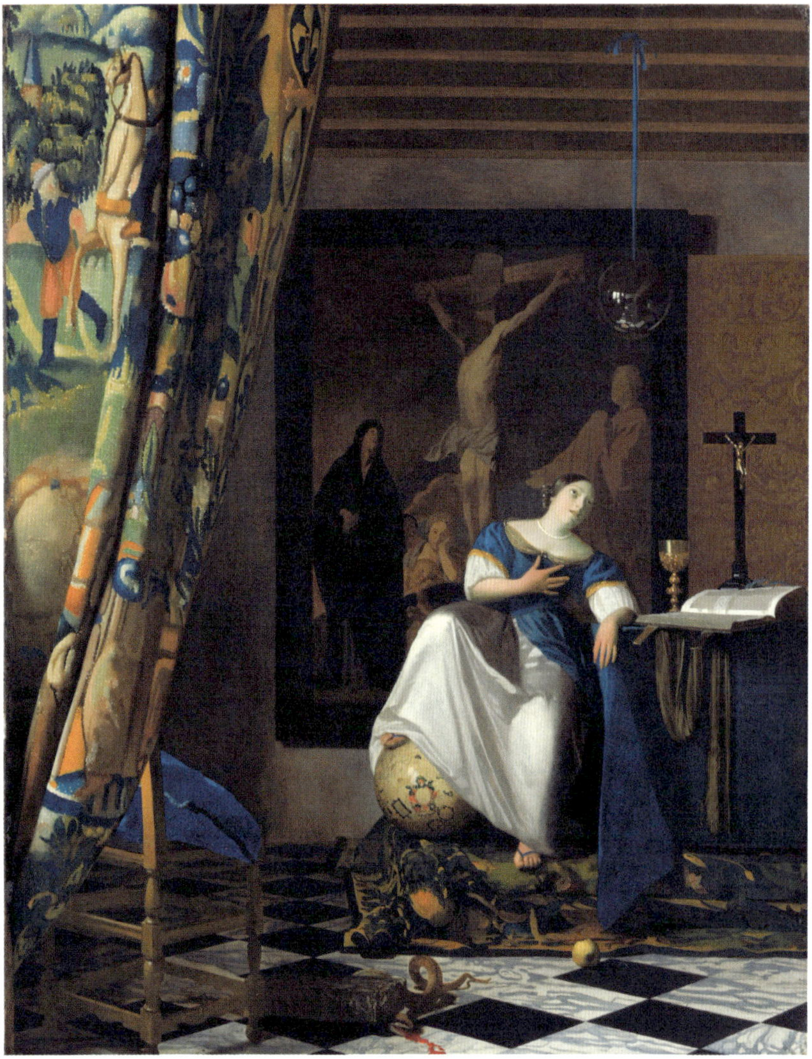

VERMEER CONVERTED to Catholicism at the behest of his future wife's mother; his eleven children were all named after Catholic saints. His *Allegory of the Catholic Faith* (*c.* 1670–72) reflects the uneasy position of Catholicism in the Protestant Netherlands. The Jesuits had a base in Delft from 1612, but Vermeer's painting of a room behind a Flemish tapestry looks very much like a *schuilkerk*, a hidden church of which there were at least three in Delft. The figure representing Faith has either a Bible or a missal for the Mass at her side; with her foot on a Dutch globe of 1618, she recalls, as do other elements of the painting, Cesare Ripa's famous emblem book *Iconologia*, translated into Dutch in 1644.

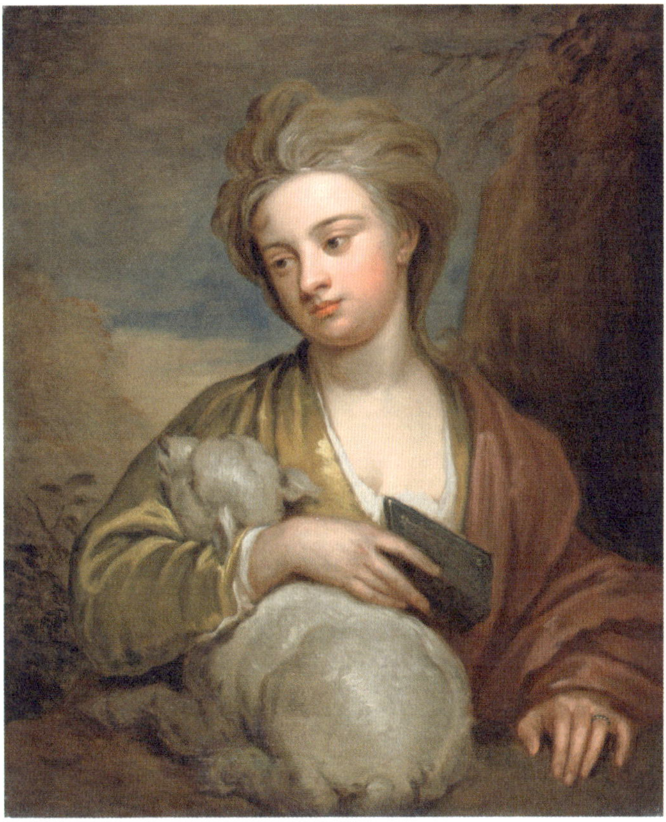

SIR GODFREY KNELLER, the Lübeck-born artist who found fame in England and painted five British monarchs in succession, beginning with Charles II, as well as Louis XIV and other European rulers, was at his most playfully hypocritical in *Portrait of a Woman as St Agnes* (1705–10), the martyred Agnes being the patron saint of chastity and survival from rape. The *New Monthly Magazine and Universal Register* explained the problem in its March 1814 issue. For 'the morals of Kneller were far from correct'. Before marrying Susanna Cawley, the daughter of a clergyman, he 'had an intrigue with the wife of a quaker, and it is said that he purchased her of the husband'. The consequence was the illegitimate Catherine Voss, almost certainly the model for St Agnes and – in another painting – for Mary Magdalene. Alexander Pope ridiculed Kneller behind his back – but not for his morals, rather his vanity.

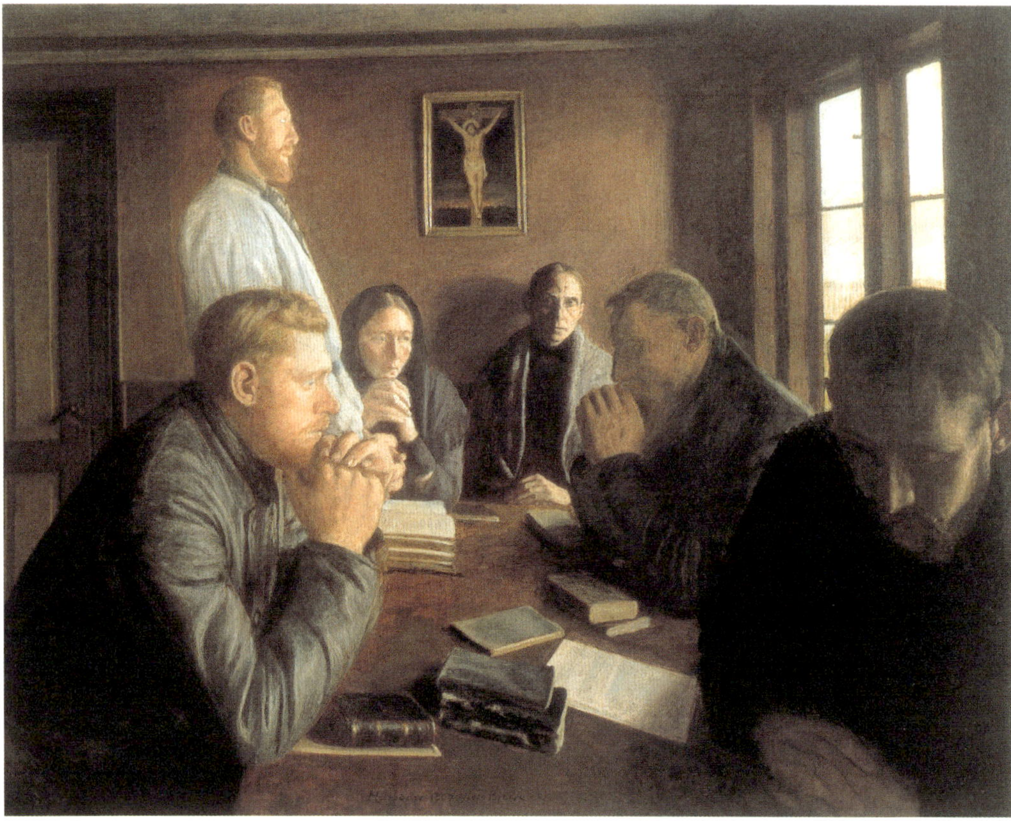

THE DANISH ARTIST Niels Bjerre studied at one point in Copenhagen, but was brought up on a farm near Lemvig. In rural communities, the religious impulse and its social expression remained strong throughout the 19th century, as the artist's *A Prayer Meeting* (1897; ABOVE) indicates. Bjerre appears to have been suspicious of strident new ideologies; like many others not yet fully exposed to modern doubt, he tried to represent 'the truth'. In that objective, books were as vital as ever for participants and artist alike.

THE MASS SUFFERING of 20th-century war damaged religious, as well as social, cohesion. A hungry Georg Scholz, back from fighting in France and Russia and full of the revolutionary, left-wing spirit of Germany at the end of the Great War, was referred to a compost heap by a farmer when he tried to get food for his family. The grotesque subjects of *Industrial Farmers* (1920; OPPOSITE), the likes of whom had prospered by hoarding during the war, are probably about to feed a pastor, visible through the window with an anticipated dinner pasted into his belly. Ironically, while the Nazis judged Scholz degenerate, he himself converted to Catholicism in the 1930s.

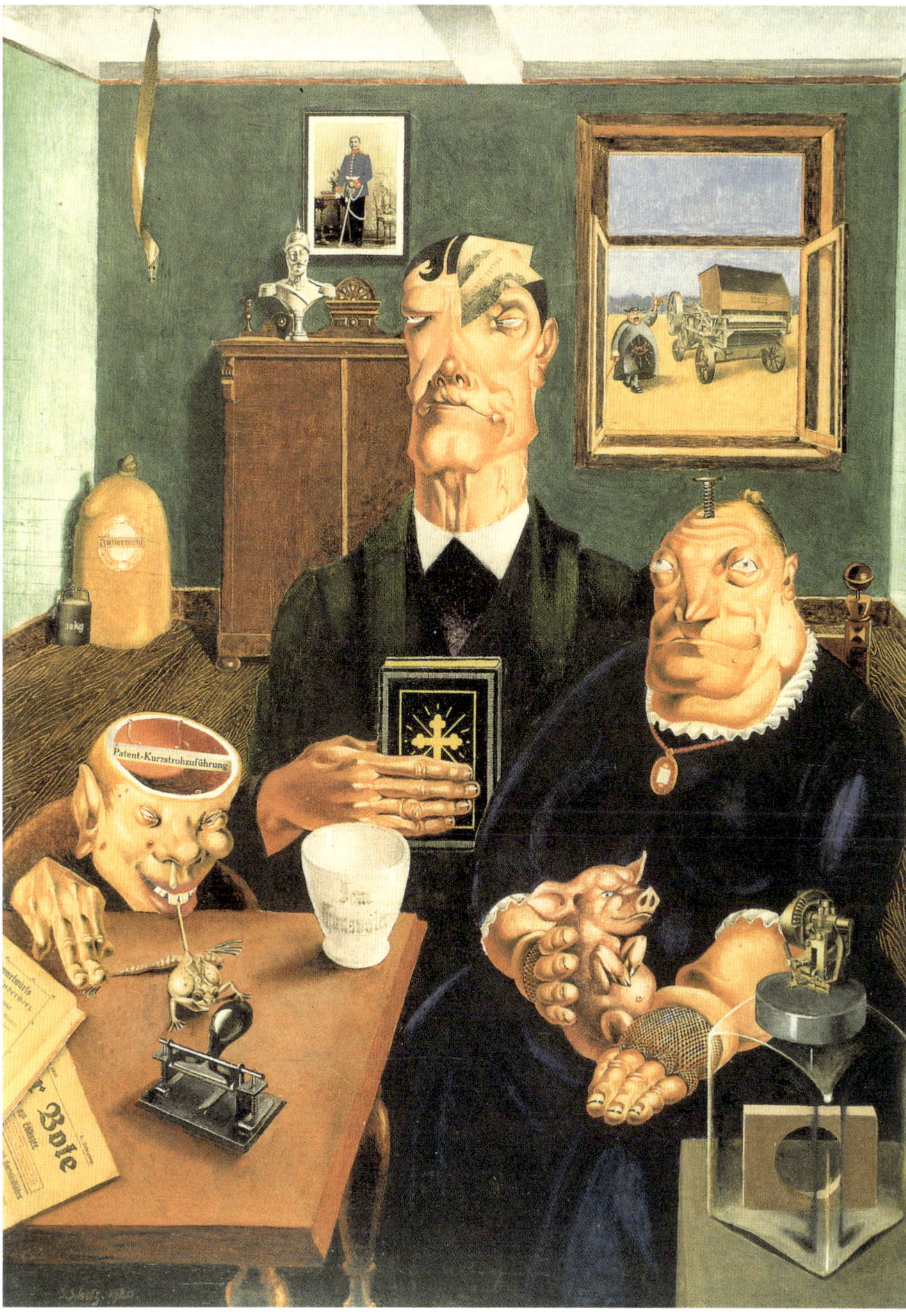
Patent-Kurzstrohzuführung

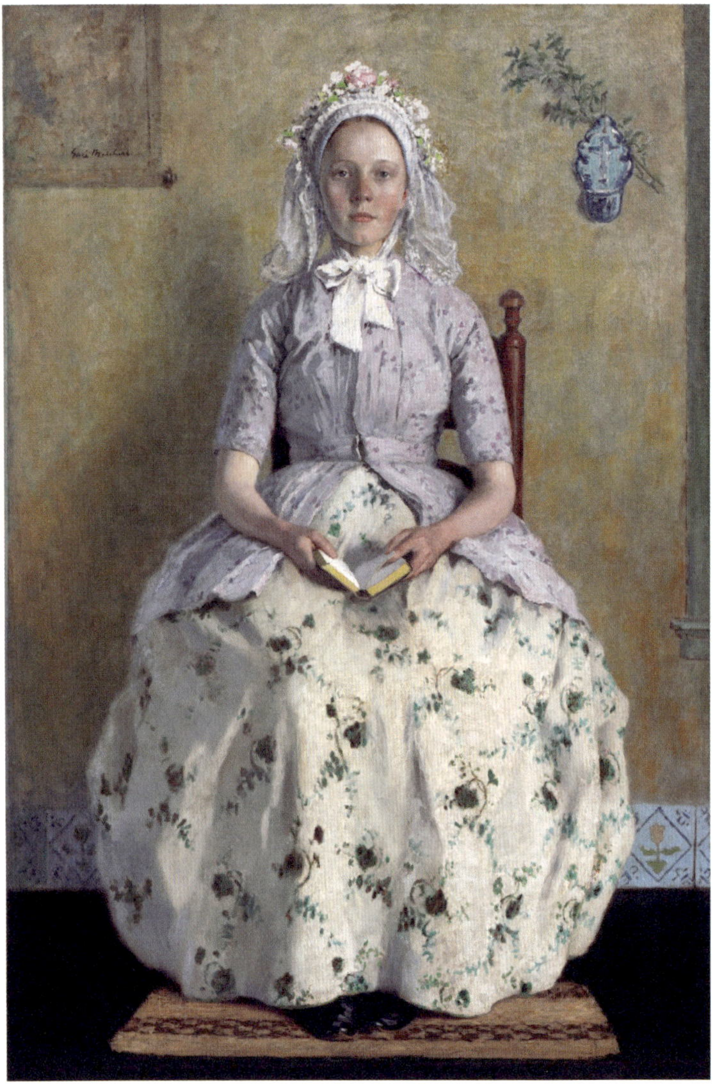

SOMEWHERE ON INTERSTATE 95 in Virginia is a faded sign to the last home of the Detroit-born artist Gari Melchers. Melchers had left the United States to study in Düsseldorf and Paris before arriving at the artists' colony in the Dutch village of Egmond aan den Hoef, where another American artist, George Hitchcock, also lived (see p. 185). Modelled on the young Petronella van den Burgh, *The Communicant* (*c.* 1900), its subject about to enter full communion with her church, was characteristic of Melchers's work in his North Sea studio. Is the strength of that unflinching gaze by the adolescent girl the simple product of the book she holds? God was not quite dead, despite Nietzsche, as the 20th century began.

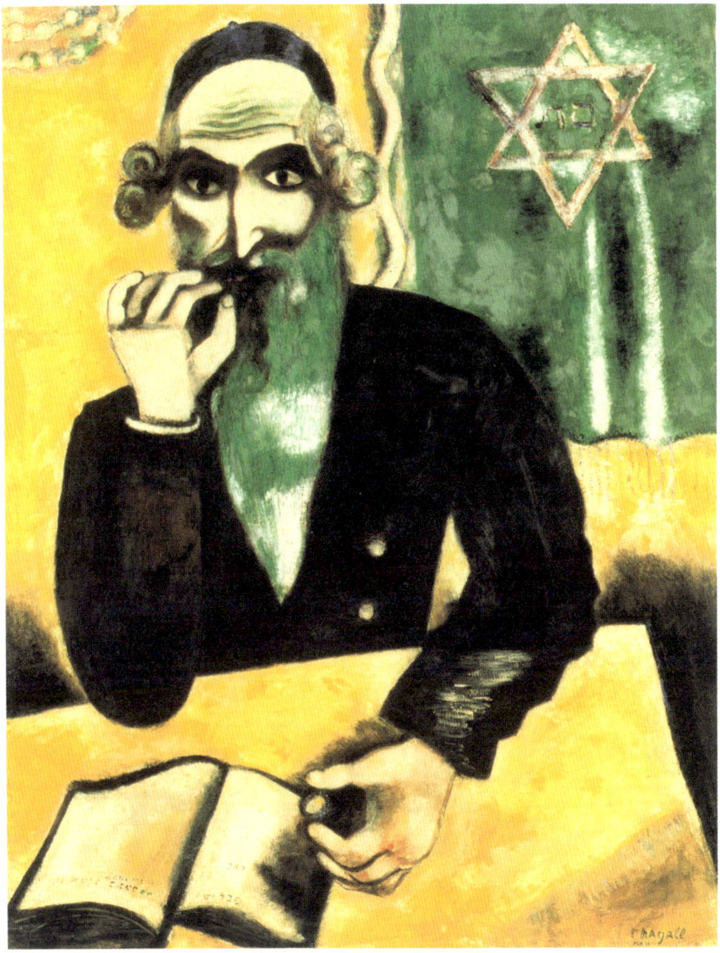

THERE ARE SEVERAL VERSIONS of this painting by Marc Chagall of a rabbi who stops reading for a moment to take a pinch of snuff; each dates from between 1912 and the late 1920s. Many art historians would agree with Robert Hughes that Chagall was 'the quintessential Jewish artist of the 20th century', and under Hitler his painting of a rabbi was ridiculed as a cart took it through the streets in June 1933; the artist himself spoke of the dream 'of all humanity'. More relevant to the intense colours of this work is Picasso's observation in the 1950s that, when Matisse died, Chagall would be the only artist left to understand what colour is.

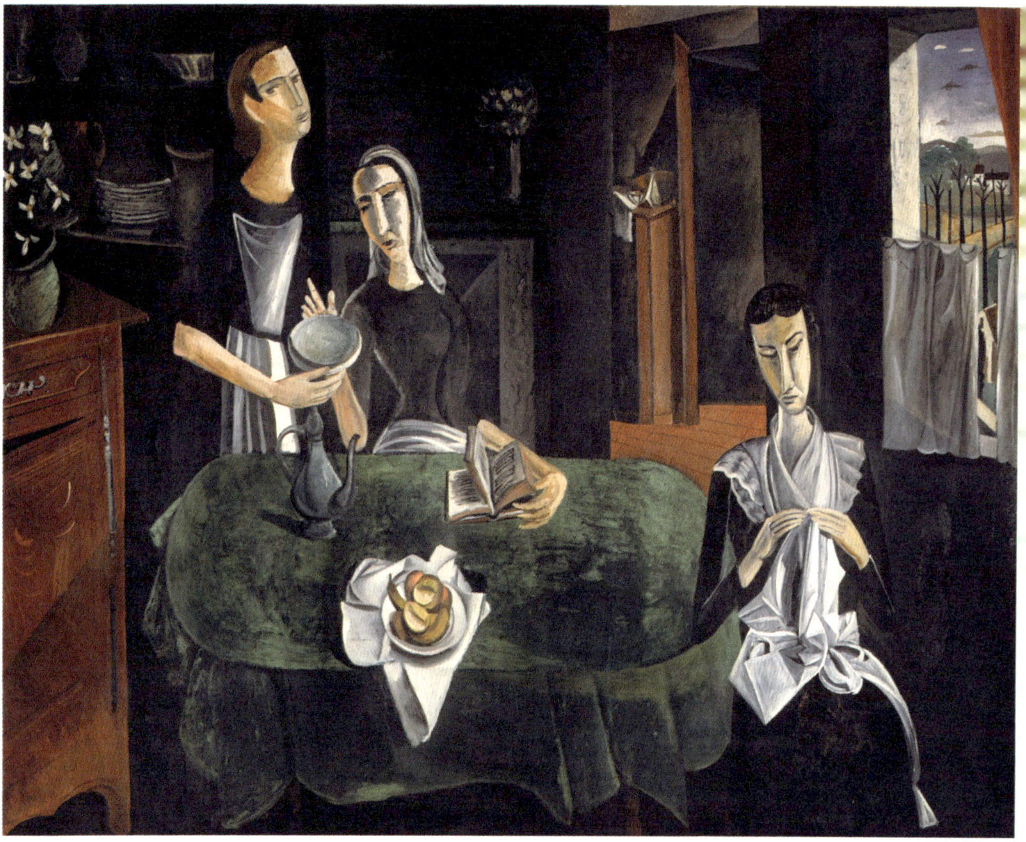

WHEN ANDRÉ DERAIN EXHIBITED with Galerie Paul Guillaume, Paris, during the First World War, the writer and critic Guillaume Apollinaire identified his religious grandeur. Many of the artists who made the future in the early 20th century, unlike most of their 21st-century counterparts, studied the art of the past. Derain and Matisse had worked together in the summer of 1905, and the results were dubbed 'wild beasts' – *les fauves*. But in the same year, the Louvre purchased a painting by the 15th-century Avignon master Enguerrand Quarton, and the composition of Derain's *Saturday* (1911–13) is influenced by Quarton's *La Pietà de Villeneuve-lès-Avignon* (1455), just as the space carries reminders of Annunciation scenes. In an apparently domestic context, a hand is raised in benediction over a bowl, while a place is kept in the text used for the sacrament. The significance of the day Saturday relates to the day of the most intense sorrow at Christ's death during Holy Week. Religion, art and the book were not yet parted.

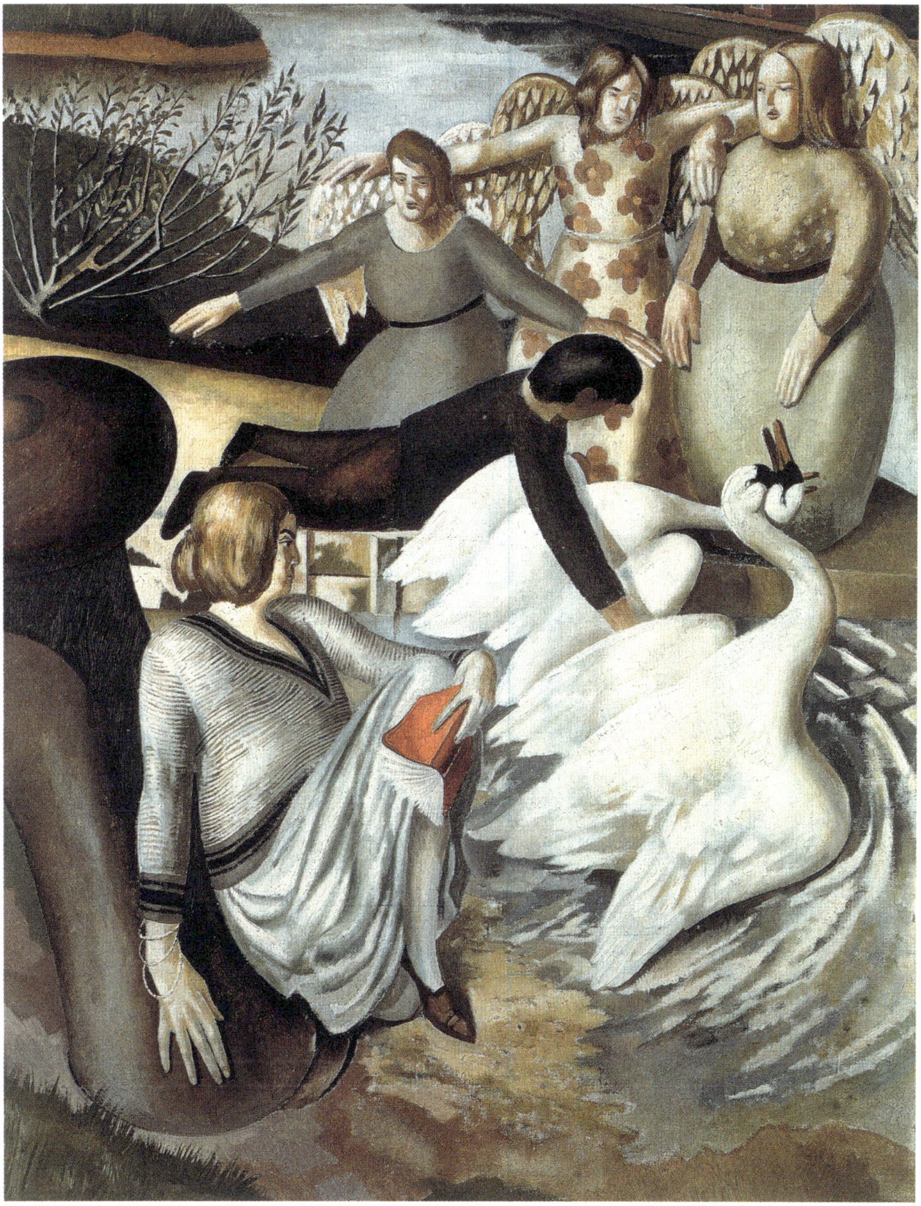

THE PERENNIAL QUESTION: how much do artists and writers draw on real-life experience? Stanley Spencer's answer, in relation to his *Separating Fighting Swans* (*c.* 1932–33), showed the characteristics of much of his work, finding the divine mixed with everyday events, obsession, compassion, in fact with everything. His passion for Patricia Preece, here holding a book, who would become his second wife in an unconsummated marriage; his own separation of two fighting swans in a park in Poole, Dorset; a memory of a sloping beach; his own earlier drawings of angels – all combine in a strange religious image in which one of the angels offers caring benediction.

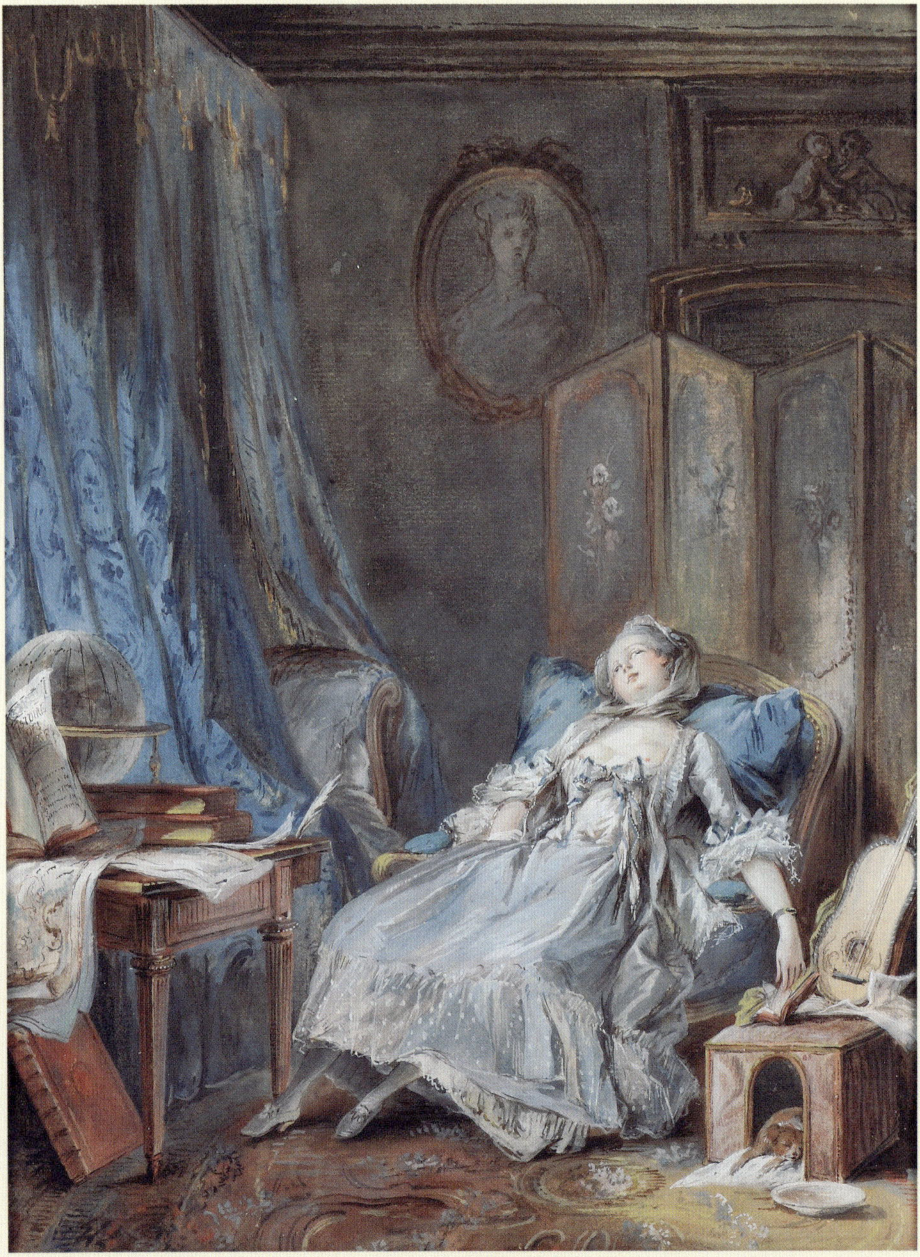

GALLERY 2

‘BOOK-LOVE’ *and* *the* HOME

ROBERT WILLMOTT (1809–1863), whose *Pleasures, Objects, and Advantages of Literature*, first published in 1851, was so popular that five editions of it appeared in German over the next seven years, once summed up 'book-love': 'a home feeling – a sweet band of family union – and never-failing source of domestic enjoyment'.[1] No wonder that artists would associate books with every aspect of home life, with a strong emphasis on an intimacy that was sometimes private, often a bond between families, and yet capable of underpinning a happy experience when outsiders visited – this last so well expressed by Jean-François de Troy's painting *Reading Molière* (*c.* 1728), in which six people listen to a reading in a Rococo salon.[2]

Reading in a home environment has a long history: in a 13th-century illuminated manuscript, a monk can be seen reading in bed. But it took a very long time for artists to move the domestic reader away from the book as symbol of social status, knowledge or devoutness to something literally more 'homely'. Nancy Lawson was one of the few free black people in the American South before the end of slavery; in W. M. Prior's portrait of her from 1843, she appears book in hand in a formal pose, with equally formal clothes that give prominence to the fashionable laces of the period.[3]

MANY MALE 18TH-CENTURY WRITERS warned, as Condillac did, that the 'impressionable' brains of women could make reading novels dangerous for them. His fellow *philosophe* Diderot was rarer in complaining about artists who corrupted. Diderot had in mind Pierre-Antoine Baudouin, whose *La Lecture* (*c.* 1760) shows an obviously erudite lady, judging by the substantial folios and globe, but fully aroused by her dropped novel – perhaps one of Crébillon's tales of erotic seduction. Baudouin's father-in-law, François Boucher, had been a little less salacious in his own *L'Odalisque blonde* (1752), the subject of which, book beside her, is said to be one of Louis XV's mistresses, Louise O'Murphy.

Change, as ever, did not come simultaneously everywhere. Many paintings continued to speak of status and formality at home, with books seen but not enjoyed. Solitary figures are common. The multitalented Louis Carmontelle (1717–1806) may depict – in a portrait dated 1764 – the Count of Schomberg as a relaxed figure, his edition of Voltaire for the moment set aside,[4] but this is not the home life that would eventually emerge for the bourgeois world (in this case in Germany) of *Westermann's Monatshefte*, a literary periodical first published in the 1850s. Nor did François Boucher's 18th-century depictions of furniture suited for reading, the *duchesse* and the *bergère*, convey the sense that they were suitable for relaxed, happy families at home.

During the long march of the middle classes in the 19th century, with its affirmation of family values, sentimentality did threaten to become a dominant motif, although this is a pejorative way of putting it because the association between happiness and reading was a genuine one. Nevertheless, the subtlety of art and artist ensured that the counterpart to the happy domestic scene was apparent in Gustave Caillebotte's *Interior, Reading Woman* (1880; pp. 134–35), which conveys both literally and symbolically the unease between husband with book and wife with magazine. Similarly, while reading groups were often embraced with enthusiasm, Philibert-Louis Debucourt's aquatint *Les Visites* (1800) showed books as playthings for frivolous aristocrats courting their female companions. Sweets were also on offer.[5]

Other artists did reveal a deep fascination with reading. Honoré Daumier, in particular, left behind a multiplicity of images showing how, in all classes, book love permeated the home – in bed and bath, in kitchen and sitting or drawing room. Pierre Bonnard's *La Lecture* (1905; p. 145) depicted a servant reading, and his other paintings of domesticity showed how important books had become as a constant for all household members.[6]

There was something straightforwardly believable about the painting attributed to the Naples-born American artist Nicolino Calyo of the Haight family (*c.* 1848), a formal family portrait with book on mother's lap. The same applied to the later Eastman Johnson painting of the Hatches of New York in their Park Avenue library (1870–71), in which Alfrederick Smith Hatch – a prominent Wall Street financier – and family engage in multi-generational activities, but are 'enclosed' by a boy reading to the left, a girl to the right.[7]

The ever-versatile book, in the work of so many artists, managed to encompass fun, friendship and family ties, but also quiet reflection, or isolation, or discord in the place where we live: our home. In this, as in all else, it helped us to understand ourselves.

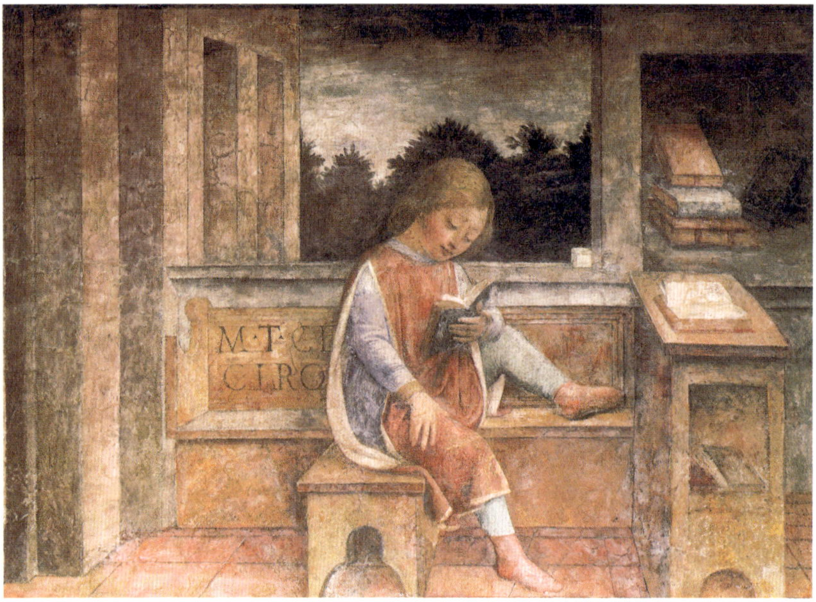

THIS FRESCO, of a young Cicero reading, is the only known work with no religious context by the most prominent Lombard painter of the second half of the 15th century, Vincenzo Foppa. Created around 1464, its significance is not that it reveals ancient Rome as it was; on the contrary, precocious Cicero – identified by 'M.T.', Marcus Tullius Cicero – is a very Renaissance figure both in clothing and in the atmosphere of his humanist *studiolo*. It is rather that the book he reads, the open book on the table, the books in the niche to the right not only symbolize but also embody knowledge, regardless of the century. The message endured, although the painting was lucky to survive; it was commissioned for the Medici Bank in Milan – a present from the Duke of Milan, Francesco Sforza, to Cosimo de' Medici – which was torn down in the 1860s in order to create another cultural monument: La Scala.

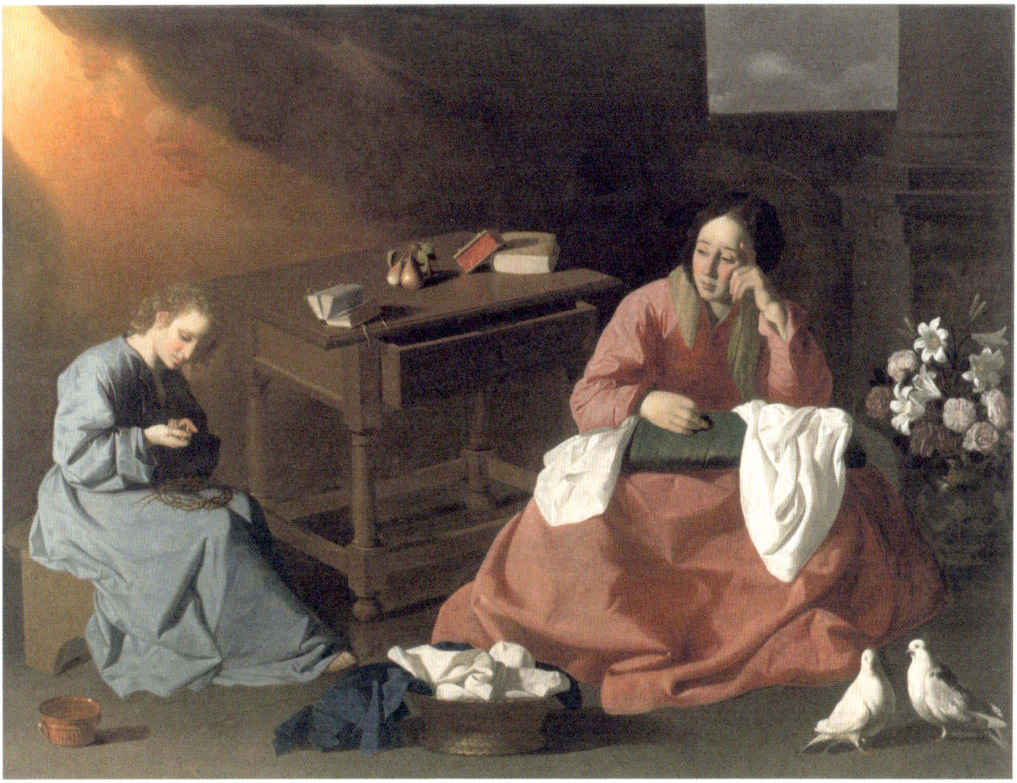

READING AT HOME would take a long but certain journey after the Reformation before it quintessentially evoked an image of domestic cosiness in modern times. But here is a start, ironically a product of the Spanish *Contrarreforma*, or Counter-Reformation. Francisco de Zurbarán's *Christ and the Virgin in the House of Nazareth* (*c.* 1640) uses familiar domestic items to express the decrees of the Council of Trent (1545–63), the Catholic gathering at which the Counter-Reformation took shape. The setting is informal, but there is no ambiguity about the symbols. The Virgin Mary (right, identified by lilies and roses) is tearful in anticipation of her son's fate. The adolescent Christ, creating a wreath of brambles, pricks his fingers on a thorn, his destiny taking him to his crown of thorns and crucifixion. And the table, with its books, transfers the altar to the home.

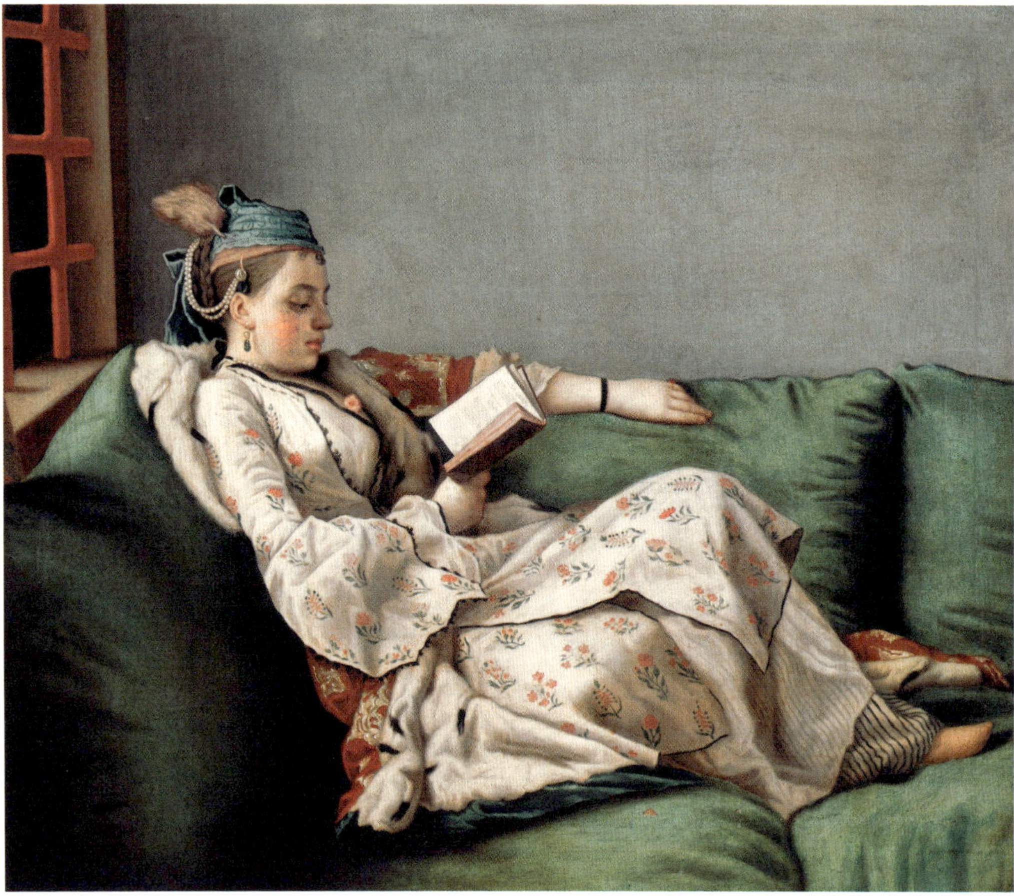

MARIE ADÉLAÏDE OF FRANCE (1732–1800), daughter of Louis XV, is thought to be the subject of this painting by the Swiss artist Jean-Etienne Liotard because of an inscription on the back. She had an up-and-down relationship with her father, especially when she and her siblings attempted to prevent Louis's affair with Madame de Pompadour; she never married and had an unhappy old age, but at the time of Liotard's portrait of her in fashionable Turkish costume (*c.* 1748–52) she was close to her father. The artist had fallen in love with Constantinople while travelling with Viscount Duncannon and other British aristocrats in the 1730s. He adopted Turkish ways to the extent that he became 'le Peintre Turc', complete with beard and Turkish dress. Joshua Reynolds put it less kindly when he reflected that one 'might smell something of the Quack from his appearance'.

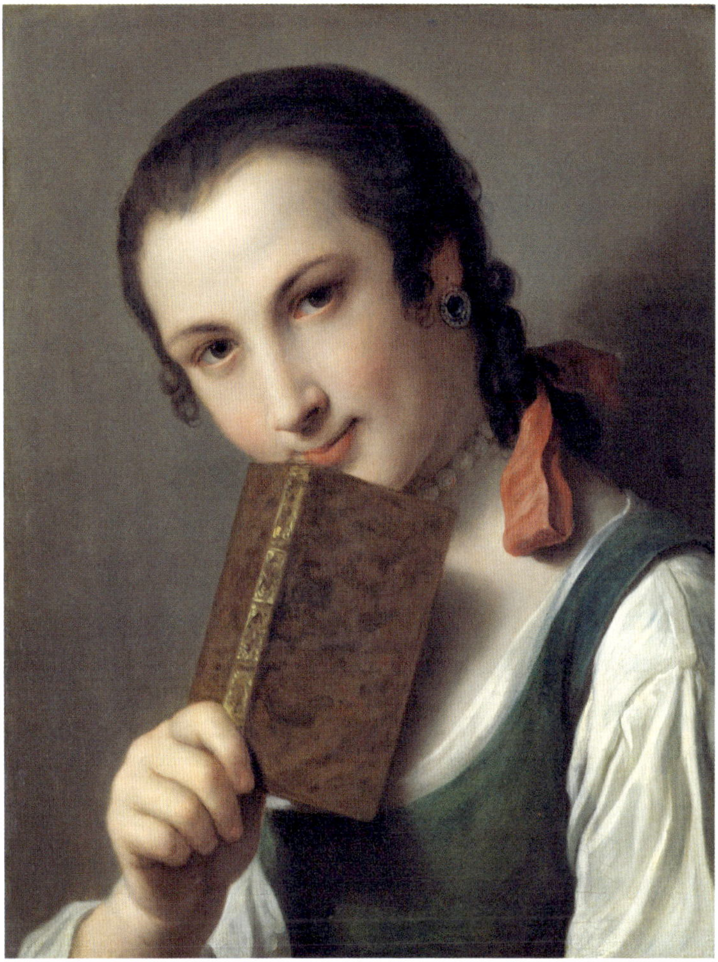

DEMURELY COQUETTISH, alluringly shy young women with a book were a familiar subject for the 18th-century portraitist. The Verona-born Pietro Rotari (1707–1762), who was influenced by Jean-Etienne Liotard when he went to Vienna in the 1750s and saw his work, painted many such girls, sometimes just revealing the pursed lips behind the book and – in at least one case – leaving only the eyes to encourage intimacy. We have come a long way from Bronzino's *Portrait of a Young Girl with a Book* (*c.* 1545; p. 124). Rotari was popular in the courts of Dresden, St Petersburg and Vienna; Mary Farquhar, one of a number of well-educated women who wrote about art during the 19th century, decided it was a case of charm and 'the deficiencies of others', rather than his own 'absolute virtues'.

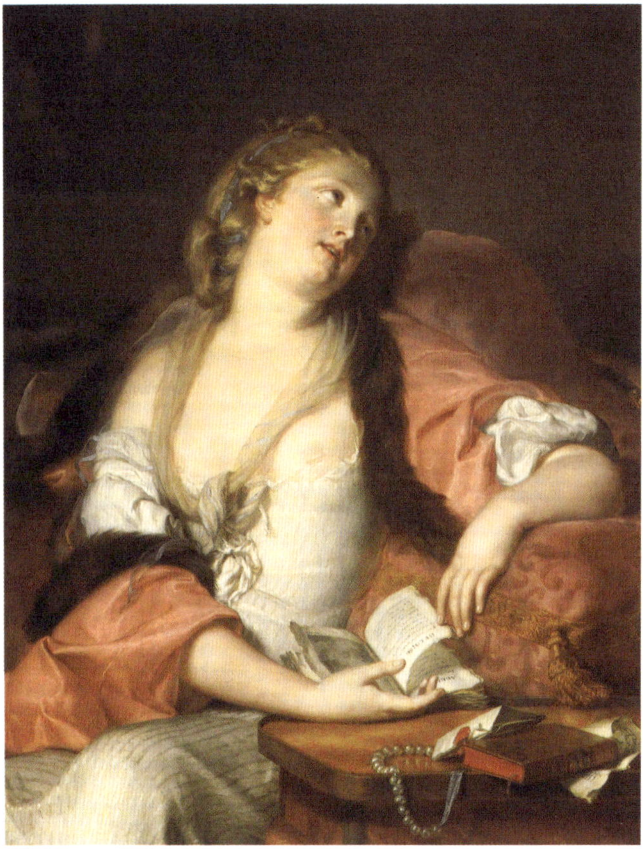

IN 1771, J. D. T. de Bienville's *Nymphomania, or a Treatise on Uterine Frenzy* noted that, for women, reading could result in convulsions. That book was so demonstrably not imbued with the spirit of the great, and sad, 12th-century love story of Héloïse and Abelard, the letters between whom are being read here in a painting (*c.* 1780) by Auguste Bernard d'Agesci. 'I preferred love to wedlock, freedom to a bond', wrote Héloïse in the first letter. On the table in the painting, next to a billet-doux, is a copy of *L'Art d'aimer* by the artist's unrelated namesake Gentil-Bernhard, so-called by Voltaire because of Bernhard's inconsequential erotic verses. Swooning, out-of-control women were favourite subjects for early novelists, but 18th-century male powerbrokers recommended (as in an article in the British *Critical Review* in December 1764) readings under patriarchal control within the family group.

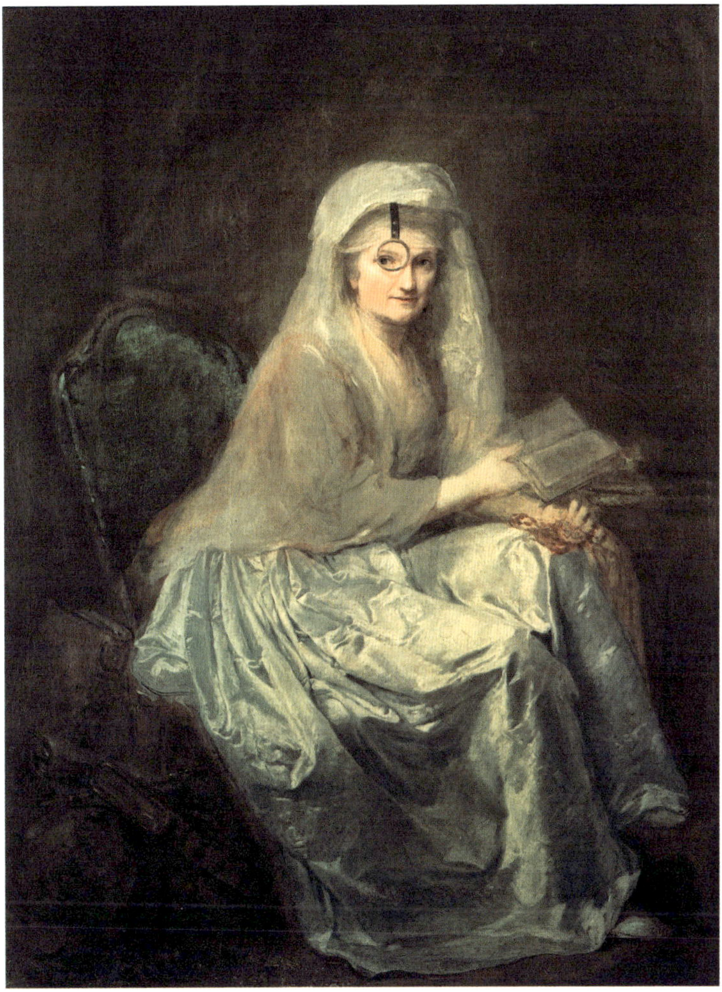

IT WAS SOMETHING to get Diderot to pose for you naked, although the philosopher's turbulent relationship with the lady he called 'Mme Terbouche' later led him to suggest that his support for her – including as an artist's model – made everyone think he had slept with 'a not exactly pretty woman'. Anna Dorothea Therbusch, born in Berlin of Polish stock, painted this self-portrait around 1776–77. It was as a myopic, middle-aged woman that she had left her innkeeper husband and three grown-up children to make her way as a court painter. In 1765, in Paris, she tried to prove that women were capable of better things than being flirtatious fluffheads, and that great artists were not all male gods. She failed, but it was a magnificent failure.

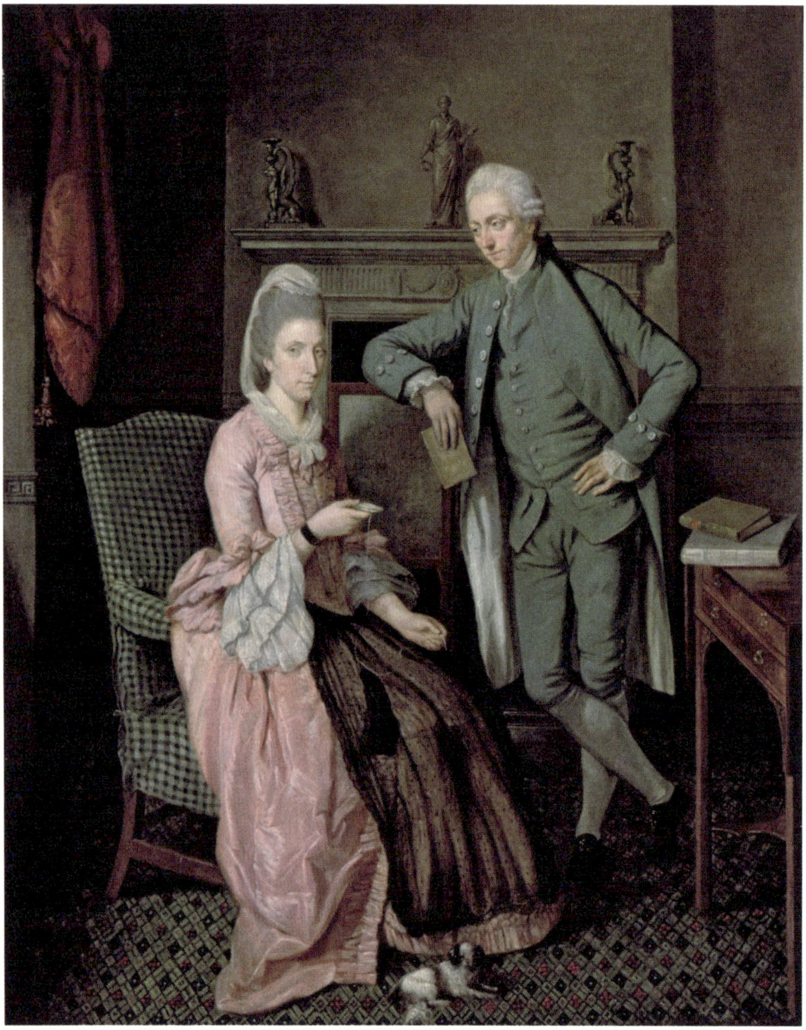

ATTRIBUTED TO RICHARD BROMPTON, this conversation piece (*c.* 1770s) was typical of the genre – group portraits in which genteel behaviour was also seen in genteel possessions, among them here books and neoclassical figures on the mantelpiece. Usually, such paintings did not fully reflect the artist's own life. In the case of Brompton, wrote the artist and art teacher Edward Edwards in 1808, 'his vanity continually led him to follies'. It started well, with an introduction by the Earl of Northampton to the Prince of Wales and a life in George Street, Hanover Square, and ended as court painter to Catherine the Great, but embraced debtor's prison along the way.

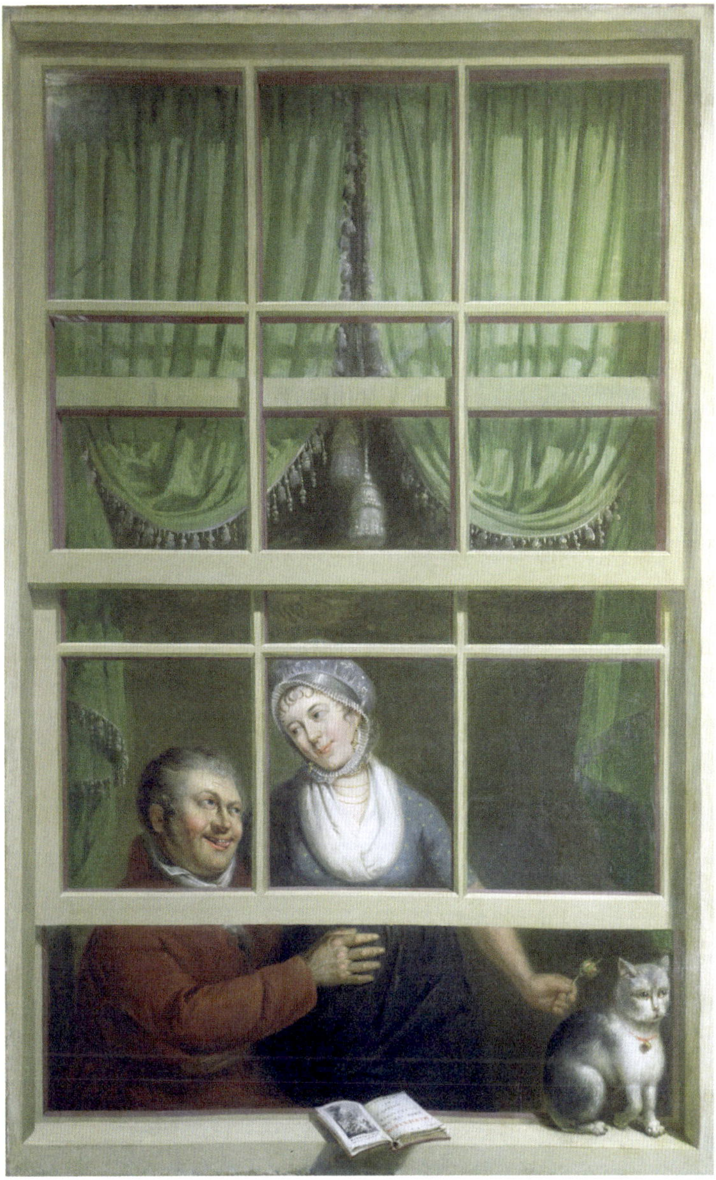

PIETER FONTEYN'S *The Fallen Woman* (1809) is poised between 18th-century amoral manipulation of women and 19th-century public respectability (accompanied by private indulgence), in which 'fallen women' could be 'rescued' by being put to work. The open book in Fonteyn's image refers to the 'siege and bloody conquest of the fort Rosenheim' – perhaps a reference to the Austrian defeat at Rosenheim in Bavaria in the aftermath of the French victory at the Battle of Hohenlinden (1800), or the bloody aftermath of the Battle of Campo Tenese in 1806, when the French pursued the Neapolitan Royal Army general Rosenheim. But here the only battle is for the virtue of the woman, who holds the yellow rose of infidelity.

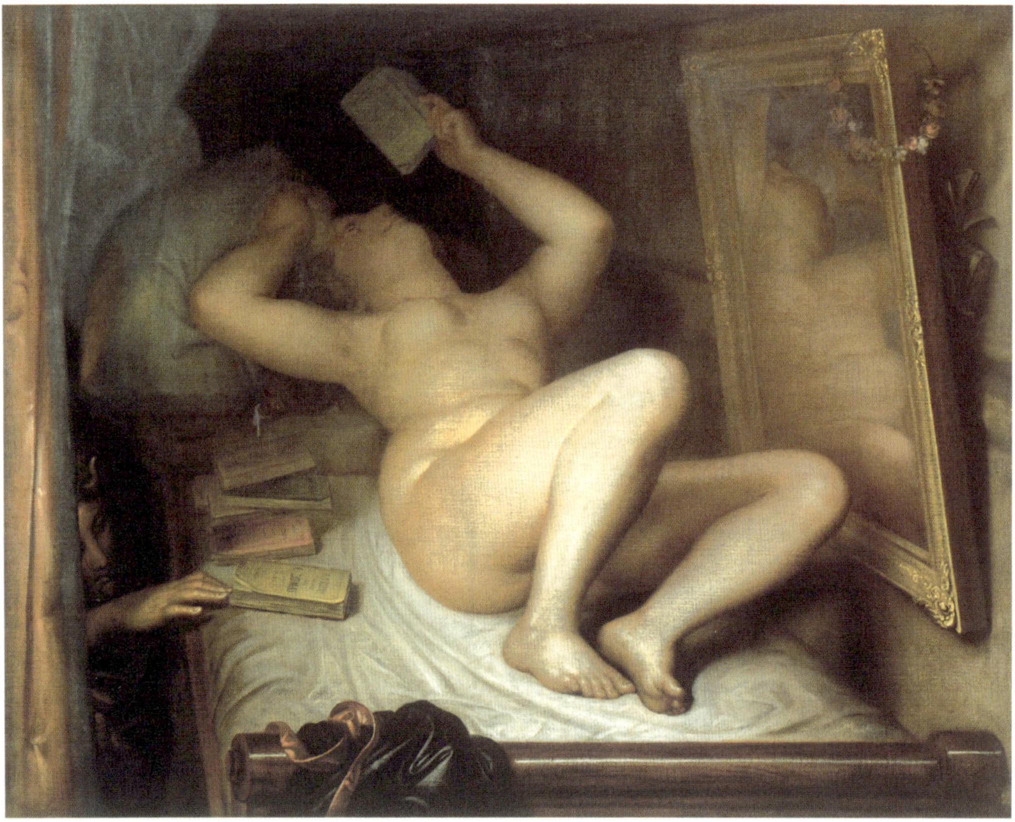

EROTIC DANGER from corrupting novels was never far from the artist's male gaze as supposedly impressionable girls and women found more and more pleasure in reading fiction. In *The Reader of Novels* (1853), the Belgian artist Antoine Wiertz chooses his pose with care, the woman sprawled back, legs slightly apart, her body reflected in the mirror while a sinister figure peeps out from behind the curtain to push more arousing literature towards her. This was Rubens with melodrama, but perhaps unsurprisingly so: at the end of the 1820s, Wiertz had spent time in Paris with French Romantics, one of whom, Théodore Géricault, had fuelled his hero-worship of the Flemish master.

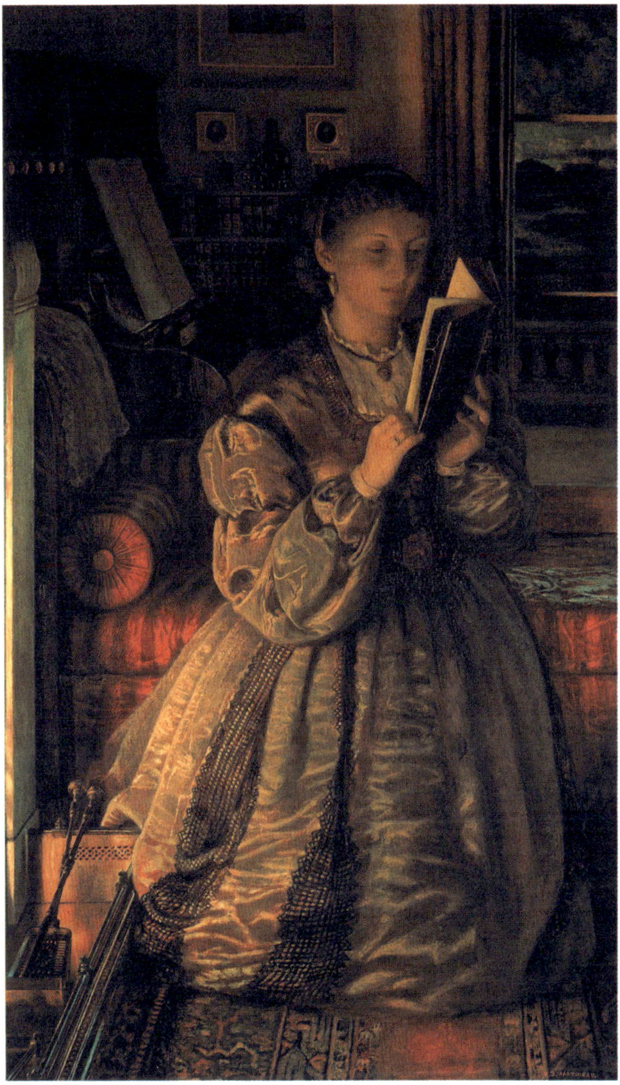

'A GRACEFUL GIRL, who, as the daylight falls, kneels before the fire to devour by its blaze the close of the sensation story that absorbs her', said *The Times* on 27 May 1863 of Robert Braithwaite Martineau's *The Last Chapter*, exhibited at the Royal Academy that year. 'Sensation' novels, full of adultery, elopement, secret or scandalous passions, were the opium of the day, exemplified by Mary Elizabeth Braddon's *Lady Audley's Secret* (1862) and its sequel, *Aurora Floyd*, published in the same year as Martineau's painting. But Martineau, who had studied under Holman Hunt and shared his studio in the previous decade, captures something more valuable than Wiertz (OPPOSITE). While it could be said that the iconography is religious, no sacrilege is meant in *The Last Chapter*: this reader is enigmatically happy, not addicted and in danger. She expresses the joyful truth that a good book is a great pleasure.

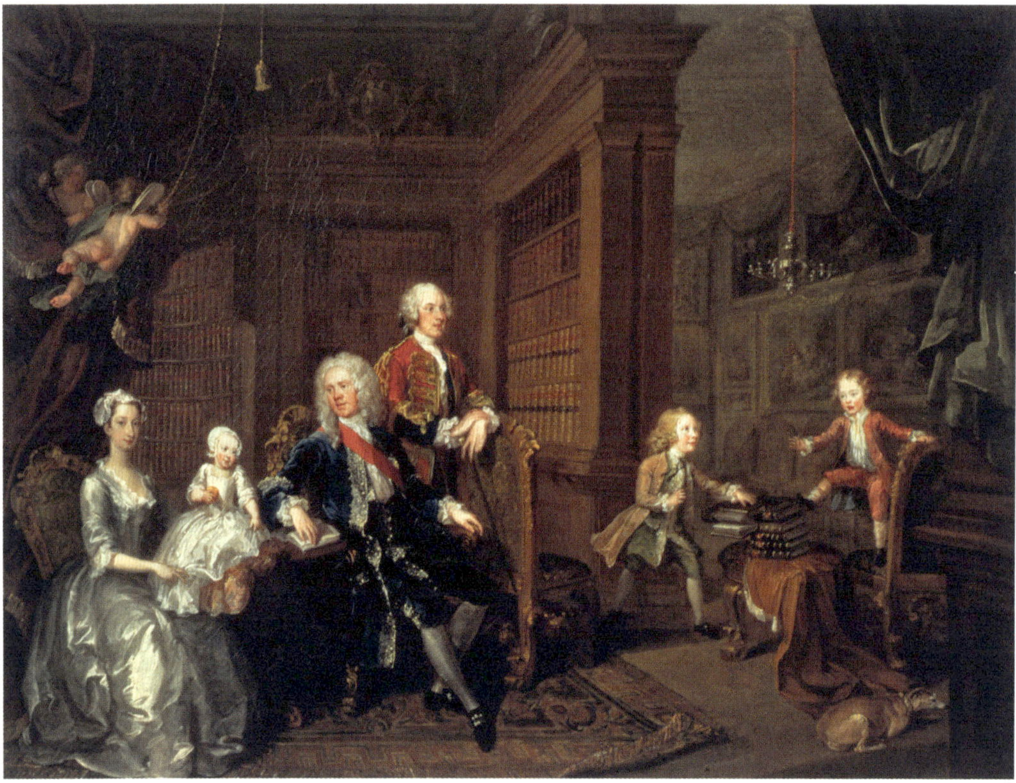

HERE IS A MANY-SIDED tale of family life, with books a key contributor. Its starting point is sombre, for William Hogarth's painting of the Cholmondeley family (1732) acts as a memorial to the mother at left, putti over her head. Lady Mary, daughter of Britain's first prime minister, Sir Robert Walpole, had died of consumption the previous year in Aix-en-Provence. Her husband, George, Viscount Malpas and 3rd Earl of Cholmondeley, looking towards her, exudes the seriousness of adult life, reflected not just in coming to terms with grief, but also in the depth of knowledge contained in the library shelves. The boys, Robert and George, threaten the pile of books to the right, the innocence of childhood not yet displaced by the earnest education they will undoubtedly receive. The dog on the floor, with its unerring sense of mood, cannot bear to look.

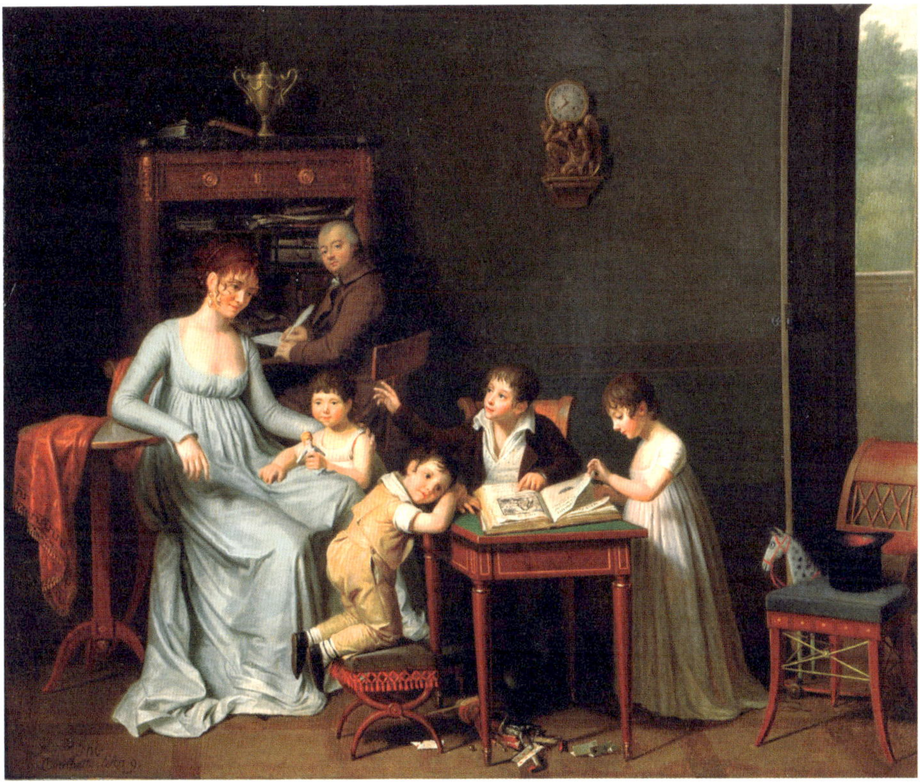

A BREAK FROM REVOLUTION as the 19th century begins. The artist, Joseph-Marcellin Combette, was from the Jura, created as a *département* during the French Revolution. Memories of turbulence are far from this harmonious family scene, father clearly, but not unkindly, a patriarchal figure, mother modesty itself, helping the children to play – and, of course, through a book to learn.

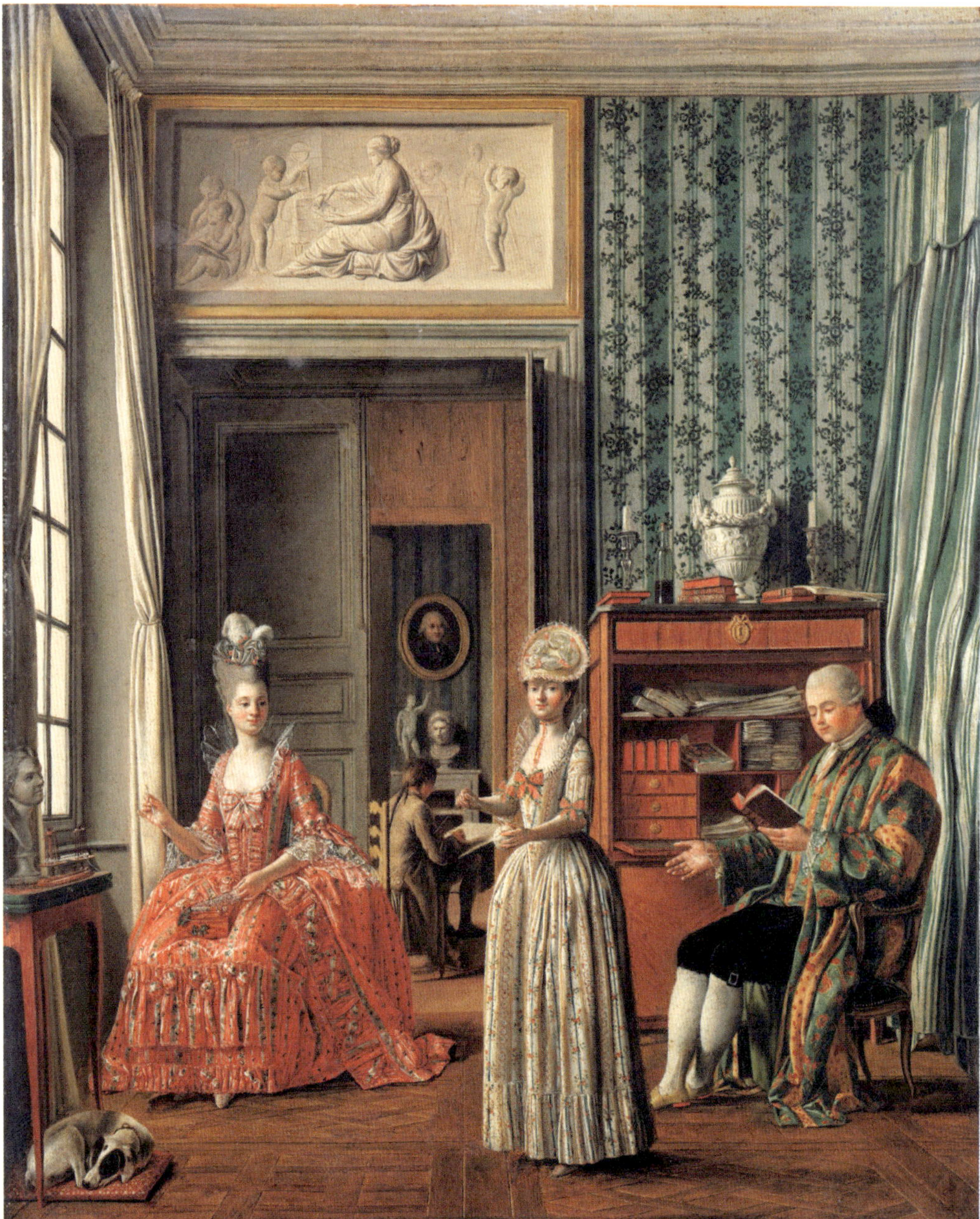

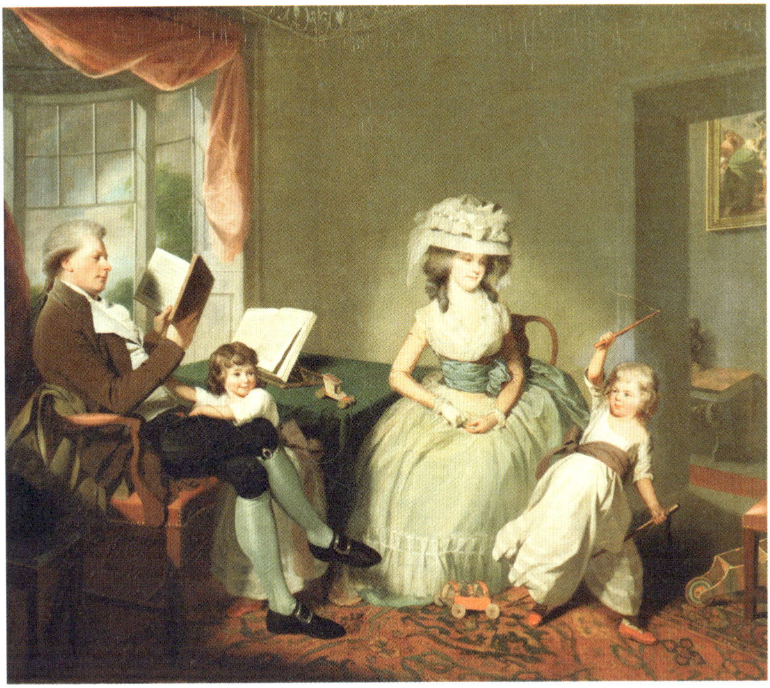

EVIDENTLY, A PATIENT FATHER'S reading is not too disrupted by playful children (ABOVE), although the mother seems to be wondering whether there is a little too much exuberance. Sir William Beechey's *Mr and Mrs Hayward with Their Children* (1789) was painted after the artist had left provincial Norwich to make his fortune in London. He took a house in Brook Street, Mayfair, and, after becoming official portrait painter to Queen Charlotte, went on to paint other members of the royal family. This was an artist 'gratified by general celebrity', as the *Gentleman's Magazine* said in its 1839 obituary. History speedily became less kind: Samuel Redgrave's book on the English School, first published in 1865–66, summed him up as 'respectable second rank'.

HOW SHOULD A FAMILY behave at home in Enlightenment Europe (OPPOSITE)? In this work from the late 1770s, the father reads aloud – as his hand gesture suggests – to his wife and daughter, engaged in making decorative netting for dresses. In another room, the son is seen sketching a classical bust. The grisaille over the door shows a similar scene in a different era, including reading. The recipe is one of sophisticated composure and decorous behaviour, sedulous and diligent – with a book at its heart. The unknown artist reflects the influence of Johann Heinrich Tischbein the Elder (1722–1789), court painter in Hesse-Kassel.

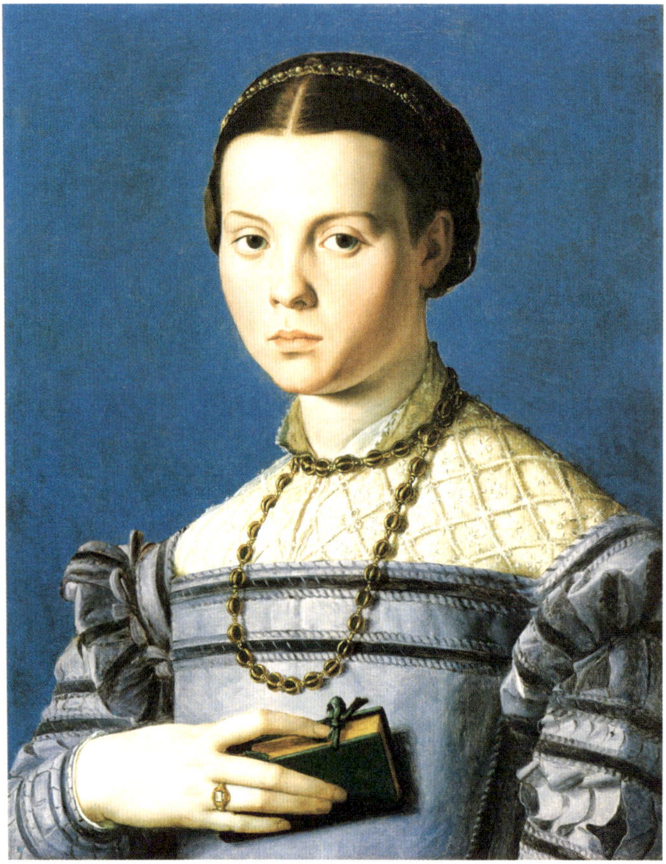

AGNOLO DI COSIMO, the Mannerist artist we know as Bronzino, court painter to Cosimo I de' Medici, shows us detached – many have said 'icy' – reserved and sophisticated elegance in his *Portrait of a Young Girl with a Book* (*c.* 1545; ABOVE). Also a poet, Bronzino revered Petrarch, whose sonnets to Laura two centuries earlier are open in a similar work by Bronzino: a portrait of Laura Battiferri (*c.* 1555–61). The subjects of both paintings express what Petrarch called 'unapproachable, unattainable beauty', referring to an unrequited love of his own. Two centuries later (SEE OPPOSITE), the world had moved on – a little.

IN GEORGE ROMNEY'S commissioned portrait, Elizabeth and Sophia Cumberland read *The Fashionable Lover*, the latest play by their father, Richard. The older girl can perhaps see the point of the play; the younger is bound to be a little puzzled by both fashion and love.

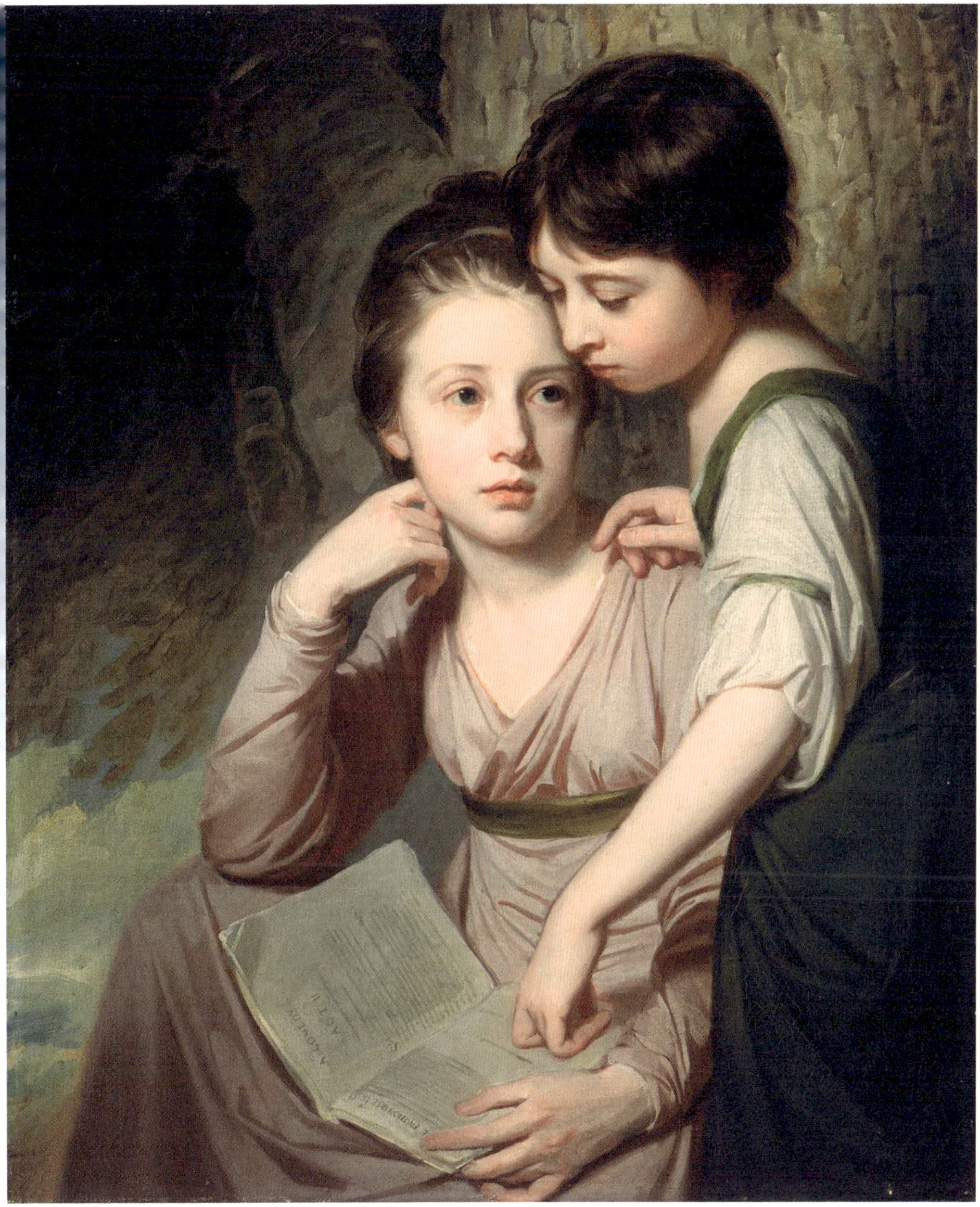

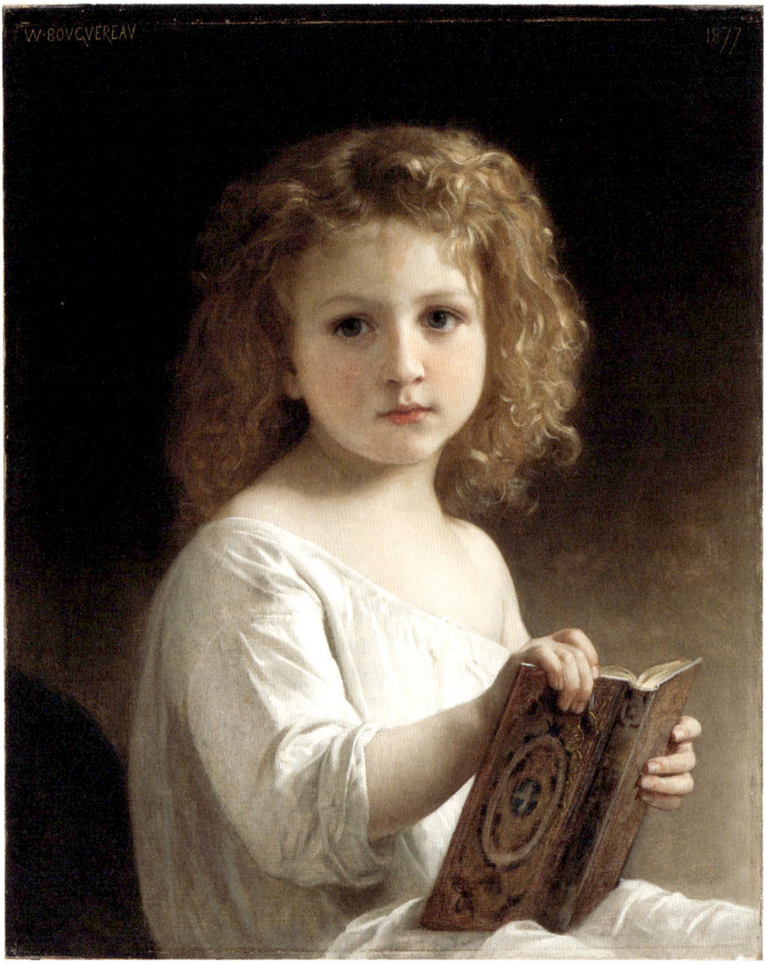

WILLIAM-ADOLPHE BOUGUEREAU, painter of *The Story Book* (1877), was much derided by the artists of his generation who wanted to move art on. There was even a term, 'Bouguereauté', to describe – as the Impressionists saw it – works that shared the deceitful artifice and contrivance of Bouguereau's style. Gauguin was especially hostile – happy, he said, only when he came across two Bouguereaus in an Arles brothel: the only place they were fit for. Behind the sentimentality of this painting, however, was a sad family tale, for Bouguereau had lost his five-year-old daughter to tuberculosis in 1866, a son had died in 1875, and, in the year of *The Story Book*, both his wife and his infant son also died.

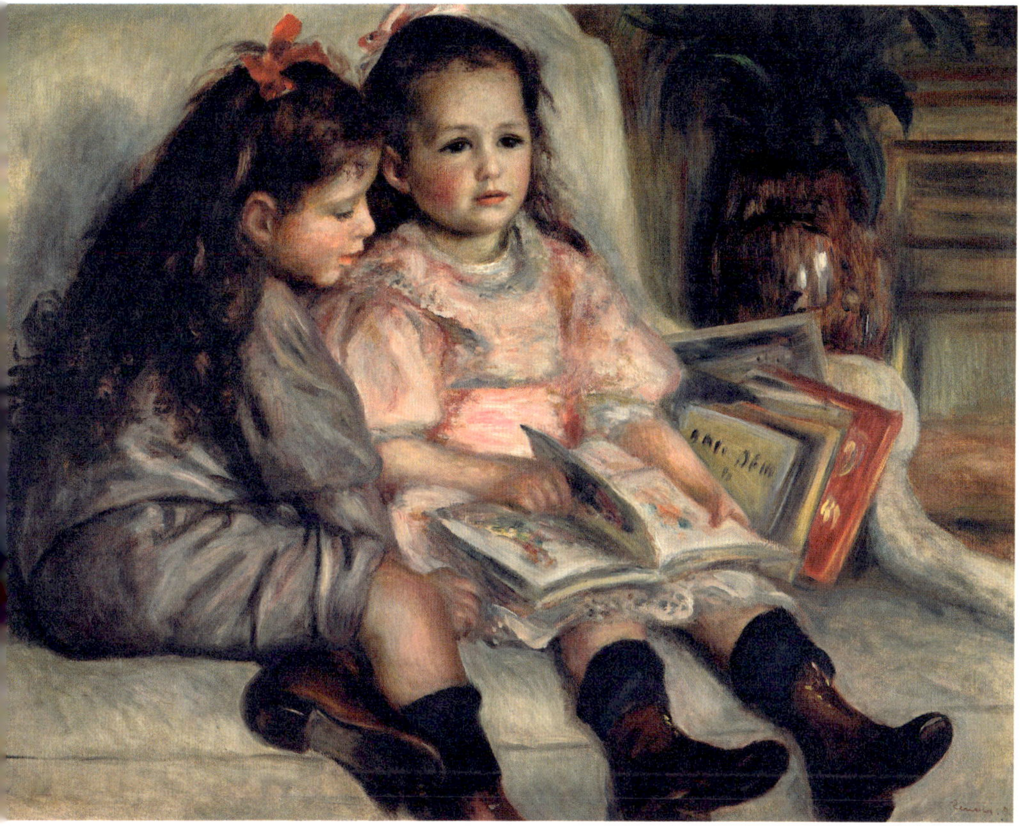

GUSTAVE CAILLEBOTTE, with Renoir's help, participated in the second Impressionist exhibition, of 1876. When Caillebotte died in 1894, Renoir was an executor of his will and cemented a friendship with Caillebotte's brother Martial – against the hostility to the Impressionists of the academicists – through their negotiations with the French state to accept the Caillebotte collection. Here, Renoir paints Martial's children in 1895. Despite the gender ambivalence – Jean, a boy, is on the left – the immemorial battle of the sexes is fully reflected in Geneviève's attempt to make it difficult for her elder brother to read either the open book or the others pushed to the side.

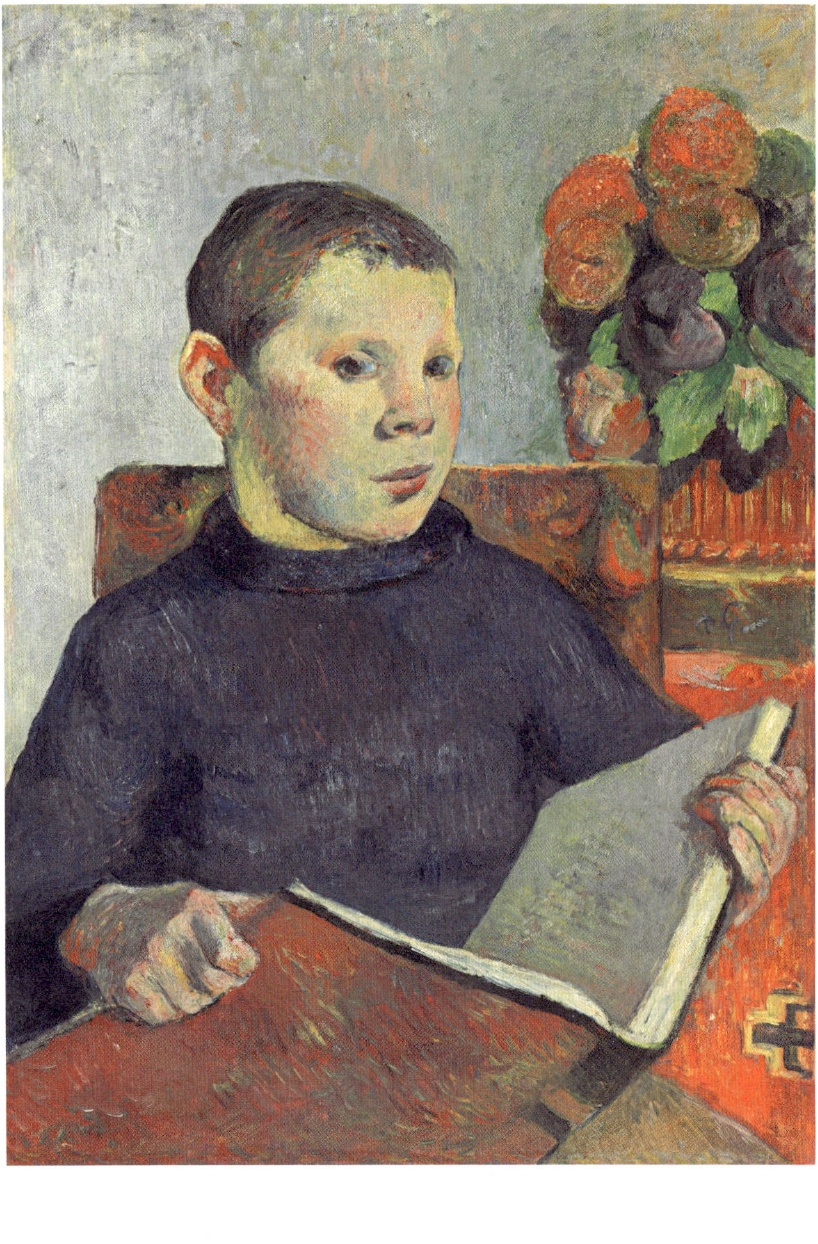

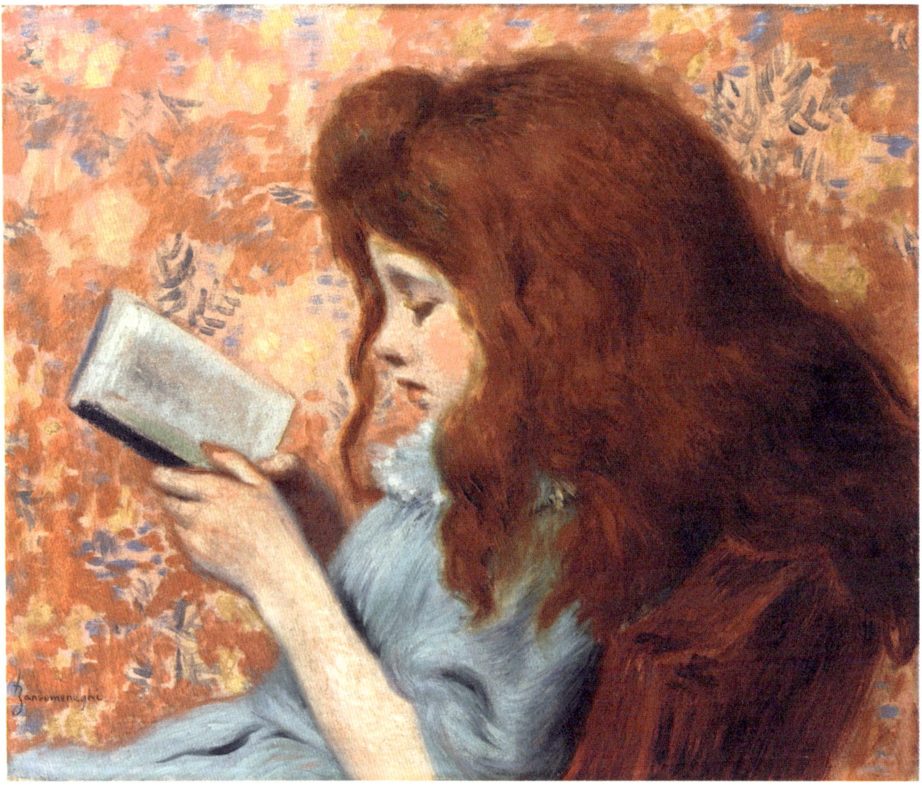

FEDERICO ZANDOMENEGHI'S *Young Girl Reading* (1880s; ABOVE) was another indication of the view that sensitivity and intelligence went with reading. The Venetian-born Zandomeneghi, unlike his fellow Italian artists, embraced the Impressionists, becoming friends with Degas and Renoir after going to Paris in 1874.

GAUGUIN WAS NOT BEING MISLEADING when he once confessed that he had practised his art at the expense of his family. Nevertheless, about the time of this portrait of his favourite son, Clovis (*c.* 1886; OPPOSITE), he observed that Clovis was 'a hero', who 'asks for nothing, not even to play, and goes to bed quietly'.

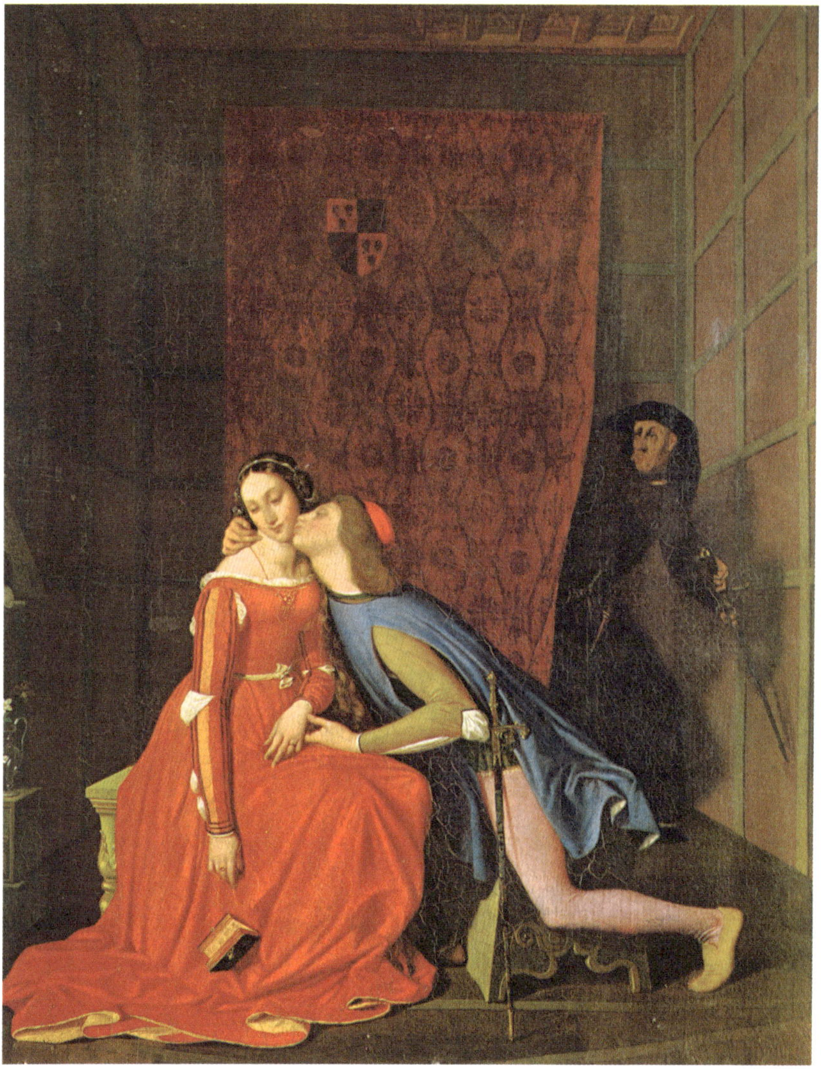

FOLLOWING THE PUBLICATION of a new French translation of Dante's *Inferno*, Ingres painted at least seven versions of Dante's account of Paolo and Francesca (this one from 1819). Other artists, from Dante Gabriel Rossetti to Ernst Klimt, were equally captivated by the story, in which a book is the absolute key to the tragedy, for 'time and time again' it was 'reading that led our eyes to meet'. Francesca, daughter of a Ravenna nobleman, was forced to marry the much older Giovanni Malatesta. Paolo, who reads of Lancelot and Guinevere with Francesca, was Giovanni's younger brother. The romance led to a forbidden embrace – and their murder by a vengeful husband.

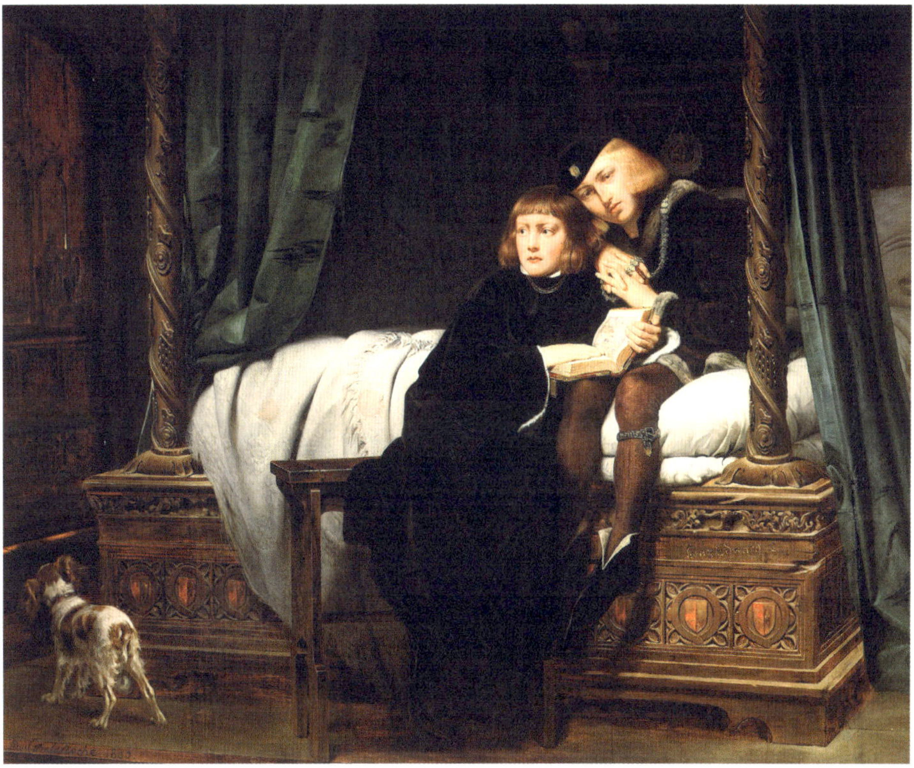

HISTORY PAINTING, so popular in the 19th century, often gave a role to books in situations of great drama. Paul Delaroche's *The Princes in the Tower* was much applauded in the Paris Salon of 1831 after the arrival of a more popular French monarchy under Louis Philippe. The young English king Edward V (right), together with his brother, Richard, are about to be murdered, an especially terrible crime against a monarch sanctified by God; the book is an illuminated prayer book, with an Annunciation scene on the left-hand page. The brothers' fate, popularized so effectively by Shakespeare's *Richard III*, had its French parallel in the childhood death of the uncrowned Louis XVII in the Paris Temple in 1795. His mother, Marie Antoinette, was painted by Anne-Flore Millet, Marquise de Bréhan, awaiting the guillotine – not with a prayer book, but with a life of the executed Mary, Queen of Scots.

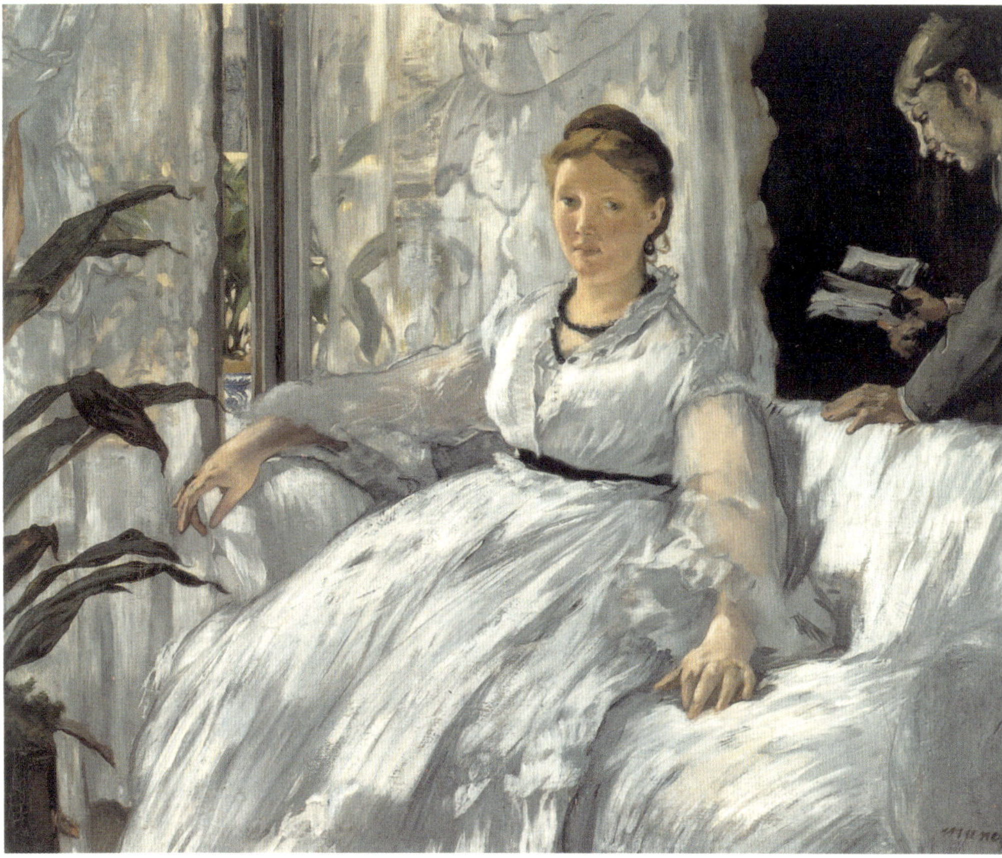

WHY MADAME MANET – the Dutch-born pianist Suzanne Leenhoff – is so detached from her reading son, Léon Köella-Leenhoff, in Edouard Manet's painting of 1868 is as mysterious as the history of the household. Manet's father, Auguste, a judge, had introduced Suzanne to the Manet brothers as piano teacher when she was nineteen and Edouard was seventeen. Léon was born in 1852; Edouard was his godfather. No one knows for certain whether the child, born out of wedlock, was Edouard's son or his father's or neither. In any event, he became the most painted of Edouard's male subjects. Suzanne and Edouard were finally married in 1863, after Auguste's death.

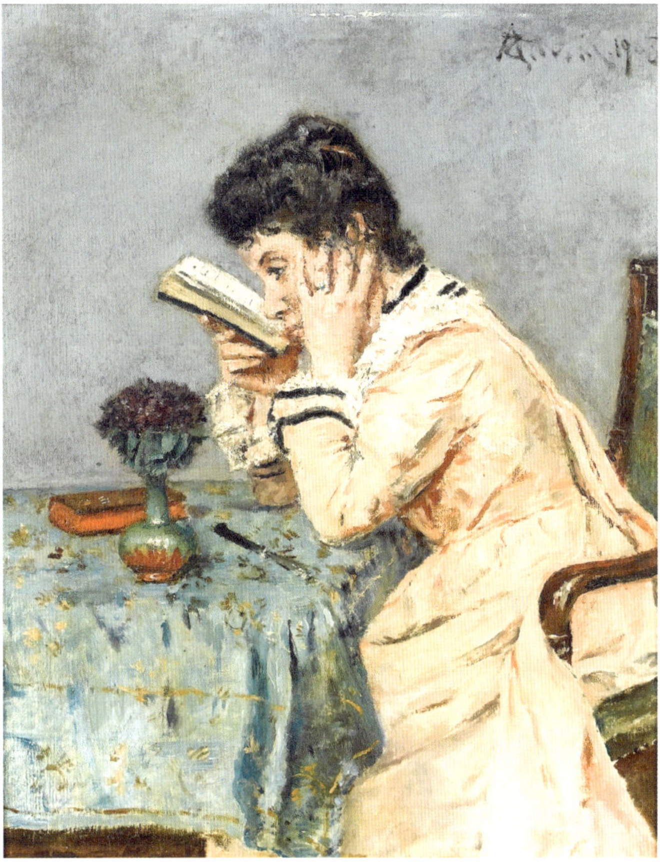

THE EARLIEST USE of the word 'myopia' is usually attributed to the Greek physician Galen in the 2nd century CE. A British army commander in the early 19th century was not alone in attributing shortsightedness among his officers to reading, a condition not affecting his usually illiterate men. Later that century, the great growth in reading, especially in education, reinforced the connection, leading in Germany to the regulation of typesize in textbooks. The Brussels-born Alfred Stevens, whose *La Myope* dates from 1903, was earlier a regular with Manet, Degas, Baudelaire and others at the Café Guerbois in Paris; Delacroix was best man at his wedding. Stevens's considerable reputation in the second half of the 19th century was founded on the painting of elegant women in tune with the times. This one suggests that the growth in knowledge about how to use lenses to correct defects in eyesight was not favoured by everyone.

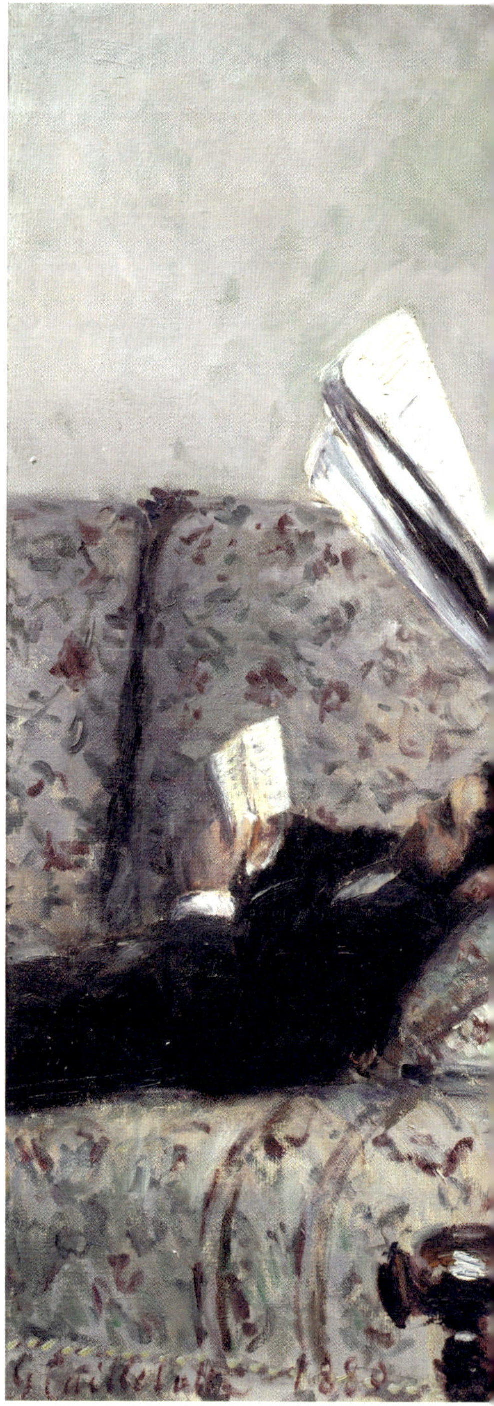

GUSTAVE CAILLEBOTTE'S *Interior, Reading Woman* (1880) amused the critics. Henri Trianon thought the man on the sofa looked like a doll, a child's toy, Paul de Charry that we were looking at a dwarf and a giant; Paul Mantz suggested the couple were expressing the ultimate sensuality: separation of bodies. This was a lonely time for Caillebotte, living with his brother Martial, although it has been suggested that the woman reading *Le Charivari*, or perhaps *L'Evénement*, is Charlotte Berthier, a younger, lower-class lover of the unmarried Gustave. Renoir's portrait of her from 1883, while not quite evidence, suggests it might be so.

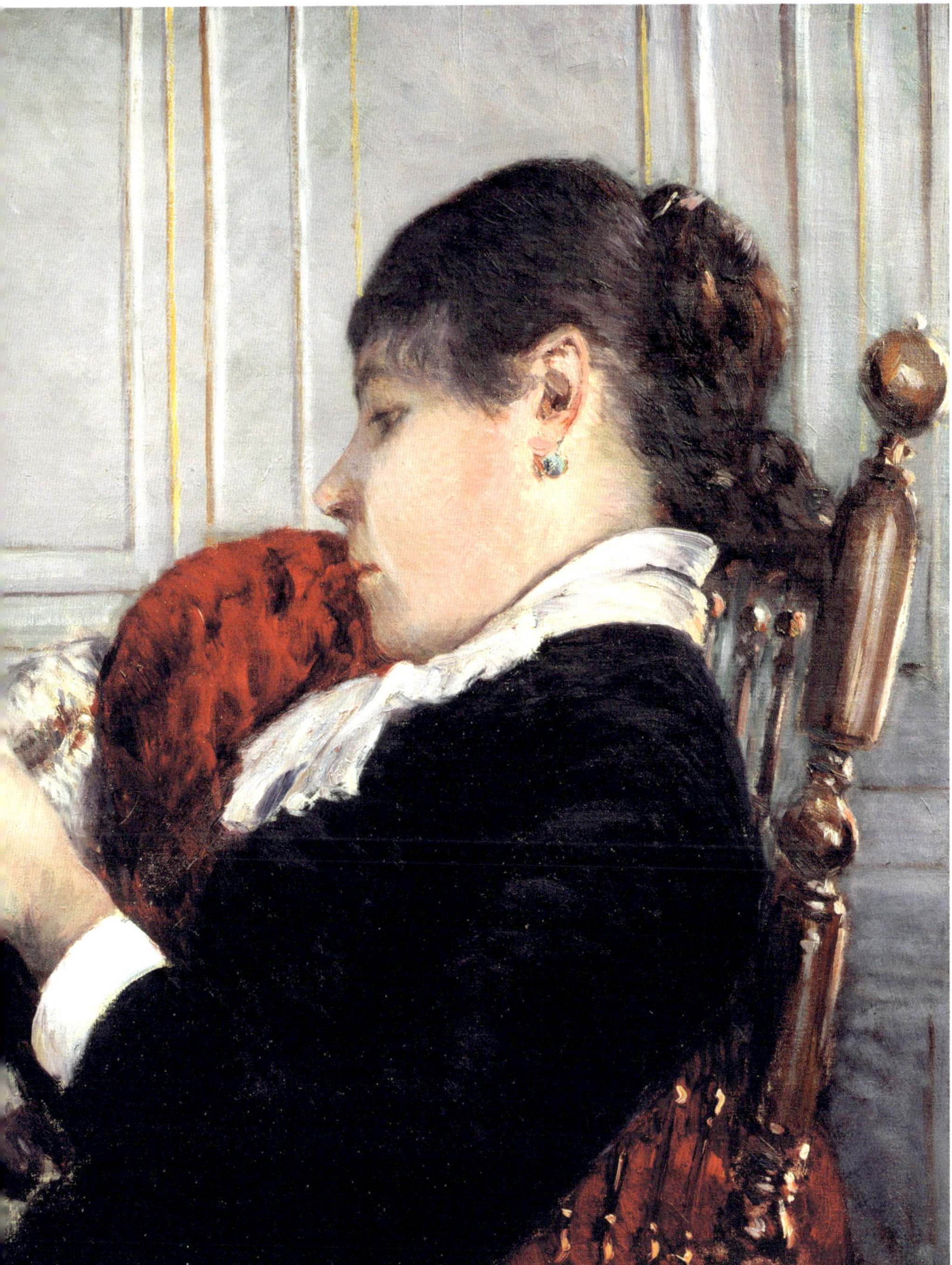

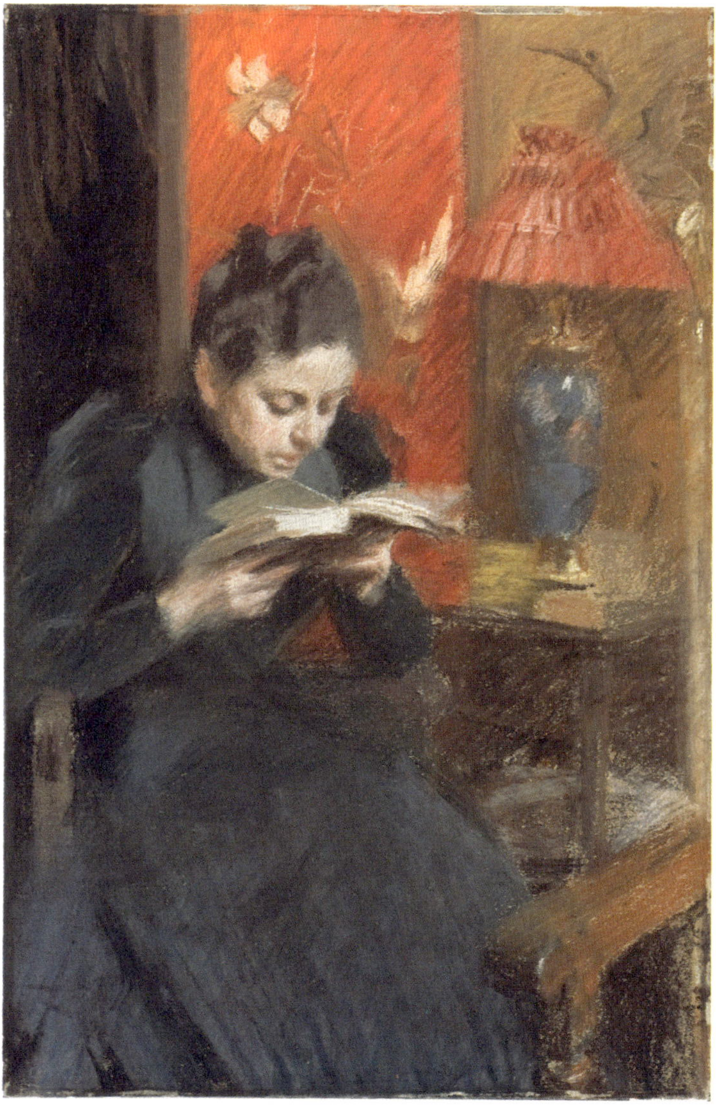

THE EVER-SUPPORTIVE, calming, wholly admirable Emma Lamm encountered Anders Zorn when she asked her mother for a portrait of herself in the early 1880s. The girl from a rich Jewish merchant family and the artist from a farming community made a marriage whose success provides a contrast to the turbulence so often found in a painter's *ménage*. This later portrait was from 1889.

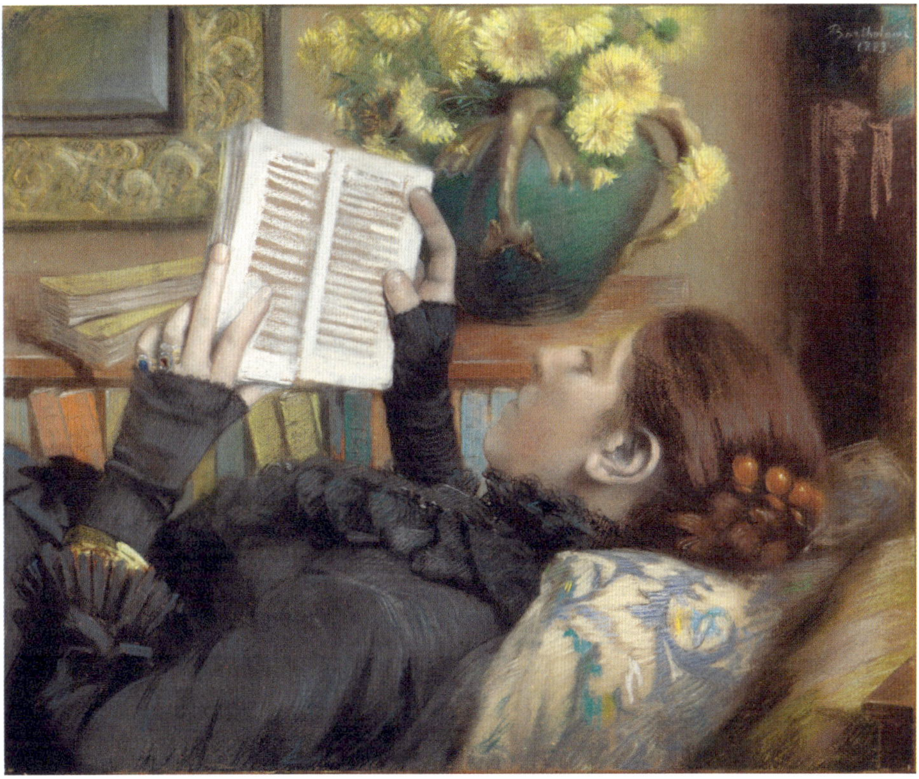

BOOKS – AND A GREAT LOVE AFFAIR. Périe (Prospérie) Bartholomé, daughter of the Marquis de Fleury, was well read, sophisticated, attractive, but fragile in health. The artist and writer Jacques-Emile Blanche recalled evenings with her in which sparkling discussion of books and music and art delighted intellectuals and bohemians alike. Périe's husband, Albert, produced this pastel-and-charcoal portrait of her in 1883. When she died four years later, Albert's friend Degas supported his transition to sculptor, starting with a monument for Périe's tomb in the old cemetery of Bouillant, Crépy-en-Valois.

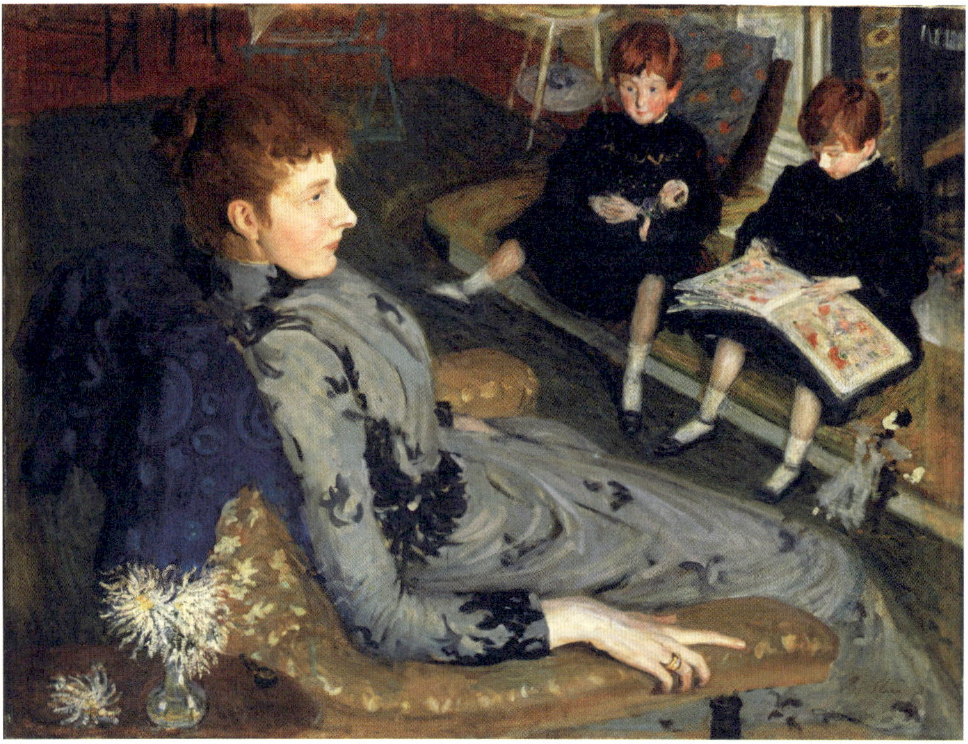

THE ONLY RELAXED and contented figure in this 1891 painting by Philip Wilson Steer, of Mrs Cyprian Williams and her two daughters, is the one enjoying the book. Steer, together with Mrs Williams herself and the commissioner of the portrait, Francis James, were all artists associated with the newly founded alternative to the Royal Academy, the New English Art Club, of which James Jebusa Shannon (SEE OPPOSITE) was also a member.

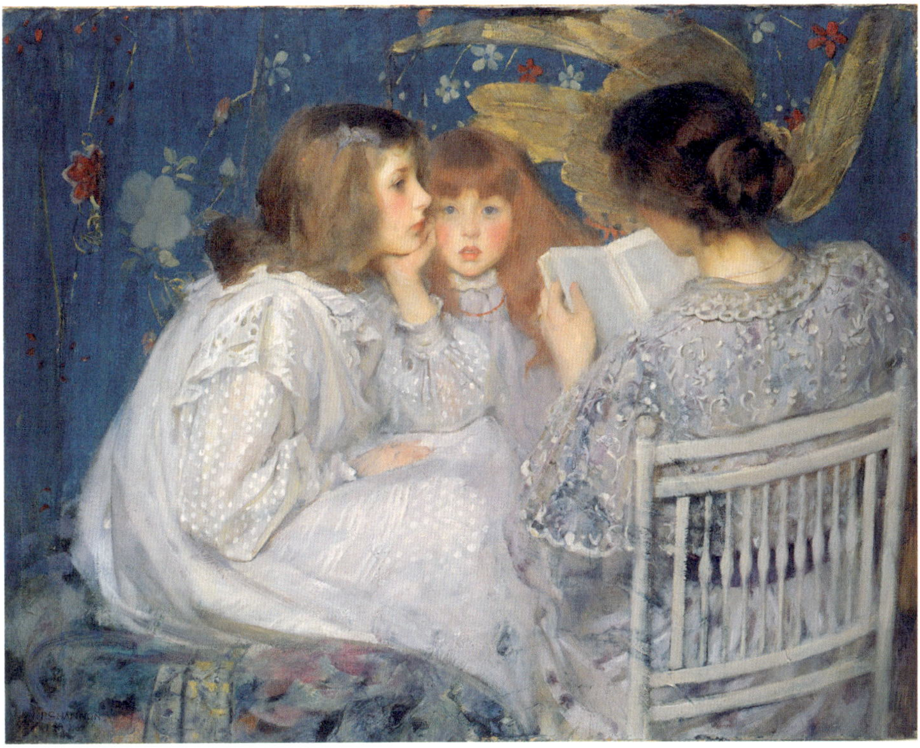

RUDYARD KIPLING'S *The Jungle Book* was published the year before James Jebusa Shannon's *Jungle Tales* was painted (1895). The American-born artist had moved to London in the 1880s, and his wife's reading to their daughter, Kitty (in profile), and her friend clearly holds the young girls' attention as they dream of adventures in distant lands.

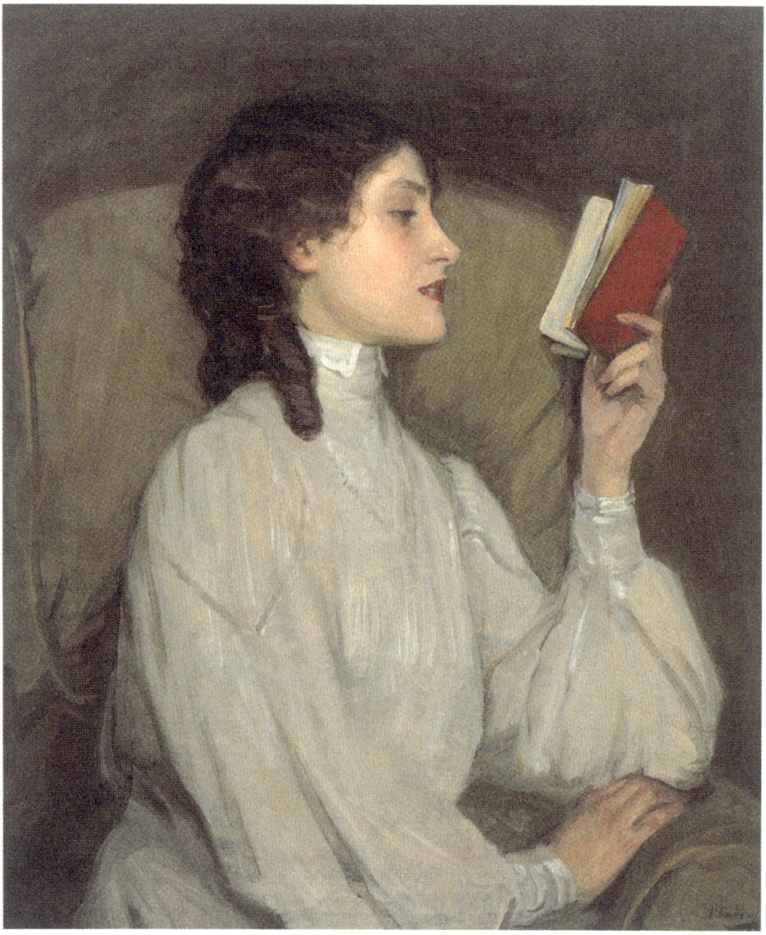

SIR JOHN LAVERY encountered sixteen-year-old Mary Auras on Berlin's Unter den Linden in 1901. She became the subject of a number of new-century portraits by him – a modernized encapsulation of beauty, here expressed in *The Red Book* (*c.* 1902). It worked: according to the English writer Arnold Bennett, Miss Auras received five proposals in three months.

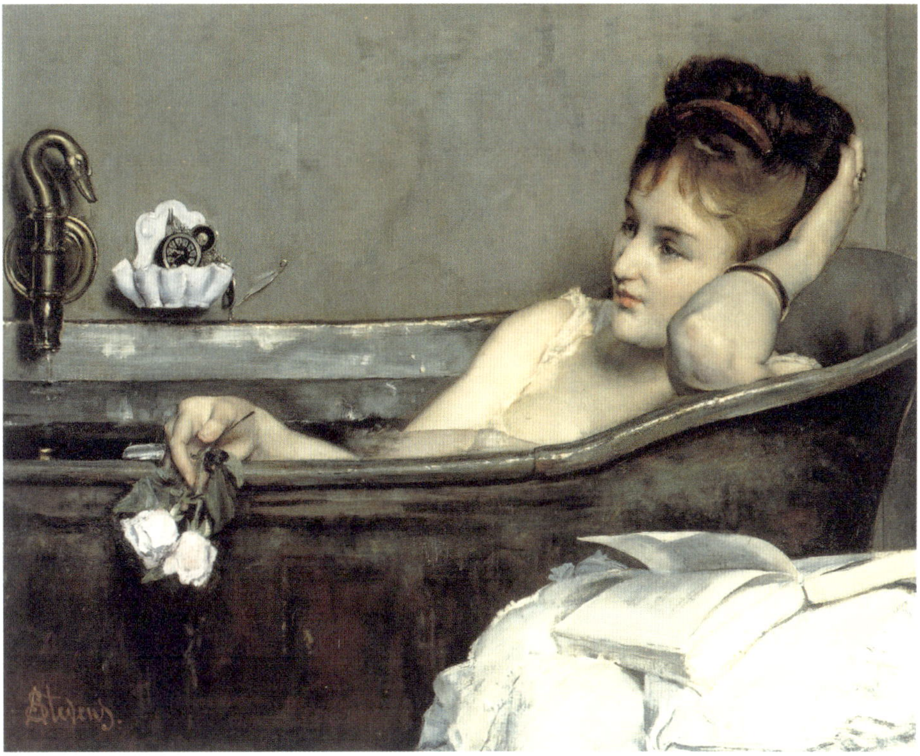

ONE'S BATH: the best place, suggests Alfred Stevens's *Le Bain* (1873–74), to muse on life and love, accompanied by an imagination-inducing novel. The novel, by definition, was fiction; the scene in the painting, by this skilled reflector of Parisian chic, was almost certainly not invented.

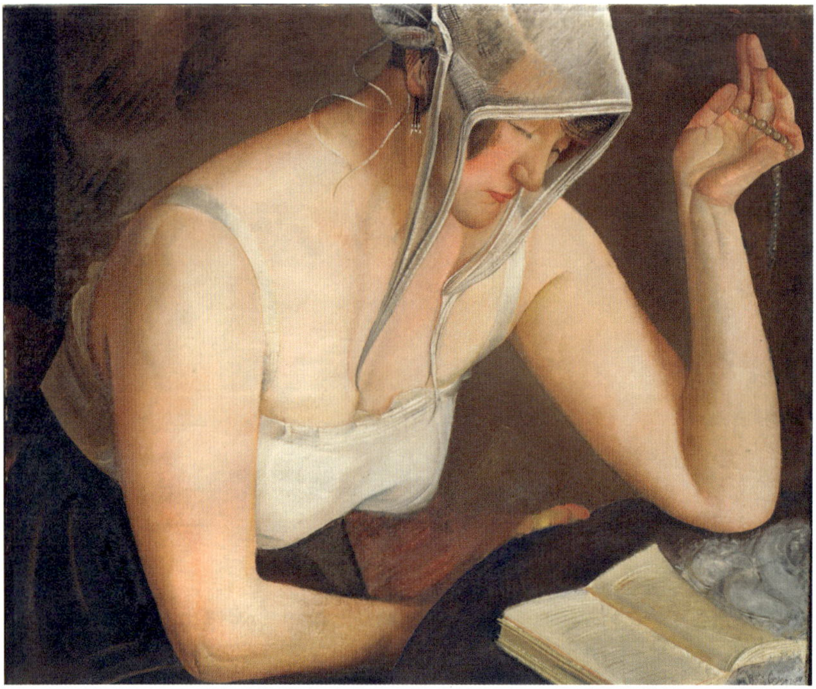

RUSSIA BEFORE REVOLUTION had a notable bohemian art and literary scene. The artist Boris Grigoriev, in these sometimes interchangeable worlds, himself published a novel at that time. As an émigré after the revolution, he travelled widely. *Woman Reading* (*c.* 1922; ABOVE) is a very unsentimental and perhaps very Russian view of domestic pleasure, in keeping with the female images of Grigoriev's set of lithographs from 1920, *Russische Erotik*. 'Savage, but not without genius!' the once acclaimed French novelist Claude Farrère said of Grigoriev.

IS THE MISCHIEVOUS INTRUDER in the room of a chambermaid (OPPOSITE) engaged in a dalliance? The evident distress of the maid, clothing in disarray, her shoes removed (which could signify that a sexual act has taken place), perhaps indicates guilt for the son of the house, calling for discretion about his actions before he takes his books to school. An only recently noted small label on the back of the work points to this being a painting, to some extent consistent in style and subject matter with his *oeuvre*, by Jean-Baptiste Greuze (1725–1805): *The Companion*. More likely still is that it was painted by a follower of Greuze, or of Etienne Aubry (1746–1781), or perhaps by an English artist imitating the genre.

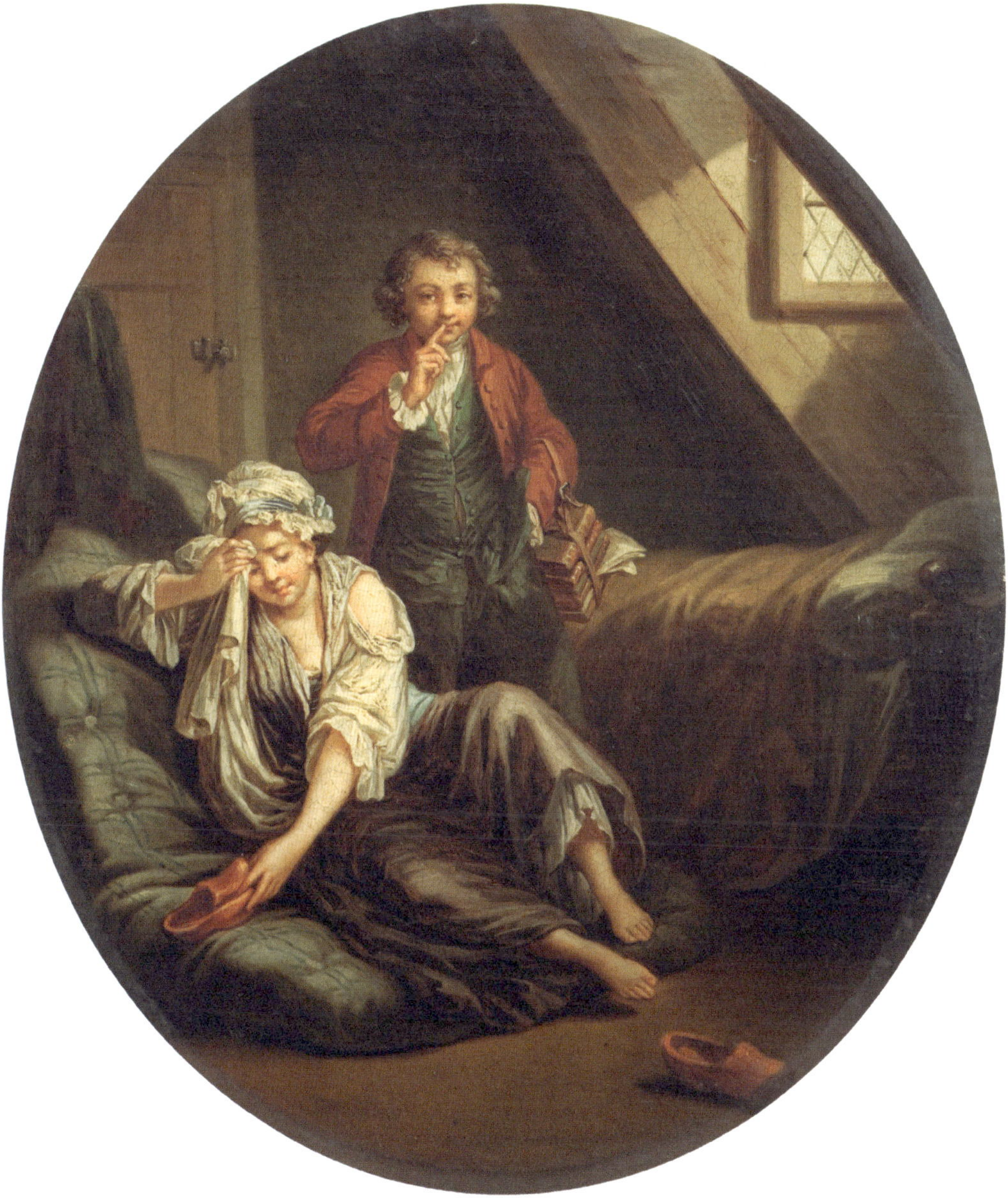

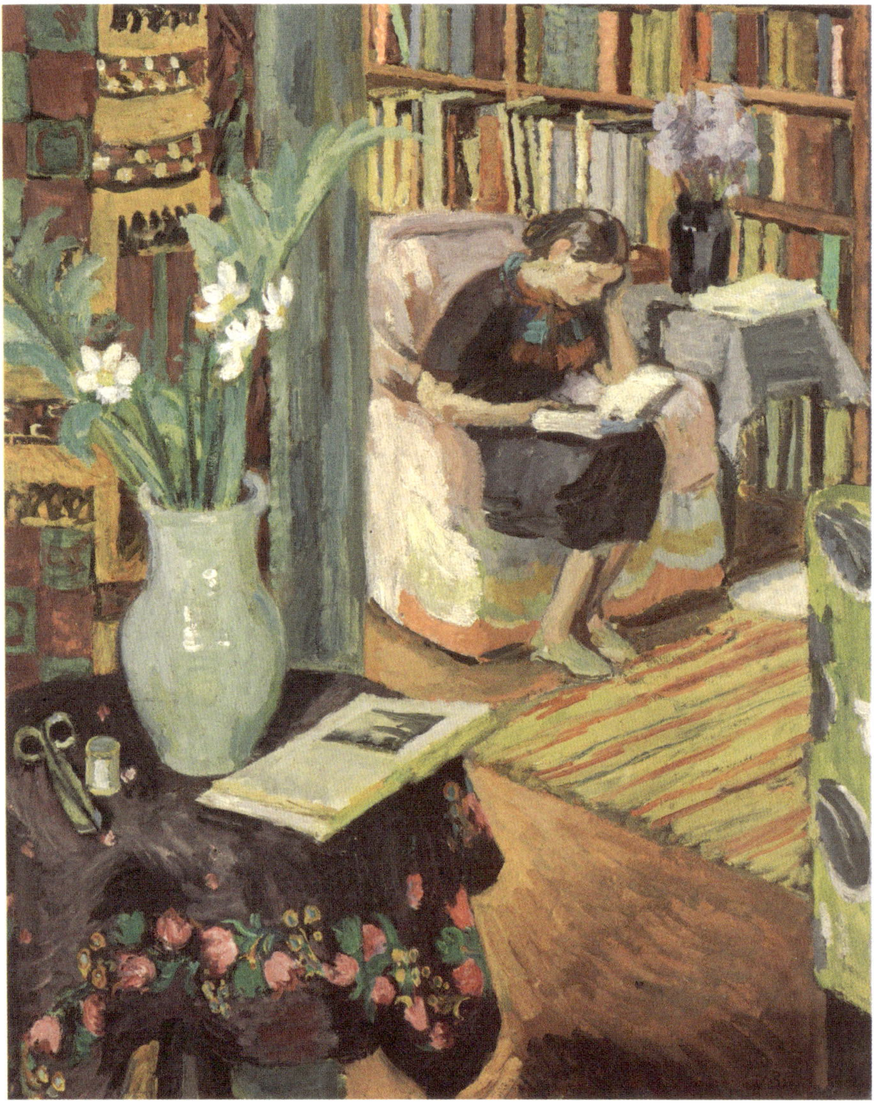

DO PAINTINGS tell better stories than books? Shortly before Vanessa Bell painted *Interior with Artist's Daughter* (*c.* 1935–36), her younger sister, Virginia Woolf, in a 1930s homage to Walter Sickert, suggested that biographers were 'tripped up' by 'those miserable impediments': facts. No one in her time would 'write a life as Sickert paints it'. Still, we might not guess that Angelica, the bookish daughter in Bell's painting, was fathered not by Clive Bell but by Duncan Grant, who had moved to the Bells' East Sussex home, Charleston, with his lover David Garnett, who was himself both present at Angelica's birth and later her husband. The 'silent kingdom of paint', as Woolf called it, is enigmatic and revealing at the same time.

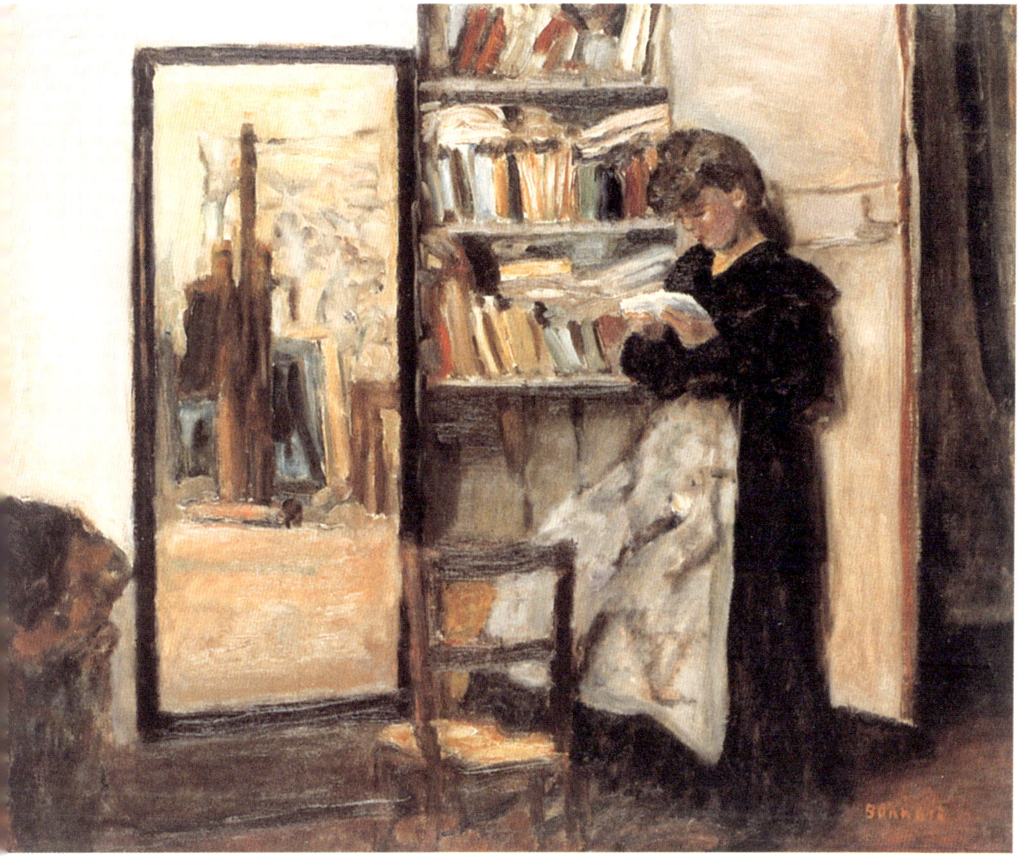

BOOKS ARE PERFECT for quiet moments, and with increased literacy that at last applied to servants, as well as their masters and mistresses. And no one better captured privacy within a domestic scene than Pierre Bonnard, here with *La Lecture* (1905). As he once explained, he took his subjects from the people and surroundings of his life. He would look at them; he would take notes; he would reflect. His great skill is to make us feel we are not intruding on what is nevertheless personal.

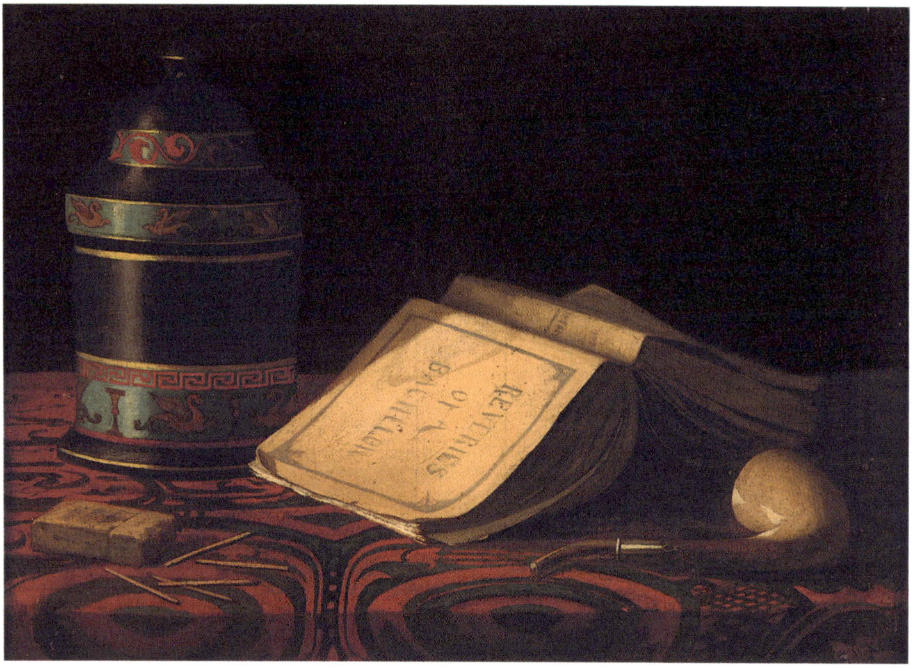

'CAN A MAN STAKE his bachelor respectability, his independence and comfort, upon the die of absorbing, unchanging, relentless marriage, without trembling at the venture?' The Yale-educated Donald Grant Mitchell had a bestseller with his 1850 *Reveries of a Bachelor, or A Book of the Heart*, published under the pseudonym Ik Marvel. The artist behind this work, Charles D. Sauerwein, answered Mitchell positively by leaving Baltimore for Europe in 1860 and marrying a nineteen-year-old French girl.

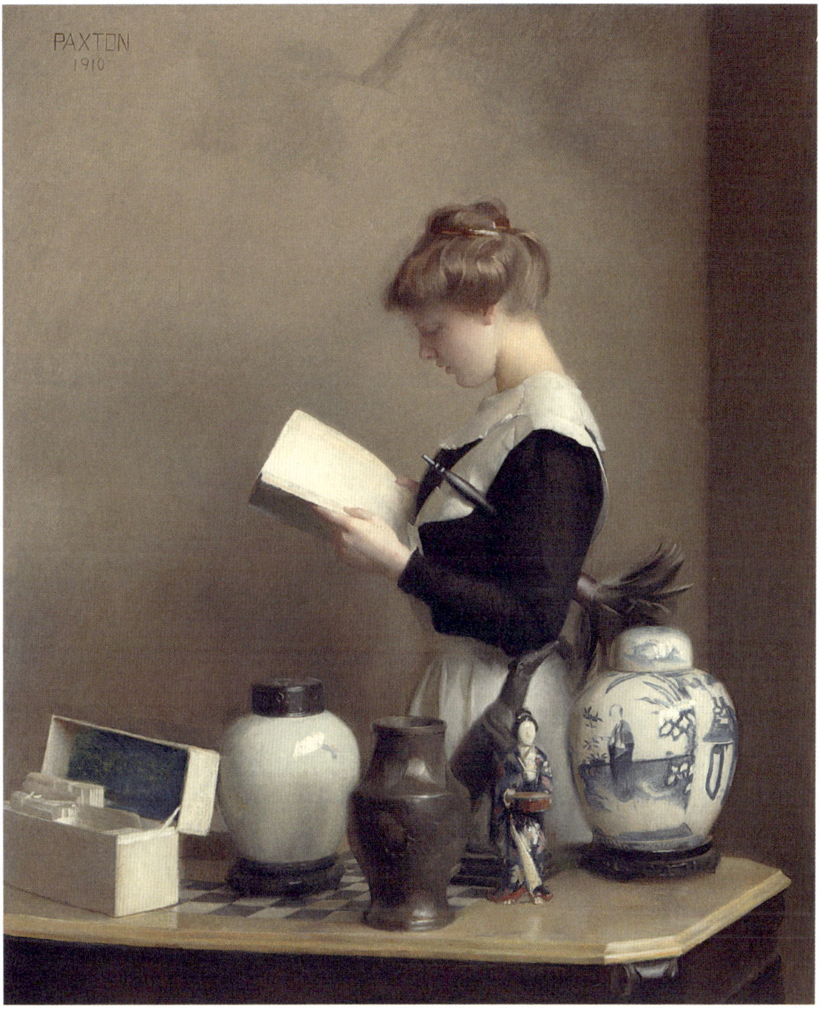

THE BALTIMORE-BORN William McGregor Paxton gravitated to the City of Refinement, Boston, and painted – in addition to US presidents Grover Cleveland and Calvin Coolidge – a stream of women rather like Christopher Newman's 'the best article in the market' in Henry James's *The American* (1877): beautiful, orderly, refined. By extension, the characteristics of a suitable bride could also be applied to Paxton's *The House Maid* (1910), here with the equally refined collectibles from New England's Chinese and East Asian trading relationships.

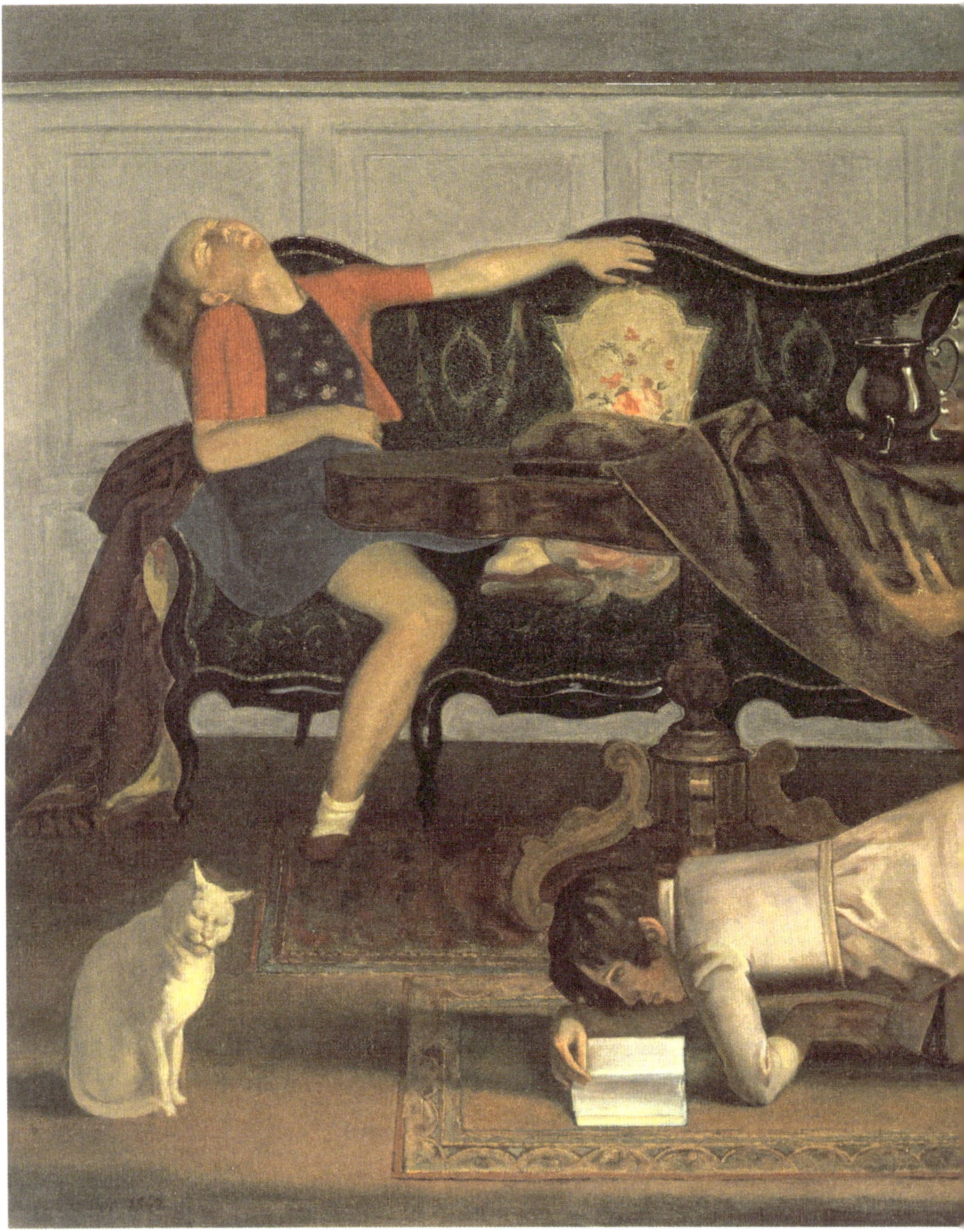

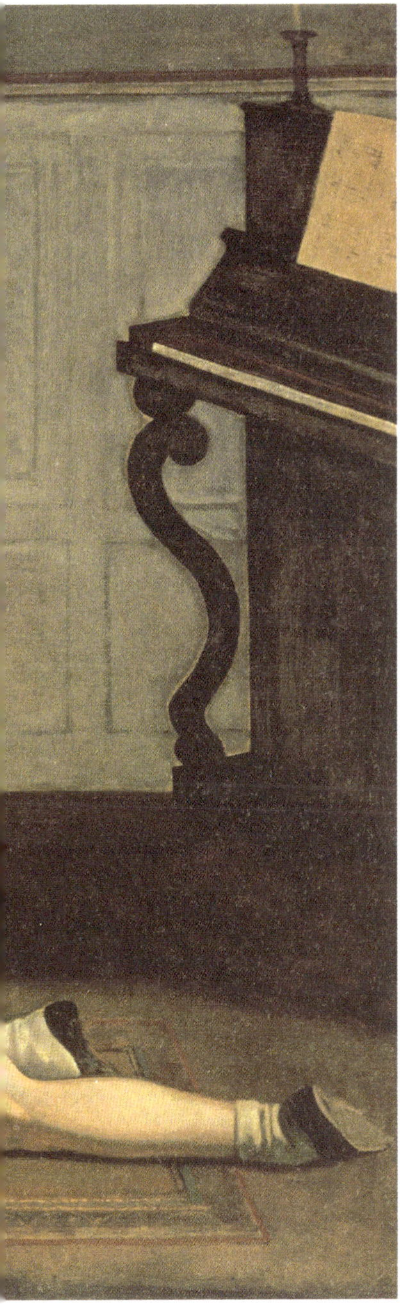

IN 1940, WHEN GERMANY invaded France, the Polish-French artist Balthus settled on a farm near Aix-les-Bains. *The Living Room* (1942) is one of two major works begun in his time there. The model for both figures was Georgette, daughter of a local farmer, who described – according to the curator Sabine Rewald – how the artist had made her kneel on the floor, in the same position as he had used for Thérèse Blanchard in *The Children* (1937). The intensity of Georgette's depiction was somewhat at odds with her later statement that 'I do not care for books', but it was certainly tiring work and, when at last rested, she would fall asleep on the sofa.

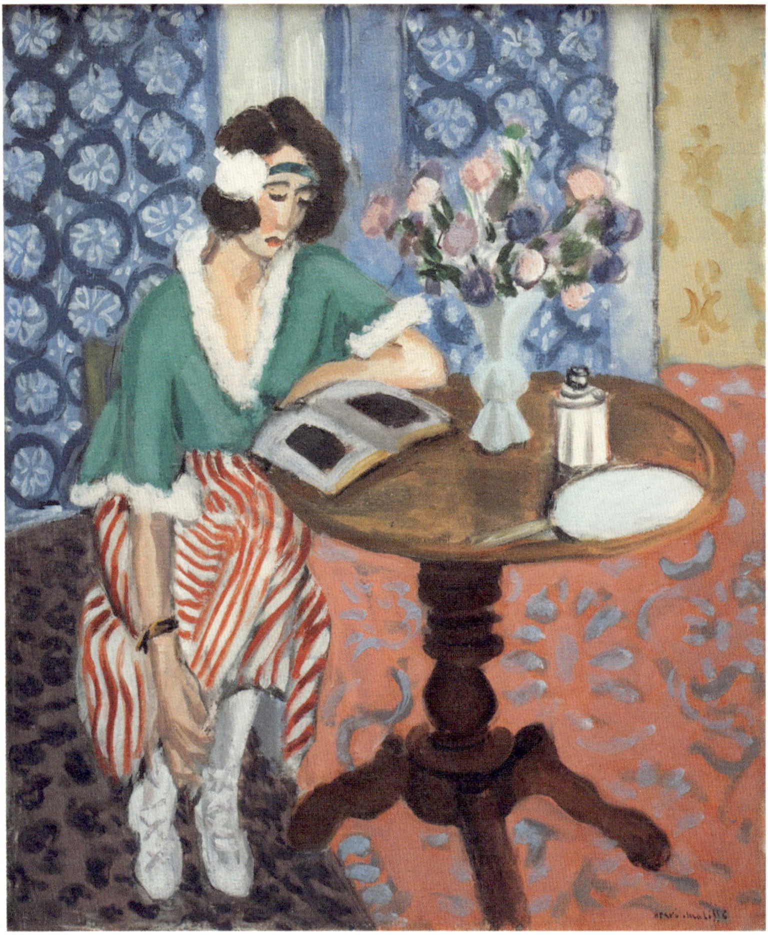

FROM HIS EARLY WORK *Woman Reading*, painted when he was not yet twenty-five, to *Woman Reading in a Garden* (1902–03) and *The Reader at the Guéridon* (1921; ABOVE), it is plain that Matisse's subjects were serious about books. He himself was a great reader, with a classical education. Even his dozen or more *livres d'artiste*, featuring his own artwork, had a dual function – to be collected as art objects, but also to be read.

THE RUSSIAN ÉMIGRÉ Frosca Munster, with whom Christopher Wood – the painter of this 1929 portrait of her (OPPOSITE) – had an intense love affair, was described by Boris Kochno, secretary to the inspired creator of the Ballets Russes, Serge Diaghilev, as having the same serene beauty as one of Piero della Francesca's subjects. On the table in Wood's portrait is Emil Ludwig's biography of Napoleon, not a bad model for an artist who told his mother he wanted to be the greatest painter who had ever lived. Wood committed suicide when he was twenty-nine – unlike Stalin, who told Ludwig in an interview that 'Marxism never denied the role of heroes'.

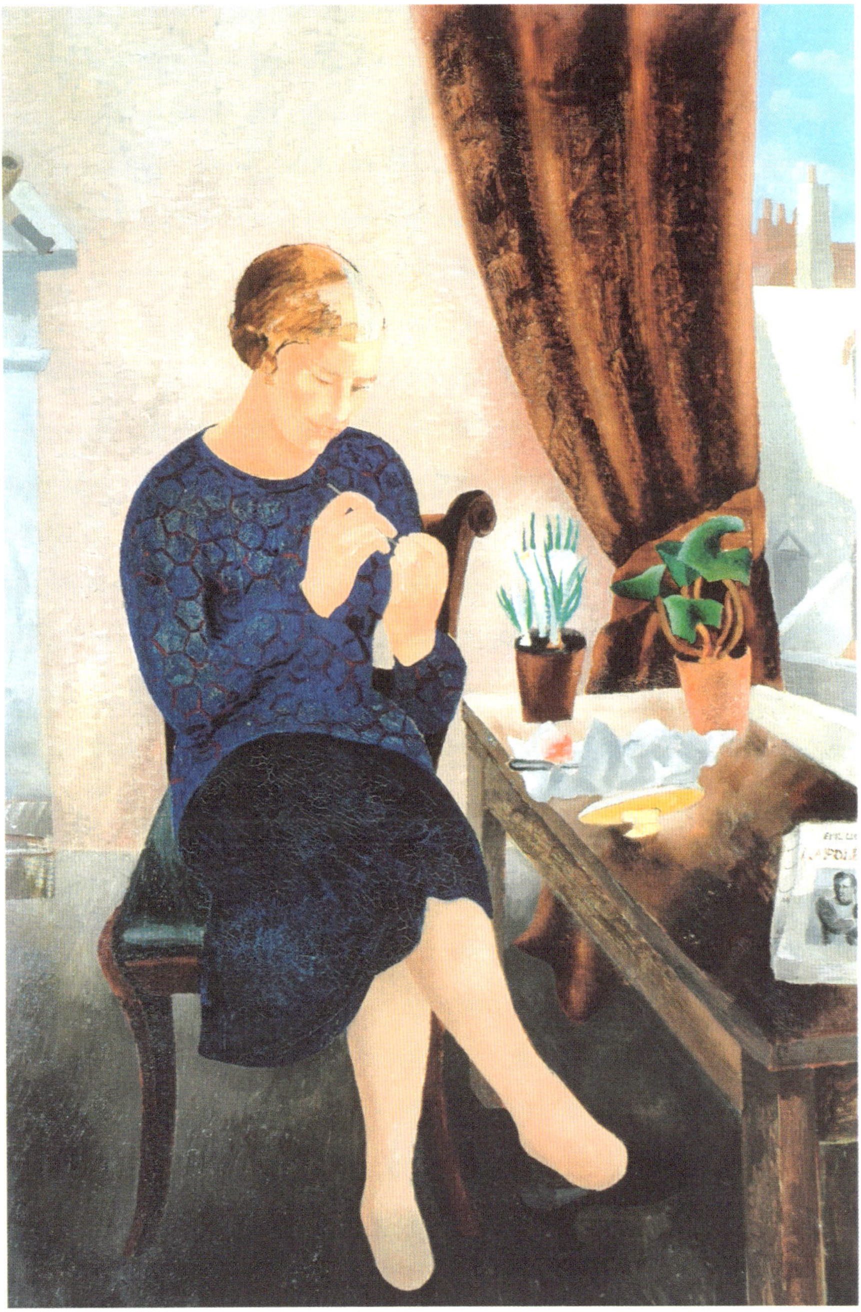

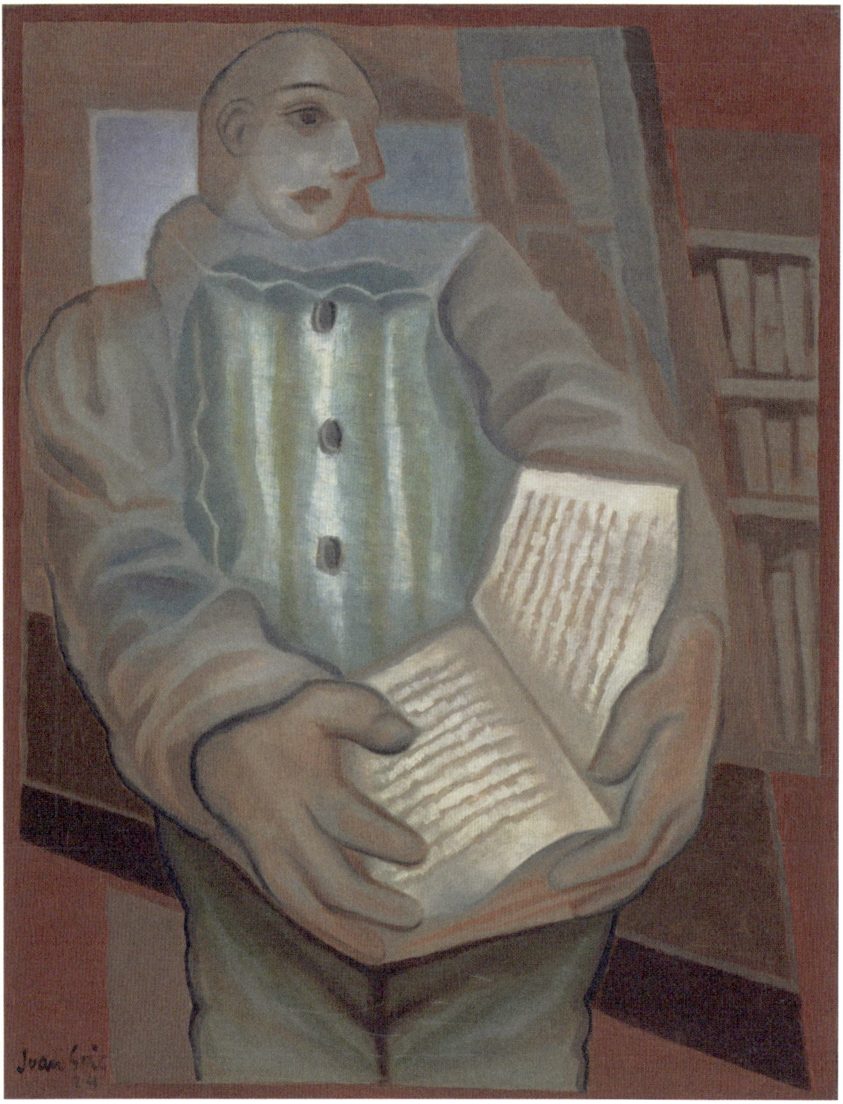

WHAT COULD THE oh-so-sad clown from the *commedia dell'arte* be reading? Juan Gris painted *Le Pierrot au livre* around the same time as he designed costumes and set for Diaghilev and a Ballets Russes production that had its premiere in 1924. According to his dealer, Daniel-Henry Kahnweiler, Gris was 'a great reader', addicted to the Spanish Baroque poet Luis de Góngora and, from the ranks of more recent Spanish-language writers, Valle-Inclán and the Nicaraguan poet Rubén Darío. He 'worshipped Mallarmé' and the obscure, French, Tobias Smollett-like novelist Pigault-Lebrun, as well as the wildly popular fictional criminal Fantômas. But he died, as melancholy as his Pierrot, just too late to seek a different succour from reading Kant's careful and brilliant encapsulations of modern life's philosophical agendas.

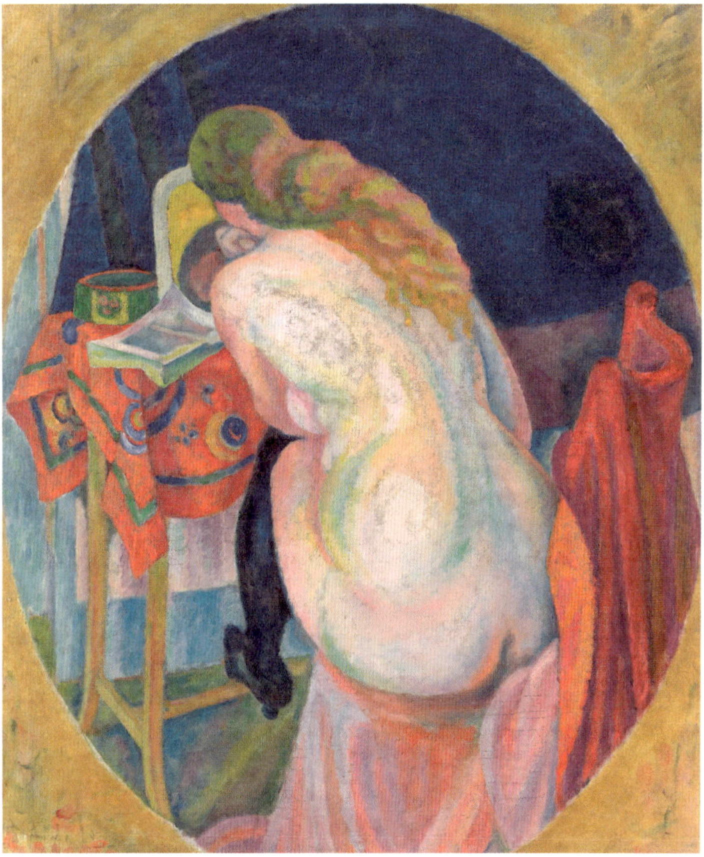

IN THE SUMMER OF 1915 Robert and Sonia Delaunay travelled to Madrid to study Old Masters in the Prado. There they saw Rubens's *c.* 1635 painting *Diana and Callisto*, an influence reflected in Robert's boudoir image of his wife, *Nude Woman Reading* (1915), the theme of which he would return to in a number of similar but increasingly less figurative works in the next five years. His interest was much more in colour and circular form than in reality – but the pleasures of reading unclothed, in private and comfort, have certainly been a reality for women and men through many centuries.

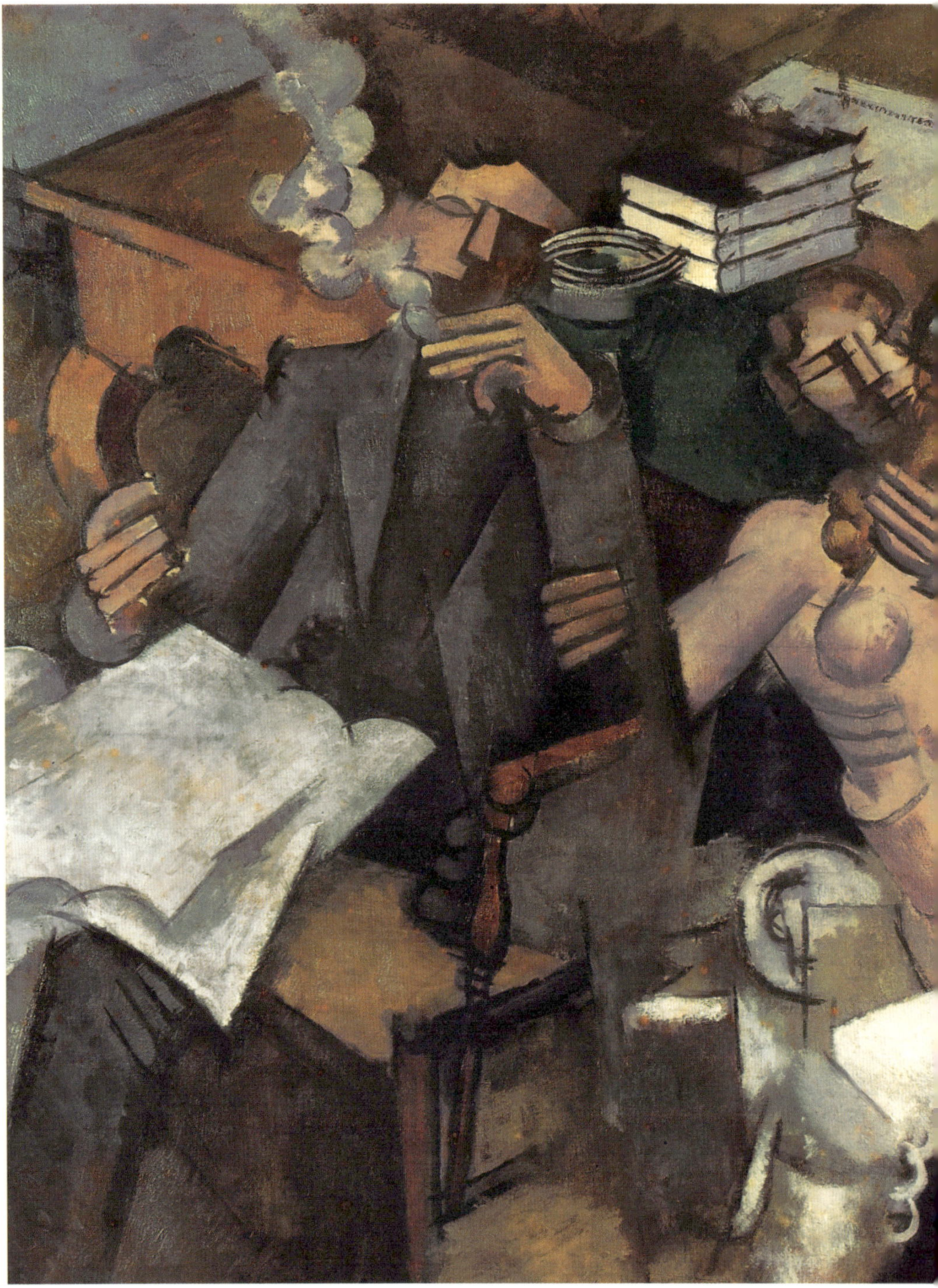

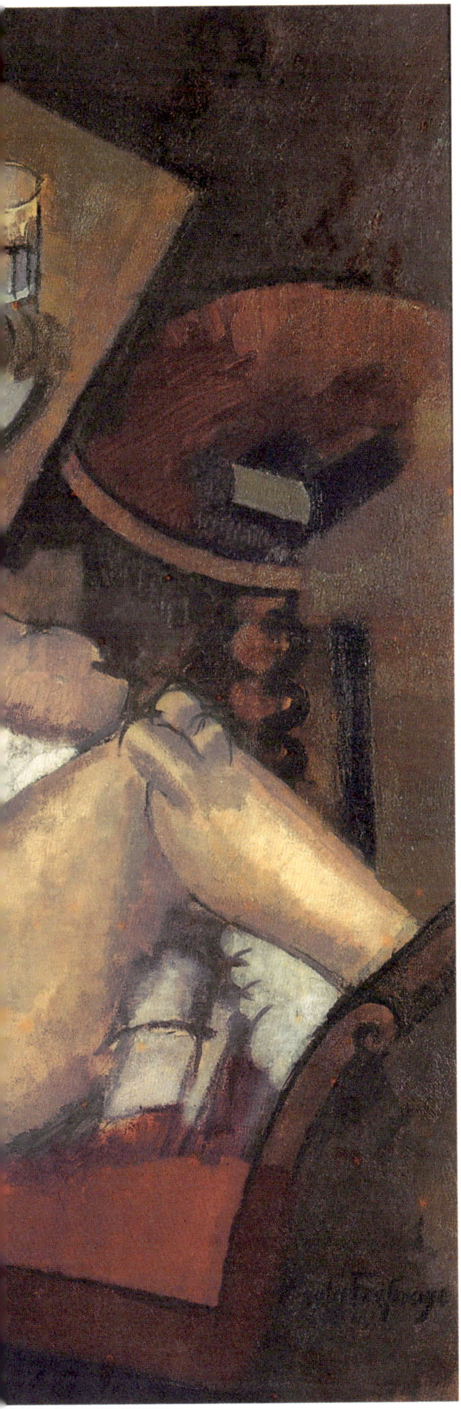

IN THE LAST YEARS before the First World War, Roger de la Fresnaye would meet in the Paris suburb of Puteaux with other artists, as well as poets and critics – the origin of the Salon de la Section d'Or, the most important Cubist exhibition before the war. This aristocratic son of a French army officer was hardly expressing a female view of matrimony in his 1912 painting *Married Life*, but the books intrude humanity into a very modern image.

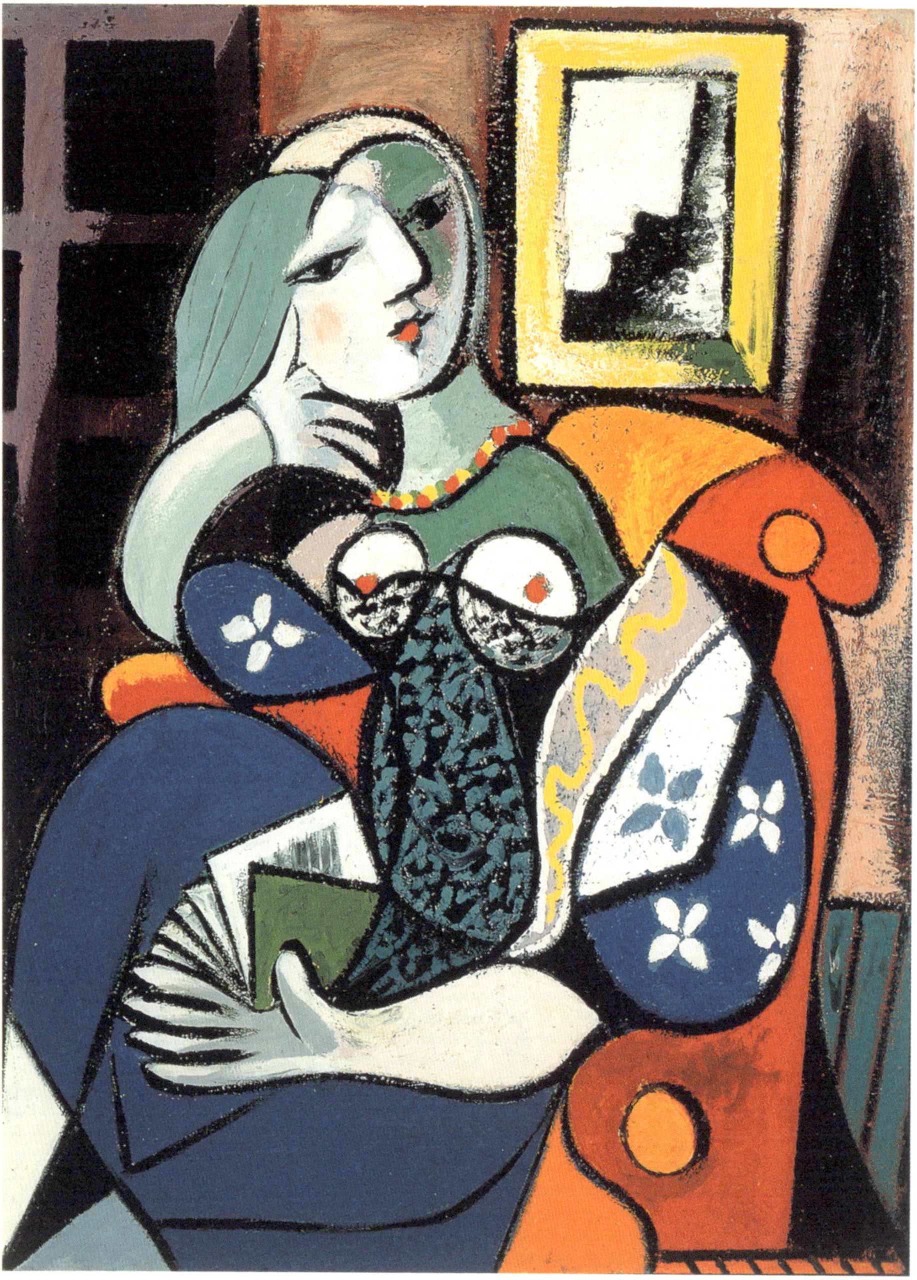

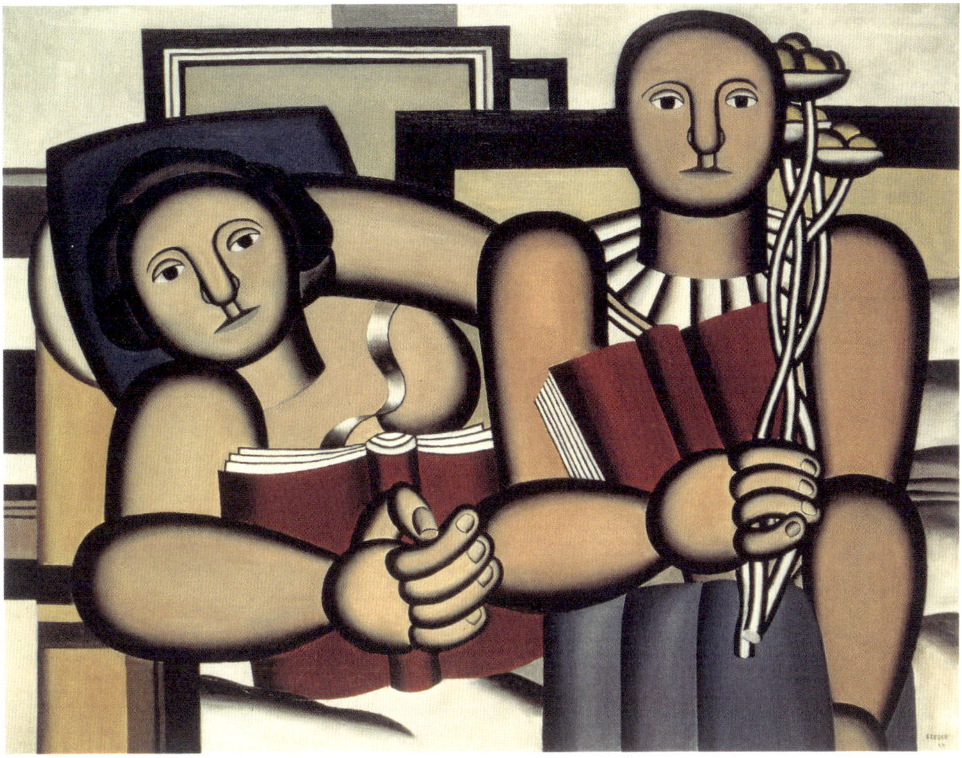

AS FRANCE TRIED TO RECOVER from the devastation of the First World War, Fernand Léger's positive feelings about technology produced depersonalized figures that were nevertheless humanized by the ever-comforting books they held – here (ABOVE) in a work from 1924, *Reading*.

BRASSAÏ SAID THAT no one ever saw Picasso with a book in his hand. But just as the Spaniard had painted a Cubist image of a woman holding a book in 1909, this depiction of his lover Marie-Thérèse Walter from 1932 (OPPOSITE) – a homage to Ingres's 19th-century portrait of Madame Moitessier – even turned the fan in Ingres's original into a book.

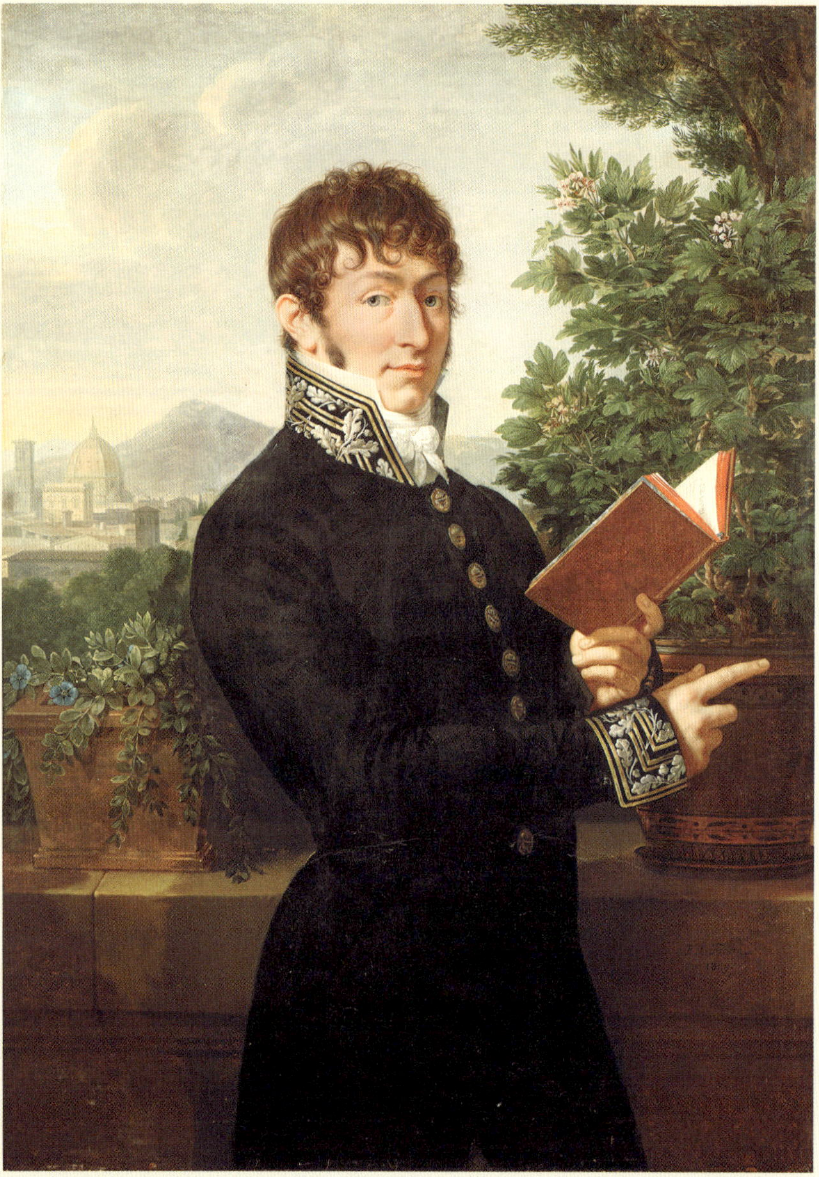

GALLERY 3

PERENNIAL PLEASURES *in* MULTIPLE LOCATIONS

AN OLD ENGLISH SONG makes a plea for 'a shadie nooke', 'With the grene leaves whispering overhead / or the Street cryes all about. / Where I maie Reade all at my ease – / Both of the Newe and Old'.[1] Finding a 'shadie nooke' in town or city after the Industrial Revolution may seem unlikely, although the degree of urbanization today gives us a false perspective. The essence of the matter was that the ever-increasing enthusiasm for, and dissemination of, books – a truly linear story that therefore might puzzle those who have known only the digital era – made more or less any environment a place for reading, unless concentrated study was the objective.

Once the bourgeois sense of structuring the day had strengthened its hold on many people's lives (but before lack of time became the threat it is today), important things – reading – could be conveniently given their place. And where? Anywhere. Noisy railway stations? Books were perfect for waiting, perfect for the journey, or simply for taking with you on your walk through a modern city: in Manet's *The Railway* (1873; p. 176), a little girl who lives in an apartment overlooking the Gare Saint-Lazare watches the smoke as a train passes, while Victorine Meurent – in Manet's last painting of his model for *Olympia* (1863) – sits with open book.

Sometimes, the railways took their passengers to the seaside. In his autobiography, William Powell Frith identifies his 1854 painting *Ramsgate Sands*

AS TRAVEL, for cultural education and for pleasure, began to increase in the 18th century, Italy became a magnet not only for Englishmen on the Grand Tour but also for other European aristocrats. The French artist François-Xavier Fabre, pupil of Jacques-Louis David, moved to Florence during the French Revolution. His clients and other tourists would have been happy to receive book-based advice from this guide, L'Intendant Delonay, high above Florence very early in the 19th century.

(the Kentish town became reachable for a day excursion from London in the 1840s) as featuring his first contemporary subject.[2] In the crowded scene, at least nine people are reading – books and newspapers – and managing to enjoy the overall conviviality while not letting it intrude on their relaxing pastime.

After the return of French émigrés from England in 1815, a habit that was, to an extent, a feature of the English country house was depicted in one of Eugène Lami's watercoloured lithographs, *La Vie de château* (1833), in which a male reader beguiles most of his companions with a reading from Victor Hugo.[3] The country house was, by definition, in rural surroundings. In time, the middle classes appropriated what had long been known to their erstwhile rulers: the joys of nature were a perfect accompaniment to the imagination books fostered.

As early as Vincenzo Foppa's 15th-century fresco *The Young Cicero Reading* (p. 110), which is set inside but gives prominence to the landscape through the window, reading connected itself to the idea of letting the beauty of nature help ponderings about life.[4] In the 18th century, this was explicit in Joseph Wright of Derby's woodland painting of Sir Brooke Boothby meditating with his book (p. 163), pointing to his mentor's name, Rousseau, on its spine. Could nature be controlled? It seemed so in a George Stubbs painting of 1768–70: *Lady Reading in a Wooded Park*. The subject wears a fashionable embroidered dress of Spitalfields silk, unbothered by good-mannered, if not genteel, intrusions of nature – the ferns and wild flowers to the side, the convolvulus just intruding over the garden seat among the trees.

Intentionally or not, the idea of silent figures completely absorbed in their own world of books in a landscape was sometimes a touch darker. Corot, who painted so many images of reading in nature, and despite using books as a symbol of redemption, on occasion loses his reader in the murkiness of a wood, or distracts attention away from them by the sombre power of his landscapes.

More typical is Karolina Max a century later in a painting by the Hungarian artist Gyula Benczúr, *Woman Reading in a Forest* (1875; p. 181), or the young woman lying on the grass in Winslow Homer's *The New Novel* (1877; pp. 182–83), a painting that has attracted many speculations about the artist and his model. Safer to say that identifying with high emotion in a book is something that can easily be encouraged by the joys of reading out of doors.

Once upon a time, the only appropriate place for the book was the church, the palace or the school. In the 18th century, reading for pleasure was first discovered by the social elite, with the invention of the novel, then made part of everyday life by the creators of modernity: the bourgeoisie. Their favoured artists looked around, as artists do – and found readers everywhere.

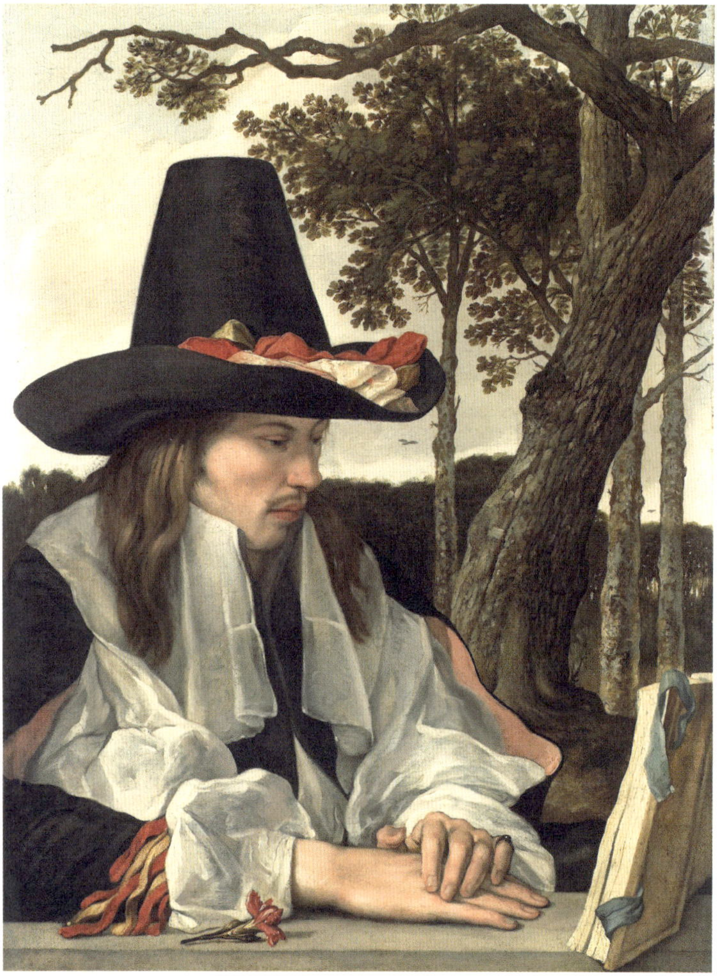

ROMANCE IS IN THE AIR for this young man, fashionably adopting the French look and perhaps reading love poems, or so the red carnation would suggest. But the setting does not suggest either a joyful union or a garden of love. Is this a prospect of love found, or an introspective reflection on love lost? An anonymous painting of the Dutch Golden Age, *c.* 1660, it does not entirely lose formality, but moves it on to enable us to identify with the unknown individual in human terms. Like so many paintings, it had a tangled later history, recorded at one time in the collection of Loughcrew, County Meath, in Ireland, bought or stolen by Hermann Goering in the Second World War, and now, appropriately, in the Rijksmuseum.

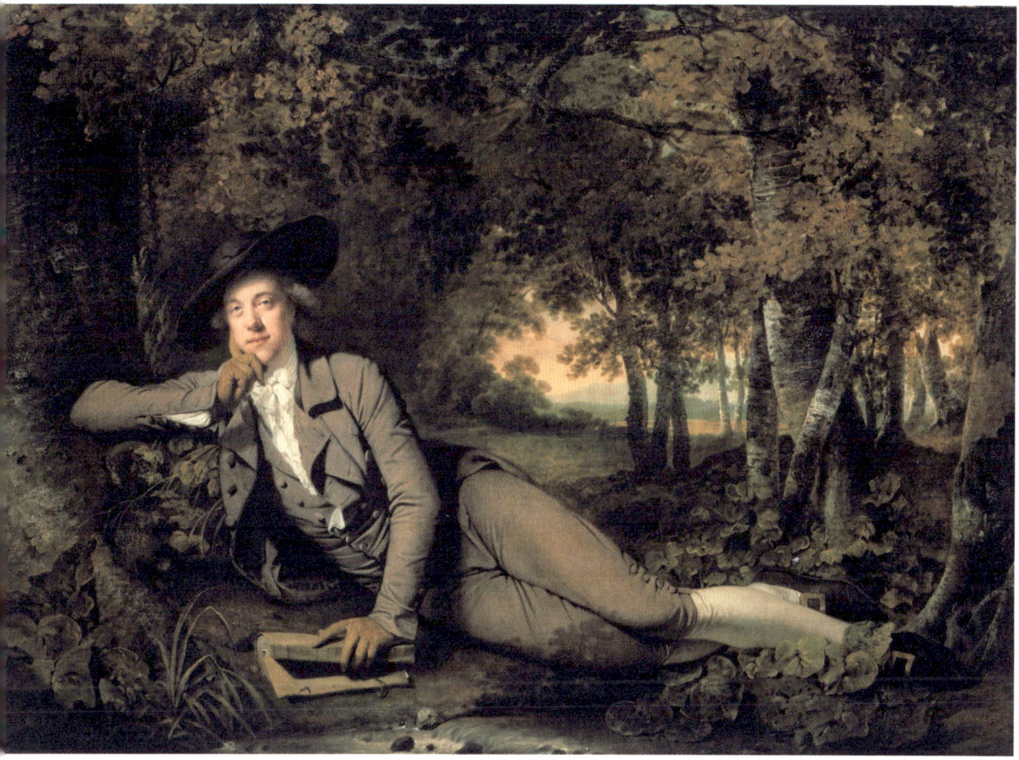

SIR BROOKE BOOTHBY, who as a young man met Rousseau during the great philosopher's stay at Wootton Lodge, Staffordshire, was later entrusted (at his own expense) with the publication of the first volume of Rousseau's autobiographical *Dialogues*. In Joseph Wright of Derby's commissioned painting (1781), the amateur poet points at Rousseau's name on the spine of a book. He escapes from triviality to commune with the untamed landscape – or, as the art historian and writer Quentin Bell acidly put it in *On Human Finery* (1947), here was 'a Natural Man who is also the eldest son of a baronet'.

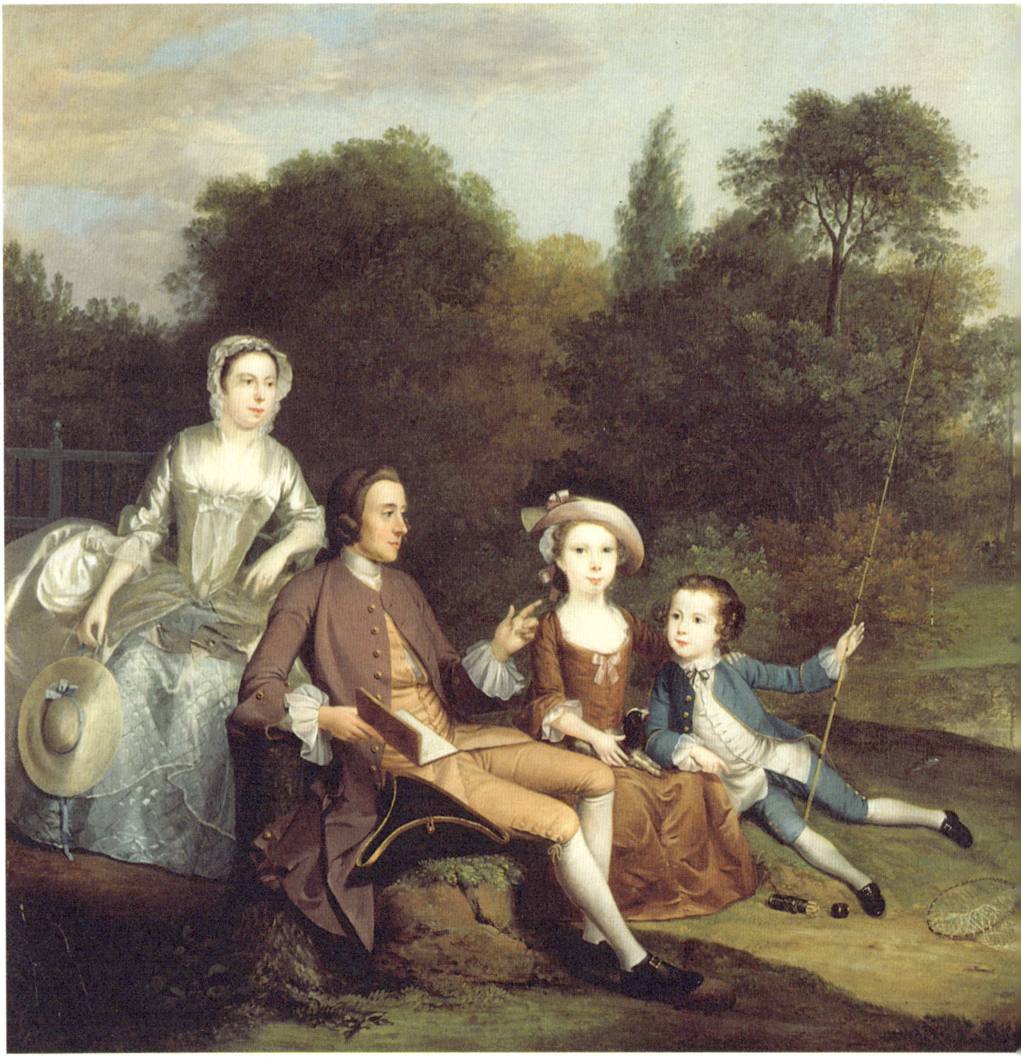

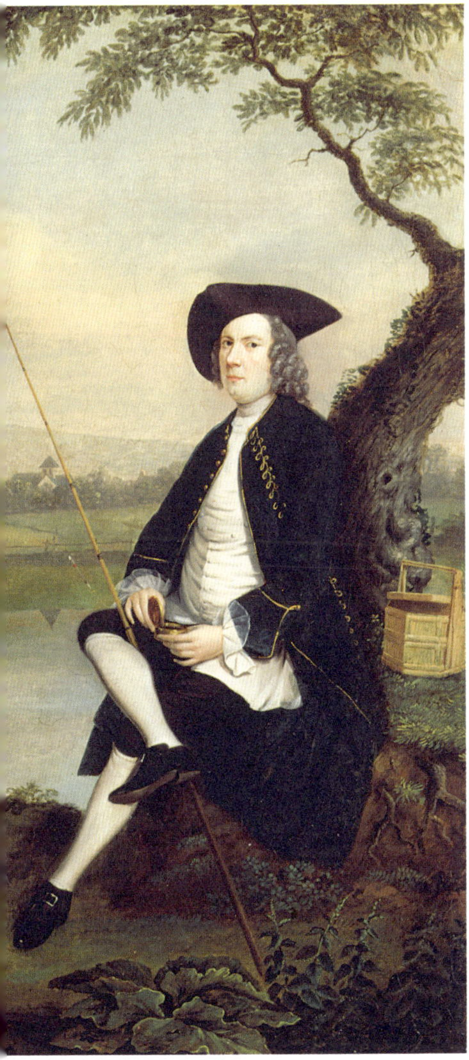

ACCORDING TO Frederick Peter Seguier, in his 1870 dictionary of painters, the artist Arthur Devis made good use of 'books bound in old brown calf, which are lying on tables or on bookshelves'. Here he takes them outside in a portrait of the Cambridgeshire Swaine family from 1749 – the patriarch John Swaine the Elder, London linen draper, to the right, his son, of the same name, and family to the left, with the ever-versatile book looking as comfortable in the countryside as the angler's rod or other rural pleasures.

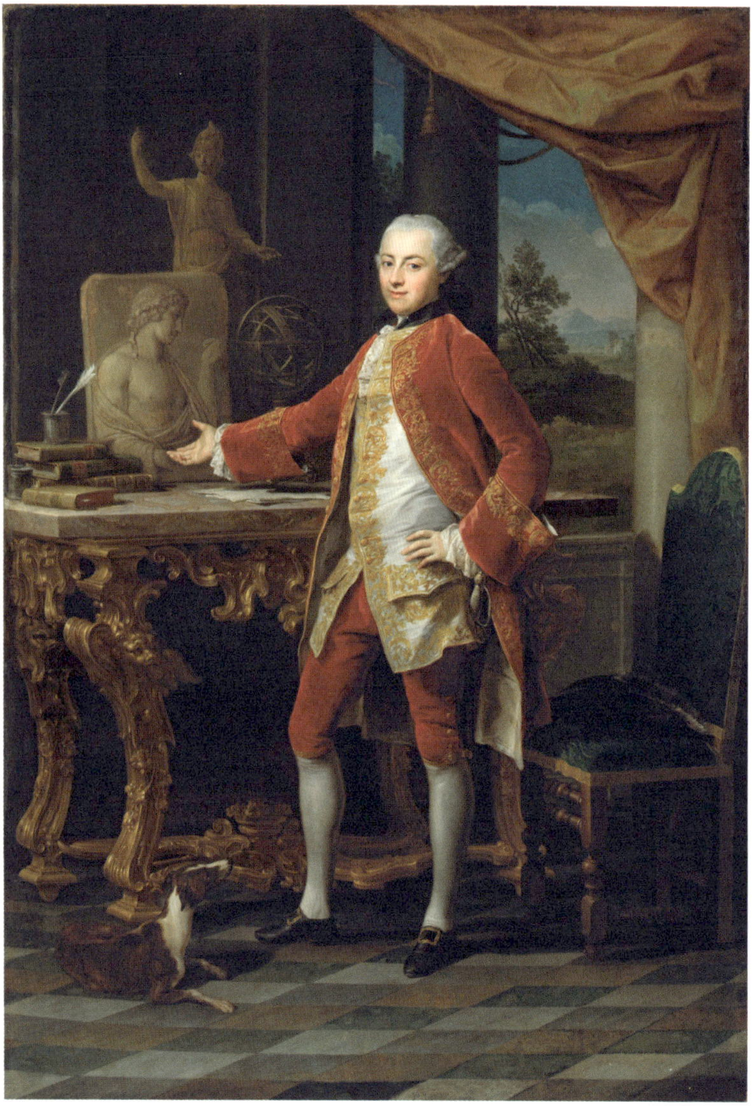

IN JAMES BOSWELL'S *Life of Samuel Johnson*, we find the eminent writer making the following entry in his journal on 11 April 1776: 'A man who has not been in Italy is always conscious of an inferiority, from his not having seen what is expected a man should see.' It had been a Roman Catholic priest, Richard Lassels, who had introduced the notion of a Grand Tour to study antiquities and architecture in his Paris-published *Voyage of Italy, or A Compleat Journey through Italy* (1670). The young man in Pompeo Batoni's portrait (*c.* 1760–65) is perhaps French, judging by his costume. Batoni painted many travellers in Rome on the Grand Tour. He sets the tone by including in the painting the second part of Homer's *Odyssey*, together with guidebooks to Rome and a biographical study of artists.

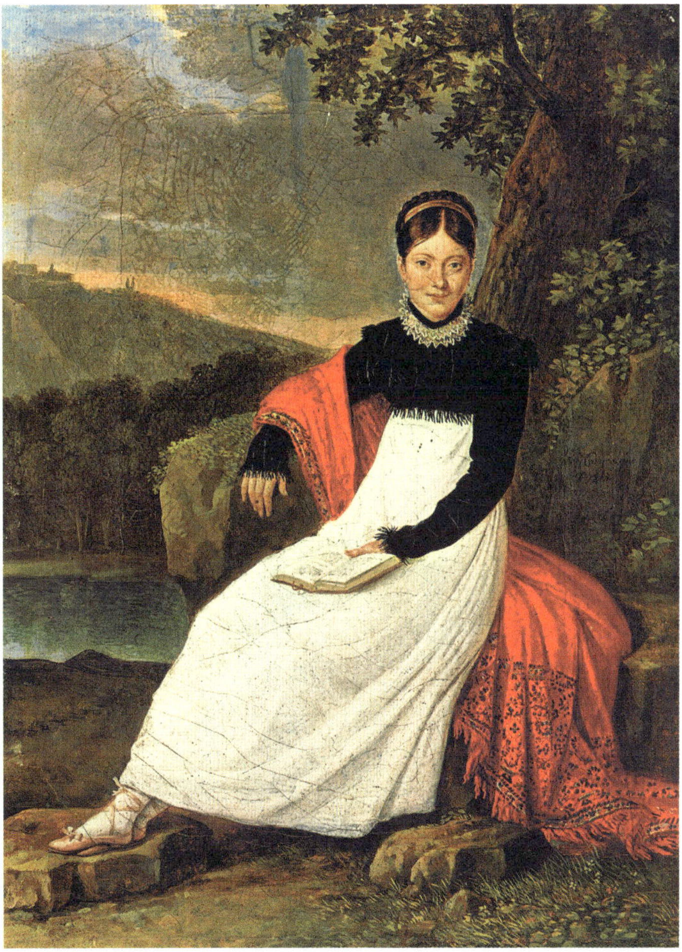

CAROLINE BONAPARTE, Napoleon's sister and inveterate plotter against the emperor's first wife, Joséphine, became Queen of Naples as a result of her marriage to one of Napoleon's generals, Joachim Murat. In this portrait of Caroline in a woodland setting by Giuseppe Cammarano (1813), the peaceful presence of the book served as a contrast to the turbulence of the time, for – after bouts of changing sides – Joachim was executed and Caroline went into exile. The Sicilian Cammarano, according to the cultured one-time British ambassador to Naples Lord Francis Napier, 'was a bad painter of royalty and Olympus', but 'an excellent man'.[5]

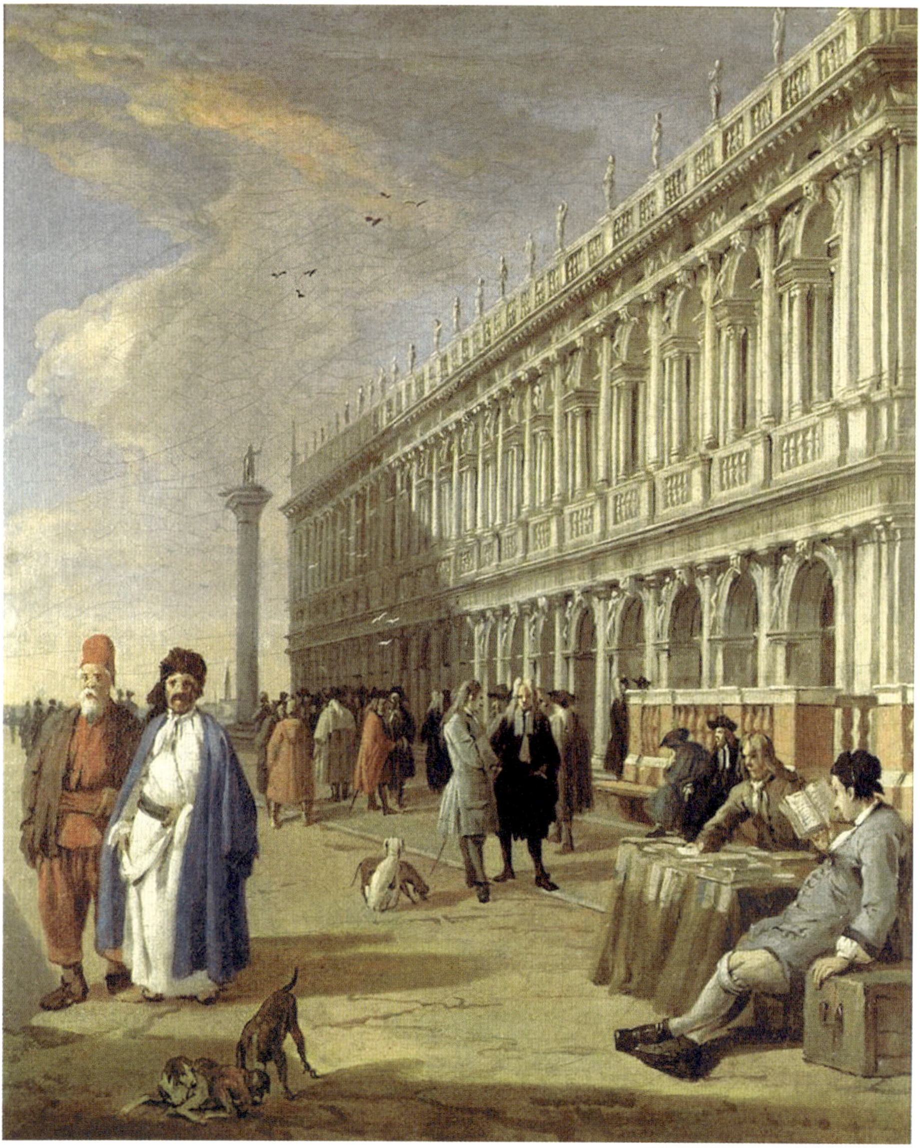

THE PIAZZETTA IN VENICE – an extension to the Piazza San Marco at its south-eastern corner, leading to the lagoon – was painted in the early 18th century by Luca Carlevarijs, who pioneered cityscapes, *vedute*, before Canaletto and Francesco Guardi. Later, Ruskin called the Piazza 'the living books of history', but here were real people – hawkers, beggars, elegant aristocrats – and real books on the stall. The Giunti, a Florentine family of printers, had a press in Venice as early as 1489 and focused on liturgical texts there, selling them (according to the census) on the Piazza on Sundays. That was as well, since for centuries regulations had guarded against selling by itinerant *vagabondi* and *ciarlatani* amid the excitable commerce of city squares.

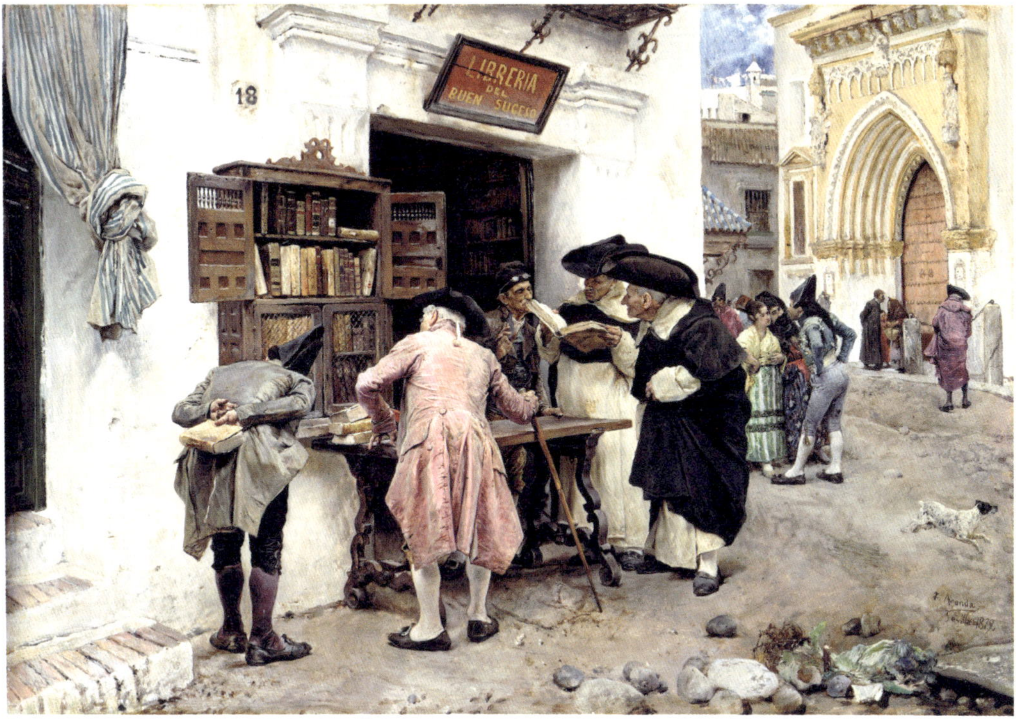

THE JOYS OF READING were almost matched by the joys of finding a new volume: the pleasure of anticipation. José Jiménez y Aranda painted *The Bibliophiles* in 1879. He moved to Paris two years later, but – unlike his brother, Luis, who seemed very much at ease in the French cultural milieu – he later returned to Spain, first to Madrid and eventually to his native Seville.

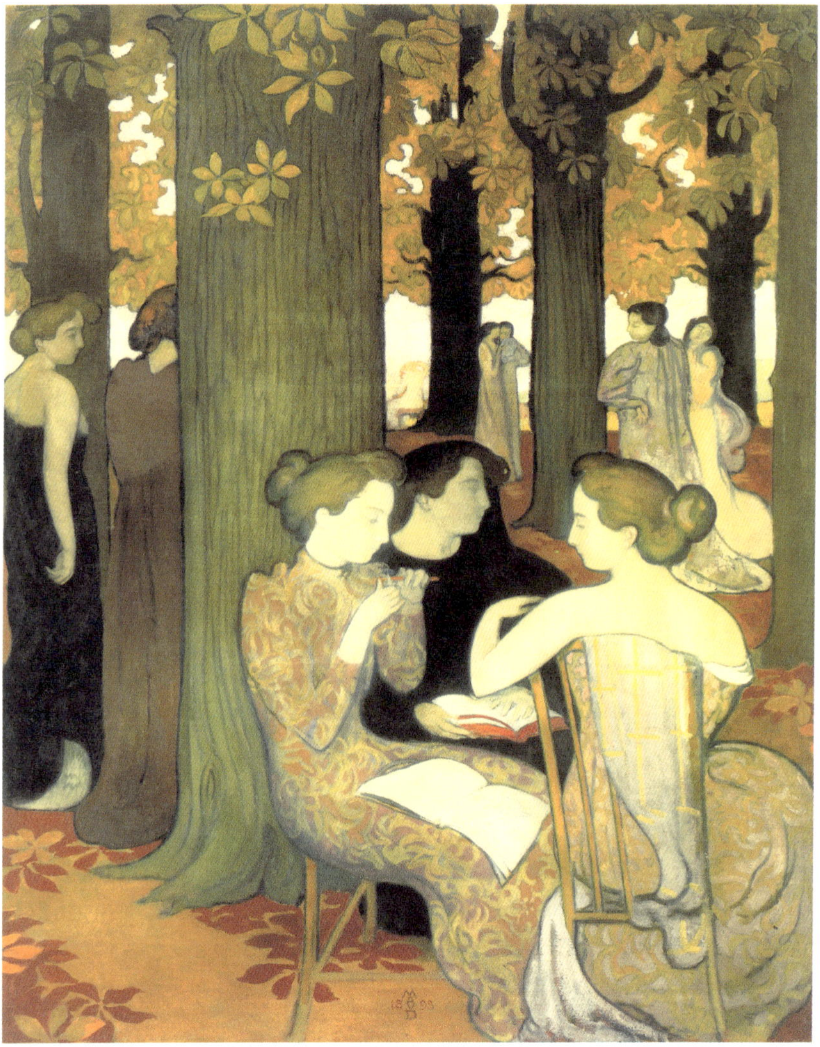

HERE ARE THE MUSES of Greek mythology, inspirers of arts and sciences. Or are they? Maurice Denis has them dressed in clothes fashionable in 1893, the year in which he painted *Les Muses*. And this sacred wood, close to the artist's home town of Saint-Germain-en-Laye, is in fact where he got married that same year. In the foreground, his wife, Marthe Meurier, appears in three seated guises: as muse of love in a ballgown; of art with open sketchbook; of faith with open religious tract and conservative hairstyle.

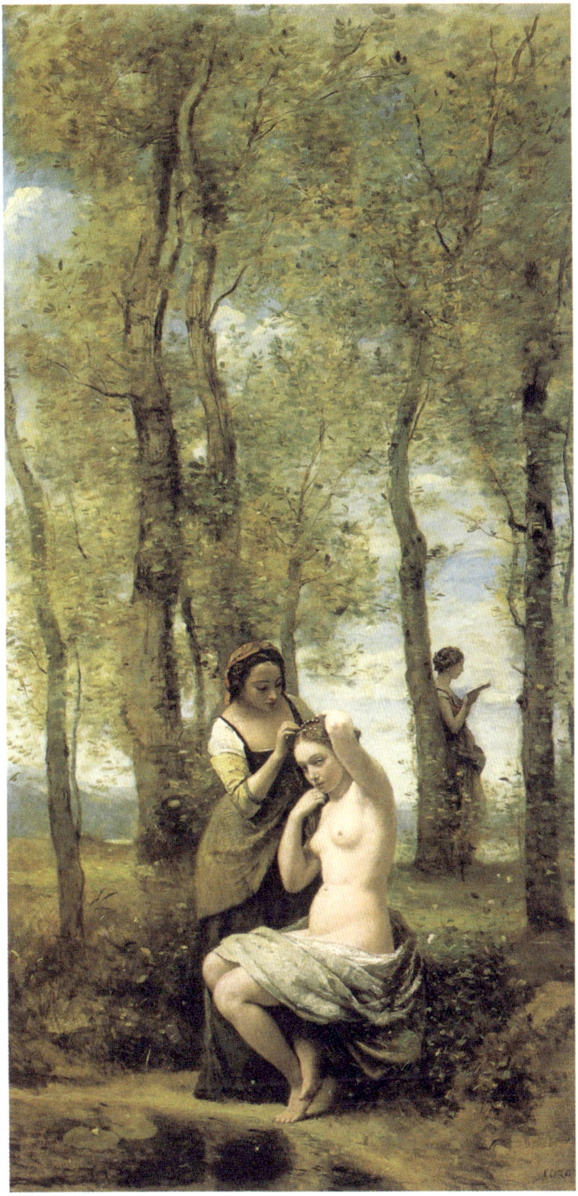

'LOOK A BIT AT how they are enjoying the country, those poor children', said Corot to the French art critic and historian Théophile Silvestre.[6] The apparently curious addition of a figure reading in the background in the artist's *La Toilette* (1859) was in fact a deliberate symbol of an Arcadian ideal in which an escape was possible from the tawdriness of everyday life into the countryside. Still, although Corot was hugely popular with Manet, Degas and many others, Zola once suggested that he should kill off the nymphs of his woods and replace them with peasants.

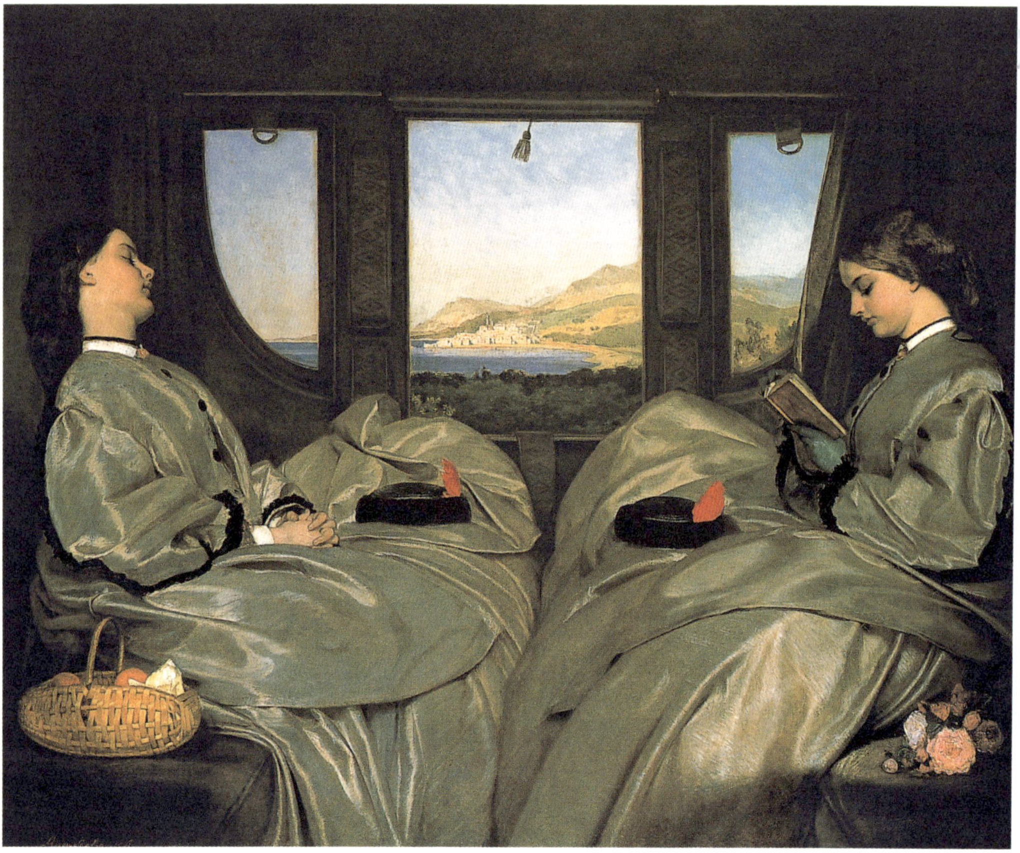

READING ON TRAINS quickly became as popular as the railways themselves. Some moralizers hinted at a wasted opportunity if travelling companions read or slept, missing the changing scene out of the window. Here, in 1862, the scene may have been Menton, near Monte Carlo, with which the artist, Augustus Leopold Egg, became familiar in his search for a warmer climate to help his poor health.

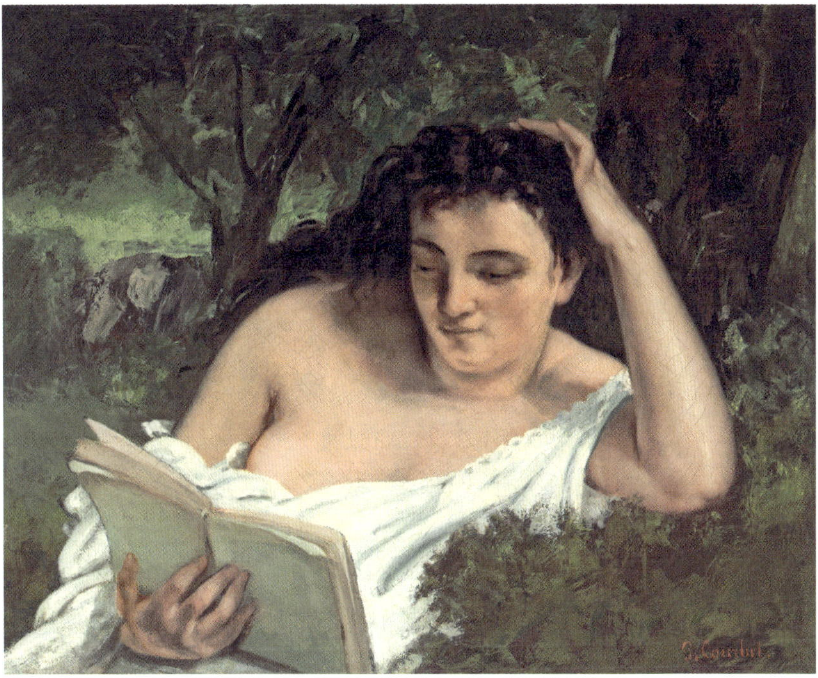

READING OUTSIDE became more and more common in the 19th century and – mostly – more and more relaxed. There is a certain irony in this depiction of a young woman reading (*c.* 1866–68) by a great artist of the realist tradition, Gustave Courbet. Its subject is so lost in the unreal world of her book that she is wholly unselfconscious of her appearance.

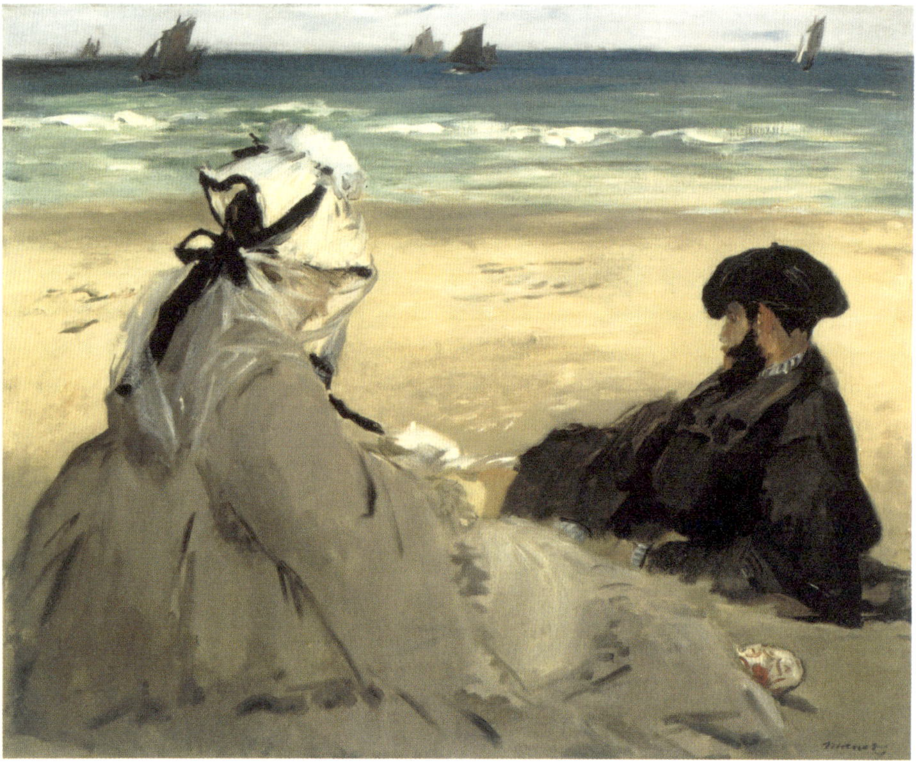

THE 19TH CENTURY and the railway brought books to the seaside. Manet's *On the Beach* has sand ingrained in the paint. The artist's wife, Suzanne, reads intently while Manet's brother Eugène – later to marry Berthe Morisot – stares seawards at the little resort of Berck-sur-Mer, where the family spent three weeks in the summer of 1873.

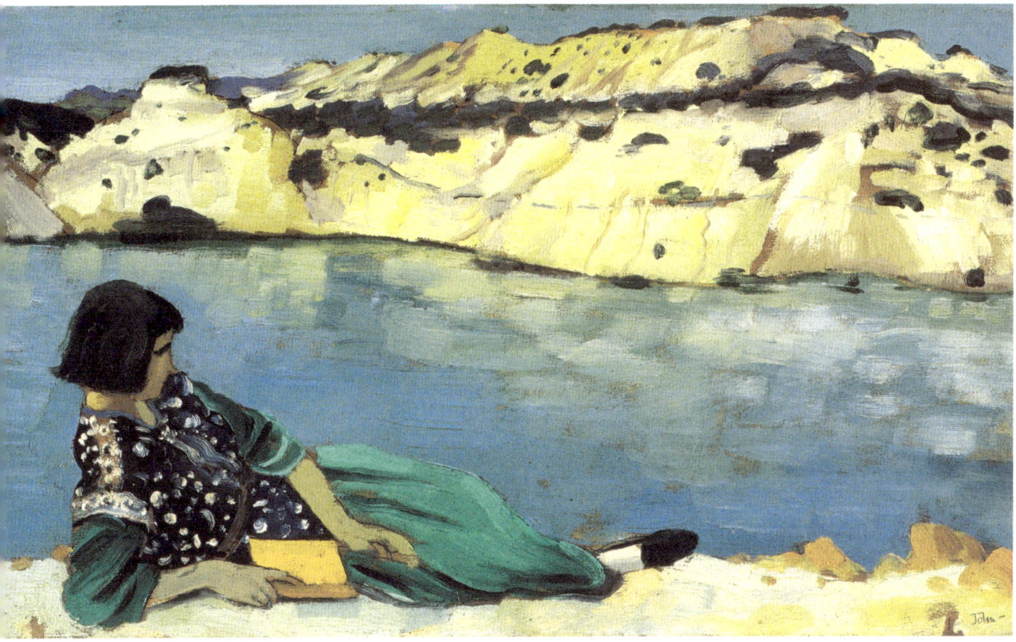

AUGUSTUS JOHN moved to Dorset with his common-law wife, Dorelia – in the previous decade, Rodin's model and mistress – in August 1911. Here, in *The Blue Pool*, she reads next to a lake in the old clay pits of Wareham Heath, in which, according to John, the suspended clay particles gave the water its intense blue at all times.

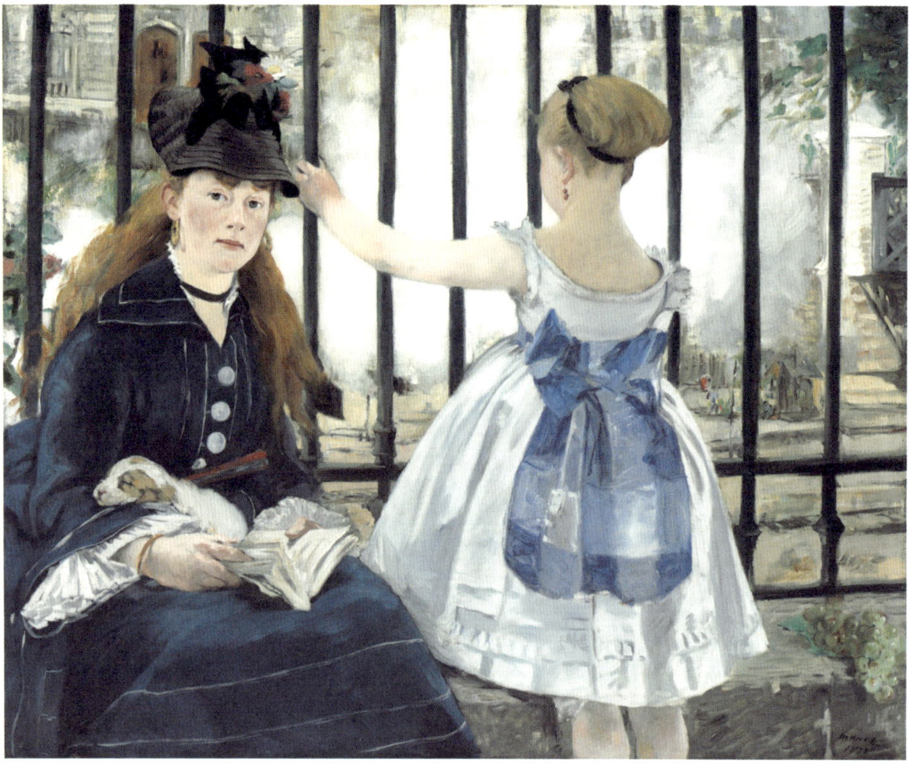

IN MANET'S STUDIO on rue de Saint-Pétersbourg, just visible in the top left-hand corner of the artist's *The Railway* (1873), the windows and floors shook from the trains at Gare Saint-Lazare. The arrival of the railways and urban development of every kind provided multiple new opportunities for proponents of ancient pleasures: painters and readers. Victorine Meurent, once the model for Manet's *Olympia*, is with the youngest daughter of his artist friend Alphonse Hirsch, whose garden overlooked the station.

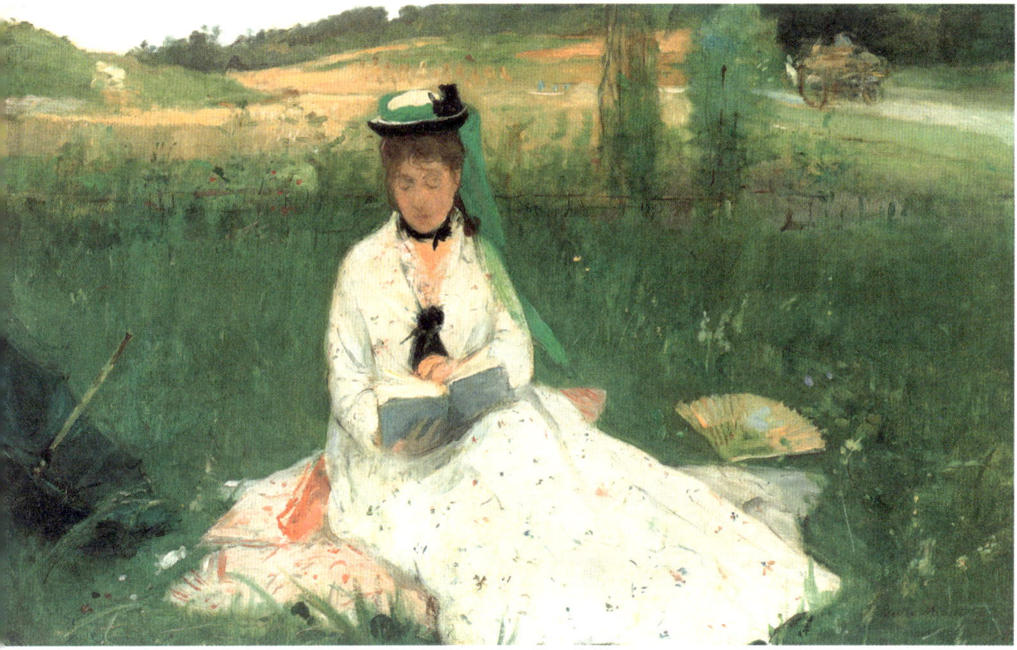

GUSTAVE GEFFROY (p. 237) called Berthe Morisot one of '*les trois grandes dames*' of Impressionism (the others being Mary Cassatt and Marie Bracquemond). She had already painted her sister Edma Pontillon, with her mother reading, in 1869–70; here, in a work from 1873, the grass of Edma's considerable garden at Maurecourt, Île de France, is a happy location for the twin pleasures of reading and dressing fashionably. But neither sister was frivolous about their study of art, and Berthe had written to Edma about seeing a painting by Frédéric Bazille that had achieved what they had so often attempted – a figure in the outdoor light. Berthe, great-grandaughter of Jean-Honoré Fragonard, included this depiction of Edma in her selection for the first Impressionist exhibition (1874).

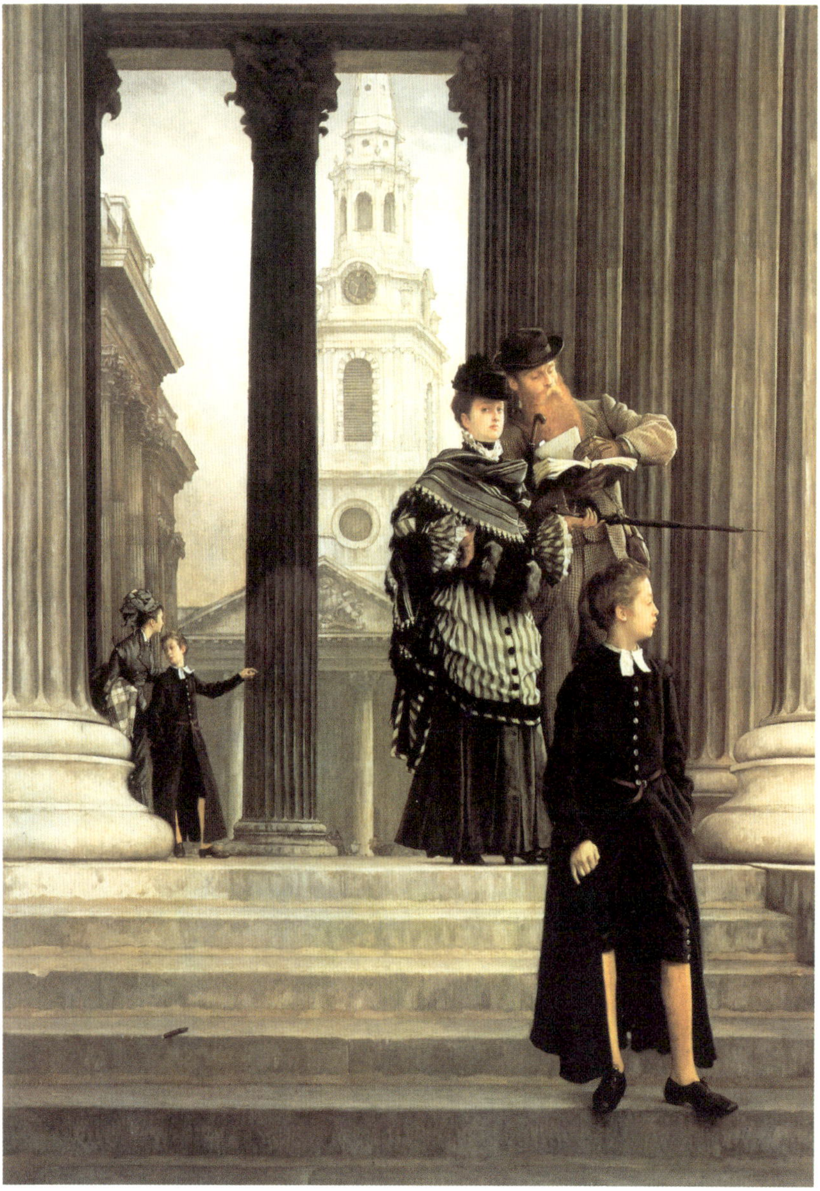

THE GREEK-REVIVAL PORTICO of the National Gallery – a place William Hazlitt suggested was a cure for 'low-thoughted cares and uneasy passions' – provides the setting for James Tissot's *London Visitors* (1874).[7] *The Times*, in its Royal Academy review in May of that year, was not enamoured by 'this clever French painter' – 'clever', in English parlance, being a rude word. Tissot had playfully painted a dropped cigar on the steps of the portico, so while the male figure is a perfect advertisement for the new publishing world of guidebooks, his companion is distracted, perhaps by the owner of the cigar. A later version of the painting omitted the risqué object.

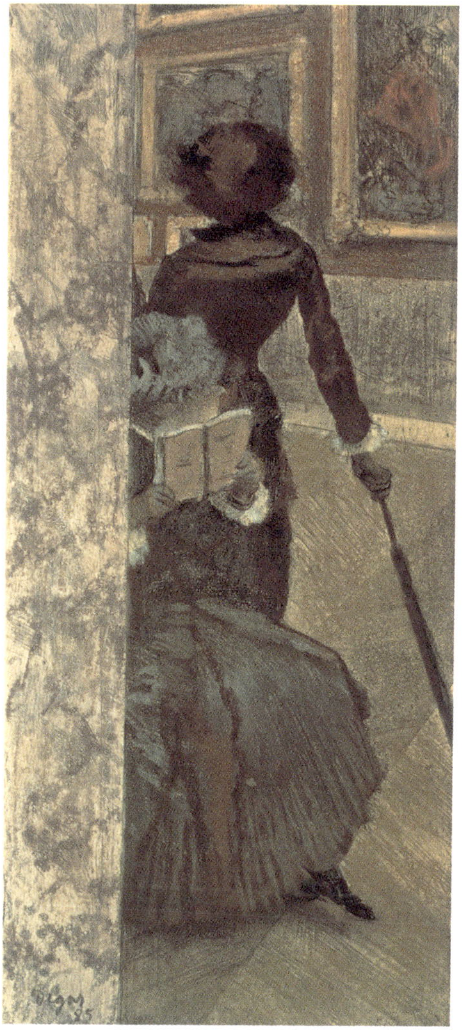

DEGAS'S 1885 PASTEL of Mary Cassatt at the Louvre – here in the Paintings Gallery – is remarkable for many reasons. He manages to depict his friend (they collected each other's work) just by showing her from the rear; the pastel is one of a series of prints, drawings, other pastels and two paintings all treating in different ways the same theme; and its striking composition owes much to the many meetings Degas had at Madame Desoye's La Porte Chinoise, a *boutique à la mode* at 220 rue de Rivoli dealing in goods from the Far East, to discuss the principles of Japanese art. The seated figure, with indispensable guidebook – book, as always, in the service of art – is probably Cassatt's sister, Lydia.

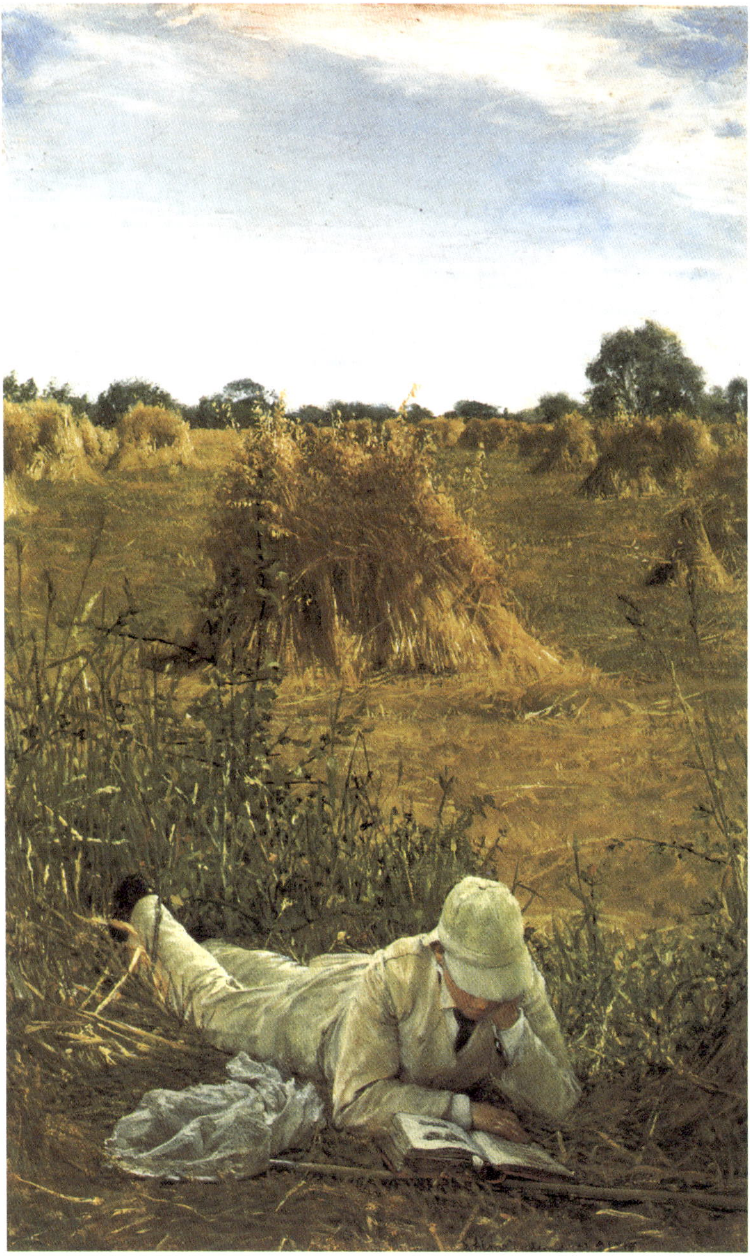

THE DUTCH-BORN Alma-Tadema paints a cornfield at Godstone, Surrey, to show how a book – on butterflies, with accompanying net – allows complete privacy and pleasure in an English kind of Arcadia, complete with messy cornstacks. The young reader, in the summer before he goes up to Cambridge (1876), is Sir Henry Francis Herbert Thompson, who later managed distinguished careers in medicine, law and Egyptology.

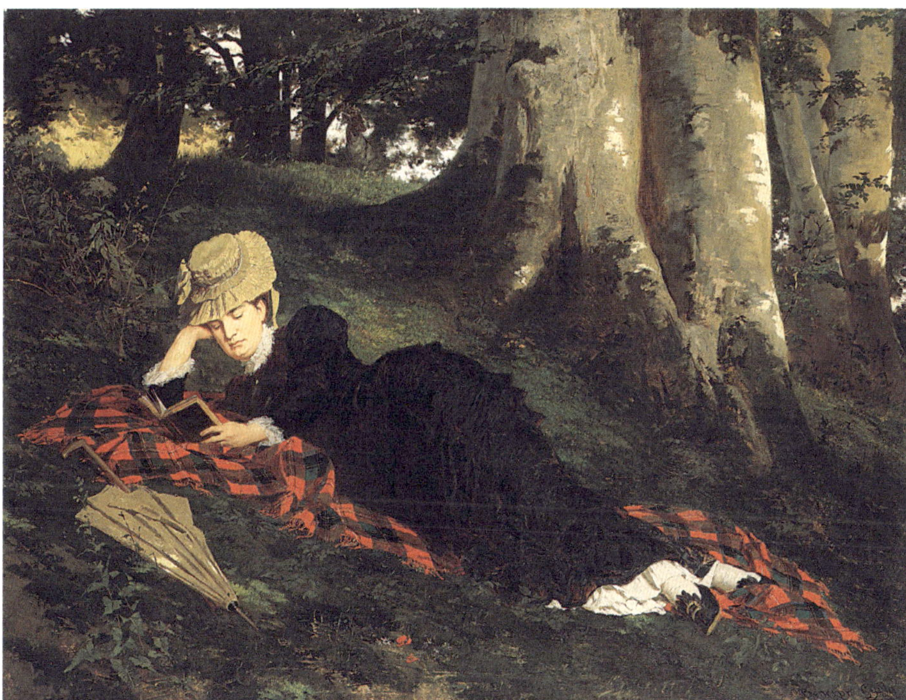

KAROLINA MAX – the probable subject of this 1875 painting and wife of the artist, Gyula Benczúr – is clearly a modern figure, in the same pose as Sir Brooke Boothby a hundred years earlier (p. 163) but without his narcissism. Benczúr, a Hungarian national, spent part of his career in the German territories; his commissions there included several from Ludwig II of Bavaria. This work was painted in Munich, where he was a professor of fine art.

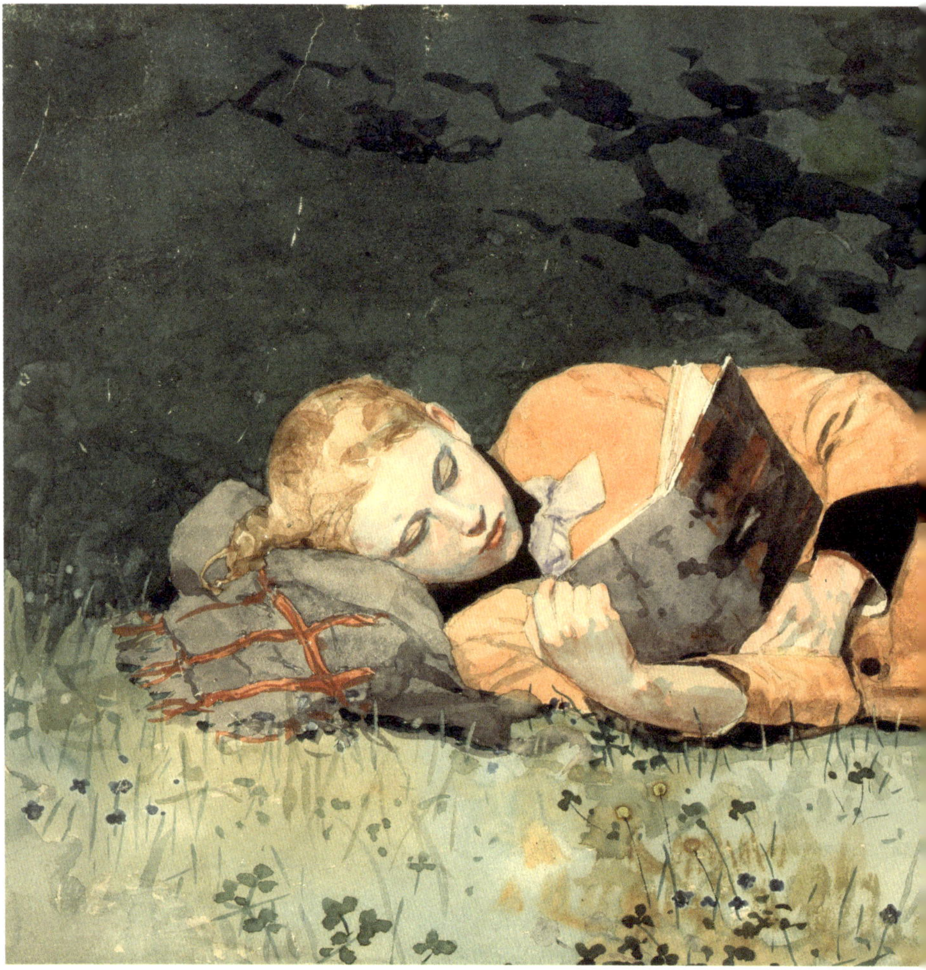

A PICTURE TELLS many stories. For the American missionary the Reverend Hollis Read, railing against Satan in 1872, the novels favoured by young women were 'garbage', full of 'a moral poison' and inciting 'carnal passion'. For the artist – Winslow Homer, the bachelor of the three Homer brothers, here with *The New Novel* (1877) – there is the sense that this is the red- or blonde-haired girl he coveted in the 1870s. No one has convincingly identified her, but when she disappears from his work, he becomes reclusive and solitary, warding off biographers and becoming misanthropic. But the girl sees it differently; like so many others, she has the joy of a good book out of doors.

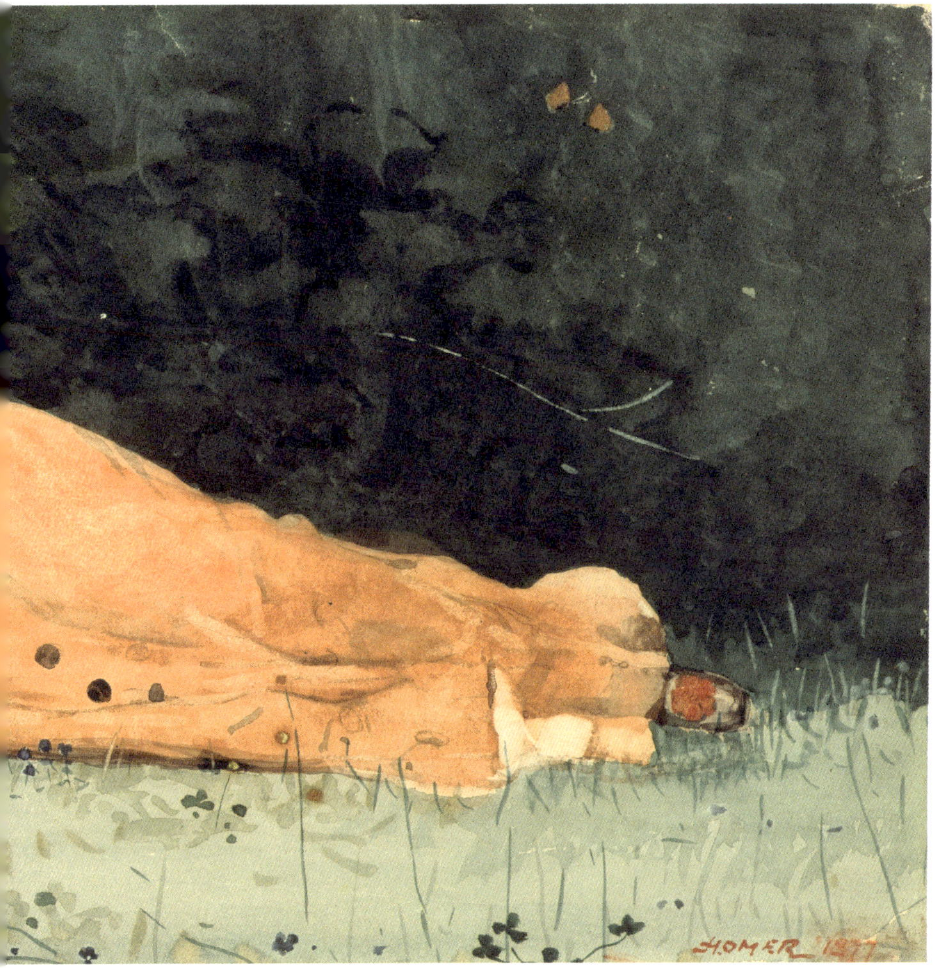
HOMER 1877

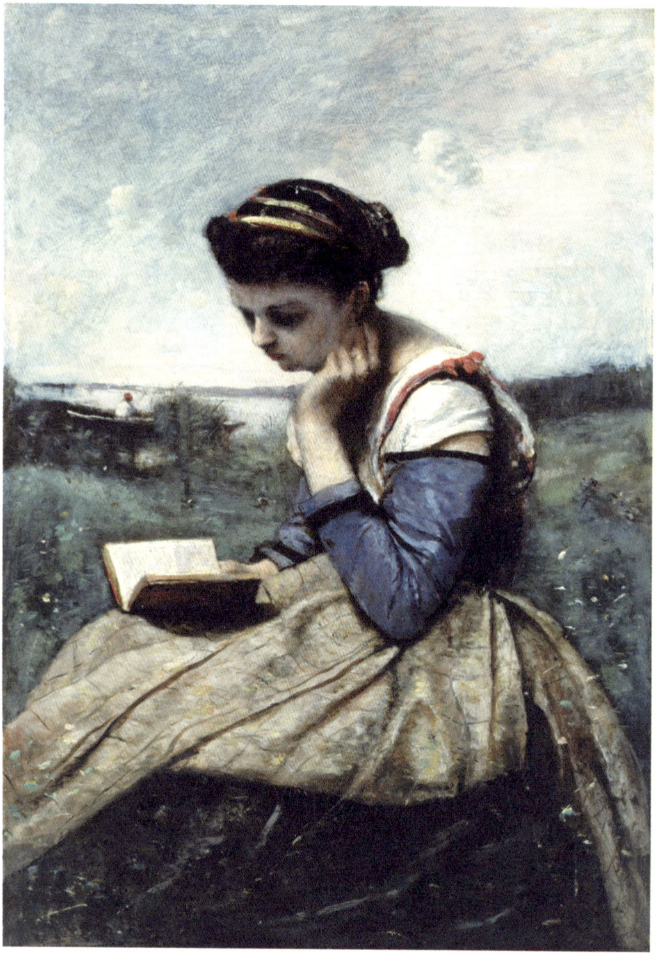

IT HAS BEEN SUGGESTED that no one painted as many books as Corot. This particular work did not find favour with Théophile Gautier at the Salon of 1869. The prolific poet, novelist and dramatist was not complimentary about the figure (Corot later reworked the landscape – but not the woman). Books were always a positive symbol for Corot, although another 19th-century French critic, Théophile Silvestre, asserted that he rarely read himself and was more interested in the shapes and colours of the books he bought along the Parisian quays: the book, as ever, as a multi-functional object. This work echoed Raphael, Corot's great love, and specifically *La Belle Jardinière* (1507), in which the Madonna holds a book in a landscape.

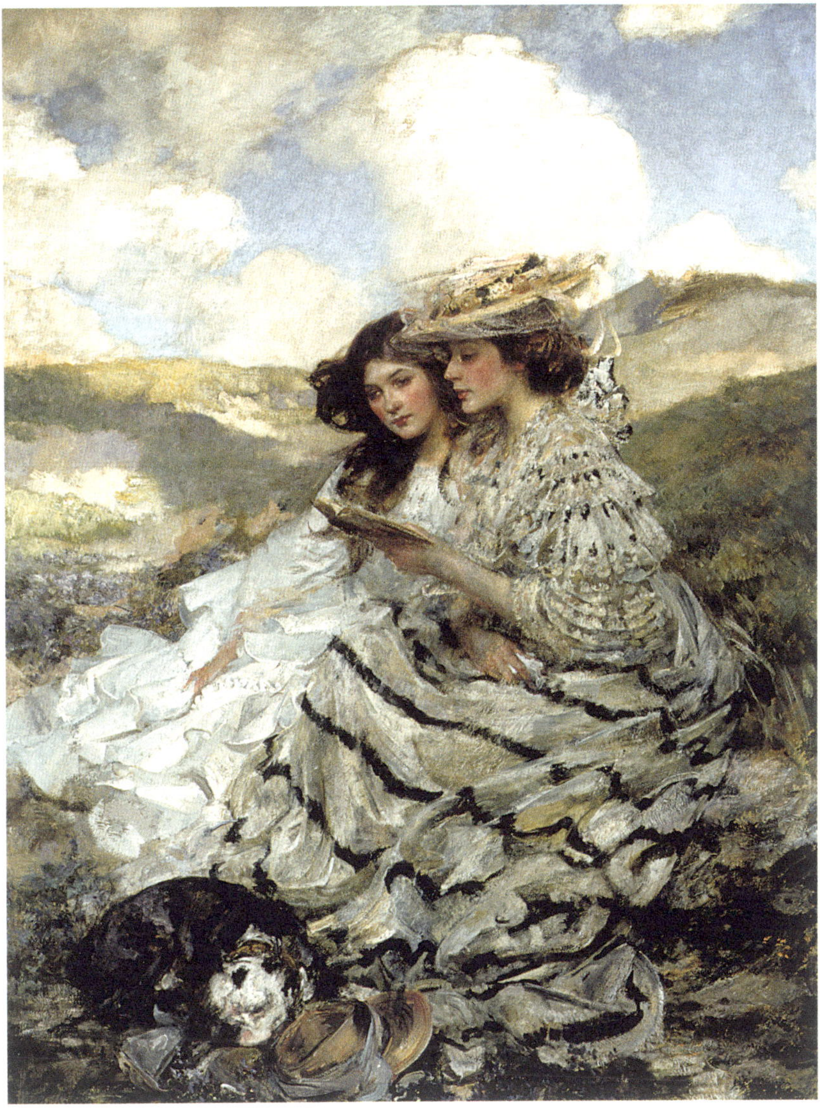

JAMES JEBUSA SHANNON proudly numbered among his subjects Mrs John D. Rockefeller and Queen Victoria (in 1895 *Munsey's Magazine* called him 'An American Painter of the English Court'). *On the Dunes*, from the early years of the 20th century, shows his wife and daughter, Kitty (see also p. 139), and may have been painted when the family stayed with the American artist George Hitchcock and his wife Henriette ('Gorgeous' and 'Miggles' according to Kitty Shannon) at Schuylenburgh, a house owned by the Hitchcocks near Egmond aan den Hoef, in the Dutch province of North Holland.

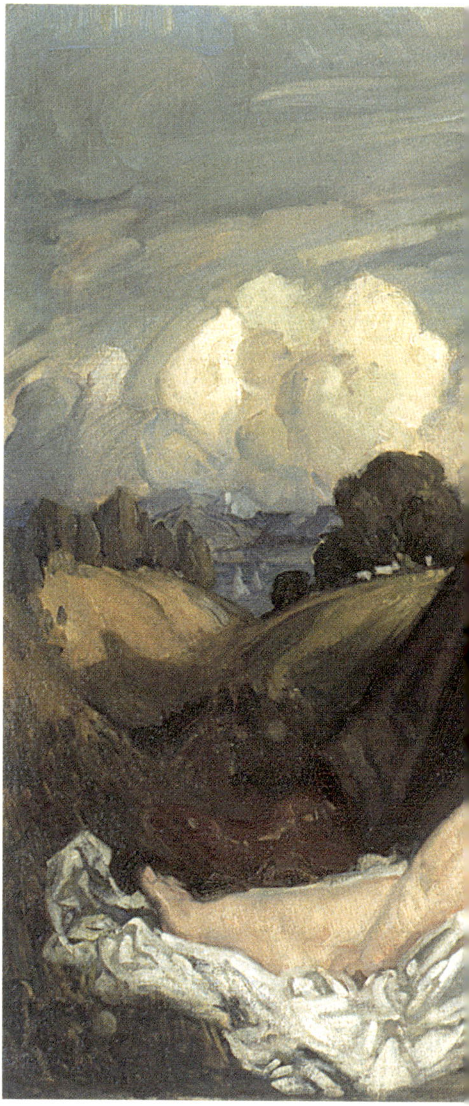

GEORGE WASHINGTON LAMBERT, son of a Baltimore railway engineer, was born in St Petersburg but lived much of his adult life in Australia. On one level, *The Sonnet* (*c.* 1907) – as the artist recorded – was heavily influenced by Giorgione's/Titian's *Le Concert champêtre* (*c.* 1509); the nude woman is a transcendental creation of the sonnet the man reads. The transgressive conundrum is that while the man is Lambert's artist-friend Arthur Streeton and the nude is Kitty Powell – an actress who posed for Lambert and took his drawing classes – the detached figure is another of his artist-friends, Thea Proctor, with whom, rumour suggested, he was romantically involved over many years.

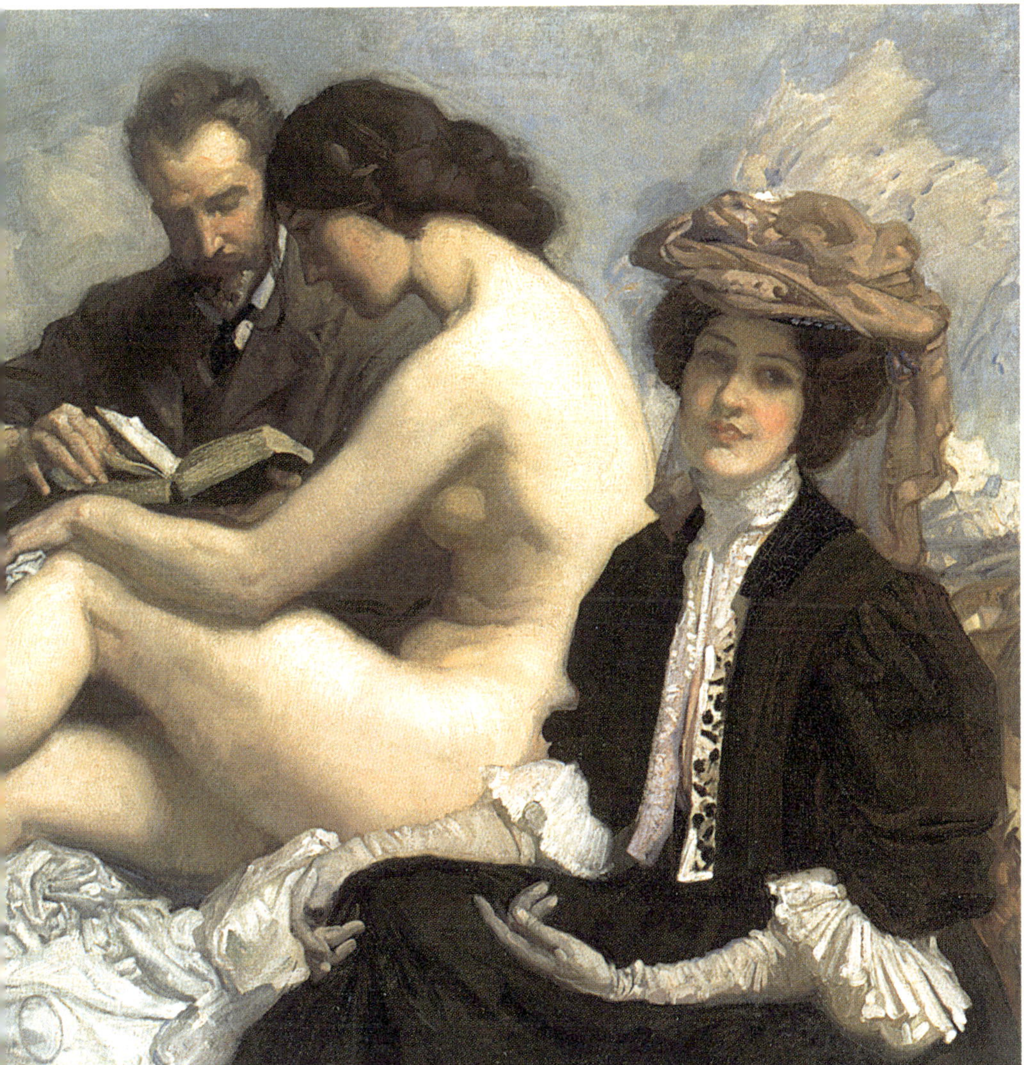

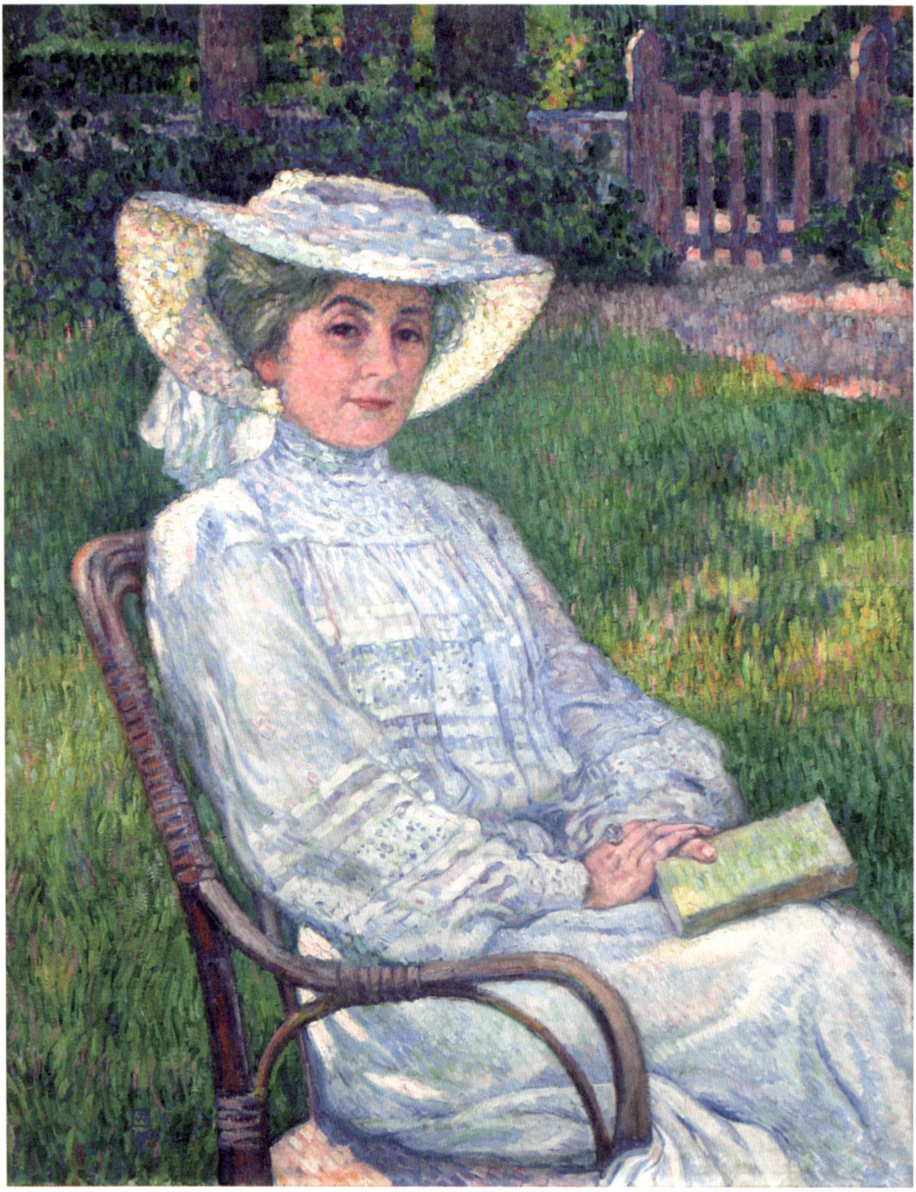

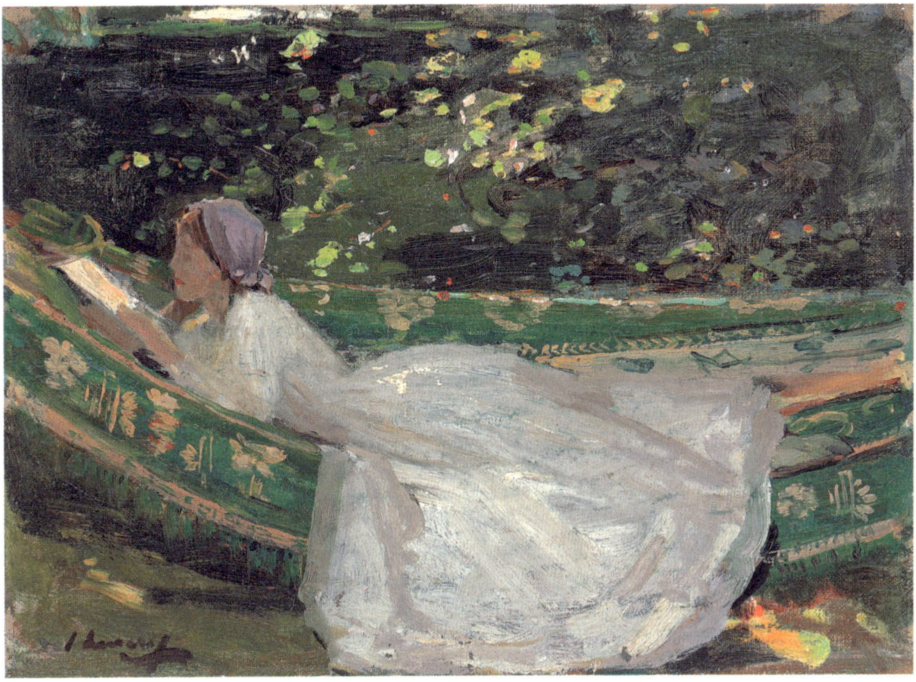

TWO THINGS PERFECTLY express 19th- and early 20th-century ideas of summer garden pleasures: the hammock, and a girl reading in a hammock (ABOVE). From Winslow Homer's *Girl in a Hammock* (1873) to this painting by Sir John Lavery, *The Green Hammock* (*c.* 1905), the scenes are uniformly beautiful, beguiling and the epitome of repose.

THE WRITER MARIA MONNOM (OPPOSITE), who came from the family of the eponymous Belgian publisher, married Théo van Rysselberghe in 1889 and, through him, met André Gide, with whom she had an 800-letter correspondence. Van Rysselberghe often painted his wife with a book; Gide fathered his only child – in secret – with their daughter, Elisabeth. The worlds of art and literature were often closely entwined.

ORDER AND DISORDER in Edvard Munch's *Christmas in the Brothel* (1904–05). The Madame reads; her dressed-up girls talk; the Christmas tree is ready – but the artist paints himself passed out from alcohol. The cancellation of a commission for a portrait of the father-in-law of Munch's German patron, Max Linde, had resulted in anxiety, drinking and a visit to a Lübeck brothel.

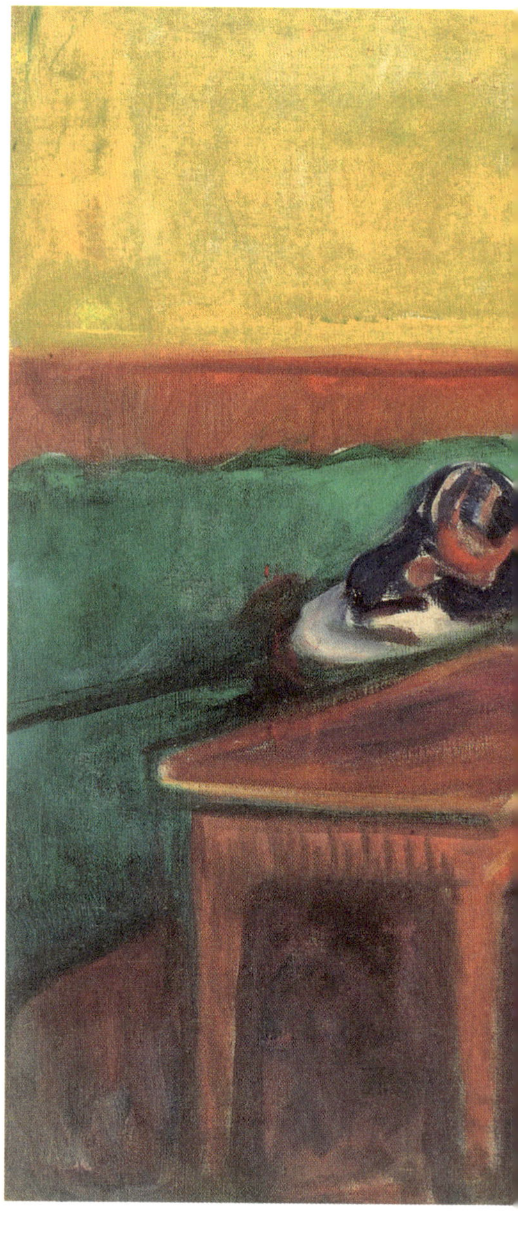

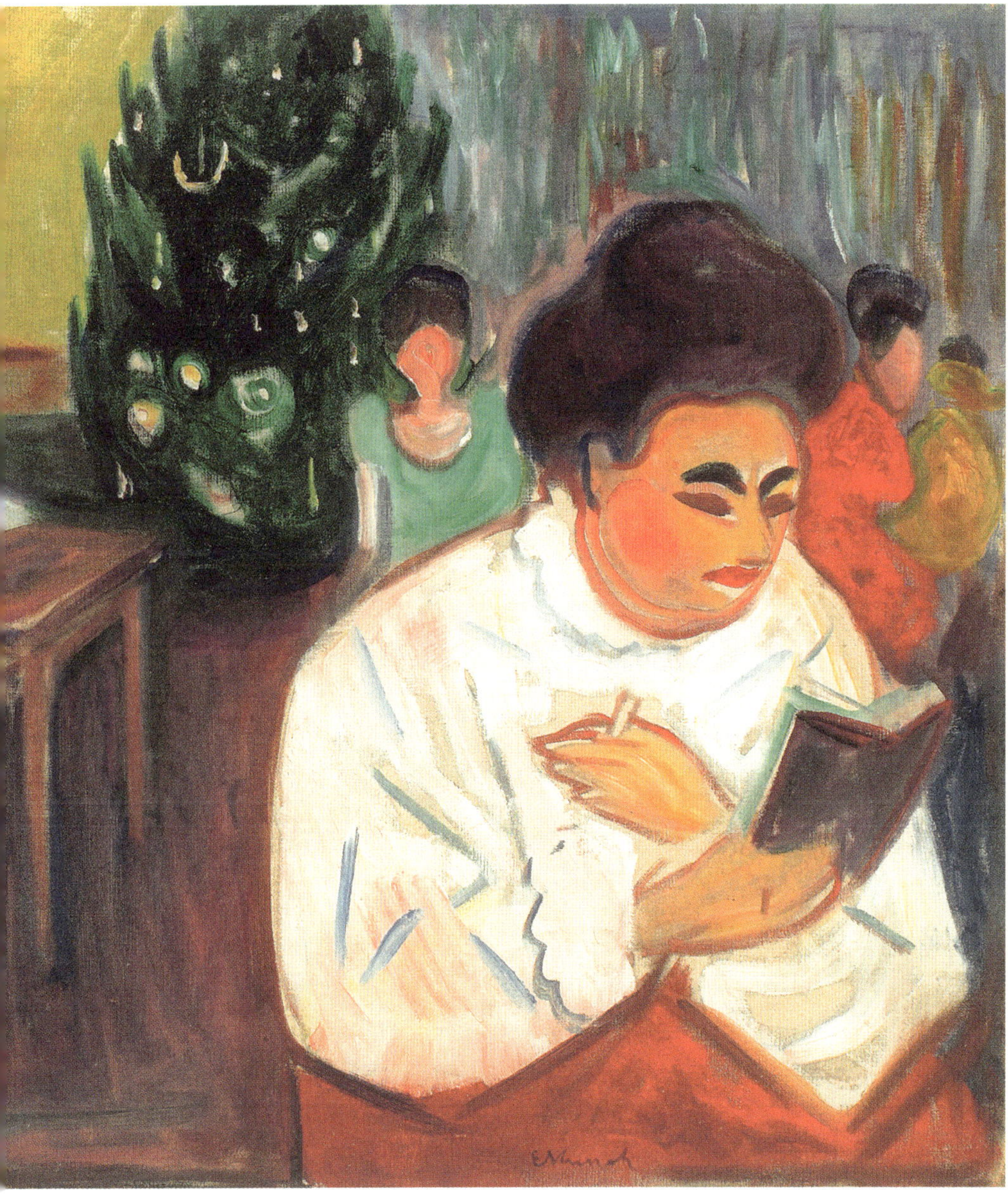

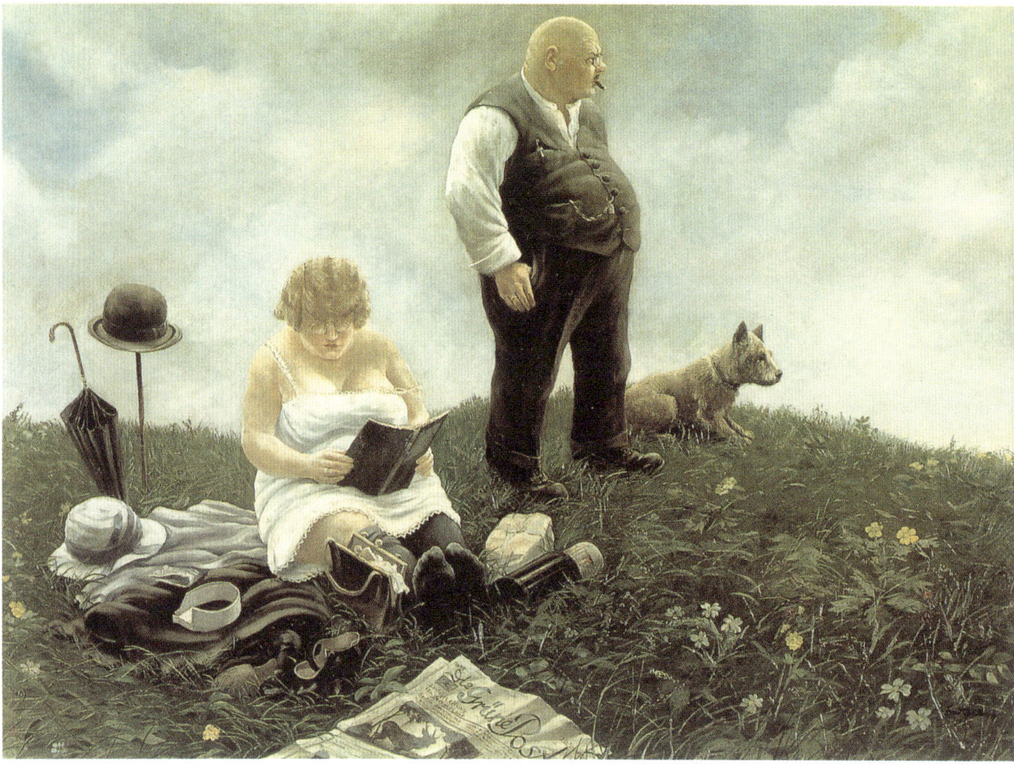

THE CRUEL OBJECTIVITY of a *Neue Sachlichkeit* Sunday afternoon in 1930 (ABOVE). Fred Goldberg, who also lived earlier and later in his life in California, satirizes the discontented picnic of the petite bourgeoisie. The newspaper is the Berlin *Die grüne Post* (The Green Mail), 'Sunday newspaper for City and Country'. At least the content of the book seems sufficiently interesting to compensate for the uncomfortable reading position.

GUY PÈNE DU BOIS, AT VARIOUS TIMES ARTIST, writer and critic of art and music, looked back in *Life* magazine in June 1949 to his time at the New York School of Art in the same class as Edward Hopper and George Bellamy, heavily influenced by the radical realist ideas of Robert Henri, but also with plentiful experience of New York in 'low Bowery dives'. A one-time neighbour of F. Scott Fitzgerald in Westport, Connecticut, he would retreat to his New York studio for peace and quiet. This Third Avenue scene (OPPOSITE) dates from 1932.

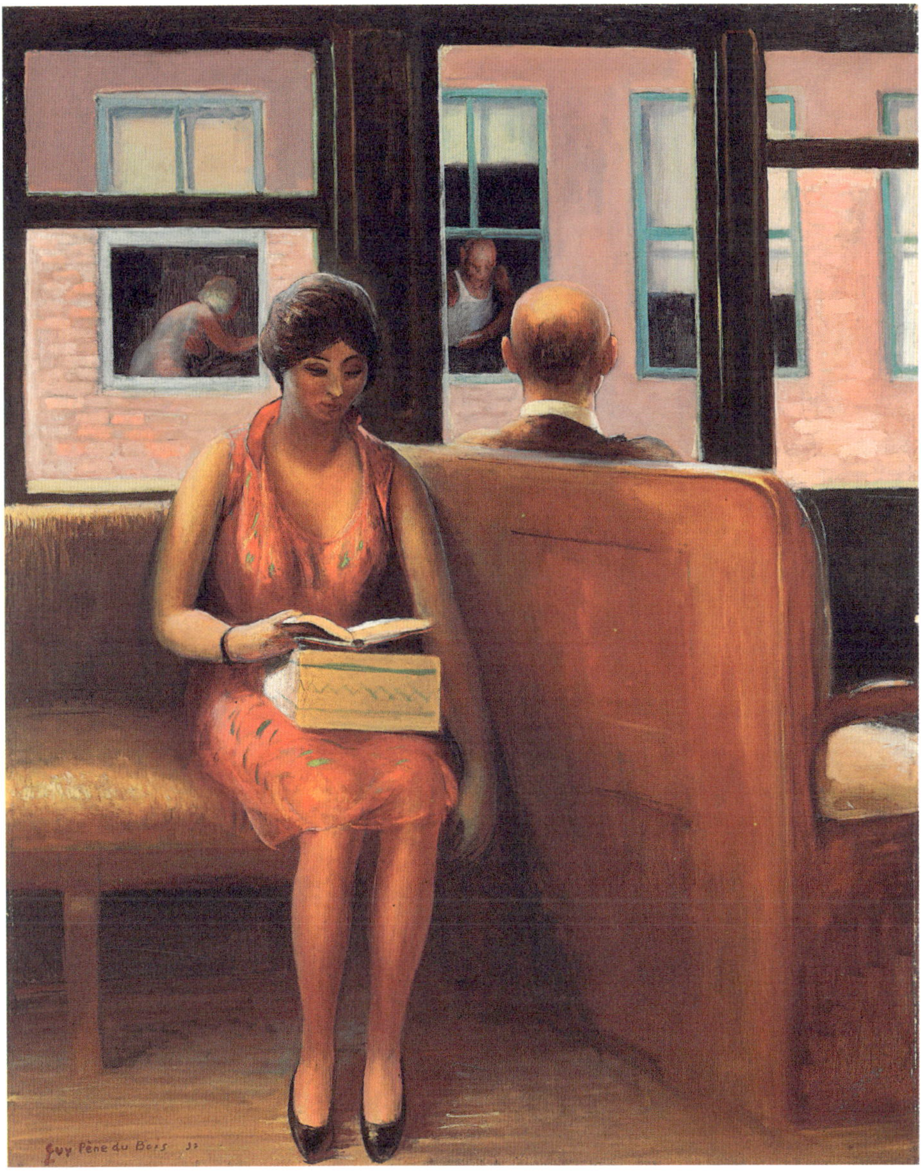
Guy Pène du Bois

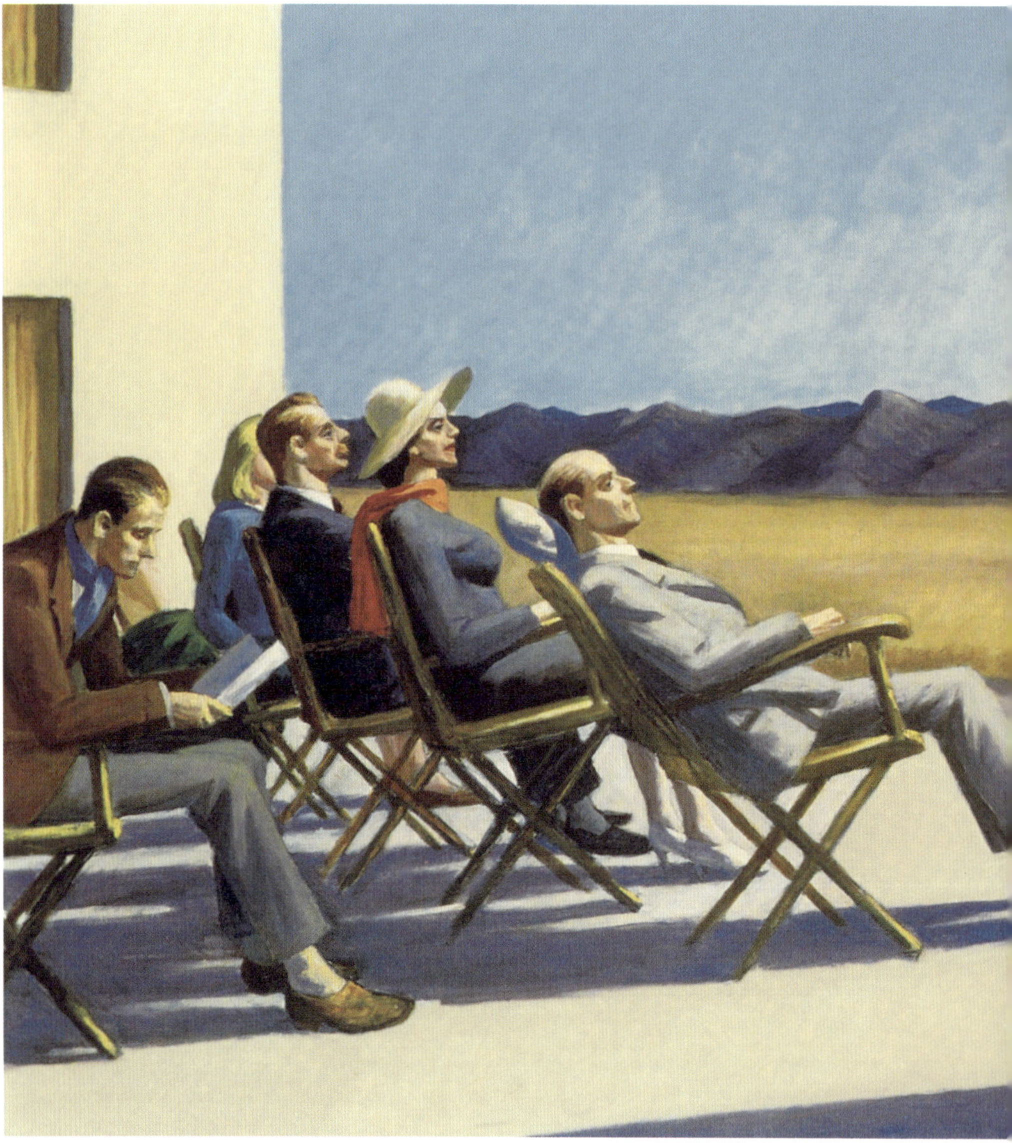

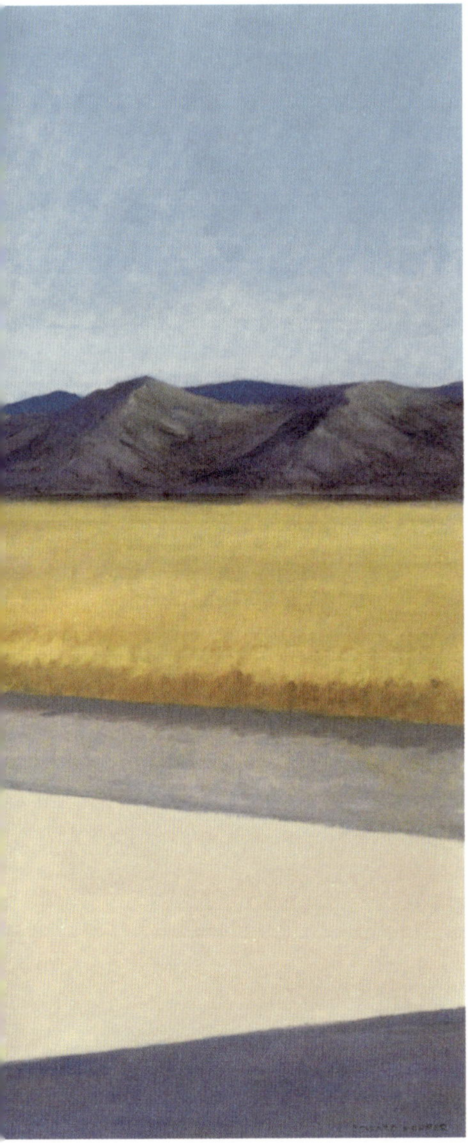

EDWARD HOPPER, according to his own account, had watched people in Washington Park Square, New York, and transferred them to the American West for *People in the Sun* (1960). Here are five people in completely separate worlds, not much joy in any of them, but – if structure, form and shape are the chief preoccupations of the artist – the man with the book is the only one with the power of escape.

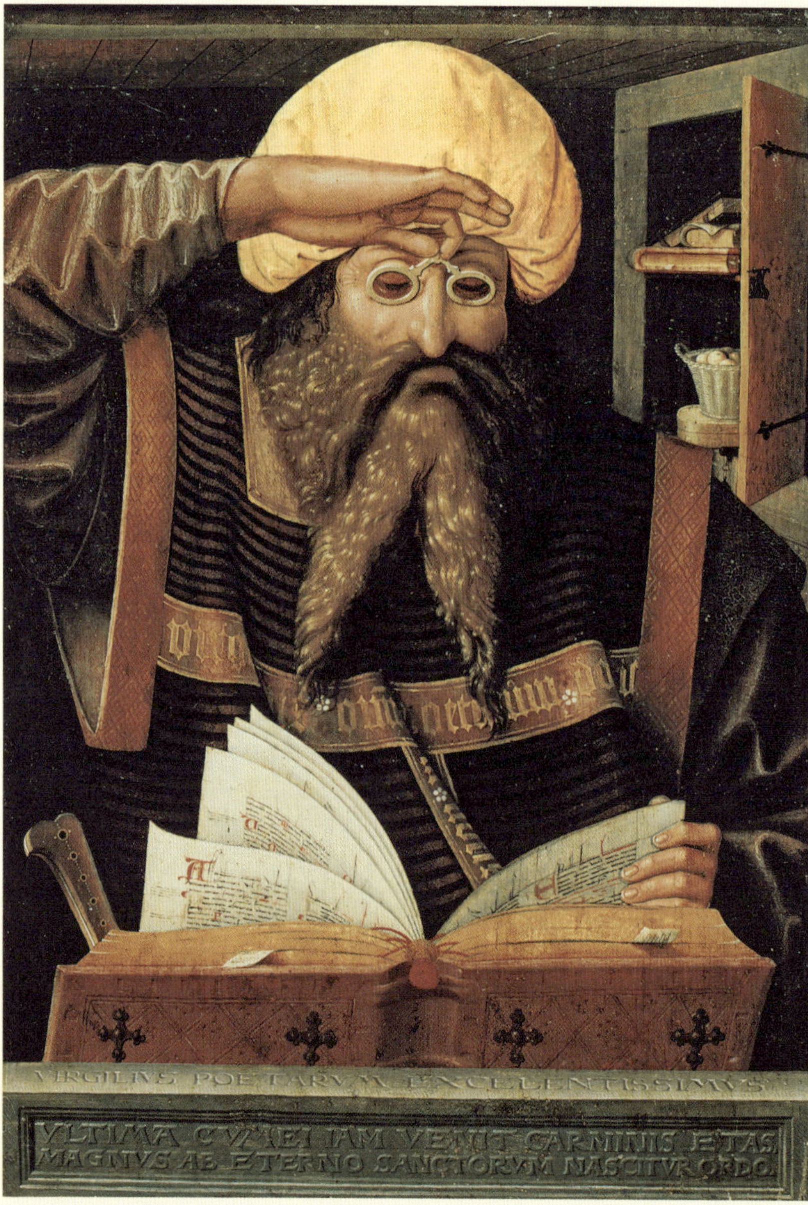
VIRGILIVS POETARVM EXCELLENTISSIMVS
VLTIMA CVMEI IAM VENIT CARMINIS ETAS
MAGNVS AB ETERNO SANCTORVM NASCITVR ORDO

GALLERY 4

'ALL *that* MEN HELD WISE'

LEIGH HUNT, in his 1823 article 'My Books', suggested that compressed within books could be found 'the assembled souls of all that men held wise'.[1] Nearly two thousand years ago, the elder Pliny's *Natural History* – an encyclopaedia of knowledge before encyclopaedias – suggested that civilized life and its practices could not be maintained without a vehicle in which they could be recorded. That was not just what the book did; it was also something that gave it status as the home of authority, of knowledge and of education.

Proud owners of soon-to-be-superseded contemporary high-tech devices might reflect on how the papyrus scrolls of Aristotle's library, created in the 4th century BCE, were thought valuable enough by the Roman general Sulla for them to be removed to Rome several hundred years later. And if there was any doubt about it, Christianity then endowed the book with ultimate authority as a means of expressing the Word of God. St Francis of Assisi, by espousing poverty, could not contemplate ownership of books, but within a few years of his canonization in 1228 he was depicted over and over again with a book (to the annoyance in the 19th century of Isaac D'Israeli, who thought it had 'disgusted the sensibilities

---

DURING THE RENAISSANCE the book carried the authority both of the Church and of a more secular world to come. On the one hand, humanism pushed the pagan classical world to the centre of education; on the other, this painting (*c.* 1538) by Ludger tom Ring the Elder, anachronistically depicting Virgil with eyeglasses and a bound book, showed the Church harnessing pre-Christian figures for its own purposes: St Augustine and other early Christian Fathers associated Virgil's *Eclogue 4* (*c.* 40 BCE) with a prophecy of Christ's birth. Either way, the sovereignty of the book as the endorsed source of knowledge was reinforced.

of taste' to depict anachronisms, among which he also included the Virgin Mary with a book on the table).[2] Nevertheless, Bonaventura Berlinghieri's tempera painting of St Francis and scenes from his life, in the church of San Francesco, Pescia (1235), emphasizes the poverty through the saint's sackcloth robes, but now he holds the Gospel.[3] Even many centuries later, Dante Gabriel Rossetti's *The Girlhood of Mary Virgin* (1848–49) symbolized the virtuous knowledge inherent in her person by means of an impressive stack of books.[4]

Renaissance humanism introduced a new element: secular knowledge. The use of the book in portraits was a *sine qua non* for articulating intellect visually; the study was no longer the province only of a St Augustine or a St Jerome. As the vehicle for recording and transmitting the new knowledge, whether Copernicus's *On the Revolutions of the Heavenly Spheres* or Vesalius's *On the Fabric of the Human Body*, both published in 1543, the book represented authority.[5] Whether the prominent volume in Rembrandt's *The Anatomy Lesson of Dr Tulp* (1632) is Vesalius's treatise or perhaps the then more recent publication on the human body by Adriaen van der Spiegel (1627), its presence showed the vital importance of using the book to transmit practical knowledge with authority.[6]

Not that art became lost to morality, or became indifferent to the challenges of worldliness and the higher virtues. In Quentin Metsys's *The Moneylender and His Wife* (1514; p. 205), the husband busies himself with weighing jewelry, gold and pearls, an attraction sufficient to distract his wife from her prayer book. But not everything was symbolic. The second edition of Vasari's *Lives* (1568), at least to an extent, reflected a new desire to move from unverified story to fact.

Knowledge and authority linked directly to education. Those at a disadvantage in life could still find escape through reading: Daniel Chester French's sculpture *Dr Gallaudet and His First Deaf-Mute Pupil* (1888), in Washington DC, shows the renowned educator of the deaf with his pupil beside him holding an open book.[7] Nor were all pupils reluctant. M. Carey Thomas's journal for August 1878 – now in the archives of Bryn Mawr College, Pennsylvania, of which Thomas would become second president – describes her delight ('the purest happiness') in reading continuously for four days, each hour passing as if it were a second.[8] Equally, there could also be an imperative about education: in the troubled Germany of the early 20th century, the notion of self-improvement – to be found in bookshop or library – was seen as an urgent necessity for the sake of the nation.[9]

The importance of the book was not lost on the great innovators of 20th-century art; it was not simply a record of the past but a vehicle for revolution, as the Russian avant-garde demonstrated so effectively in the 1920s and 1930s. Once upon a time, the mythical Egyptian king Thamus, according to Socrates, feared for the effects of writing on human memory.[10] He need not have worried: through the book, writing saved memory. The digital zeitgeist, however, has ushered in the post-truth age, and partly for a mundane reason. Its disciples became used to the idea that knowledge and entertainment should be free, pushing down consumer prices to unsustainable levels and thereby threatening the search for objectivity. Throughout its history, the book has remained the epitome of knowledge, authority and education without having that problem.

No wonder that Shakespeare's Prospero decides that his library is 'dukedom large enough'.[11]

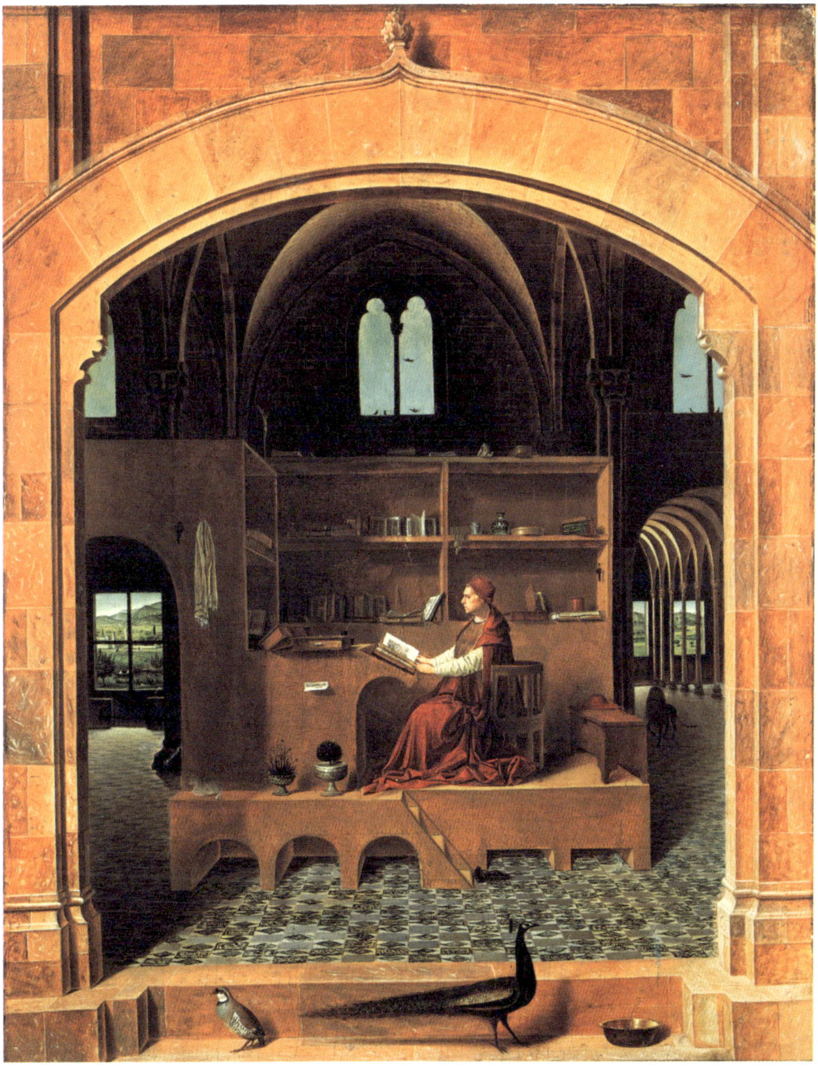

WHO BETTER THAN St Jerome to associate 'the book' with authoritative knowledge? His 4th-century translation of the Bible into Latin – the Vulgate – gave those able to read a common source for the Word of God stretching over hundreds of years of the book's early history. In this painting (*c.* 1475) by Antonello da Messina, one of many from the Renaissance of St Jerome in his study, an additional element is present: the comforting company provided by a book. Other comforting possessions can also be seen, including slippers (at the foot of the steps), plants, cat and towel.

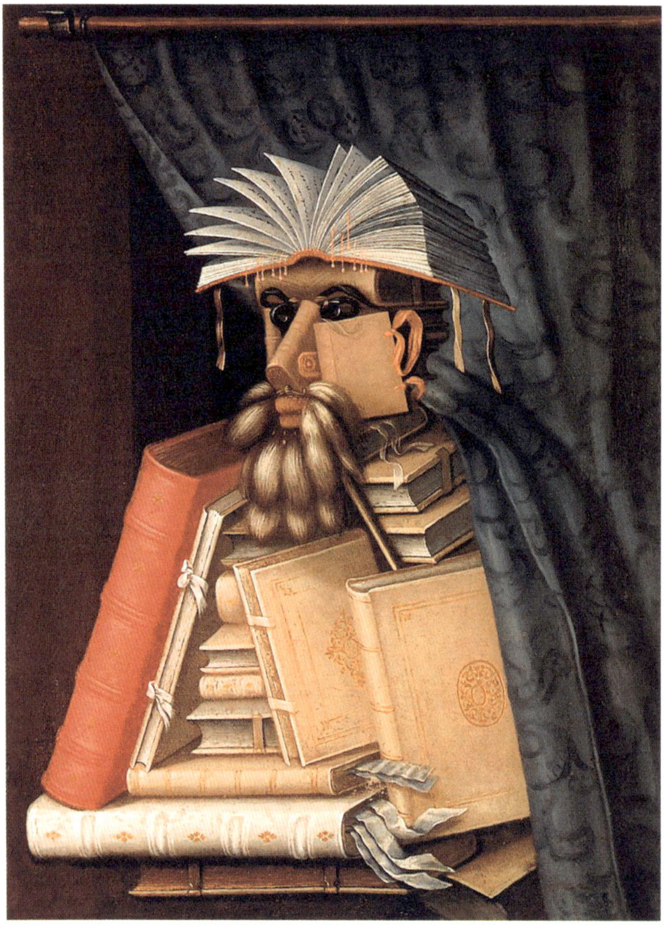

ARCIMBOLDO'S *The Librarian* (1560s; ABOVE) is thought to be a portrait of the humanist Wolfgang Lazius, who – like the artist himself – was attached to the Habsburg court of Emperor Maximilian II. Some have seen it as a satire on the world of books, but this was also the era of the Swiss scholar Conrad Gessner, whose four-volume *Bibliotheca universalis* (1545–49) recorded the rise of the book by attempting a universal catalogue of everything that had been produced in the first century of printing.

MORE THAN FOUR HUNDRED YEARS after Machiavelli lost his long-held position in the chancery of Florence and retreated to his farm to 'step inside the venerable courts of the ancients' and pen *The Prince*, Joseph Stalin settled down to read a copy of the book, annotating it as he read. The early Mannerist Rosso Fiorentino, 'Il Rosso', supposed painter of this portrait of Machiavelli (OPPOSITE), found a place in Vasari's *Lives*; Machiavelli's book continued to be so influential on so many that Henry Kissinger was once forced to deny that he was one of them (the books of Spinoza and Kant meant more to him).

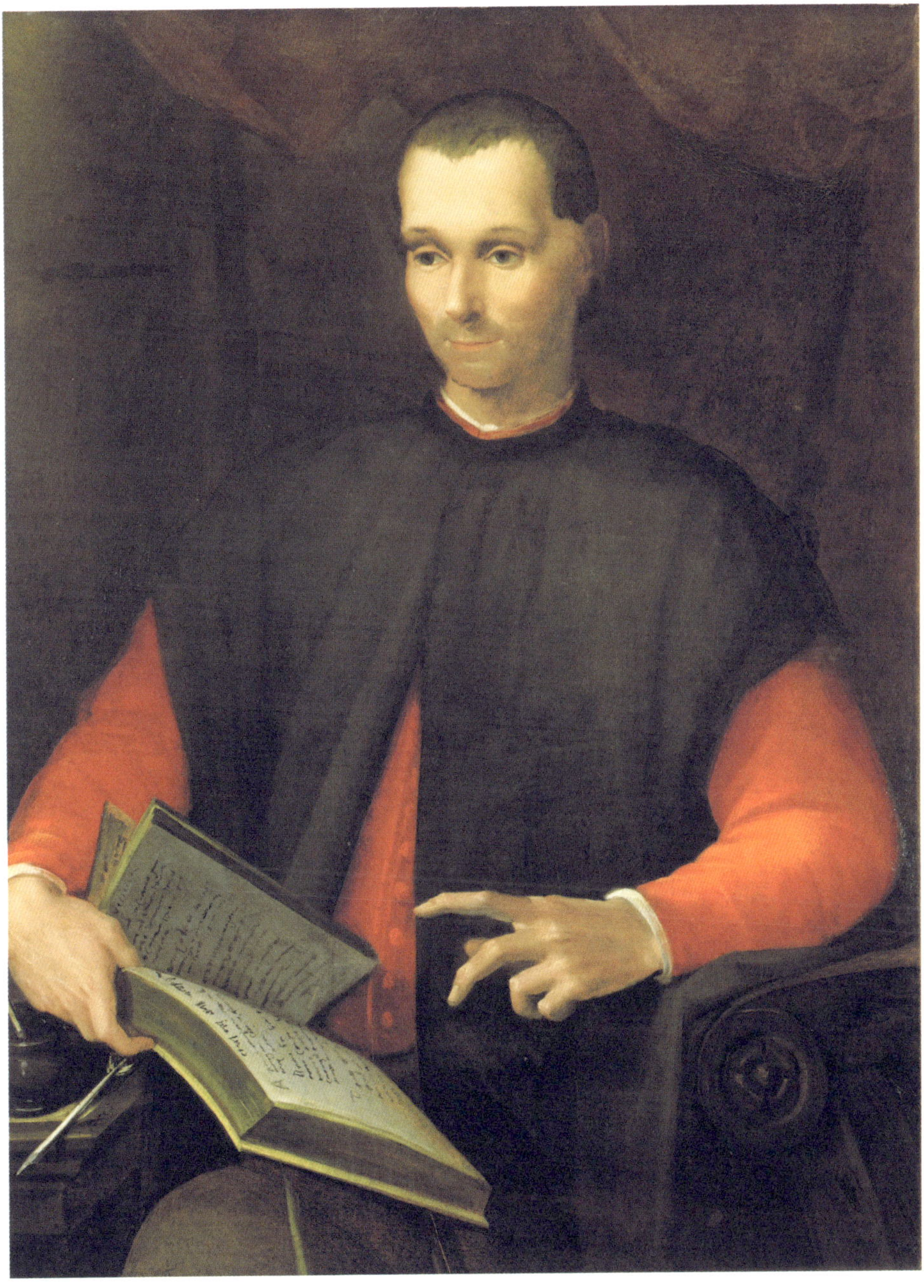

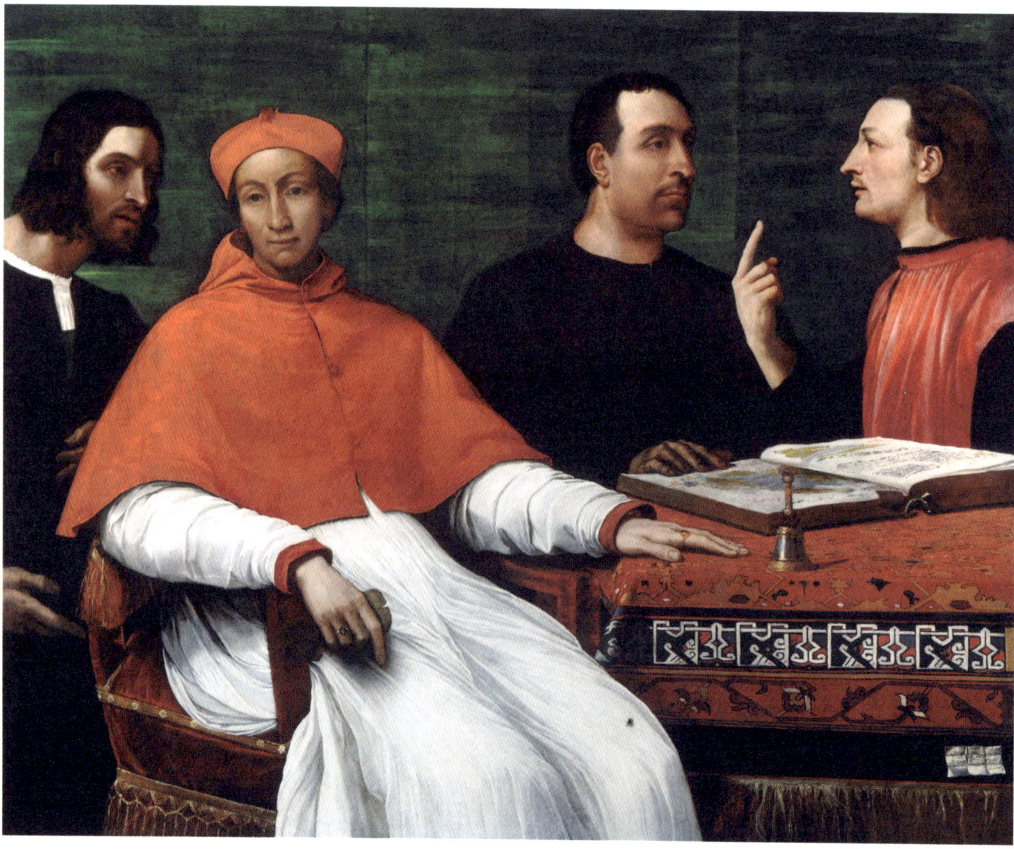

A BOOK SIGNALS a crucial moment in the history of the world – and, for different reasons, in the life of Cardinal Bandinello Sauli. The date is 1516. Sebastiano Luciani, later to acquire the tag 'del Piombo' (of the lead) as Keeper of the Papal Seal, paints the soon-to-be-imprisoned – for knowledge of a plot to assassinate Pope Leo X – cardinal. On the far right is Vasari's friend and Renaissance historian Paolo Giovio, caught between two worlds: the need for papal patronage and a secular, empirical spirit of investigation. On the table is an *isolario*, a book about islands, for this is the era of exploration, discovery, new-found lands and new trading routes. On the one hand, the authority of the book – the Bible – can be transferred to another – one of scientific exploration – to help missionary activity over the next five centuries; on the other, there is a glimmer of a secular, rational future, making use of scientifically derived knowledge. Books carry the authority to support both.

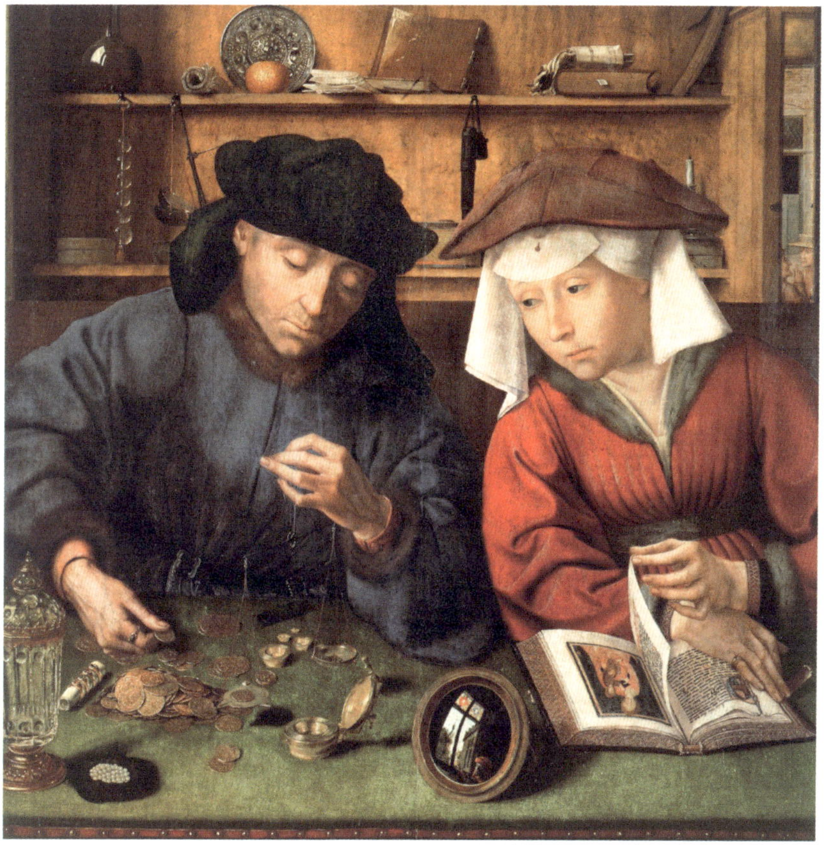

QUENTIN METSYS, born in Leuven in 1466, died in the great commercial centre of Antwerp in 1530. Antwerp, at that time at the heart of trade between northern and southern Europe, was well used to the different currencies used by Italian bankers or Iberian merchants, but how should we interpret *The Moneylender and His Wife* (1514)? Is the wife being lured away from her spiritual study of the Virgin and Child by worldly riches? Or could it be that a prayer book was helpful in providing a moral sense for behaving reasonably when greed threatened? Whatever the answer, the tiny figure in the red hat – perhaps the artist – in the convex mirror in the foreground is himself reading a book.

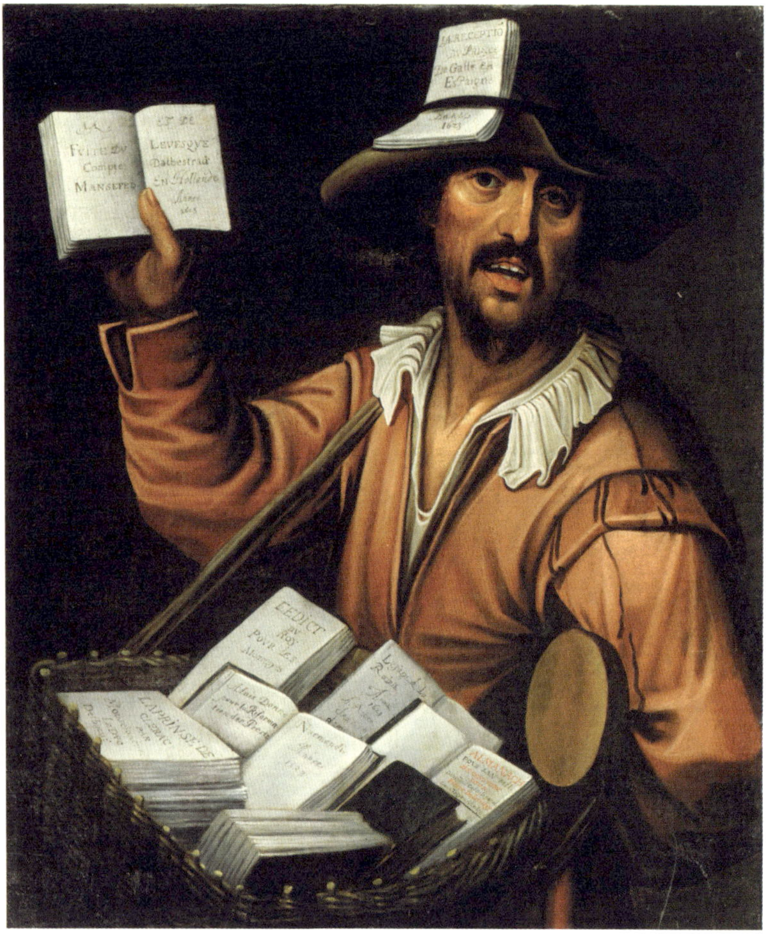

A 17TH-CENTURY *colporteur*. Book-pedlars were much persecuted, but flourished after the invention of printing. Without rent or other overheads, they could undercut competitors in price – if not quite being the Amazon of their day – and played an important role in bringing books first to merchants and landowners and eventually to the working classes. In October 1817, the Prefect of Aube in north-east France warned the Mayor of Troyes of the animosity of the merchants towards pedlars on market days, for Troyes was the home of the *Bibliothèque bleue*, a series of cheap, mass-produced books equivalent to chapbooks in England and *Volksbuch* in Germany. Still, not long after, the Jewish pedlar Simon Lévy moved from his native Alsace to Paris – Lévy being the father of the brothers who founded the well-known publishing house of Calmann-Lévy. The *colporteurs* were the quiet engine of book dissemination. No wonder that Guy de Maupassant's short story 'Le Colporteur', published in *Le Figaro* in the year of his death, 1893, begins with the sight of a book-pedlar on a Savoyard path along Lac du Bourget.

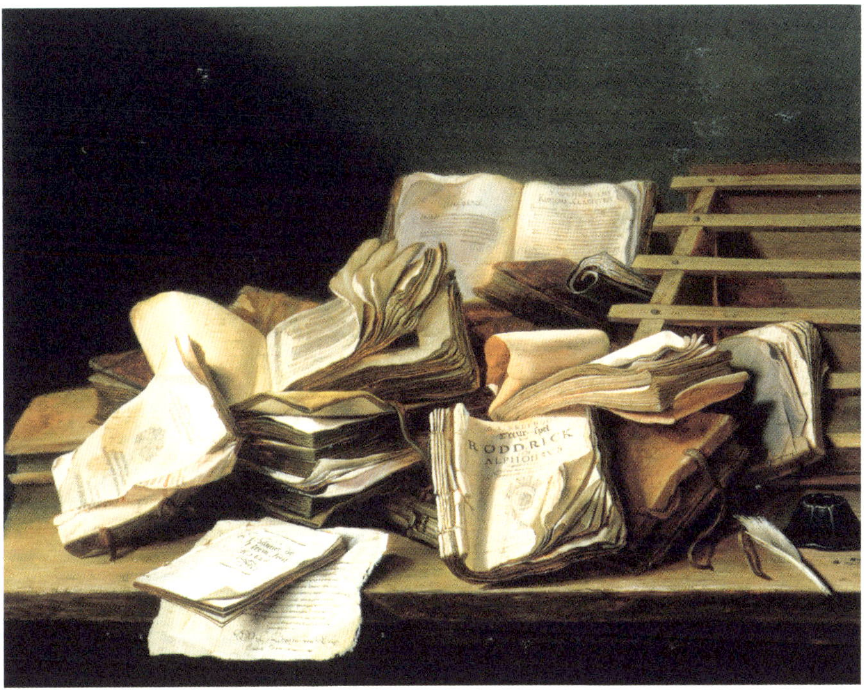

LEIDEN WAS THE HOME of the oldest university in the Netherlands, and Jan Davidsz. de Heem's *Still Life with Books* (1628) would have been well understood there, its melancholy, battered volumes a sure sign of the perishability of all things human. De Heem, whose stepfather was a bookbinder and bookseller, painted at least six other similar works while in Leiden, where there was a fashion for relatively monochromatic paintings, and also for the use of the handle of the brush or a sharp tool to scratch the paint to simulate the pages of a book – a technique De Heem shared with the young Rembrandt and the young Jan Lievens. Visible are a volume by the jovial Jacob Westerbaen (top, centre), who was writing comic love poetry at the time, and *Roddrick and Alphonsus* (centre right) by the poet and playright G. A. Bredero; also on show is the artist's signature in the tract overhanging the table at bottom left. Colour infused De Heem's later still lifes in a way that – along with a sense of controlled disorder – appealed to Matisse, who did his own version of one in the Louvre.

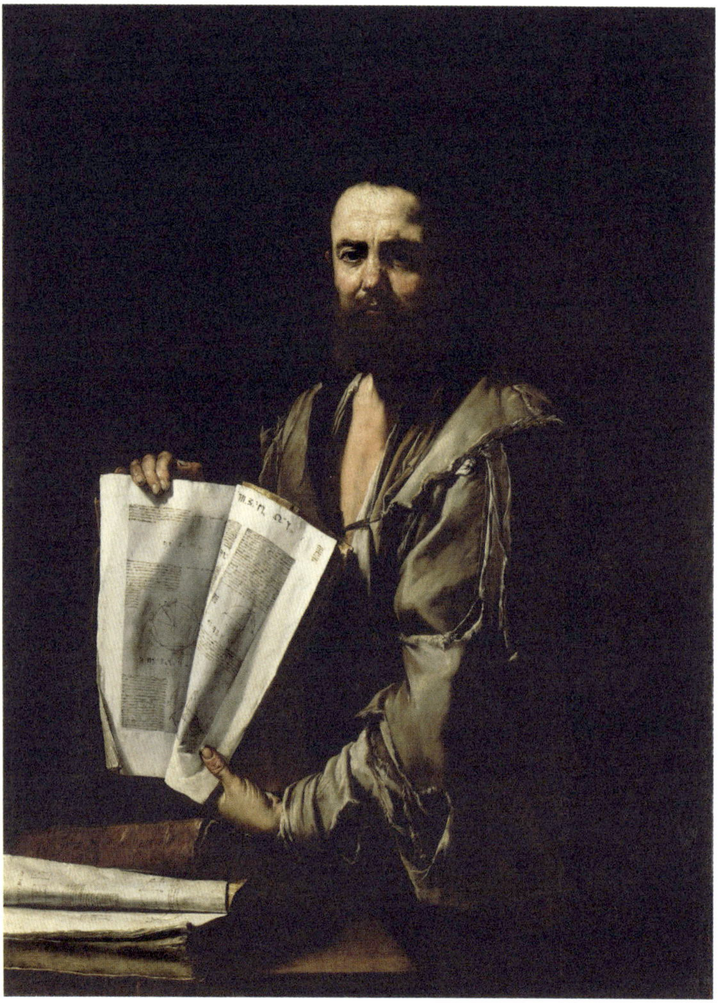

THE ITALIAN EARLY BAROQUE ARTIST Ludovico Carracci noted the impact of Jusepe de Ribera, a 'young Spaniard working in the manner of Caravaggio', not long after his arrival in Italy from Valencia. As ever, in Jusepe's portrait of Euclid, probably from the first half of the 1630s, the book connects past, present and future. Euclid's mathematical tract *Elements* (*c.* 300 BCE) remained the key textbook, certainly for geometry, for well over two thousand years, while the artist's depiction of an unkempt scholar, caring for nothing but the intellect, not only reflected aspects of Hellenistic philosophy and the 17th century's revived interest in Stoicism as a moral basis for existence, but also gave us an image relevant to us at all times.

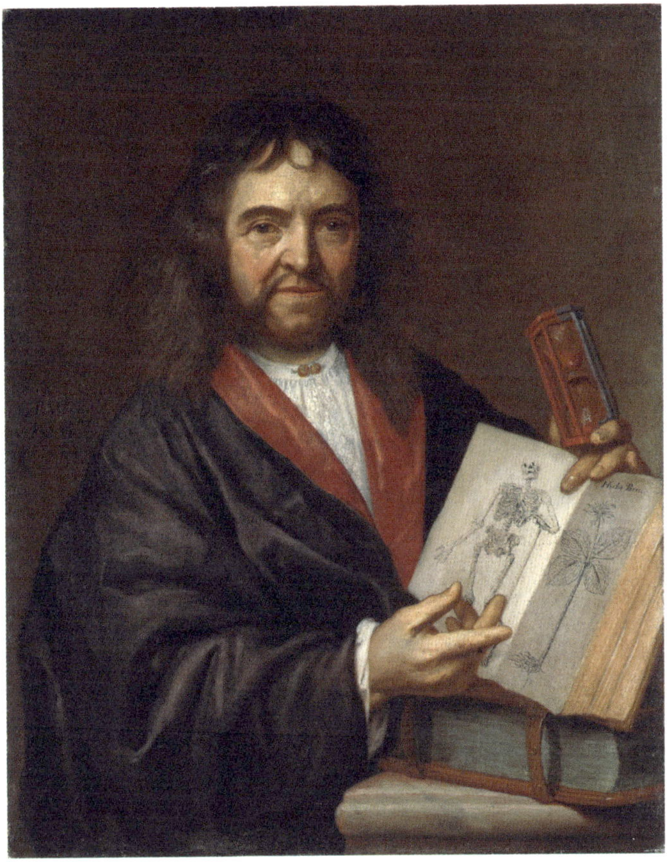

IN THIS CASE, there is some uncertainty as to whether the artist, Caspar Kenckel, was Swedish or German, and whether the subject, Olof Rudbeck, is the younger or elder (the consensus seems to be the latter, but he looks a very young fifty-seven at the date of the painting, 1687). Aged just twenty-one, Olof Rudbeck the Elder (1630–1702), son of a bishop, discovered the lymphatic gland and circulation of the lymphatic fluid. Professor of medicine in Uppsala, botanist, engineer, architect and historian (notably in his four-volume treatise suggesting that Sweden was the lost Atlantis), he passed on knowledge, curiosity and skill to his son, Olof Rudbeck the Younger (1660–1740). The son succeeded the father as professor of medicine, taught Linnaeus, and was himself an explorer and scientist of distinction from an early age. The book in the painting is open at a drawing of a skeleton taken from Vesalius's 1543 study of the human body, opposite what is probably a medicinal plant from *Herbario nuovo* by Castore Durante (1529–1590).

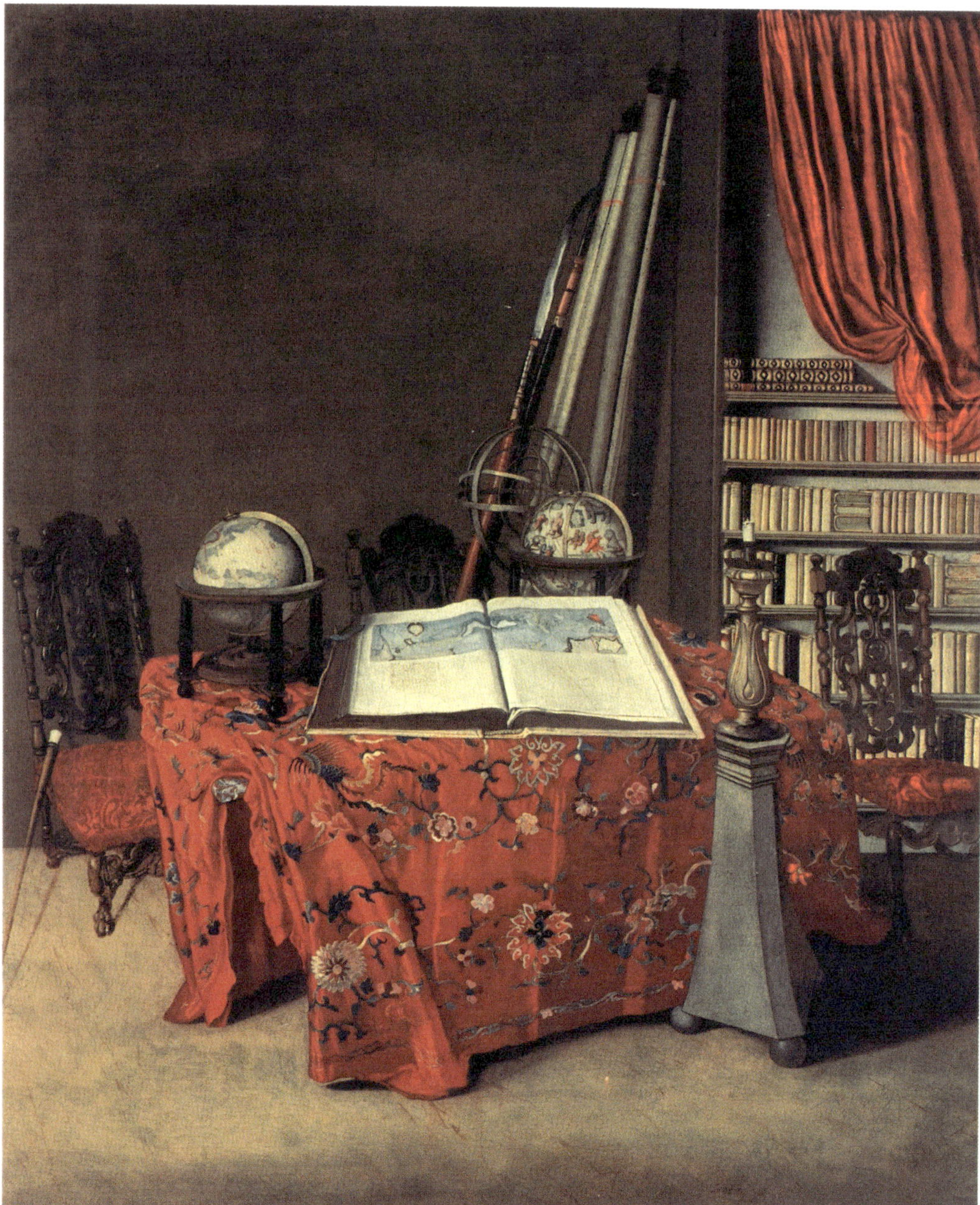

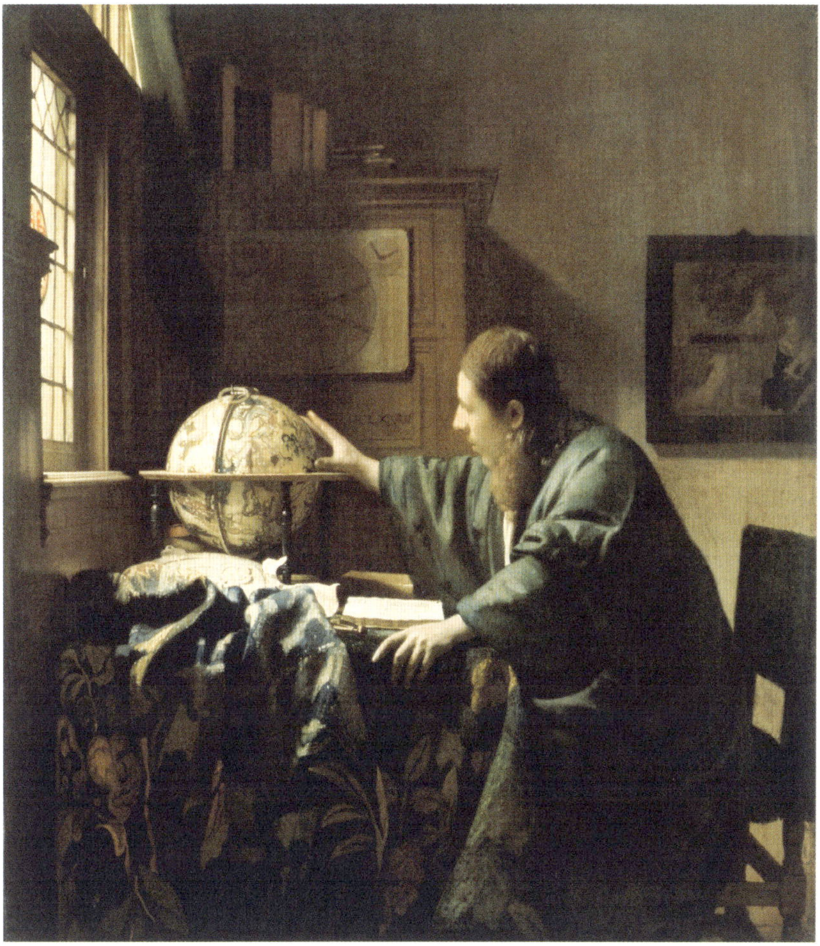

HOW EFFECTIVE BOOKS were at navigating a passage between the new world, opened up by the discoveries of 17th-century science, and the old world – still very much alive – of divine wisdom. The open book in Vermeer's painting *The Astronomer* (1668; ABOVE), a companion to the later *The Geographer*, shows a section of Adriaan Metius's *Institutiones stronomicae geographicae*, which prescribed geometry, mechanical instruments – and 'inspiration from God'. Some think the figure was based on Vermeer's contemporary Antonie van Leeuwenboek, a pioneer of the use of the microscope in studying living organisms.

BOOKS BECAME A WINDOW on the world, a message reinforced in this depiction of a library in 1711 (OPPOSITE) by the globes and by an open Blaeu atlas, as well as by the Chinese silk and Japanese ceramics. The artist, the Dutchman Jan van der Heyden (1637–1712), painted three such scenes late in life; at his death, an inventory recorded that he himself owned 184 volumes, including a number of substantial folios.

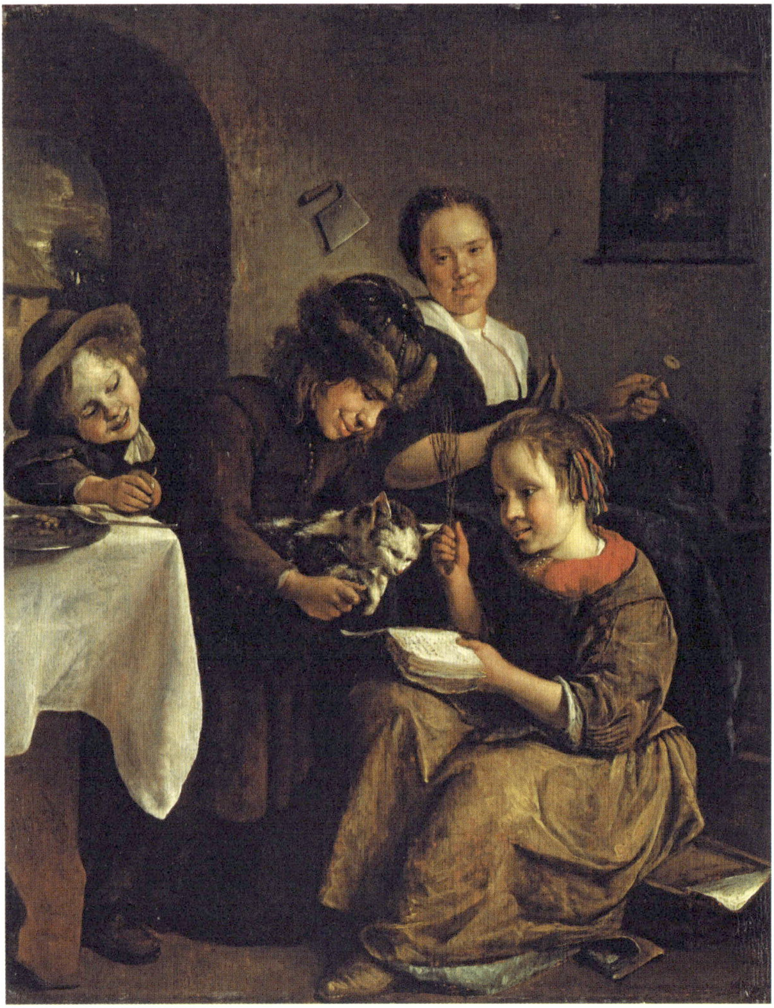

THE LEIDEN-BORN ARTIST Jan Steen, who was also for a while the owner of a tavern and a brewery in Delft, liked to depict the chaotic humour of everyday life at home, the messiness of his domestic interiors giving rise to the Dutch saying '*een huishouden van Jan Steen*'. Here, in a work painted between 1665 and 1668, children teach a cat to read, although – just to ensure cats had all the essential skills – Steen also painted a cat being taught to dance. The idea was a little dangerous, given that cats were often thought to be harbingers of danger, or to provide a warning against behaving badly, especially to children.

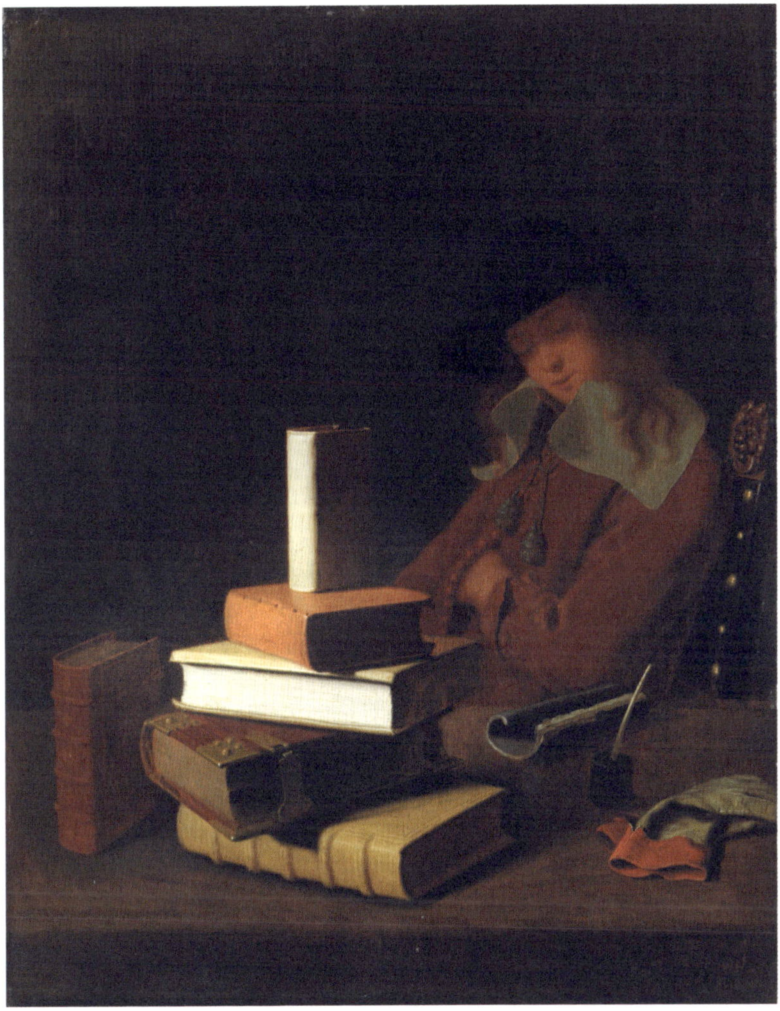

ONCE UPON A TIME, SLOTH, being one of the Seven Deadly Sins, had only religious connotations, as in the painting on that subject in the Prado (*c.* 1500), attributed to Bosch. But in *The Sleeping Student* (1663), Constantin Verhout – active in Gouda in the 1660s – has a different motive. It was more common for 17th-century Dutch artists to paint girls and women asleep as a symbol of slackness, but few had been given the chance to read. For boys, Protestant Holland believed that an educated population led to a prosperous country. The pile of books here reeks of non-naturalistic new modernity, while the student is being gently chastised for his own good.

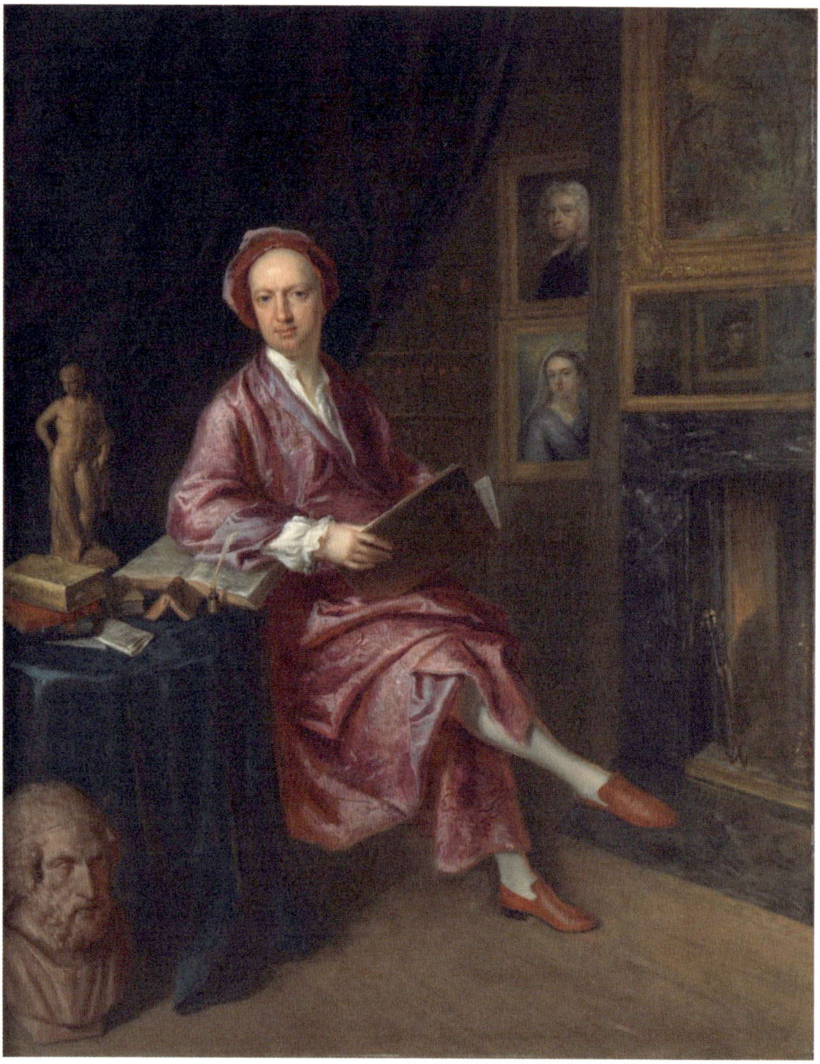

JONATHAN RICHARDSON painted this portrait of his son around 1734. Richardson's writings on art inspired Johsua Reynolds, were translated into French, and were praised by the German art historian Johann Winckelmann. Richardson encouraged the idea of painting as an intellectual activity in which a portrait should 'reveal the mind as well as the visual appearance' of the subject. He also coined the term 'connoisseur' as a 'science for gentlemen'. Like father, like son: the younger Richardson did the Grand Tour in Italy in 1721, gathering information on 'statues, bas-reliefs, drawings and pictures', which he later developed into a book with his father, to be used by collectors and wealthy tourists.

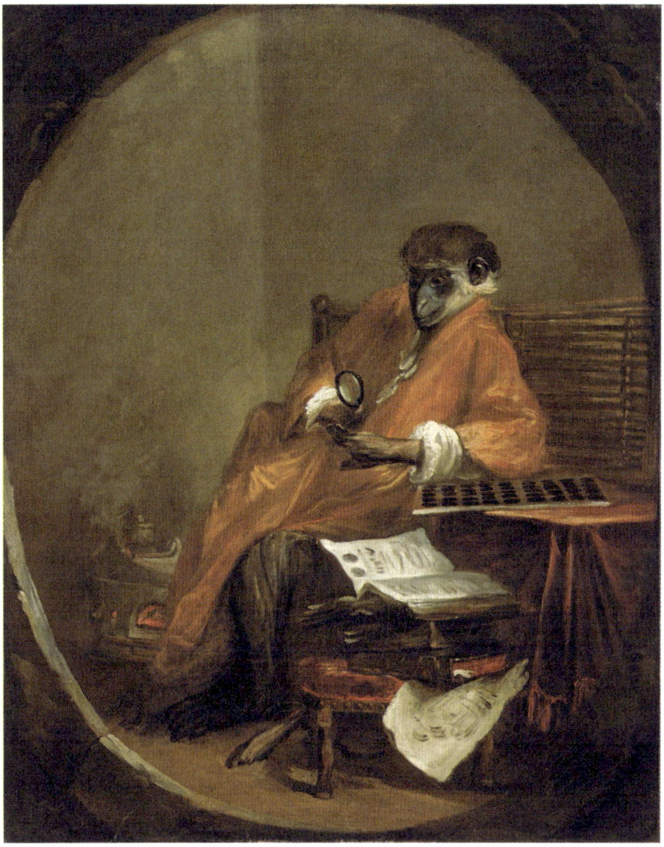

ANIMALS HAVE HAD A BAD PRESS in Western culture. Monkeys were demons within Christianity, but not much changed as secular ideas began to spread: whether symbols of insanity or lust, or described as repulsive deformations of humans, they were not depicted with sensitivity. In Henry Fuseli's *The Nightmare* (1781), a simian form comes to take possession of a woman. Chardin, as ever, brought subtlety, here in *Le Singe antiquaire* (*c.* 1725–45). The 18th-century fashion for singeries (works of art in which monkeys are shown imitating human behaviour) had already been expressed by Antoine Watteau and others. A friend of Chardin, the poet Charles-Etienne Pesselier, explained the satirical purpose of the artist's work: the antiquarian collector should look up from his medals and books to see the achievements of the present day. Similarly, in Chardin's *Le Singe peintre* (*c.* 1739–40), where the monkey artist tries to paint a statue and draws his own image, he is guilty of old-fashioned copying of others, rather than reflecting nature.

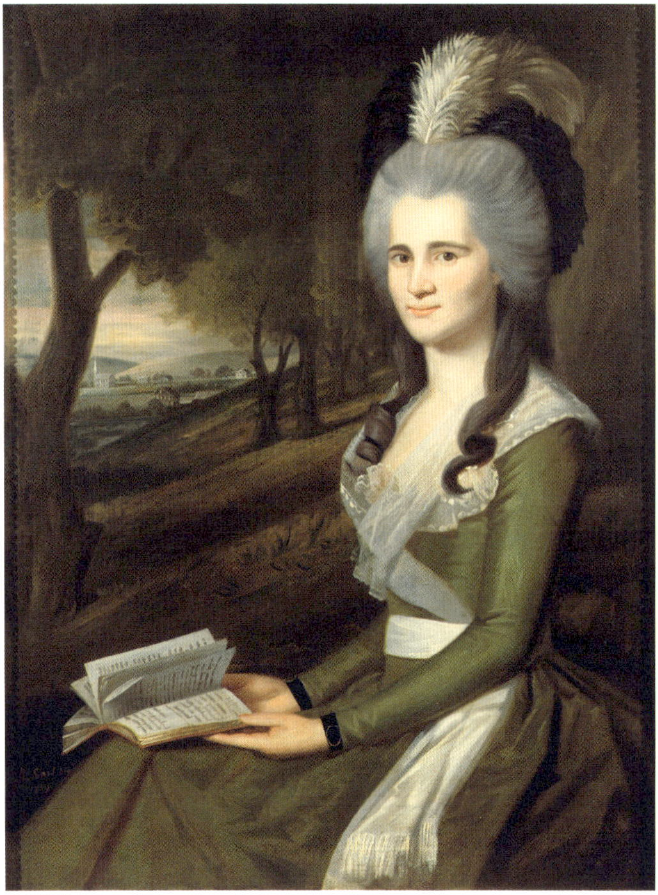

EVERYTHING IS FASHIONABLE about Esther Boardman, sister of Elijah (OPPOSITE), in Ralph Earl's portrait of her from 1789 (ABOVE): the hat with feather trim; the *lévite* dress, popularized by Marie Antoinette in particular in the 1780s; and the book of poetry. No colleges in America admitted women at that time; a little over a century later, four-fifths did.

RALPH EARL, FROM WORCESTER COUNTY, Massaschuetts, had a chequered career: in London with artist Benjamin West not long after American independence; plucked from debtor's prison in New York to paint this portrait in safer Connecticut in 1789; and descending into alcoholism in later life. Elijah Boardman, who had fought in the Revolutionary War when only sixteen, later a senator and here a merchant draper, combines textiles (with prominent British tax stamp) with Shakespeare's plays, Milton's *Paradise Lost* and the *London Magazine* for 1786 in his New Milford store.

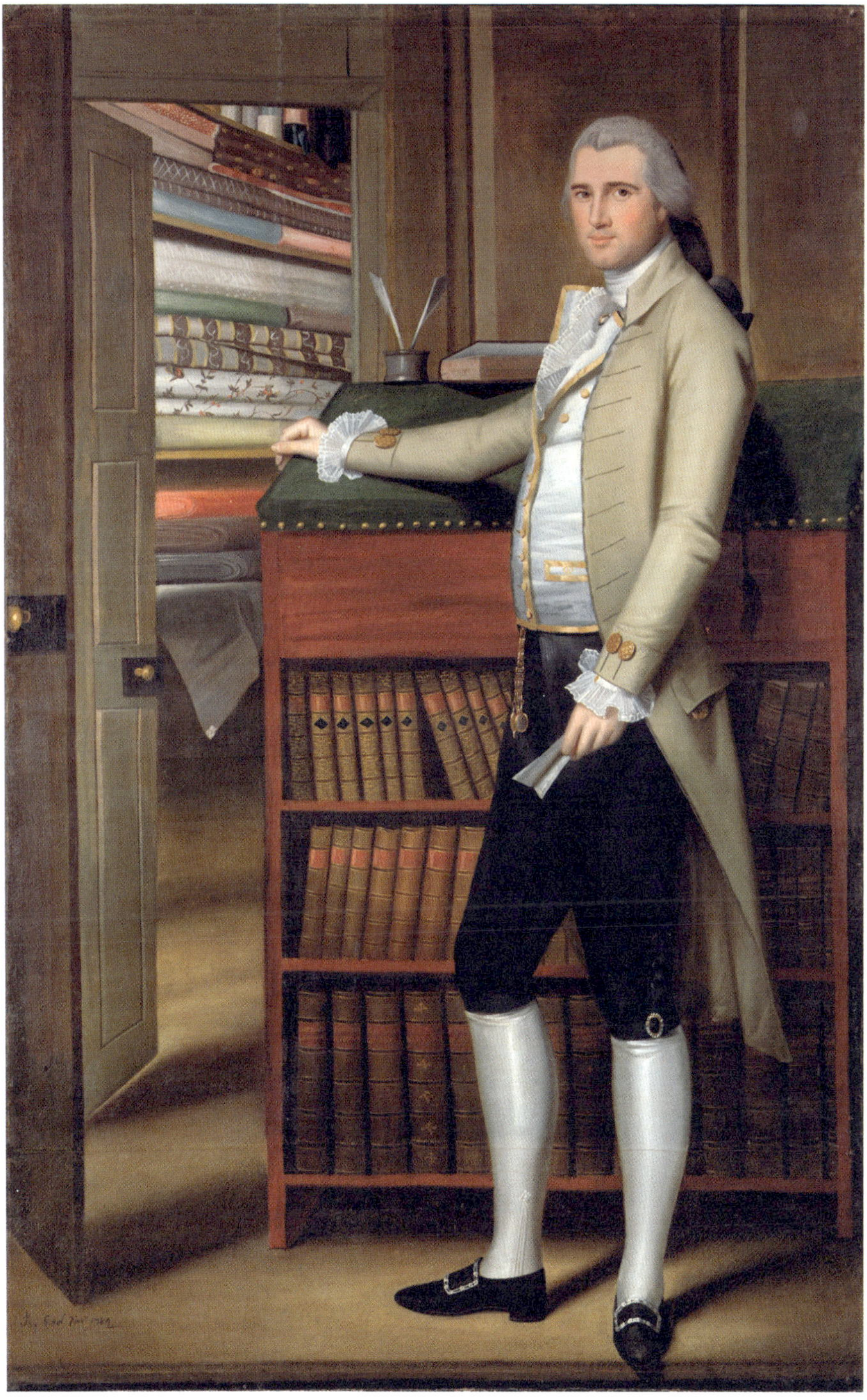

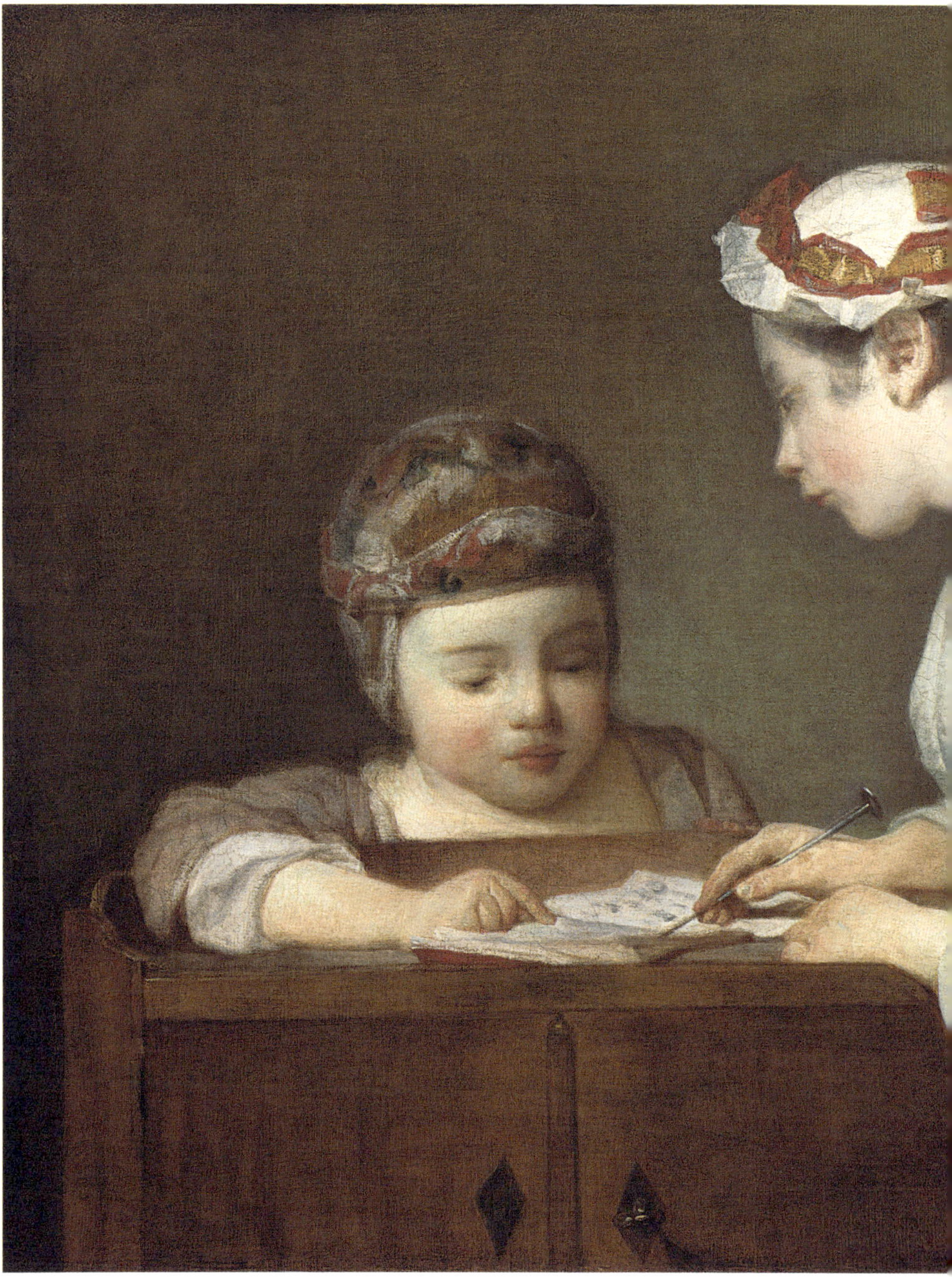

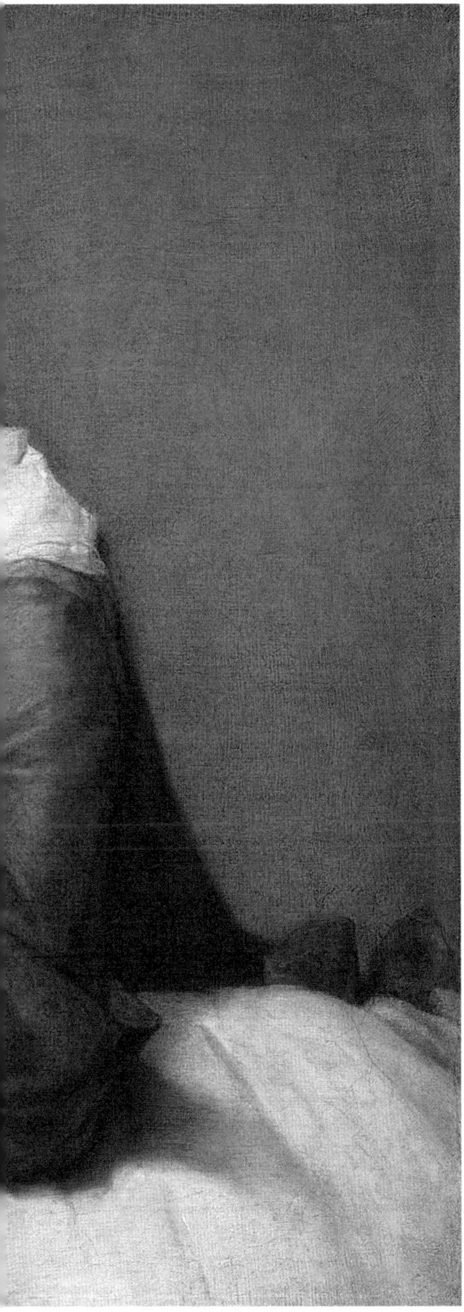

THERE ARE AT LEAST THREE extant versions of Chardin's *The Little Schoolmistress* – one each in Dublin, London and Washington DC (the version pictured here) – as well as a further variant engraved for '*le gros public*' by François-Bernard Lépicié in 1740. They all made the same point, with an exquisite skill that inspired Lucian Freud to make his own painting and etching of the subject well over two and a half centuries later. The young pupil, possibly the child of Chardin's furniture-dealer and cabinet-maker friend Monsieur Lenoir, and painted with less definition, must aspire to the level of attainment of the young woman, conceivably a sibling. Education and the book were inseparable.

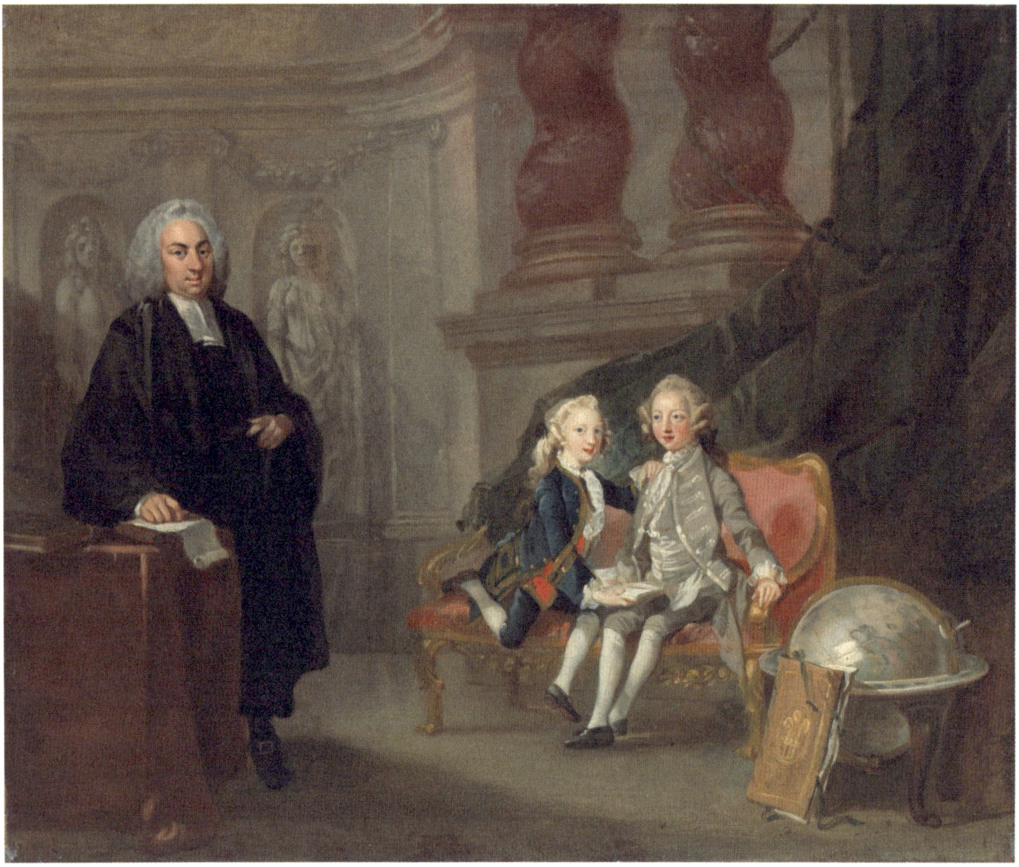

GEORGE III IS SEEN here as a boy (at far right) in about 1748–49, in a painting that exists in several versions by a founder of the Royal Academy, Richard Wilson; also pictured are George's brother Prince Edward, later Duke of York and Albany, and their tutor, the formidable Dr Francis Ayscough. George was a great lover of books: he renewed the royal collection and left some 65,000 volumes to the British Museum as the foundation for a national collection. Indeed, books and education were essentials for the royal heir. He was the first British monarch to study science; he was taught maths, agriculture, constitutional law and other subjects; and he could read and write German and English before he was eight years old.

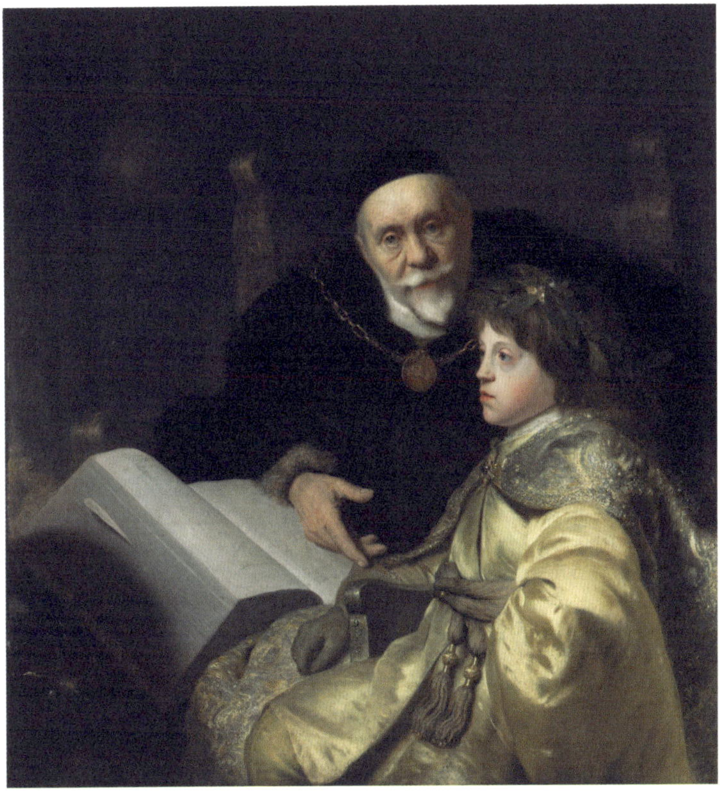

WHEN PRINCE CHARLES LOUIS OF THE PALATINATE arrived at the English court of his uncle Charles I – his mother's younger brother – on 21 November 1635, he was received graciously. 'May your flame flie': the playwright and actor Thomas Heywood's courtly homage, which also made comparisons with Charlemagne, encouraged the eighteen-year-old exile. The mood was not to last: the prince was intent on restoration of his lands, lost by his intellectual, mystic father in conflict with the Habsburg emperor Ferdinand II, and fell out with the unresponsive Charles I. This portrait of Charles Louis in 1631, with his tutor Wolrad von Plessen, locating the two figures in a distant past through their clothing, reflected a common theme for its Dutch artist, Jan Lievens, close associate of Rembrandt. It is believed to represent them as Aristotle and the young Alexander the Great. The boy dreams; the teacher connects with the viewer; the anachronistic book (if this is indeed the 4th century BCE) retains its serious intent.

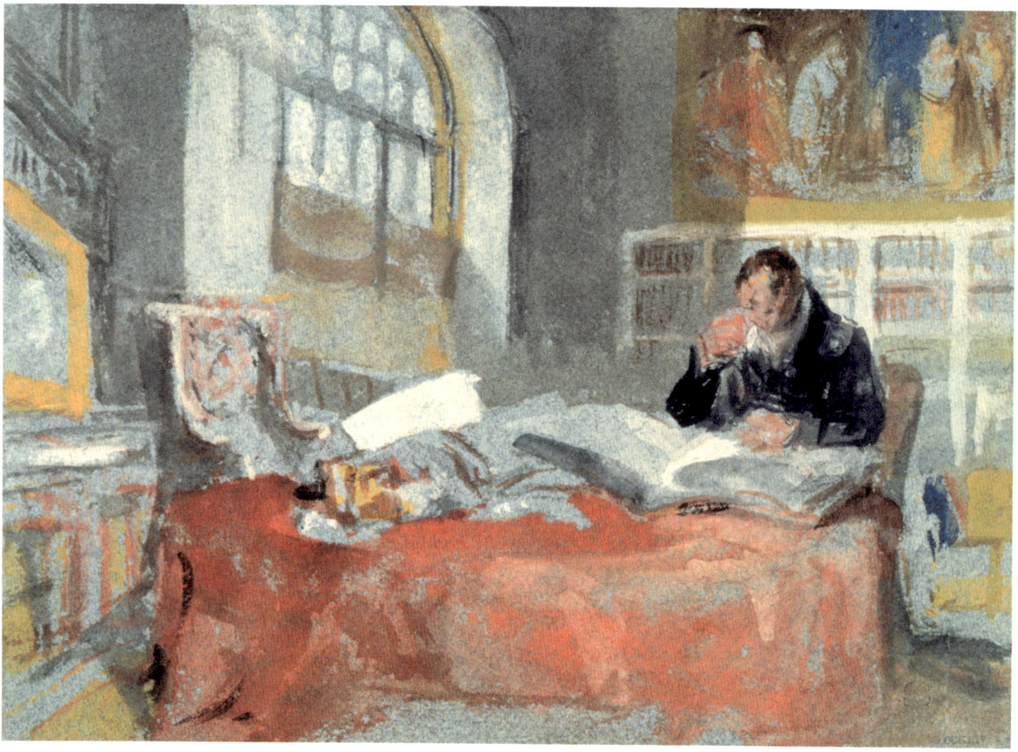

BEHIND J. M. W. TURNER'S informal gouache and watercolour of the Old Library at Petworth House in Sussex (1827) was a long story – not without some falling out – of friendship between the great artist and a great art patron and collector, George Wyndham, 3rd Lord Egremont. But even the larger-than-life libertine aristocrat ('in his time Petworth was a great inn', observed the renowned diarist Charles Greville) was not allowed to enter the studio Turner was given at the house without first identifying himself. Turner was present at Wyndham's funeral in 1837 – in borrowed mourning dress.

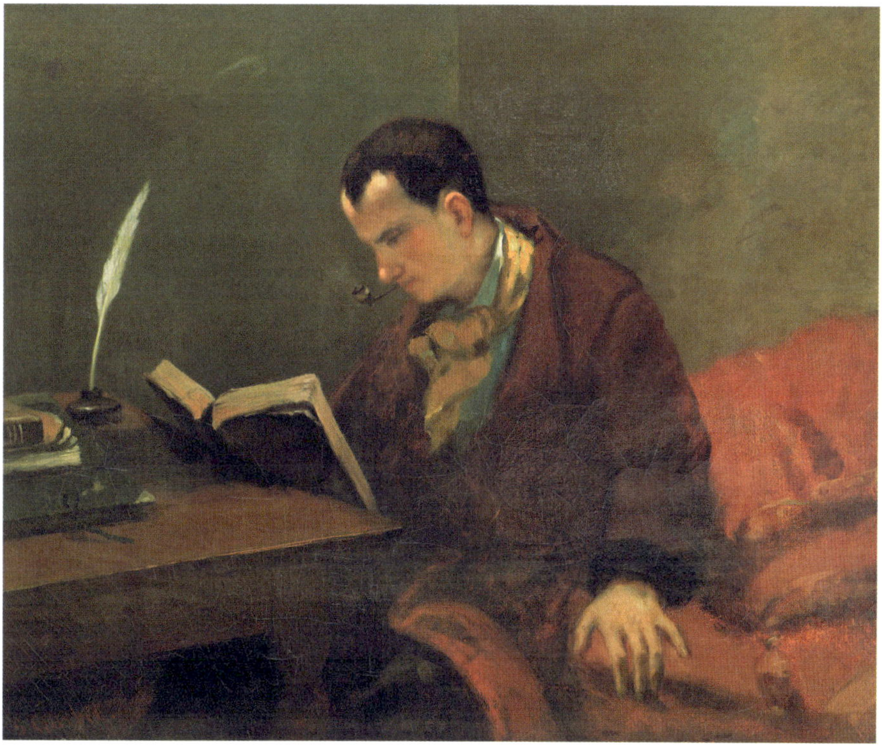

IT TOOK A BRAVE ARTIST to tackle a portrait of the many-sided chameleon (ham actor, according to French author Jules Vallès) Charles Baudelaire. In Gustave Courbet's 1848 painting, realism has been applied more to the book and quill than to the subject, perhaps as well, since the forthright writer declared that photography was a mere refuge for a painter 'too ill-endowed or too lazy to complete his studies'. Courbet confessed that he did not know how to finish the portrait: 'every day his face changes'. The two drifted apart, and later, when reviewing the Salon of 1859, Baudelaire suggested that portraiture – not at all a 'modest' art – needed not only intelligence and the skills of a historian but also 'the power of divination'.[12]

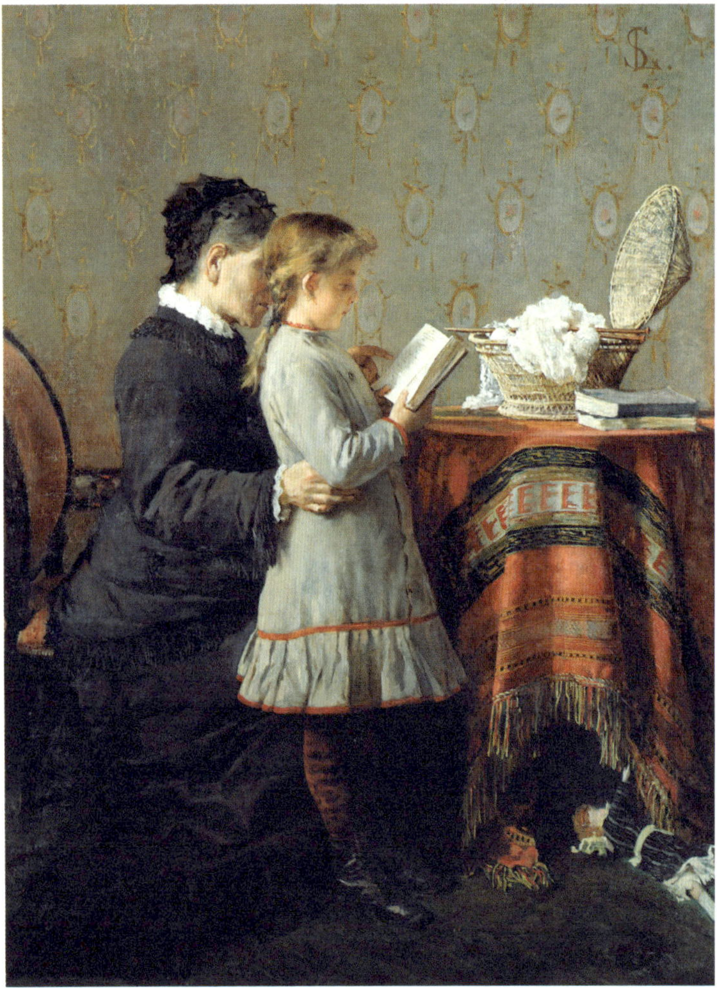

MODERN STUDIES have shown how education in Renaissance Florence had a strong focus on commercial and mathematical skills, although other Tuscan towns concentrated on grammar and Latin. But many centuries later, when the Tuscan artist Silvestro Lega painted *The Reading Lesson* (1881), middle-class values across the Western world prioritized reading skills as an essential for making the modern world.

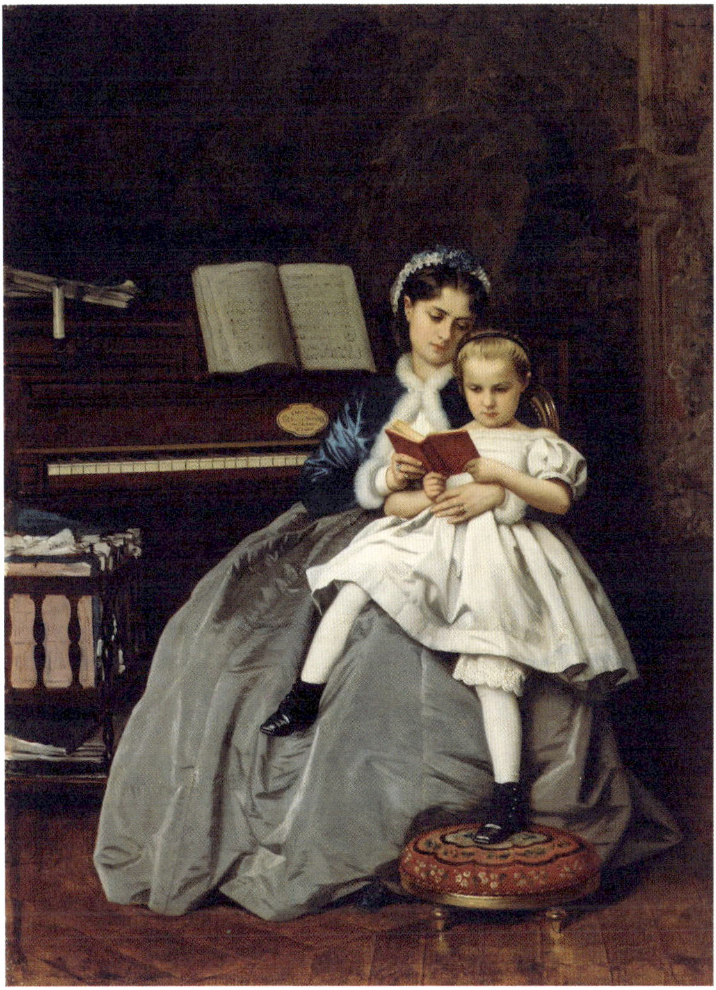

BY THE TIME Auguste Toulmouche painted *The Reading Lesson* (1865), education in France, beginning with the importance of learning to read, had become ingrained as a Second Empire precept for the bourgeoisie. Clearly, neither mother nor child were what Zola called 'Toulmouche's delicious dolls'; other paintings by the artist matched that description.

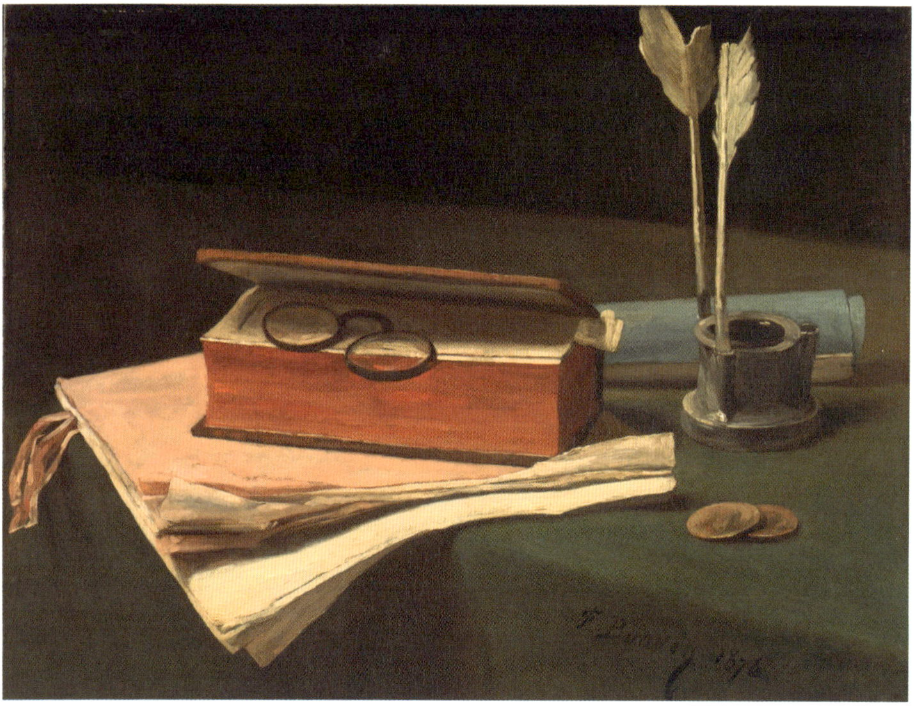

FRANÇOIS BONVIN, who worked in the Paris police headquarters until 1850 and was largely self-taught, had two great advantages: the support of the collector Louis La Caze, who welcomed him – with Degas, Manet and other artists – to his salon on rue du Cherche-Midi; and his own determined study of the art and artists of the past – Dutch and Flemish 17th-century vanitas paintings, as well as Chardin and the genre scenes of Pieter de Hooch in particular. This still life (ABOVE) dates from 1876.

THE ITALIAN BAROQUE ARTIST Guercino came from Cento, between Bologna and Ferrara, where he painted this portrait (*c.* 1626–28; OPPOSITE) of the lawyer and city councillor Francesco Righetti. Righetti, himself an author, holds Julius Clarus's influential handbook on criminal law; on the shelves are parts of key works in the history of Western jurisprudence. For many centuries, the title of a book was variously placed on the tail-edge or the fore-edge – or in the position familiar to us today: the spine. Matters of design apart, legal publishing reinforced the authority of books.

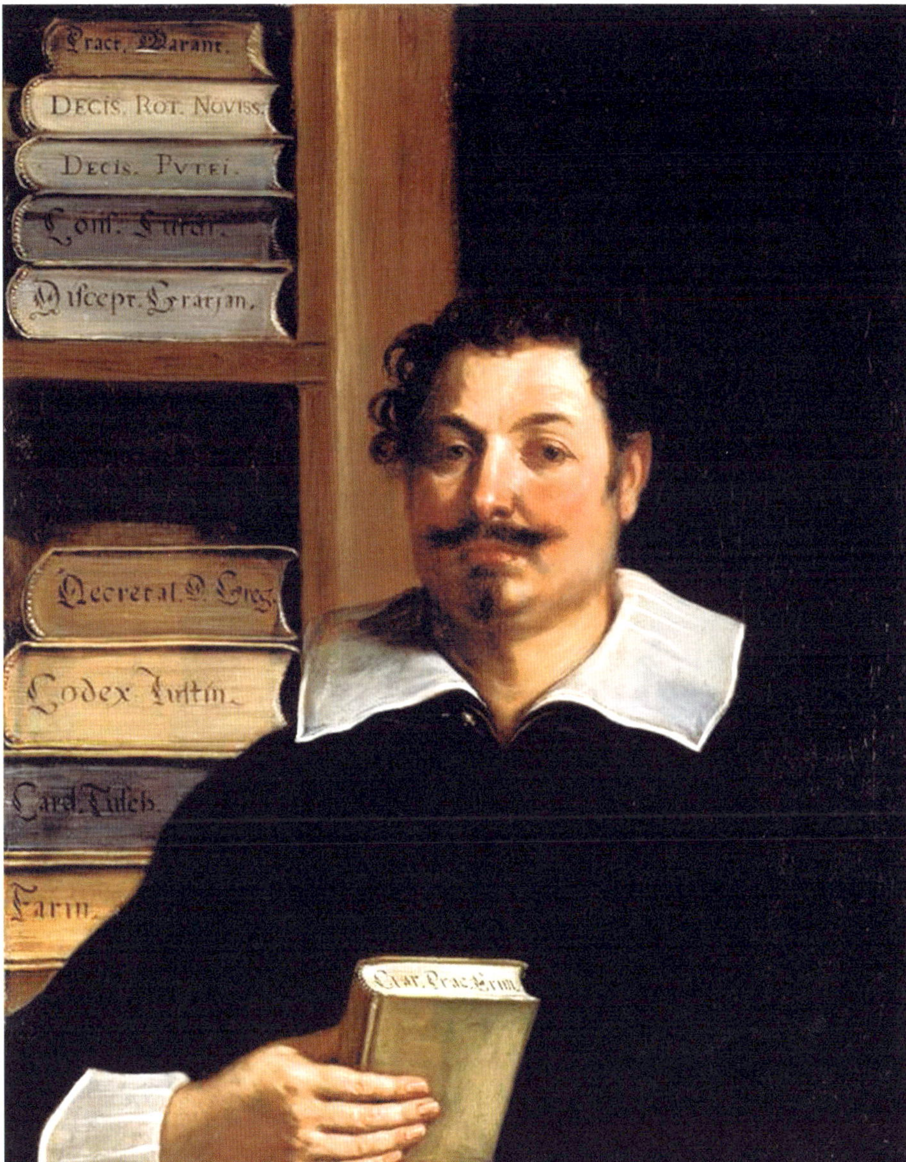
DECIS. ROT. NOVISS.
DECIS. PVTEI.
Codex

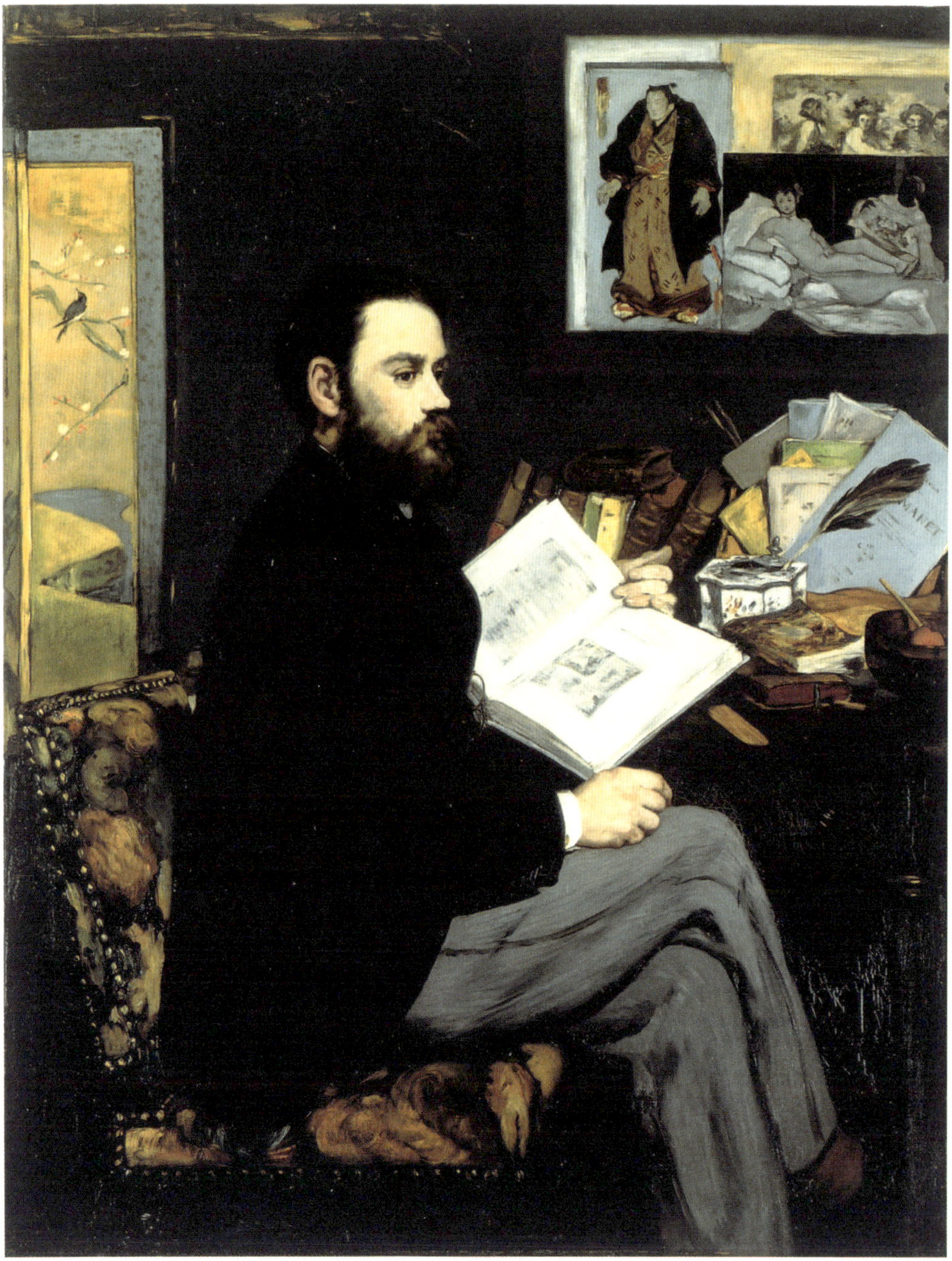

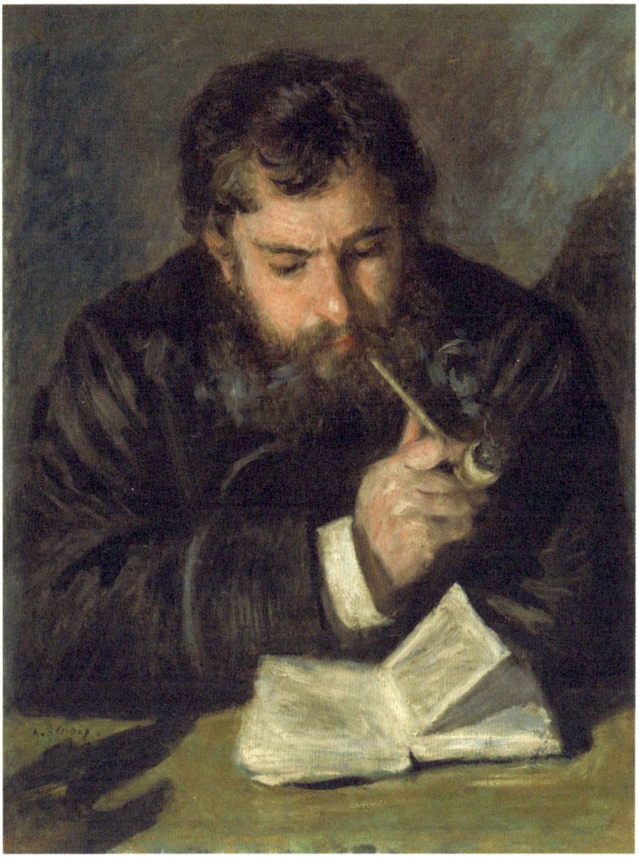

ARTISTS ALSO PAINTED other artists with books. The Swiss painter Charles Gleyre numbered among his irreverent pupils Renoir and, briefly, Monet in the 1860s, which was how the two young artists met, together with Alfred Sisley and Frédéric Bazille. Both Renoir and Monet struggled in their early career. Renoir painted this portrait of Monet (ABOVE) in 1872, and another – also with pipe, but less intense and with the subject reading a newspaper – in the same year.

THE MEETING OF Edouard Manet and Emile Zola in February 1866, via an introduction from the landscape painter Antoine Guillemet, proved timely for both parties. An article by Zola, later extended (its blue cover is visible on the table in the painting, OPPOSITE), defended Manet against his many critics; the publication of *Thérèse Raquin* in 1867 made Zola a celebrity; and Manet painted his portrait the following year, the writer holding – in all probability – the first volume of one of the artist's favourite books, Charles Blanc's *L'Histoire des peintres*. In May 1868 Zola wrote of the long sittings with Manet, the artist bright-eyed, rigid-featured and with an absorption so complete that it was as if he were not there. The French artist Odilon Redon described the result as more a still life than a portrait of a person.

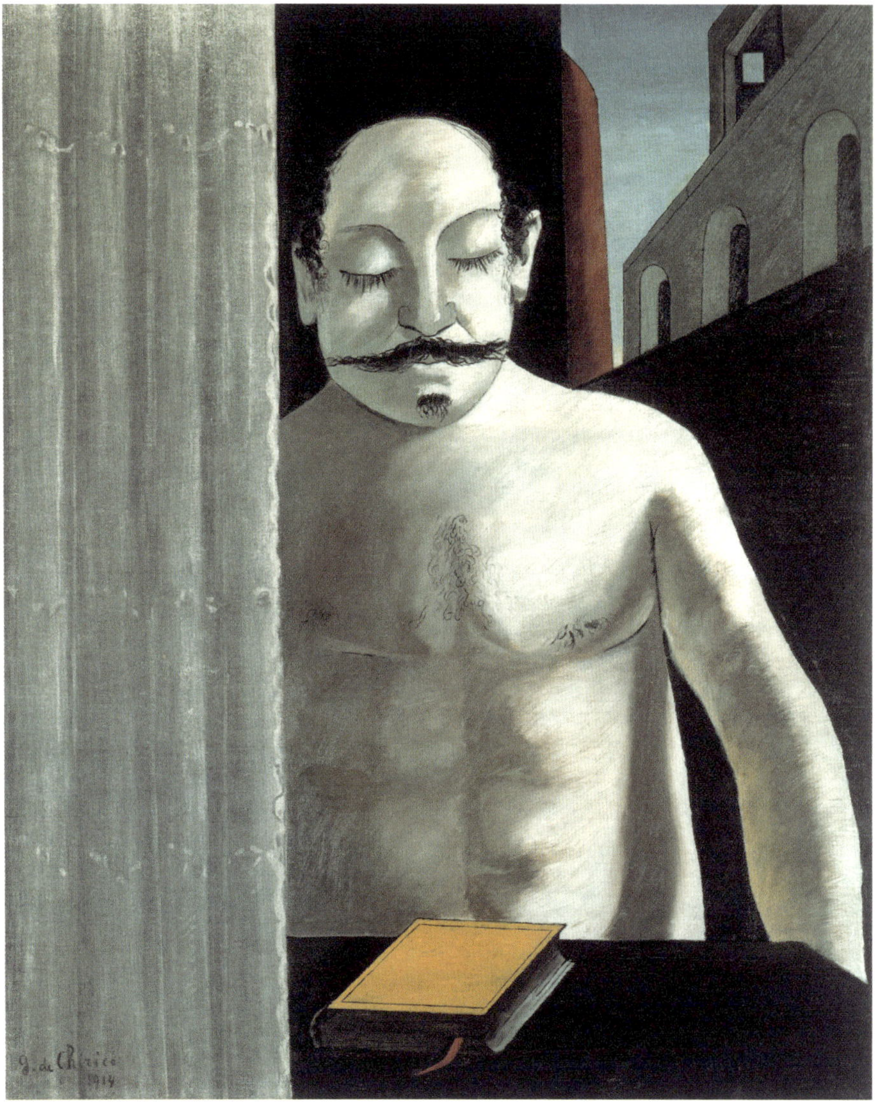

THE BOOK TOOK ON new symbolic functions in the 20th century. Giorgio de Chirico's *The Child's Brain* (1914), which so hypnotized André Breton when he saw it in a Paris gallery window as he passed on a bus that he felt compelled to buy it, is believed to reflect Freud's theories of castration anxiety and the Oedipus complex. Is this De Chirico's father, with moustache of masculinity and long, feminine eyelashes, engaged in hidden masturbation? And is the red ribbon marker a penis, with the book itself his parents' lovemaking?

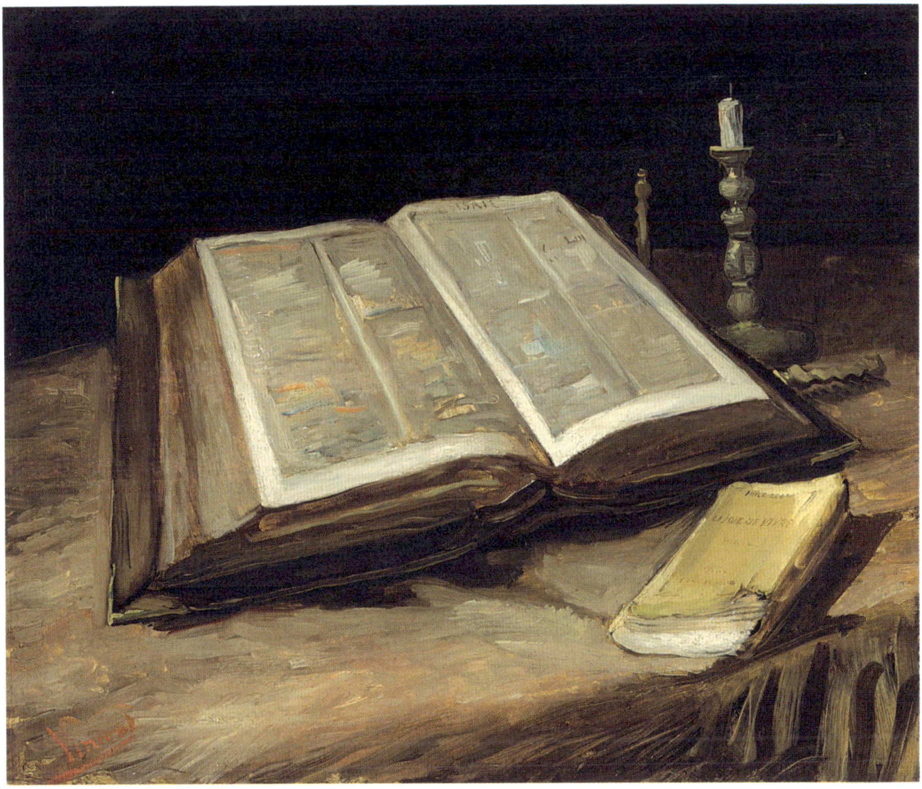

VAN GOGH CONTRASTS two starkly different approaches to life in his 1885 still life: the blind faith of his strict pastor father, who had just died, reflected in an 1882 printing of the Bible, open at Isaiah 53, full of the suffering and rejection of Christ; and the world of Zola's recently published *La Joie de vivre* in front of it, a world in which writers, as Van Gogh said, 'paint life as we feel it ourselves'.[13] Not that there was any more joy in Zola than in Isaiah: the novel is full of unhappiness, malice, betrayal and suicide, albeit with a brave attempt by the central character, Pauline Quenu, to keep hope alive.

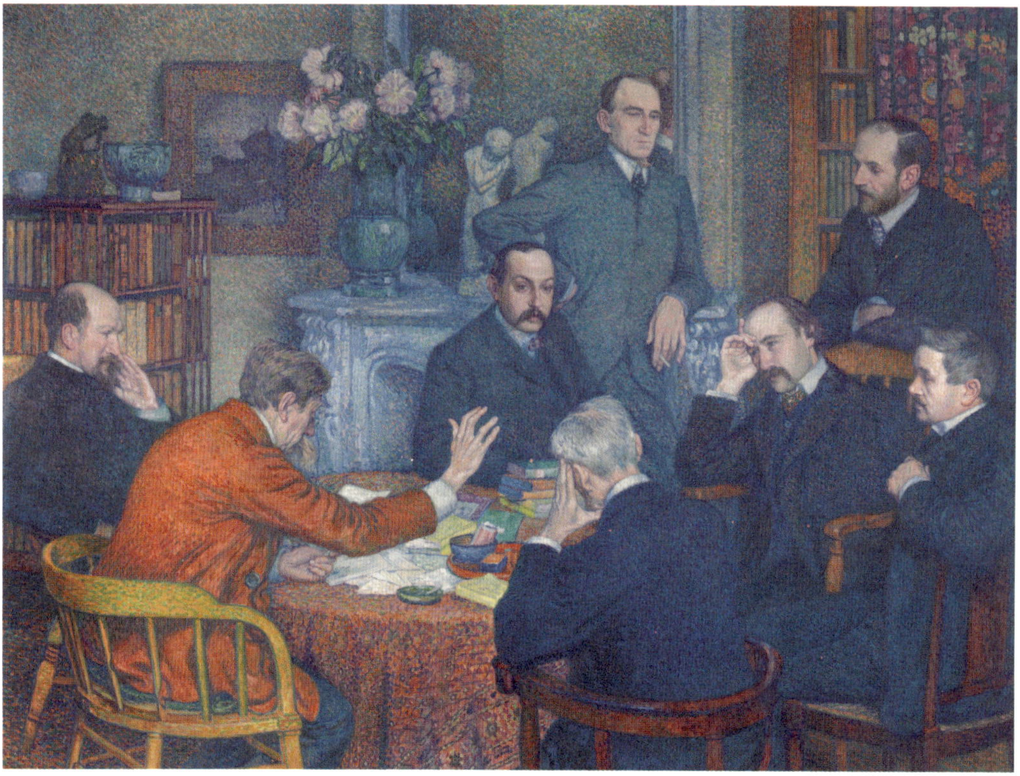

READING COULD BE both a private and a social activity; it could also combine pleasure with intellectual excitement. In Théo van Rysselberghe's *The Reading* (1903; ABOVE), Emile Verhaeren – a Belgian-born Symbolist poet and the artist's lifelong friend – reads to a distinguished gathering that includes (at far right) the essayist, dramatist and poet Maurice Maeterlinck, who would win a Nobel Prize less than a decade later.

CONVENTIONALLY, Gauguin's 1889 portrait of his apparently admiring artist friend Jacob Meyer de Haan (OPPOSITE), designed to decorate part of a door at their lodgings in Gauguin's 'first Tahiti in France' – Le Pouldu on the Brittany coast – was a tribute to Meyer de Haan's esoteric knowledge.[14] Perhaps instead the lasciviousness of his gaze had something to do with the way in which the Jewish hunchback, in competition with Gauguin, had won the affection of Marie Henry, their landlady; and perhaps the themes of Milton's *Paradise Lost* and Thomas Carlyle's heavily anti-semitic *Sartor Resartus* on the table were not acknowledgments of his learning.

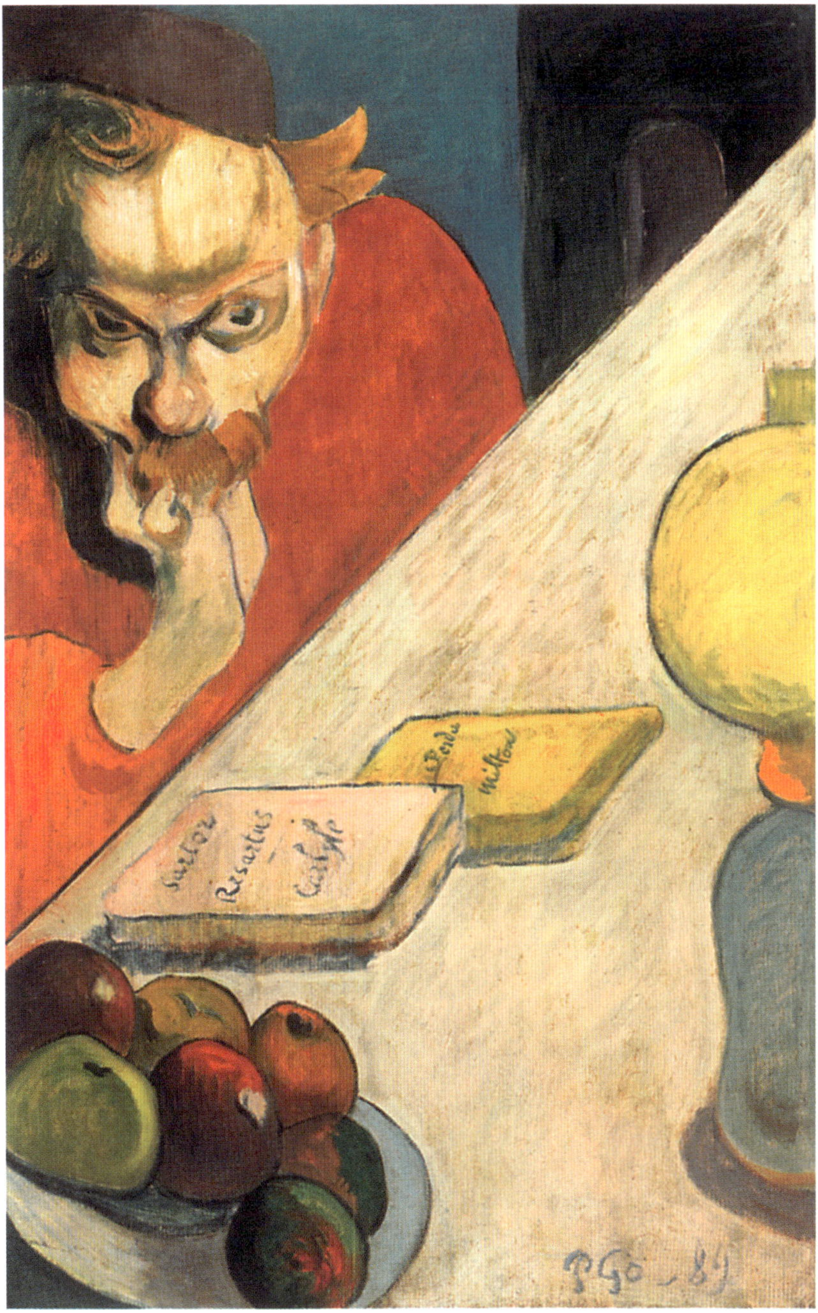
Sartor
Resartus
Milton

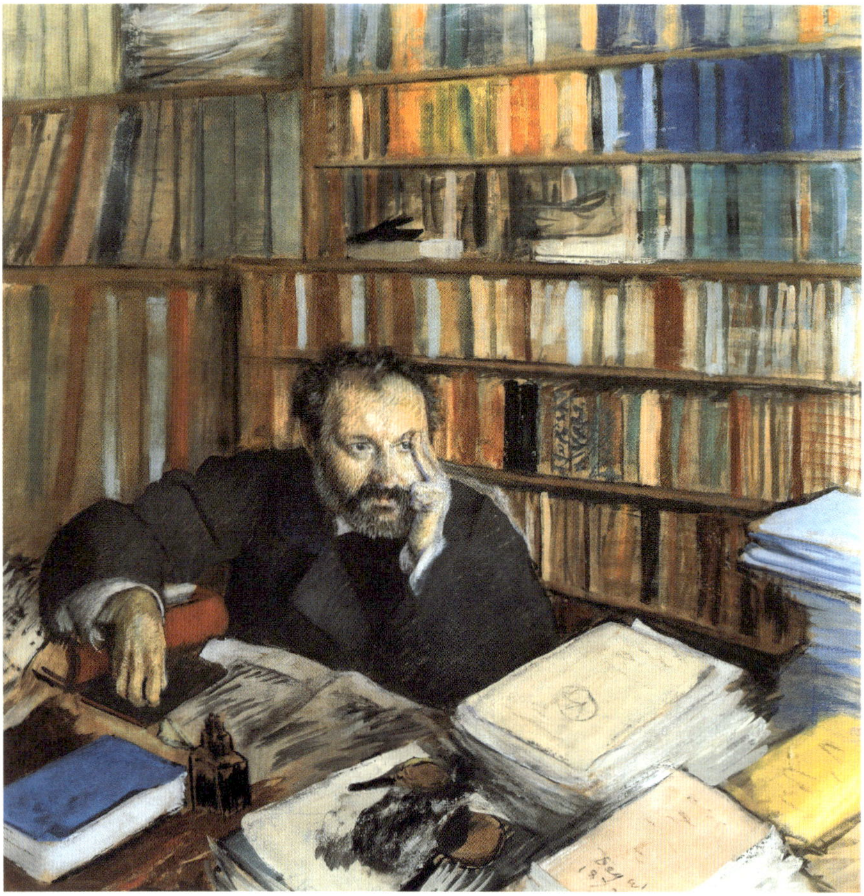

LIFE WAS SOMETIMES TURBULENT for the creative habitués of the Café Guerbois, Paris. The art critic and novelist Edmond Duranty – here depicted in his study by Degas in 1879, so happy with his books – was challenged to a duel in the café by Manet after one of his reviews. Zola was Manet's second; Duranty was wounded; but the friendships continued. Duranty's essay 'The New Painting', published at the time of the second Impressionist exhibition in 1876, was the first true attempt to give intellectual coherence to the new style of painting of 'modern life'. He referred to Degas as a man of the rarest talent and intellect, and indeed the ideas expressed seem very much those of Degas himself. Later, approaching death, Duranty dealt with that poignant dilemma of bibliophiles everywhere, what to do with one's books. He sold most of them – and died a year later.

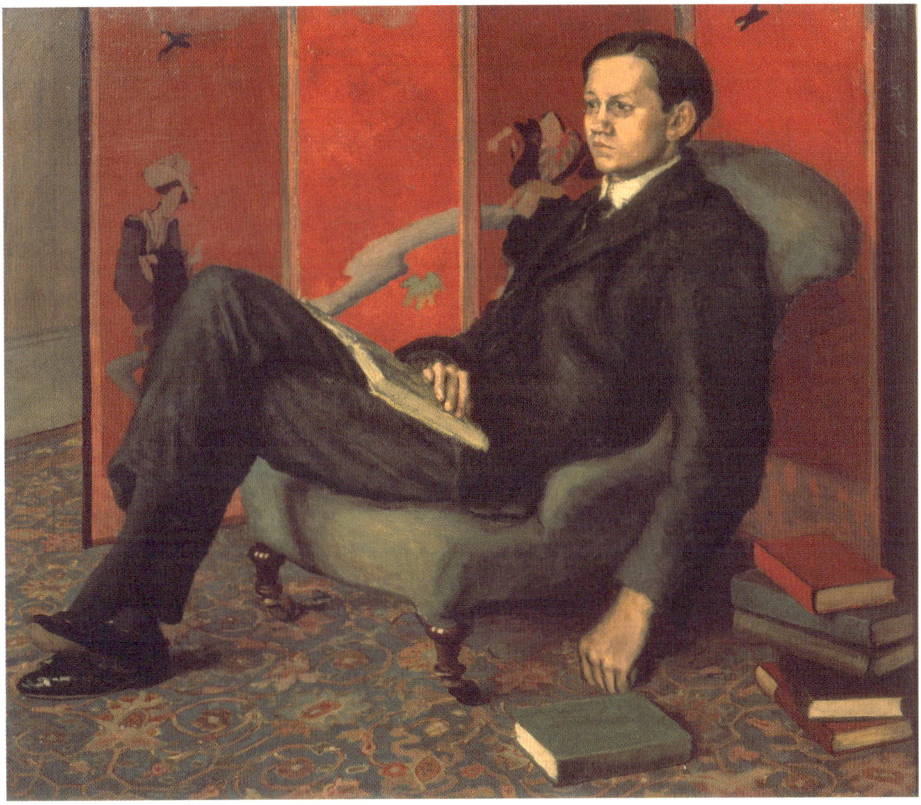

THE BLOOMSBURY SET reinforced the centuries-long message that art, books and writers were central to life. Duncan Grant paints his cousin James Strachey, younger brother of Lytton, in 1910, just down from Cambridge and writing for *The Spectator*. Later, Strachey's translation, made with his wife, Alix, of the complete works of Freud into English was so widely praised that weighty consideration was given to translating it back into German. Grant painted many people reading, including James's sister Marjorie, overcome with emotion after finishing Dostoevsky's *Crime and Punishment*.

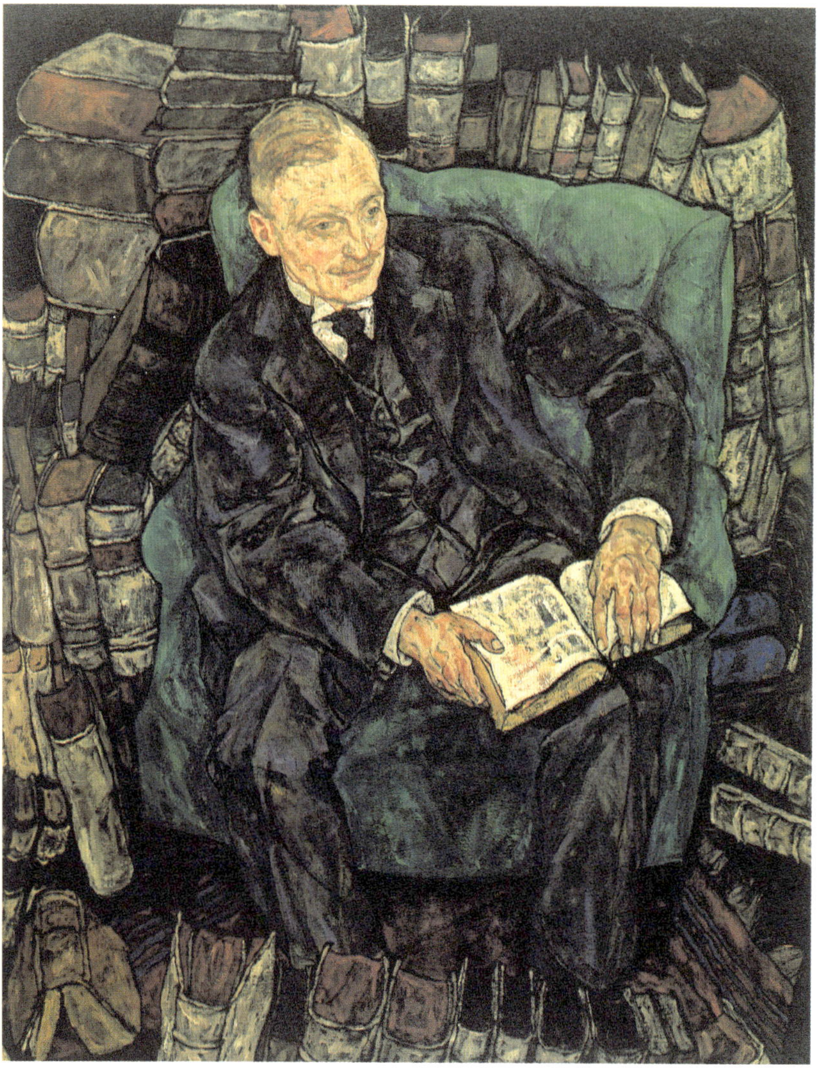

THE VIENNESE INDUSTRIALIST Hugo Koller becomes the gentle scholar, surrounded by his books, in Egon Schiele's portrait of 1918 – the year before the artist died. Schiele enjoyed some of the rare books in Koller's large library at his country house in Oberwaltersdorf, just south of Vienna. Koller's Romanian wife, Broncia Koller-Pinell, herself an artist whose reputation would later suffer when the Nazis came to power, painted Schiele and his wife around this time.

GUSTAVE GEFFROY WAS a novelist and an art historian, the first biographer of Monet (who was so little forthcoming that he gave one-word answers to all of Geffroy's questions). It was Monet who introduced Cézanne to Geffroy, a relationship that resulted in this 1895 portrait but was not a happy one. Despite three months of regular sittings, 'the meagre result' (as Cézanne wrote to Monet in July) left hands and face unfinished, and the two men never met again. The Cubists disagreed with Cézanne's own self-deprecating verdict, and, with hindsight, we can see why.

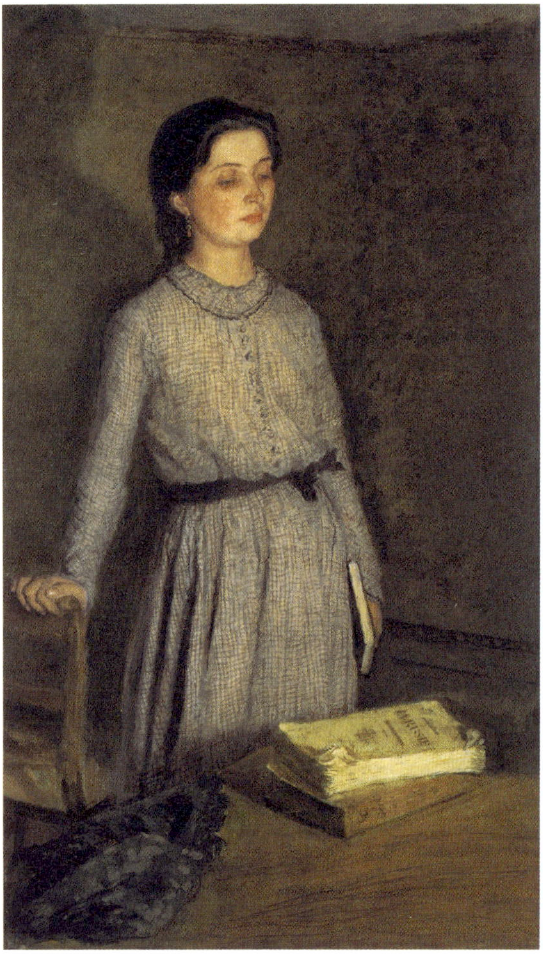

DOROTHY MCNEILL, 'Dorelia', wintered in Toulouse on a walking tour with Gwen John in 1903. The critic Laurence Binyon, famous for his First World War poem 'For the Fallen' (1914), summed up John's portrait of Dorelia, *The Student* (1903–04; ABOVE), to perfection in the *Saturday Review*. For this was 'intensity', as he said, but of a 'quiet and shy' kind, not common in contemporary art, yet so much more important than flashy brilliance. The travel books – one of them *La Russie* – draw our gaze to Dorelia's face: functional furnishing.

'NERVY', 'RAWLY EROTIC', 'highly wrought', 'unrelenting', 'angst-ridden', 'on the edge' – these are the kinds of words critics have applied to Egon Schiele. This 1914 painting of his desk (OPPOSITE) came after an unhappy prison experience for displaying indecent drawings. Sometimes, when he shows some of his books, or in his landscapes of the hilly fields of Krumau, Austria, we can experience a calmer view of his prodigious abilities. Even so, perhaps the phallic arrangement of and fetish feel to the objects he owned, as here, hinted at his true tastes.

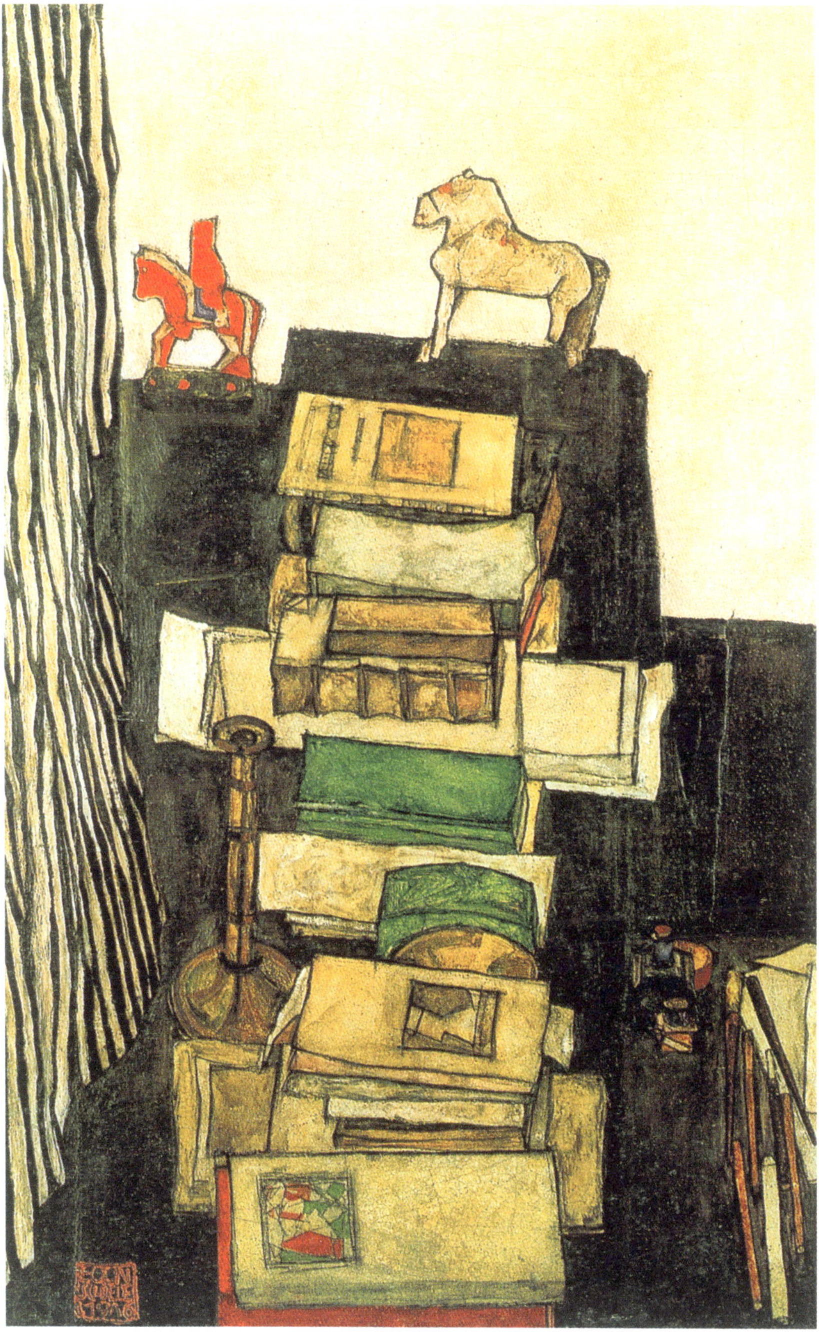

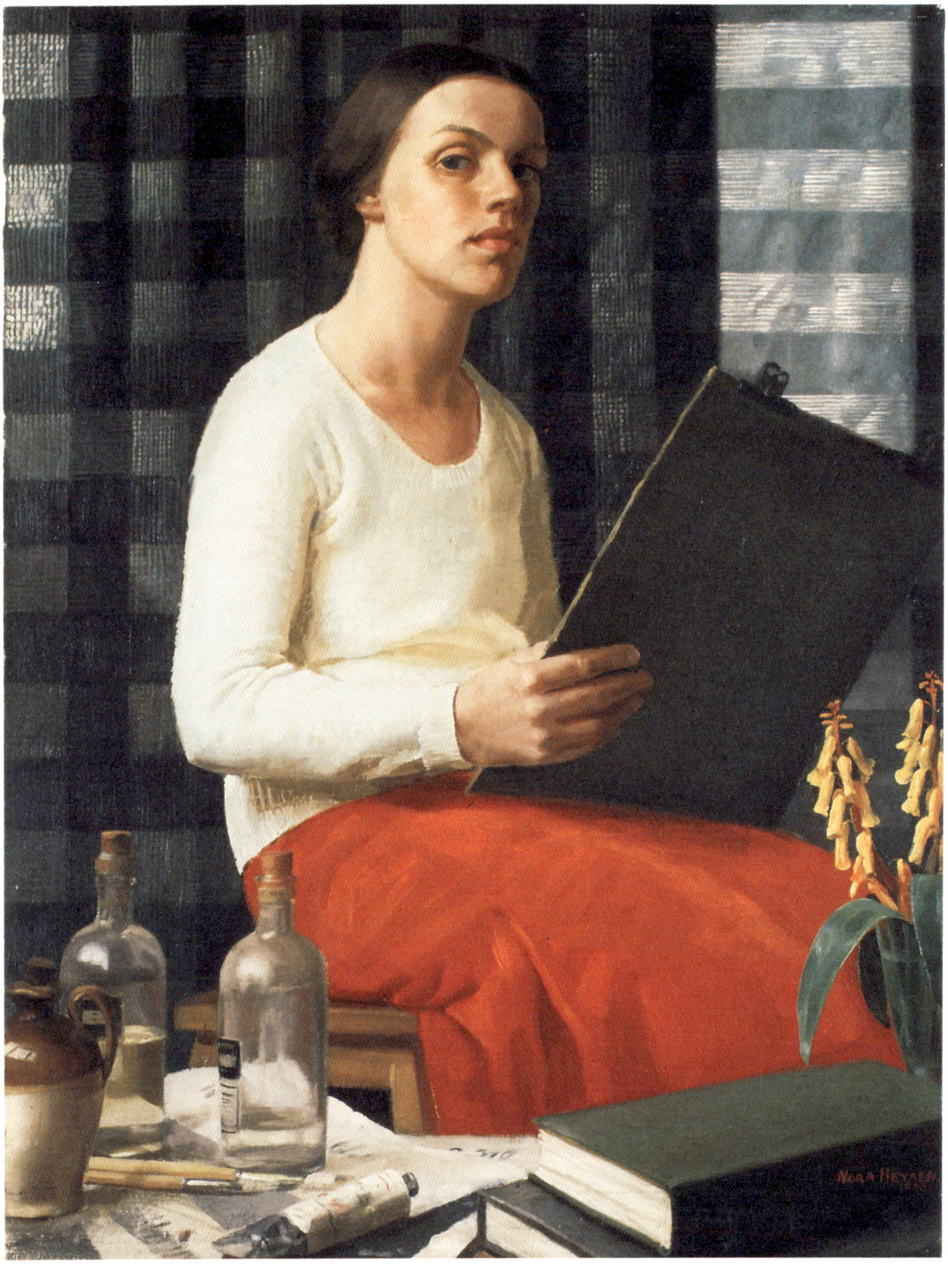
NORA HEYSEN

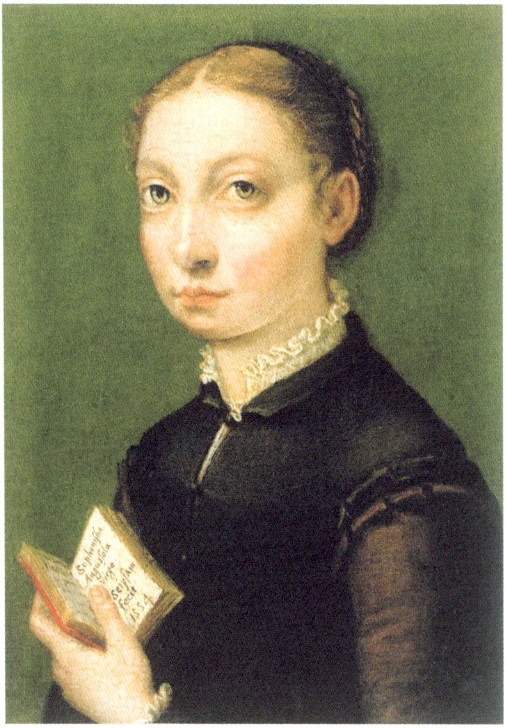

SOFONISBA ANGUISSOLA, from a noble family of Cremona in northern Italy, managed to impress both Michelangelo, whom she met in Rome in 1550, and Vasari, who declared that she applied herself 'with greater study and better grace than any other woman of her time'. Heavily supported and encouraged by her father, but hardly finding the 'footing of perfect equality with men' that the great 19th-century cultural historian Jacob Burckhardt identified as a feature of the Renaissance, she managed in this self-portrait (ABOVE) to display what Castiglione had called *discreta modesta* while asserting her achievement in the book of love sonnets or devotion she holds open at the inscription, 'The Virgin Sofonisba Anguissola made this herself in 1554'.

HOW MUCH CHANGED for women artists in the almost four hundred years between Sofonisba Anguissola (ABOVE) and Nora Heysen's self-portrait of 1933 (OPPOSITE)? Sadly, not as much as we might suppose. Heysen, daughter of the well-known Australian artist Hans Heysen, did win the prestigious Archibald Prize, under the auspices of what became the Art Gallery of New South Wales, but the headline in the *Australian Women's Weekly* of 4 February 1939 summed up the cultural attitudes of many: 'Girl Painter Who Won Art Prize is also Good Cook'. The Australian Tonalist artist and teacher Max Meldrum suggested that it was 'sheer lunacy' to expect women to do some things as well as men, and that their focus should be family, not career. Nora Heysen's gaze, in her self-portrait, is sufficient answer.

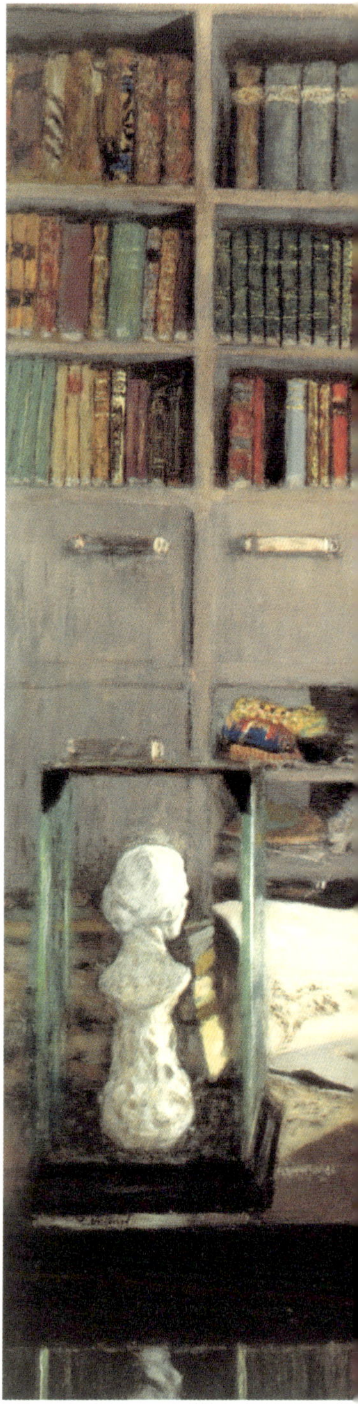

EDOUARD VUILLARD AND JEANNE LANVIN lived in the same building on rue Saint-Honoré, central Paris, in the early 1890s and were also the same age. Vuillard said that he painted not portraits but 'people at home', and this early 1930s evocation of a great figure of Parisian haute couture in the creative hub of her home-like headquarters, with pattern and other books, reflects that observation. Julian Barnes once brilliantly summed it up as 'a triumph of relevant detail'.

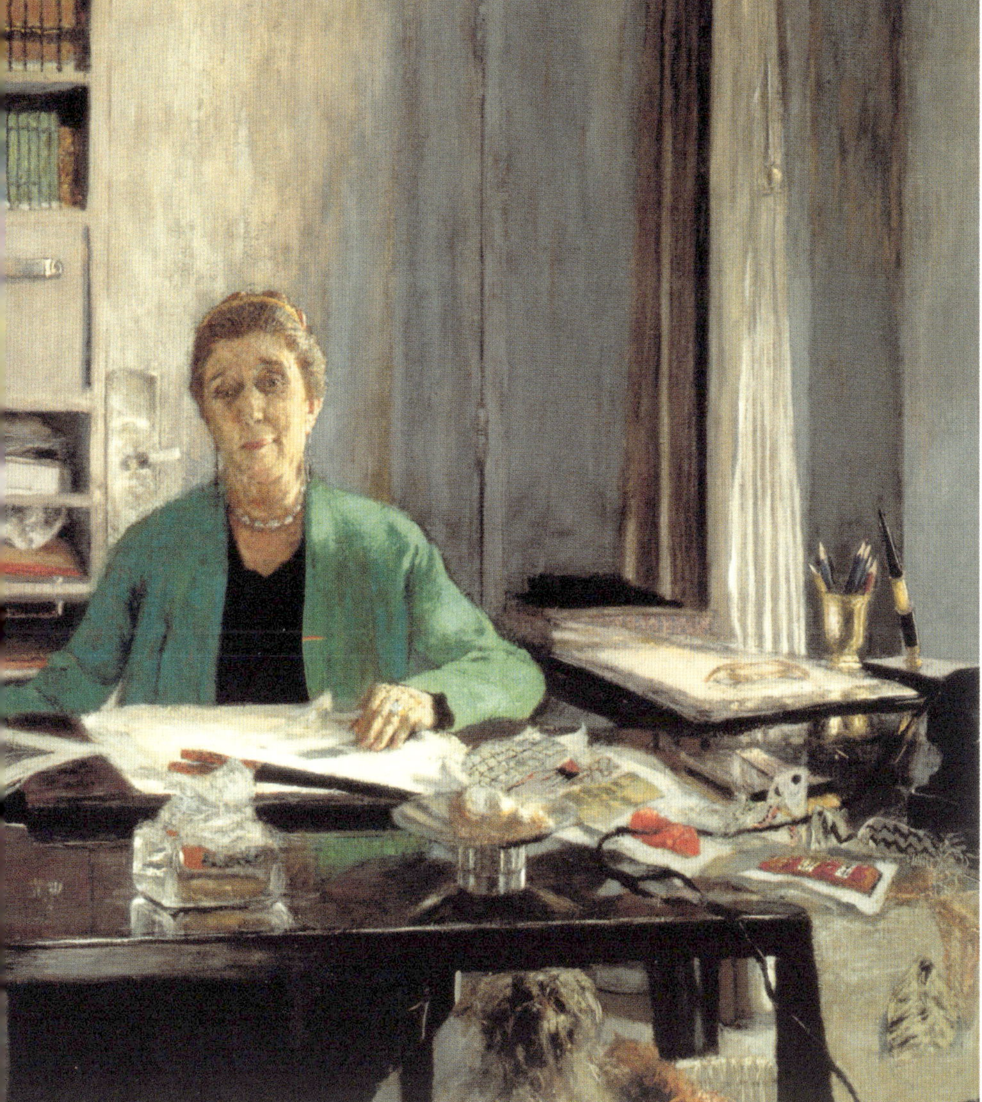

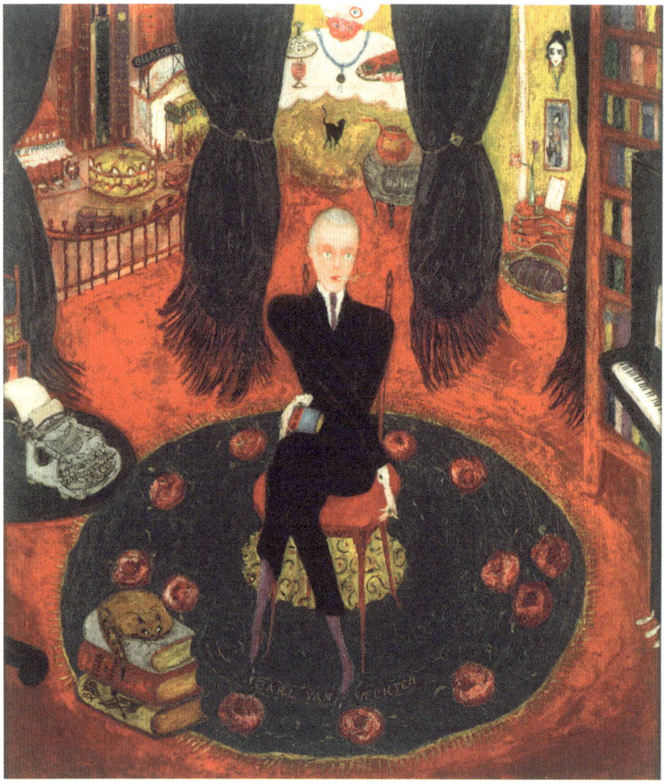

THE DELIGHTFULLY SELF-EFFACING Florine Stettheimer, who – said the curator and critic Henry McBride in his 1946 MoMA, New York, monograph on her – preferred not to exhibit but just to keep her pictures, nevertheless painted many portraits of her friends: Duchamp, Stieglitz and here, in a work from 1922, the photographer, writer, collector Carl Van Vechten. Van Vechten's cat is honoured by a seat on a pile of books. The middle book is Van Vechten's own *The Tiger in the House: A Cultural History of the Cat*, and the books and piano to his left were an appropriate backdrop for the circle of Greenwich Village bohemians, High Society high-flyers, Harlem writers and otherwise creative souls with whom he mixed.
The flamboyant Van Vechten, 'Papa Woojums', wrote to Gertrude Stein and Alice B. Toklas as 'Dear dear DEAR Woojumses! (pronounced Woo-Jums-Ez, pelase!'). His wife, Fania Mainhoff, is represented in the painting by what has been called a shrine: her dressing table. An actress, she appeared in a notorious performance of Frank Wedekind's *Spring Awakening*. The cast were arrested after one performance.

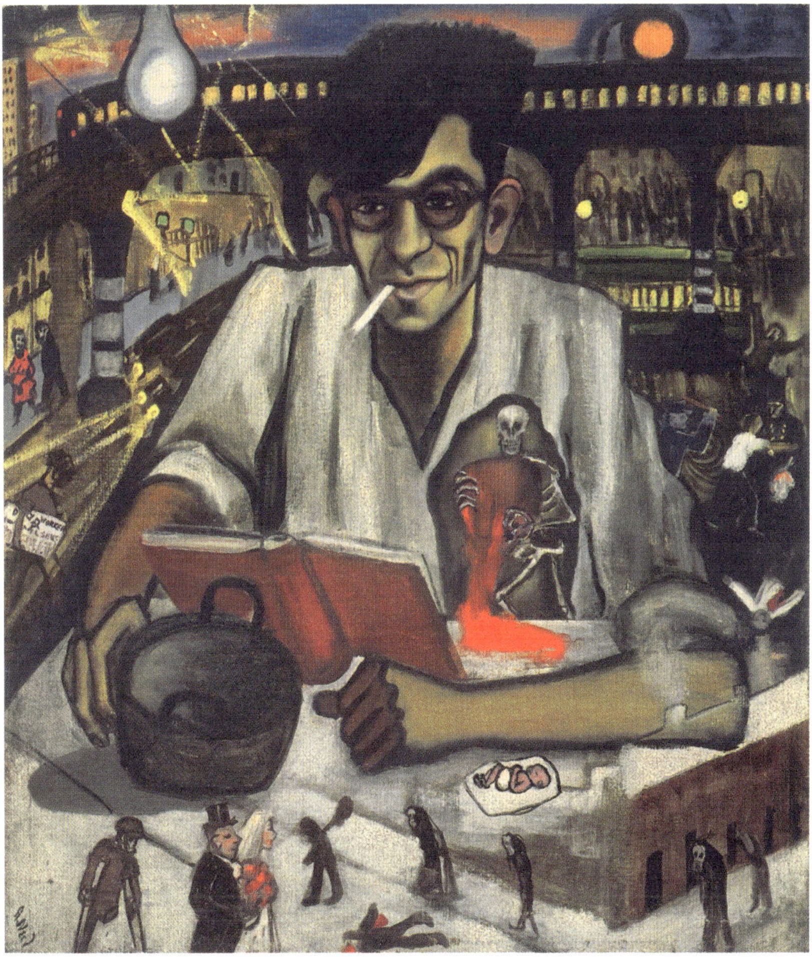

'TAKE THAT FAUNTLEROY OUT OF MY HEART', the poet Kenneth Fearing said to Alice Neel when she painted his portrait in 1935: it represented the bleeding heart of a man desperately saddened by the fate of the poor and downtrodden during the Great Depression, depicted in the foreground. Living in Greenwich Village, with her own life beset by suicidal feelings and an abusive marriage, Neel became friends with a cluster of bohemian, radical writers, Fearing among them (the Sixth Avenue elevated railway close to where he lived can be seen in the background of the painting). Only the book in the centre of the work was some kind of reassurance, just as it had been for nearly two thousand years.

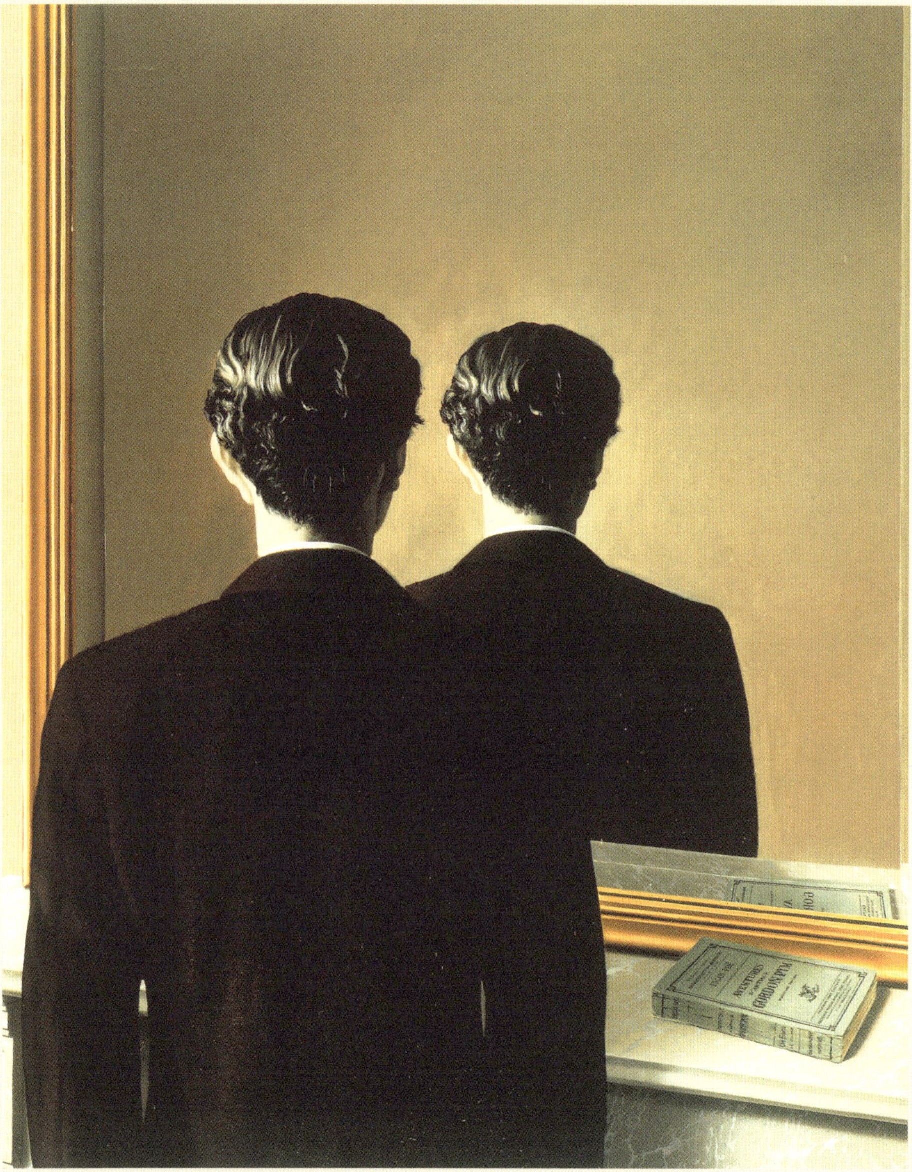

ONLY THE BOOK on the mantelpiece – a French edition of Edgar Allen Poe's *Narrative of Arthur Gordon Pym of Nantucket* – is properly reflected in Magritte's *La Reproduction interdite* (1937). Yet Poe's 1838 fantastical tale of a sea journey from Nantucket to Symzonia is itself surreal. We see what we see; we read what we read: art and books together.

NOTES

PREFACE

1 F. R. Grahame (pseudonym of Catherine Laura Johnstone), *The Progress of Science, Art, and Literature in Russia* (1865), p. 8.

2 Bertolt Brecht, 'Against Georg Lukács', *New Left Review*, 84 (1974), p. 51. Quoted in Janet Wolff, *The Social Production of Art* (2nd edn, 1993), p. 91.

3 Quoted in Alexander Ireland, *The Book-Lover's Enchiridion* (5th edn, 1888), 'Prelude of Mottoes'.

4 *Ibid.*, p. 289.

5 *Ibid.*, p. 312.

6 Richard D. Altick, *Paintings from Books: Art and Literature in Britain, 1760–1900* (1985), p. 399.

7 Quoted in Ireland, *op. cit.*, p. 200.

8 Kate Flint, *The Woman Reader, 1837–1914* (1993), p. 139.

9 Quoted in Lynda Nead, *Myths of Sexuality: Representations of Women in Victorian Britain* (pbk edn, 1990), p. 79.

10 John Ruskin, *Modern Painters* (6th edn, 1857), vol. 1, p. xxii.

11 A. Hyatt Mayor, *Prints and People: A Social History of Printed Pictures* (1971), n.p.

12 Ian Gadd (ed.), *The History of the Book in the West: 1455–1700* (2010), essay by David Cressy, p. 508.

CHAPTER 1

1 For Gutenberg, see Albert Kapr, *Johann Gutenberg: The Man and His Invention*, trans. Douglas Martin (1996); John Man, *The Gutenberg Revolution: The Story of a Genius and an Invention that Changed the World* (2002); Leslie Howsam (ed.), *The Cambridge Companion to the History of the Book* (2015).

2 Keith Houston, *The Book: A Cover-to-Cover Exploration of the Most Powerful Object of Our Time* (2016), p. 96.

3 *Ibid.*, p. 255.

4 Guglielmo Cavallo and Roger Chartier (eds), *A History of Reading in the West*, trans. Lydia G. Cochrane (pbk edn, 2003), p. 15.

5 Houston, *op. cit.*, p. 56.

6 Christina Duffy, 'Books Depicted in Art', British Library Collection Care blog, 1 July 2014.

7 Svend Dahl, *History of the Book* (2nd English edn, 1968), p. 41.

8 Joseph Rosenblum, *A Bibliographic History of the Book* (1995), p. 1.

9 Alberto Manguel, *A History of Reading* (1996), p. 294.

10 Simon Eliot and Jonathan Rose (eds), *A Companion to the History of the Book* (2007), essay by Rowan Watson, p. 486.

11 Manguel, *op. cit.*, p. 150.

12 *Ibid.*, p. 98.

13 Anthony Charles Ormond McGrath, 'Books in Art: The Meaning and Significance of Images of Books in Italian Religious Painting 1250–1400' (unpublished PhD thesis, University of Sussex, 2012), pp. 11, 12, 68.

14 Norma Levarie, *The Art and History of Books* (new edn, 1995), p. 23; Lucien Febvre and Henri-Jean Martin, *The Coming of the Book: The Impact of Printing 1450–1800*, ed. Geoffrey Nowell-Smith and David Wootton, trans. David Gerard (1976), pp. 26, 27.

15 Manguel, *op. cit.*, p. 77.

16 Linda L. Brownrigg (ed.), *Medieval Book Production: Assessing the Evidence* (1990), essay by R. H. and M. A. Rouse, pp. 103–06.

17 Jan Białostocki, *The Message of Images: Studies in the History of Art* (1988), p. 156.

18 Paul Oskar Kristeller, *Renaissance Thought and the Arts: Collected Essays* (expanded edn, 1990), p. 181.

19 Emma Barker, Nick Webb and Kim Woods (eds), *The Changing Status of the Artist* (1999), intro., p. 28.

20 Mary Rogers and Paola Tinagli, *Women and the Visual Arts in Italy c. 1400–1650: Luxury and Leisure, Duty and Devotion – A Sourcebook* (2012), p. 66.

21 Houston, *op. cit.*, p. 170.

22 Levarie, *op. cit.*, p. 67; Febvre and Martin, *op. cit.*, p. 22.

23 Levarie, *op. cit.*, p. 67.

24 Houston, *op. cit.*, p. 121.

25 Quoted in Elizabeth L. Eisenstein, *The Printing Press as an Agent of Change: Communications and Cultural Transformations in Early-Modern Europe* (pbk edn, 1980), p. 250.

26 Houston, *op. cit.*, pp. 203–04.

CHAPTER 2

1 Eliot and Rose, *op. cit.*, essay by Rowan Watson, p. 487; Cavallo and Chartier, *op. cit.*, essay by Anthony Grafton, p. 185.

2 David Finkelstein and Alistair McCleery (eds), *The Book History Reader* (2002), essay by Roger Chartier, p. 126.

3 Rogers and Tinagli, *op. cit.*, p. 213.

4 Rudolf and Margot Wittkower, *Born under Saturn: The Character and Conduct of Artists – A Documented History from Antiquity to the French Revolution* (1963), p. 54.

5 Peter Burke, *The Italian Renaissance: Culture and Society in Italy* (rev. edn, 1987), p. 60.

6 Antonella Braida and Giuliana Pieri (eds), *Image and Word: Reflections of Art and Literature from the Middle Ages to the Present* (2003), p. 3.

7 *Ibid.*, p. 5.

8 Burke, *op. cit.*, p. 155.

9 René Wellek, 'The Parallelism Between Literature and the Arts', *English Institute Annual 1941* (1942), p. 31.

10 Houston, *op. cit.*, p. 185.

11 Sandra Hindman (ed.), *Printing the Written Word: The Social History of Books, circa 1450–1520* (1991), essay by Martha Tedeschi, p. 41.

12 *Ibid.*, essay by Sheila Edmunds, pp. 25, 33.

13 Finkelstein and McCleery, *op. cit.*, essay by Jan-Dirk Müller, p. 154.

14 John L. Flood and William A. Kelly (eds), *The German Book, 1450–1750: Studies presented to David L. Paisey in His Retirement* (1995), essay by Irmgard Bezzel, pp. 31–32.

15 Hugh Amory and David D. Hall (eds), *A History of the Book in America*, vol. 1, *The Colonial Book in the Atlantic World* (2000), p. 26.

16 Dahl, *op. cit.*, p. 137.

17 Finkelstein and McCleery, *op. cit.*, essay by Jan-Dirk Müller, p. 163.

18 Gadd, *op. cit.*, essay by Andrew Pettegee and Matthew Hall, pp. 143, 162.

19 Patricia Lee Rubin, *Giorgio Vasari: Art and History* (1995), p. 106.

20 Rodney Palmer and Thomas Frangenberg (eds), *The Rise of the Image: Essays on the History of the Illustrated Art Book* (2003), essay by Sharon Gregory, p. 52.

21 Rubin, *op. cit.*, p. 50.

22 Philip Jacks (ed.), *Vasari's Florence: Artists and Literati at the Medicean Court* (1998), p. 1.

23 Rubin, *op. cit.*, pp. 290–91.

24 *Ibid.*, p. 148.

25 Jacks, *op. cit.*, p. 1.

26 Rudolph and Margaret Wittkower, *op. cit.*, p. 12.

27 Levarie, *op. cit.*, p. 288.

28 Eliot and Rose, *op. cit.*, essay by Megan L. Benton, p. 495.

29 Manguel, *op. cit.*, pp. 296–97.

30 Eisenstein, *op. cit.*, p. 248.
31 *Ibid.*, pp. 247–48; Białostocki, *op. cit.*, p. 153; Febvre and Martin, *op. cit.*, p. 95.
32 Eisenstein, *op. cit.*, p. 233.
33 *Ibid.*, p. 254, quoting Anthony Blunt, *Artistic Theory in Italy, 1450–1600* (1962), p. 56.
34 David J. Cast (ed.), *The Ashgate Research Companion to Giorgio Vasari* (2014), p. 263.
35 Joanna Woods-Marsden, *Renaissance Self-Portraiture: The Visual Construction of Identity and the Social Status of the Artist* (1998), p. 22.
36 Barker, Webb and Woods, *op. cit.*, intro., p. 20, essay by Kim Woods, pp. 104, 110; Białostocki, *op. cit.*, p. 159.
37 John C. Van Dyke, *A Text-Book of the History of Painting* (new edn, 1915), preface to 1st edn [1894].
38 Palmer and Frangenberg, *op. cit.*, essays by Anthony Hamber, p. 224, and Valerie Holman, p. 245.
39 Białostocki, *op. cit.*, p. 153.
40 Kristeller, *op. cit.*, p. 190.

CHAPTER 3

1 Roger Chartier (ed.), *A History of Private Life*, vol. 3, *Passions of the Renaissance*, trans. Arthur Goldhammer (1989), p. 128.
2 John Bury, 'El Greco's Books', *Burlington Magazine*, vol. 129, no. 1011 (June 1987), pp. 388–91.
3 Białostocki, *op. cit.*, p. 154.
4 Altick *op. cit.*, p. 18.
5 Finkelstein and McCleery, *op. cit.*, essay by Roger Chartier, p. 122.
6 *Ibid.*, essay by E. Jennifer Monaghan, p. 299.
7 Gadd, *op. cit.*, essay by David Cressy, p. 501.
8 David H. Solkin, *Painting out of the Ordinary: Modernity and the Art of Everyday Life in Nineteenth-Century Britain* (2008), p. 117.
9 Quoted in Ireland, *op. cit.*, p. 101.
10 Albert Ward, *Book Production, Fiction and the German Reading Public, 1740–1800* (1974), p. 29.
11 Denis V. Reidy (ed.), *The Italian Book 1465–1800: Studies Presented to Dennis E. Rhodes on His 70th Birthday* (1993), essay by Diego Zancani, p. 177.
12 Quoted in Flint, *op. cit.*, p. 22.
13 Charles Sterling, *Still Life Painting: From Antiquity to the Twentieth Century*, trans. James Emmons (2nd rev. edn, 1981), pp. 12, 63.

CHAPTER 4

1 Quoted in Cavallo and Chartier, *op. cit.*, essay by Reinhard Wittram, p. 298.
2 Chartier, *Private Life*, p. 143.
3 Ward, *op. cit.*, p. 61.
4 Cavallo and Chartier, *op. cit.*, essay by Reinhard Wittram, p. 293.
5 Ward, *op. cit.*, p. 6.
6 Finkelstein and McCleery, *op. cit.*, essay by John Brewer, p. 241.
7 Ann Bermingham and John Brewer, *The Consumption of Culture 1600–1800: Image, Object, Text* (1995), essay by Peter H. Pawlowicz, p. 45.
8 Altick, *op. cit.*, p. 1.
9 *Ibid.*, p. 54.
10 Kristeller, *op. cit.*, pp. 199–203.
11 Kate Retford, *The Art of Domestic Life: Family Portraiture in Eighteenth-Century England* (2006), pp. 38–40.
12 Solkin, *op. cit.*, p. 212.
13 Quoted in Bermingham and Brewer, *op. cit.*, essay by Peter H. Pawlowicz, p. 47.
14 Chartier, *Private Life*, p. 146.
15 Bermingham and Brewer, *op. cit.*, essay by Peter H. Pawlowicz, p. 49.
16 Finkelstein and McCleery, *op. cit.*, p. 134.
17 Matt Erlin, *Necessary Luxuries: Books, Literature, and the Culture of Consumption in Germany, 1770–1815* (2014), p. 79.
18 Ward, *op. cit.*, pp. 30, 47.
19 Amory and Hall, *op. cit.*, pp. 520–21.
20 Robert A. Gross and Mary Kelley (eds), *A History of the Book in America*, vol. 2, *An Extensive Republic: Print, Culture, and Society in the New Nation, 1790–1840* (2010), pp. 11, 14.
21 Ward, *op. cit.*, p. 107.
22 Quoted in Erlin, *op. cit.*, p. 65.
23 *Ibid.*, p. 72.
24 Pamela E. Selwyn, *Everyday Life in the German Book Trade: Friedrich Nicolai as Bookseller and Publisher in the Age of Enlightenment, 1750–1810* (2000), *passim*. For Heinzmann, see Chad Wellmon, *Organizing Enlightenment: Information Overload and the Invention of the Modern Research University* (2015), and James Van Horn Melton, *The Rise of the Public in Enlightenment Europe* (2001), esp. pp. 110–11.
25 Quoted in Cavallo and Chartier, *op. cit.*, essay by Reinhard Wittram, p. 285.
26 Roger Chartier, *The Order of Books: Readers, Authors and Libraries in Europe between the Fourteenth and Eighteenth Centuries*, trans. Lydia G. Cochrane (1994), pp. 62–63.
27 Ward, *op. cit.*, p. 59.
28 Erlin, *op. cit.*, p. 85.

CHAPTER 5

1 Altick, *op. cit.*, pp. 96–97.
2 Quoted in Dianne Sachko Macleod, *Art and the Victorian Middle Class: Money and the Making of Cultural Identity* (1996), p. 275.
3 *Ibid.*, pp. 41, 43.
4 Lynne Tatlock (ed.), *Publishing Culture and the 'Reading Nation': German Book History in the Long Nineteenth Century* (2010), p. 4.
5 Gross and Kelley, *op. cit.*, p. 6.
6 *Ibid.*, essay by Barry O'Connell, p. 510.
7 James Smith Allen, *In the Public Eye: A History of Reading in Modern France, 1880–1940* (1991), p. 165.
8 Nicole Howard, *The Book: The Life Story of a Technology* (1st pbk edn, 2009), p. 134.
9 Eliot and Rose, *op. cit.*, essay by Rowan Watson, p. 489.
10 Grahame, *op. cit.*, p. 8.
11 Cavallo and Chartier, *op. cit.*, essay by Martin Lyons, p. 313.
12 Macleod, *op. cit.*, p. 350.
13 Mark Bills (ed.), *Dickens and the Artists* (2012), p. 162.
14 Manguel, *op. cit.*, p. 110.
15 Scott E. Casper, Jeffrey D. Groves, Stephen W. Nissenbaum and Michael Winship (eds), *A History of the Book in America*, vol. 3, *The Industrial Book, 1840–1880* (2007), essay by Barbara Sicherman, p. 281.
16 *Ibid.*, pp. 290, 372.
17 Allen, *op. cit.*, p. 29.
18 Carl F. Kaestle and Janice A. Radway, *A History of the Book in America*, vol. 4, *Print in Motion: The Expansion of Publishing and Reading in the United States, 1880–1940* (2009), essay by Carl F. Kaestle, p. 31.
19 Allen, *op. cit.*, p. 161.
20 Casper, Groves, Nissenbaum and Winship, *op. cit.*, p. 31.
21 Gerard Curtis, *Visual Words: Art and the Material Book in Victorian England* (2002), p. 255.
22 *Ibid.*, p. 260.
23 These issues, and their associated writers, were discussed at the conference 'Erotics of Late Nineteenth-Century Book Collecting', University of Cambridge, Faculty of English, 28 June 2014, under the auspices of Victoria Mills.
24 William Carew Hazlitt, *The Confessions of a Collector* (1897), p. 224.
25 Octave Uzanne, *The Book-Hunter in Paris: Studies among the Bookstalls and the Quays* (1893), pp. 226, 109–10.
26 Curtis, *op. cit.*, p. 259.
27 Flint, *op. cit.*, p. 4.
28 *Ibid.*, p. 258.
29 Peter Gay, *The Bourgeois Experience: Victoria to Freud*, vol. 2, *The Tender Passion* (1st pbk edn, 1999), p. 137.
30 Flint, *op. cit.*, p. 3.
31 Quoted at www.royalcollection.org.uk/collection/403745/the-madonna-and-child.

32 Flint, *op. cit*, p. 254.
33 Quoted in Tatlock, *op. cit.*, essay by Jennifer Drake Askey, p. 157.
34 Altick, *op. cit.*, p. 140.
35 Augustine Birrell, preface to Uzanne, *op. cit.*, p. vii.
36 Braida and Pieri, *op. cit.*, essay by Luisa Calè, p. 151.
37 Quoted in Rhoda L. Flaxman, *Victorian Word-Painting and Narrative: Toward the Blending of Genres* (1987), p. 19.
38 Bills, *op. cit.*, p. 1, quoted from Ronald Pickvance, *English Influences on Van Gogh* (1974), p. 26.
39 Rosalind P. Blakesley, *The Russian Canvas: Painting in Imperial Russia, 1757–1881* (2016), p. 127.
40 Altick, *op. cit.*, p. 139.
41 Jean Seznec, *Literature and the Visual Arts in Nineteenth-Century France* (1963), p. 12.
42 Altick, *op. cit.*, p. 168.
43 Casper, Groves, Nissenbaum and Winship, *op. cit.*, essay by Louise Stevenson, p. 324.
44 Braida and Pieri, *op. cit.*, essay by J. J. L. Whiteley, p. 38.
45 Bills, *op. cit.*, essay by Hilary Underwood, p. 80.
46 Roselyne de Ayala and Jean-Pierre Guéno, *Illustrated Letters: Artists and Writers Correspond*, trans. John Goodman (2000), pp. 13, 90.
47 Dan Piepenbring, 'Victor Hugo's Drawings', *Paris Review* online, 26 February 2015.
48 David Wakefield, *The French Romantics: Literature and the Visual Arts, 1800–1840* (2007), p. 106.
49 John Rewald, *The History of Impressionism* (4th rev. edn, 1973), p. 52.
50 Françoise Cachin and Charles S. Moffett, in collaboration with Michel Melot, *Manet 1832–1883* (1983), pp. 280–82.
51 Białostocki, *op. cit.*, pp. 62–63.
52 H. R. Graetz, *The Symbolic Language of Vincent van Gogh* (1963), p. 39.
53 Białostocki, *op. cit.*, p. 63.
54 Leo Jansen, Hans Luijten and Nienke Bakker (eds), *Vincent van Gogh – The Letters: The Complete Illustrated and Annotated Edition* (2009), letter 853.

CHAPTER 6

1 Tatlock, *op. cit.*, essay by Katrin Völkner, p. 263.
2 Curtis, *op. cit.*, p. 208.
3 M. C. Fischer and W. A. Kelly (eds), *The Book in Germany* (2010), essays by Jasmin Lange, p. 117, and Alistair McCleery, pp. 127–29.
4 Kaestle and Radway, *op. cit.*, essay by Ellen Gruber Garvey, p. 186.
5 Molly Brunson, *Russian Realisms: Literature and Painting, 1840–1890* (2016), pp. 160–61.
6 Peter Burke, *Eyewitnessing: The Uses of Images as Historical Evidence* (2001), p. 75.
7 Manguel, *op. cit.*, p. 92.
8 Quoted in Gustav Janouch, *Conversations with Kafka*, trans. Goronwy Rees (1985, first published 1971), pp. 34–37.
9 Ulrich Finke (ed.), *French Nineteenth-Century Painting and Literature* (1972), p. 359.
10 Johanna Drucker, *The Century of Artists' Books* (2nd edn, 2004), p. 46.
11 *Ibid.*, p. 60.
12 Kathryn Bromwich, 'Mike Stilkey's Paintings on Salvaged Books – In Pictures', *The Guardian*, 20 July 2014.
13 David Paul Nord, Joan Shelley Rubin and Michael Schudson (eds), *A History of the Book in America*, vol. 5, *The Enduring Book* (2009), intro. by Michael Schudson.
14 Howard, *op. cit.*, p. 147.
15 Nord, Rubin and Schudson, *op. cit.*, p. 512.
16 Howard, *op. cit.*, p. 156.
17 Quoted in Ireland, *op. cit.*, p. 172.
18 Robbie Millen, 'Gilbert & George', *The Times*, 25 April 2017.
19 Jo Steffens and Matthias Neumann (eds), *Unpacking My Library: Artists and Their Books* (2017).

GALLERY 1

1 Białostocki, *op. cit.*, p. 42.
2 Catherine Nixey, *The Darkening Age: The Christian Destruction of the Classical World* (2017), provides comprehensive documentation.
3 Michael F. Suarez, S. J. and H. R. Woodhuysen (eds), *The Oxford Companion to the Book* (2010), vol. 1, essay by Brian Cummings, p. 63.
4 James Hall, *A History of Ideas and Images in Italian Art* (1983), p. 4.
5 Quoted in Braida and Pieri, *op. cit.*, p. 3.
6 McGrath, *op. cit.*, p. 11.
7 Howard, *op. cit.*, p. 21.
8 Francis Haskell, *History and Its Images: Art and the Interpretation of the Past* (3rd printing, with corrections, 1995), p. 434.
9 Manguel, *op. cit.*, p. 171.
10 Quoted in Finkelstein and McCleery, *op. cit.*, essay by Richard Altick, p. 344.
11 Howard, *op. cit.*, p. 58.
12 Jean-François Gilmont (ed.), *The Reformation and the Book*, trans. Karin Maag (1998), essay by Jean-François Gilmont, p. 482.
13 Burke, *Eyewitnessing*, p. 114.
14 Amory and Hall, *op. cit.*, essay by Ross W. Beales and E. Jennifer Monaghan, p. 383.
15 John Stuart Mill, *Considerations on Representative Government* (1861), p. 14.
16 Quoted in Christiane Inmann, *Forbidden Fruit: A History of Women and Books in Art* (2009), pp. 180–81.

GALLERY 2

1 Quoted in Flint, *op. cit.*, p. 11.
2 Chartier, *Private Life*, p. 151.
3 Casper, Groves, Nissenbaum and Winship, *op. cit.*, essay by Barbara Sicherman, p. 282.
4 Chartier, *Private Life*, p. 124.
5 Allen, *op. cit.*, pp. 159, 145.
6 *Ibid.*, pp. 143, 172.
7 The painting is reproduced in Steven Mintz and Susan Kellogg, *Domestic Revolutions: A Social History of American Family Life* (1988).

GALLERY 3

1 Quoted in Ireland, *op. cit.*, p. 52.
2 Curtis, *op. cit.*, p. 235.
3 Mayor, *op. cit.*, n.p.
4 Białostocki, *op. cit.*, p. 55.
5 Lord Francis Napier, *Notes on Modern Painting at Naples* (1855), p. 13.
6 Quoted in Gary Tinterow, Michael Pantazzi and Vincent Pomarède, *Corot* (1996), p. 278.
7 William Hazlitt, *Sketches of the Principal Picture-Galleries in England* (1824), pp. 1–22.

GALLERY 4

1 Quoted in Ireland, *op. cit.*, p. 200.
2 Isaac D'Israeli, *Curiosities of Literature* (multiple expanded editions, 1791–1849), 'Essay on Painting'.
3 McGrath, *op. cit.*, p. 105.
4 Flint, *op. cit.*, p. 17.
5 Howard, *op. cit.*, p. 71.
6 Białastocki, *op. cit.*, p. 47.
7 Curtis, *op. cit.*, p. 219.
8 Casper, Groves, Nissenbaum and Winship, *op. cit.*, essay by Barbara Sicherman, p. 293.
9 Tatlock, *op. cit.*, essay by Katrin Völkner, p. 252.
10 Houston, *op. cit.*, p. 252.
11 Chartier, *Private Life*, p. 137.
12 Baudelaire's comments were in his review 'The Salon of 1859', *Revue française*, 10 June – 20 July 1859. Courbet is quoted in Heather McPherson, *The Modern Portrait in Nineteenth-century France* (2001), p. 24.
13 Jansen, Luijten and Bakker, *op. cit.*, letter 574.
14 Quoted in Charles Chassé, *Gauguin et le groupe de Pont-Aven* (1921), p. 52.

LIST OF ILLUSTRATIONS

Dimensions are given in centimetres followed by inches, with height before width.
l = left; r = right

Kunstmuseum Basel (1738). Chagall ®/© ADAGP, Paris and DACS, London 2018 **104** André Derain, *Saturday*, 1911–13. Oil on canvas, 181 × 228 (71¼ × 89¾). The Pushkin Museum of Fine Arts, Moscow (3353). Photo Scala, Florence. © ADAGP, Paris and DACS, London 2018 **105** Stanley Spencer, *Separating Fighting Swans*, *c.* 1932–33. Oil on canvas, 91.4 × 72.4 (36 × 28½). Leeds Museums and Galleries, City Art Gallery, Leeds. © Estate of Stanley Spencer/Bridgeman Images **106** Pierre-Antoine Baudouin, *La Lecture*, *c.* 1760. Gouache, 29 × 23.5 (11 7/16 × 9¼). Les Arts Décoratifs, Paris. Georges Heine Bequest, 1919 (26829). Photo Jean Tholance/akg-images **110** Vincenzo Foppa, *The Young Cicero Reading*, *c.* 1464. Fresco, 101.6 × 143.7 (40 × 59 9/16). Wallace Collection, London **111** Francisco de Zurbarán, *Christ and the Virgin in the House in Nazareth*, *c.* 1640. Oil on canvas, 165 × 218.2 (64 15/16 × 85⅞). The Cleveland Museum of Art. Leonard C. Hanna, Jr. Fund (1960.117) **112** Jean-Etienne Liotard, *Lady Reading on a Sofa*, *c.* 1748–52. Oil on canvas, 50 × 56 (19 11/16 × 22 1/16). Uffizi, Florence **113** Pietro Rotari, *A Young Woman with a Book*, 1756–62. Oil on canvas, 46 × 36 (18⅛ × 14 3/16). Rijksmuseum, Amsterdam **114** Auguste Bernard d'Agesci, *Lady Reading the Letters of Héloïse and Abelard*, *c.* 1780. Oil on canvas, 81.3 × 64.8 (32 × 25½). Art Institute of Chicago. Mrs. Harold T. Martin Fund; Lacy Armour Endowment; Charles H. and Mary F. S. Worcester Collection (1994.430) **115** Anna Dorothea Lisiewska-Therbusch, *Self-Portrait*, *c.* 1776–77. Oil on canvas, 151 × 115 (59½ × 45¼). Staatliche Museen, Berlin **116** Richard Brompton (attr.), *Conversation Piece*, *c.* 1770s. Oil on canvas, 91.3 × 73.7 (35 15/16 × 29). Temple Newsam House, Leeds Museums and Art Galleries/Bridgeman Images **117** Pieter Fonteyn, *The Fallen Woman*, 1809. Oil on canvas, 226 × 140 (89 × 55⅛). Private collection. Photo Rafael Valls Gallery, London/Bridgeman Images **118** Antoine Wiertz, *The Reader of Novels*, 1853. Oil on canvas, 125 × 157 (49 3/16 × 61 13/16). Royal Museums of Fine Art, Brussels (1971) **119** Robert Braithwaite Martineau, *The Last Chapter*, 1863. Oil on canvas, 71.5 × 31.7 (28⅛ × 12½). Birmingham Museums and Art Gallery **120** William Hogarth, *The Cholmondeley Family*, 1732. Oil on canvas, 71 × 90.8 (27 15/16 × 35¾). Private collection **121** Joseph-Marcellin Combette, *Portrait of a Family*, 1800–01. Oil on canvas, 58 × 74 (22 13/16 × 29⅛). Musée des Beaux-Arts, Tours **122** Unknown German artist, *Domestic Scene*, *c.* 1775–80. Oil on canvas, 45.7 × 37.8 (18 × 14⅞). Metropolitan Museum of Art, New York. Bequest of Edward Fowles, 1971 (1971.115.6) **123** Sir William Beechey, *Mr and Mrs Hayward with their children*, 1789. Oil on canvas, 68.5 × 80.8 (27 × 31 13/16). Christie's Images, London/Scala, Florence **124** Bronzino, *Portrait of a Young Girl with a Book*, *c.* 1545. Tempera on panel, 58 × 46 (22 13/16 × 18⅛). Uffizi, Florence (1890–770) **125** George Romney, *Portrait of Two Girls (Misses Cumberland)*, *c.* 1772–73. Oil on canvas, 76 × 63.5 (30 × 25). Museum of Fine Arts, Boston. Robert Dawson Evans Collection (17.3259) **126** William-Adolphe Bouguereau, *The Story Book*, 1877. Oil on canvas, 59.1 × 48.3 (23¼ × 19). Los Angeles County Museum of Art. Mary D. Keeler Bequest (40.12.40) **127** Pierre-Auguste Renoir, *The Children of Martial Caillebotte*, 1895. Oil on canvas, 65 × 82 (25 9/16 × 32¼). Private collection. Josse Christophel/Alamy Stock Photo **128** Paul Gauguin, *Clovis*, *c.* 1886. Oil on canvas, 56.6 × 40.8 (22 5/16 × 16 1/16). Private collection **129** Federico Zandomeneghi, *Young Girl Reading*, 1880s. Oil on canvas, 38.8 × 46.3 (15¼ × 18¼). Christie's Images, London/Scala, Florence **130** Jean-Auguste-Dominique Ingres, *Paolo and Francesca*, 1819. Oil on canvas, 47.9 × 39 (18⅞ × 15⅜). Musée des Beaux-Arts, Angers **131** Paul Delaroche, *The Princes in the Tower*, 1831. Oil on canvas, 181 × 215 (71¼ × 84⅝). Musée du Louvre, Paris (3834) **132** Edouard Manet, *Reading (Madame Manet and her son Léon Köella-Leenhoff)*, 1868. Oil on canvas, 60.5 × 73.5 (23⅞ × 28⅞). Musée d'Orsay, Paris **133** Alfred Stevens, *La Myope*, 1903. Oil on canvas, 41 × 33 (16 × 13). Photo Bonhams **134–35** Gustave Caillebotte, *Interior, Reading Woman*, 1880. Oil on canvas, 65 × 81 (25 9/16 × 31⅞). Private collection. Photo Josse/Scala, Florence **136** Anders Zorn, *The Artist's Wife*, 1889. Pastel, 50 × 33 (19 1/16 × 13). Nationalmuseum, Stockholm (NMB 340). Photo Erik Cornelius **137** Albert Bartholomé, *The Artist's Wife Reading*, 1883. Pastel and charcoal, 50.5 × 61.3 (19⅞ × 24⅛). Metropolitan Museum of Art, New York. Catharine Lorillard Wolfe Collection, Wolfe Fund, 1990 (1990.117) **138** Philip Wilson Steer, *Mrs Cyprian Williams and her Two Little Girls*, 1891. Oil on canvas, 76.2 × 102.2 (30 × 40¼). Tate, London **139** James Jebusa Shannon, *Jungle Tales*, 1895. Oil on canvas, 87 × 113.7 (34¼ × 44¾). Metropolitan Museum of Art, New York. Arthur Hoppock Hearn Fund, 1913 (13.143.1) **140** Sir John Lavery, *The Red Book*, *c.* 1902. Oil on canvas, 76.3 × 63.5 (30 1/16 × 25). Private collection **141** Alfred Stevens, *Le Bain*, 1873–74. Oil on canvas, 73.5 × 92.8 (28 15/16 × 36 9/16). Musée d'Orsay, Paris **142** Boris Grigoriev, *Woman Reading*, *c.* 1922. Oil on canvas, 54 × 65.1 (21¼ × 25⅝). Metropolitan Museum of Art, New York. Gift of Humanities Fund Inc., 1972 (1972.146.1) **143** Anonymous, *Interior, Chambermaid and Man with Books*, late 18th century. Oil on canvas, 46 × 38 (18⅛ × 14 15/16). Harris Museum & Art Gallery, Preston **144** Vanessa Bell, *Interior with Artist's Daughter*, *c.* 1935–36. Oil on canvas, 73.7 × 61 (29 × 24). Charleston Trust, bequeathed by Ben Duncan and Dick Chapman. © the Estate of Vanessa Bell, courtesy of Henrietta Garnett **145** Pierre Bonnard, *La Lecture*, 1905. Oil on canvas, 52 × 62.4 (20½ × 24½). Private collection **146** Charles D. Sauerwein, *Reveries of a Bachelor*, 1855–70. Oil on canvas, 31 × 45 (12 3/16 × 17¾). Shelburne Museum, Vermont/Bridgeman Images **147** William McGregor Paxton, *The House Maid*, 1910. Oil on canvas, 76.5 × 64 (30⅛ × 25 3/16). National Gallery of Art, Washington DC, Corcoran Collection. Museum Purchase, Gallery Fund (2014.136.11) **148–49** Balthus (Balthasar Klossowski de Rola), *The Living Room*, 1942. Oil on canvas, 114.8 × 146.9 (45¼ × 57⅞). Museum of Modern Art, New York. Estate of John Hay Whitney (245.1983). © Balthus **150** Henri Matisse, *The Reader at the Guéridon*, 1921. Oil on canvas, 55.5 × 46.5 (21⅞ × 18 5/16). Kunstmuseum, Bern. Photo Archives H. Matisse, all rights reserved. © Succession H. Matisse/DACS 2018 **151** Christopher Wood, *The Manicure (Portrait of Frosca Munster)*, 1929. Oil on canvas, 152.4 × 101.6 (60 × 40). Bradford Museums and Galleries, UK **152** Juan Gris, *Le Pierot au livre*, 1924. Oil on canvas, 65.5 × 50.8 (25 13/16 × 20). Tate, London. Bequeathed by Elly Kahnweiler 1991 to form part of the gift of Gustav and Elly Kahnweiler, accessioned 1994 **153** Robert Delaunay, *Nude Woman Reading*, 1915. Oil on canvas, 86.2 × 72.4 (33 15/16 × 28½). National Gallery of Victoria, Melbourne. Felton Bequest, 1966 (1665–5) **154–55** Roger de la Fresnaye, *Married Life*, 1912. Oil on canvas, 98.9 × 118.7 (38 15/16 × 46¾). Minneapolis Institute of Art. The John R. Van Derlip Fund (52.1) **156** Pablo Picasso, *Woman with a Book*, 1932. Oil on canvas,

Richardson, *Portrait of the Artist's Son in his Study*, *c.* 1734. Oil paint on canvas on board, 90.4 × 71.5 (35 9/16 × 28⅛). Tate, London. Photo akg-images **215** Jean-Siméon Chardin, *Le Singe antiquaire*, *c.* 1725–45. Oil on canvas, 81 × 64 (31⅞ × 25 3/16). Musée du Louvre, Paris (3206). Photo RMN-Grand Palais (Musée du Louvre)/René-Gabriel Ojéda **216** Ralph Earl, *Esther Boardman*, 1789. Oil on canvas, 108 × 81.3 (42½ × 32). Metropolitan Museum of Art, New York. Gift of Edith and Henry Noss, 1991 (1991.338) **217** Ralph Earl, *Elijah Boardman*, 1789. Oil on canvas, 210.8 × 129.5 (83 × 51). Metropolitan Museum of Art, New York. Bequest of Susan W. Tyler, 1979 (1979.395) **218–19** Jean-Siméon Chardin, *The Little Schoolmistress*, after 1740. Oil on canvas, 58.3 × 74 (22 15/16 × 29⅛). National Gallery of Art, Washington DC, Andrew W. Mellon Collection (1937.1.91) **220** Richard Wilson, *Prince George and Prince Edward Augustus, Sons of Frederick, Prince of Wales, with Their Tutor Dr Francis Ayscough*, *c.* 1748–49. Oil on canvas, 63.5 × 76.5 (25 × 30⅛). Yale Center for British Art, Paul Mellon Collection (B1981.25.689) **221** Jan Lievens, *Prince Charles Louis of the Palatinate with his Tutor Wolrad von Plessen in Historical Dress*, 1631. Oil on canvas, 104.5 × 97.5 (41⅛ × 38⅜). The J. Paul Getty Museum, Los Angeles **222** Joseph Mallord William Turner, *A Man Seated at a Table in the Old Library*, 1827. Gouache and watercolour on paper, 14.1 × 19.1 (5 9/16 × 7½). Tate, London **223** See entry for pp. 12–13 **224** Silvestro Lega, *The Reading Lesson*, 1881. Oil on canvas, 116 × 90 (45 11/16 × 35 7/16). Private collection. Josse Christophel/Alamy Stock Photo **225** Auguste Toulmouche, *The Reading Lesson*, 1865. Oil on canvas, 36.5 × 27.6 (14⅜ × 10⅞). Museum of Fine Arts, Boston (24.1) **226** François Bonvin, *Still Life with Book, Papers and Inkwell*, 1876. Oil on zinc, 36.2 × 48.3 (14¼ × 19). National Gallery, London (NG3234)/Heritage Image Partnership Ltd/Alamy Stock Photo **227** Guercino, *Portrait of Francesco Righetti*, *c.* 1626–28. Oil on canvas, 83 × 67 (32 11/16 × 26⅜). Private collection. Photo Art Collection/Alamy Stock Photo **228** Edouard Manet, *Portrait of Emile Zola*, 1868. Oil on canvas, 146 × 114 (57½ × 44⅞). Musée d'Orsay, Paris **229** Pierre-Auguste Renoir, *Portrait of Claude Monet*, 1872. Oil on canvas, 65 × 50 (25 9/16 × 19 11/16). National Gallery of Art, Washington DC, Collection of Mr and Mrs Paul Mellon (1985.64.35) **230** Giorgio de Chirico, *The Child's Brain*, 1914. Oil on canvas, 81.5 × 65 (32 1/16 × 26). Moderna Museet, Stockholm. © DACS 2018 **231** Vincent van Gogh, *Still Life with Bible*, 1885. Oil on canvas, 65.7 × 78.5 (25⅞ × 30 15/16). Van Gogh Museum, Amsterdam **232** Théo van Rysselberghe, *The Reading*, 1903. Oil on canvas, 181 × 241 (71¼ × 94⅞). Museum of Fine Arts, Ghent. Photo Hugo Maertens, Lukas – Art in Flanders VZW **233** Paul Gauguin, *Portrait of Jacob Meyer de Haan by Lamplight*, 1889. Oil on panel, 79.6 × 51.7 (31⅜ × 20⅜). Museum of Modern Art, New York. Gift of Mr and Mrs David Rockefeller (2.1958) **234** Edgar Degas, *Portrait of Edmond Duranty*, 1879. Tempera and pastel on linen, 100.6 × 100.6 (39⅜ × 39⅜). Burrell Collection, Glasgow **235** Duncan Grant, *James Strachey*, 1910. Oil on canvas, 63.5 × 76.2 (25 × 30). © Tate, London **236** Egon Schiele, *Portrait of Hugo Koller*, 1918. Oil on canvas, 140 × 110 (55⅛ × 43 5/16). Osterreichische Galerie Belvedere, Vienna **237** Paul Cézanne, *Portrait of Gustave Geffroy*, 1895. Oil on canvas, 110 × 89 (45⅜ × 35). Musée d'Orsay, Paris **238** Gwen John, *The Student*, 1903–04. Oil on canvas, 56.1 × 33.1 (22 1/16 × 13). Manchester City Art Gallery **239** Egon Schiele, *Still Life with Books (Schiele's Desk)*, 1914. Oil on canvas, 117.5 × 78 (46¼ × 30 11/16). Leopold Museum, Vienna **240** Nora Heysen, *A Portrait Study*, 1933. Oil on canvas, 86.5 × 66.7 (34 × 26¼). Tasmanian Museum and Art Gallery, Hobart. © Lou Klepac **241** Sofonisba Anguissola, *Self-Portrait*, 1554. Oil on poplar wood, 19.5 × 12.5 (7 11/16 × 4 15/16). Kunsthistorisches Museum, Vienna **242–43** Edouard Vuillard, *Jeanne Lanvin*, *c.* 1933. Tempera on canvas, 124.5 × 136.5 (49 × 53¾). Musée d'Orsay, Paris. Bequest of the Comtesse Jean de Polignac, daughter of the model, 1958 **244** Florine Stettheimer, *Portrait of Carl Van Vechten*, 1922. Oil on canvas, 91 × 80 (35 13/16 × 31½). Yale Collection of American Literature, New Haven, CT **245** Alice Neel, *Kenneth Fearing*, 1935. Oil on canvas, 76.5 × 66 (30⅛ × 26). Museum of Modern Art, New York. Gift of Hartley S. Neel and Richard Neel (28.1988). © The Estate of Alice Neel **246** René Magritte, *La Reproduction interdite*, 1937. Oil on canvas, 81.5 × 65.5 (32 1/16 × 25 13/16). Museum Boijmans Van Beuningen, Rotterdam. © ADAGP, Paris and DACS, London 2018

INDEX

Page numbers in *italics* refer to the illustrations.